RUSSIA

TRANSYLVANIA

RUMANIA

ARABIA

DOBRUDJA

○ Bucharest

SILISTRIA ○ Constanza

BLACK

○ Varna

SEA

BULGARIA

○ Sofia

EASTERN RUMELIA

'Tirnovo

Kirk Kilisse ○

○ Midia

Adrianople

EASTERN
THRACE

Bosphorus

Therapia

IN EUROPE

WESTERN
THRACE

Scutari and
Haidar Pasha ○ Ismidt

Kavalla

○ Dedeagatch

Constantinople

Thasos ○ Enos

Samothrace

Imbros

Dardanelles

TURKEY IN ASIA

MᵗAthos

Bezika B.

Lemnos

Mitylene

Studies in Modern Diplomacy

SIR ARTHUR NICOLSON, BART.

FIRST LORD CARNOCK

Studies in Modern Diplomacy

LORD CARNOCK
A Study in the Old Diplomacy

PEACEMAKING 1919

CURZON: THE LAST PHASE
A Study in Post-War Diplomacy

Also by Harold Nicolson

DWIGHT MORROW

BYRON: THE LAST JOURNEY
TENNYSON
PAUL VERLAINE

SWEET WATERS
PUBLIC FACES

SOME PEOPLE
SMALL TALK

Constable & Company

(*Frontispiece*)

SIR ARTHUR NICOLSON BART.

1st LORD CARNOCK

From the portrait by Laszlo.

SIR ARTHUR NICOLSON, BART.

FIRST LORD CARNOCK

A Study in the Old Diplomacy

by

HAROLD NICOLSON

LONDON
CONSTABLE & CO LTD

PUBLISHED BY

Constable and Company Ltd.

LONDON

.

*The Macmillan Company
of Canada, Limited*

TORONTO

First published 1930
Second printing 1930
Third printing 1931
Fourth printing 1937

PRINTED IN GREAT BRITAIN BY ROBERT MACLEHOSE AND CO. LTD.
THE UNIVERSITY PRESS, GLASGOW

AUTHOR'S NOTE

THE material used in this book has been drawn mainly from my father's private and semi-official correspondence. The Foreign Office have also placed at my disposal the relevant official archives and I have had the advantage of consulting personally many of the protagonists in the story. The MS. of this book (which was written and completed while I was still a member of the Diplomatic Service) was submitted to the Foreign Office before publication, and was passed by them without an excision. All that they asked was that they should not in any way be regarded as having approved the opinions, personal or other, which I express.

I have consulted and quoted most of the official archives and private memoirs covering the period. The German collection, so admirably edited by Friedrich Thimme and his colleagues under the title " Die Grosse Politik der Europäischen Kabinette " is referred to in the reference notes as G.P. The equally admirable edition of British Documents by Gooch and Temperley figures as B.D. The Austrian Documents, in their full edition, were only published after this book had been sent to the publishers.

Specific acknowledgments would be invidious. I cannot refrain, however, from expressing my thanks to Mr. Stephen Gaselee, Librarian of the Foreign Office, and to the Library Staff for their unstinted assistance.

H. N.

CONTENTS

LIST OF ILLUSTRATIONS

INTRODUCTION

THIS book covers nearly half a century of diplomatic history. Arthur Nicolson entered the British Foreign Service a week before the Battle of Sedan, and left it a fortnight after the Battle of Jutland. During these forty-six years he witnessed the rise and fall of the German Empire, and saw his own country cease to be the strongest Power in the world.

He was personally identified with almost every phase in that slow, and at the time unrealised, process, by which England and Germany were gradually impelled towards their mutual destruction. It may thus be of value to trace, in terms of an individual experience and of a single personality, those recondite displacements of weight, prejudice and sympathy, which, between the year 1870 and the year 1914, produced the European War.

The old diplomatist has not been fairly treated by his posterity. If he failed to foresee the war, he is, and with full justice, called a fool : if he did foresee the war, he is, quite unjustly, considered a knave. I trust that this biography may do something to correct such false perspectives. It is unnecessary to assume that such men as Bethmann Hollweg, Grey, the two Cambons, Hardinge, Jagow, Metternich, Pourtalès, Mensdorff, Schoen, or Nicolson were less high-minded than those who gather to-day in the Salle de la Réformation at Geneva. What was wrong was the civilisation which they represented. But if we are tempted to regard our own state of mind as more humane and more enlightened, we should remember that we were taught our lesson by the death and mutilation of ten million young men. We have no cause to feel self-righteous when backed by so expensive an education.

Arthur Nicolson provides an admirable example for the study of the old diplomacy at its best.

In the first place, he had actual experience, from 1870 onwards, of all the main factors, which contributed towards the final catastrophe. In the second place his frank and gentle character furnishes an excellent mirror in which the clouds and shadows of that epoch are reflected simply, clearly, and without distortion.

Arthur Nicolson was neither imaginative nor intellectual : he was merely intelligent, honest, sensible, high-minded and fair. In temperament he was essentially English. The unhappiness of his childhood, the rigours and limitations of his early education, rendered him, even for an Englishman, unduly diffident and reserved. He curbed his instinctive tendency towards original or individual thought. He adopted, rather, the mental habits of his generation,—and among other fallacies, he imagined that virility was among the highest aims of human endeavour. He thus, in common with the vast majority of his contemporaries, came to believe that patriotism was in its turn the sublimation of the virility-ideal,—that it was the duty of every Englishman to render his own country more powerful, richer, and larger than any other country. This nineteenth century patriotism, although not entirely a vulgar thing, laid too heavy an emphasis upon the standards of power and possession : the patriots of 1850-1899 were inclined, when thinking about the British Empire, to render unto God the

things that were Caesar's.   And for this error they
paid a heavy price.

Guided as he was by such solid simple landmarks,
Nicolson's political journey falls into two distinct
periods.   There is the period, from 1870 to 1900,
when he believed in splendid isolation ; there is the
period, from 1900 to 1914, when he believed in the
German menace.   Both these periods have their successive phases.

During the period when he believed in splendid
isolation he passed through the following modifications.   He began by sharing completely the mid-
Victorian doctrine that the Continent did not matter
very much ; that Germany was delightful and related
to us dynastically ; that France and Russia were the
countries whom one ought to combat and despise.   His
experiences at Constantinople and Cairo at the moment
when we acquired Egypt led him to wonder whether
we were really strong enough to cast aside the old
Crimean combine, and permanently to antagonise both
Turkey and France.   His experiences in Persia made
him realise the immense force of Russian infiltration,
and to question whether this immeasurable tide should
not be stayed at its source in St. Petersburg rather than
in the sandy reaches of Central Asia.   His second
experience of Constantinople, a decade later, convinced
him that the old patronising assumption of German
friendliness must be qualified by the realisation that
Germany was expansive and determined.   His experiences in Morocco, his acute realisation of the shame
and implications of the South African War, coupled
with the first menacing symptoms of German naval
ambition, combined to destroy his faith in isolation

and to make him feel that England must cease to be
the enemy of all the world.

The second period is marked by similar phases of
progression. At first he thought only in terms of the
danger of continued isolation, and of the necessity of
making friends in Europe, primarily with Germany.
The rejection of our overtures to Berlin led him, as it
led the British Government, to look to France. It was
only when Germany tried to smash the Anglo-French
Agreement of 1904 that he came to regard that understanding as more than a removal of past difficulties,
and to look upon it as an insurance against future
dangers. At Algeciras he was himself able to mark
that transition. By 1906 he was already convinced of
the German menace, and his activity in Russia was
inspired as much by considerations of the balance of
power as by fears of Anglo-Russian rivalry. In 1910
he became head of the Foreign Office. His whole
efforts were directed towards rendering our understandings with France and Russia active, and not merely
passive, towards the maintenance of peace. The
German historians are perfectly correct in regarding
him as a protagonist in the so-called policy of encirclement. They are apt, however, to attribute his
efforts and convictions to an envious desire to destroy
the growing might of Germany. In this they are
mistaken. Nicolson conceived of the " German
menace " in far other terms.

It is a commonplace among a certain school of
German publicists, of whom Herr von Tirpitz may be
taken as representative, that Anglo-German rivalry was
due to British envy of German commercial and colonial
expansion. I am profoundly convinced that this sus-

picion is unjust. In the first place the British, whatever their faults, are the least envious race on earth. They are arrogant : but they are not envious. In the second place, from 1900 onwards, we were only too anxious that Germany should find a field for colonial expansion provided that she took other peoples' colonies and not our own. And in the third place it was only those people who were completely ignorant of commerce or economics (a small minority in England) who felt anything but satisfaction at the increased purchasing power of our richest customer. The belief in the " German menace " arose simply and solely from the fact that Germany, who already possessed the greatest army in the world, from 1900 onwards began to construct a fleet which was deliberately devised to challenge our naval superiority. The German mind, as is indicated by Prince Bülow's memoirs,[1] is somewhat obtuse to the mental attitudes of other countries. They do not pause to consider what apprehensions would have been raised in Germany, if we, from 1900 onwards, had embarked upon the recruiting and equipment of a vast standing army. At one breath they admit that the German Battle Fleet was devised in order to frighten England, and at the next breath they express pained astonishment at the fact that we eventually became alarmed. I do not deny that Germany had the " right " (whatever that may mean) to compete with England in naval construction. All I contend is that it was ignorant of them not to realise from the start that any such com-

---

[1] The more enlightened German publicists are under no such delusions, e.g. Brandenburg, Theodor Wolff, or Johannes Haller, whose brilliant little monograph " Die Aera Bülow " is a model of historical interpretation.

petition in a matter which threatened our existence would render England not pacific but bellicose.

It was thus under the pressure of German naval construction that Nicolson first came to fear " the German menace." What, exactly (for unless we are clear on this point the whole story will be unintelligible) did he mean by this phrase? He did not imagine that Germany wished to attack England. He did not imagine, even, that she hoped to construct a fleet which would by itself be able to destroy or subjugate the British Navy. He thought that German sea power was dangerous because it was reinforced by preponderating military power on land. He thought that, relying on the latter, she would " dominate the Continent." Here again is a phrase which requires precision. Nicolson meant thereby that Germany by threatening France or Russia with her army could force those two countries into neutrality, if not into an alliance. That the defection or subjugation of France and Russia would mean not only that our naval forces in the Mediterranean and elsewhere would be inadequate, but also that Russia would be in a position to menace us in Central Asia. Germany already had at her command the fleets of Austria and Italy. It was expected that Turkey also, a country of immense geographical if not of military value, would adhere to the Triple Alliance. The nightmare which haunted Nicolson year in year out was a continental coalition which would give Germany the fleets and armies of Russia, France, Austria, Italy, Turkey, Bulgaria, and Rumania, and thus place England in the position where she would either have to face a disastrous war or capitulate to German dictation. What, finally, did

he mean by " German dictation " ? He meant that
Germany might force England, let us say, to dismiss
Mr. Winston Churchill, as she had forced France to
dismiss M. Delcassé. He meant that Germany might
force England to cede British East Africa, or not to
renew the alliance with Japan, as she forced France to
cede Congo territory, and forced Russia to abandon
Serbia in 1909. He knew that British public opinion
would desire to resist such dictation. And he feared
that by the time the British public awoke to this necessity it would be too late.

This book will show that there was good cause to
entertain such apprehensions. I do not think that,
given the circumstances, any British public servant
could have thought, and therefore have advised,
differently. It was quite obvious that Germany believed in force, and that by force only could she be
restrained. I am honestly unable to conceive how a
man, placed in Nicolson's position, could have risked
any other diagnosis, or recommended any other treatment. Even to-day, when we are able to hold a *post
mortem*, we cannot say for certain that his diagnosis
was wrong.

This does not mean that I consider Germany responsible for the war, or that I feel anything but
dislike for that ignorant and disgraceful paragraph in
the Treaty of Versailles which endeavours to fix such
responsibility upon her. I consider, on the contrary,
that Germany is placed at an unfair disadvantage in all
discussions of the origins, as distinct from the causes, of
the war. As regards the origins (1900-1914) I consider
Germany at fault. Though even then, less at fault than
Austria or Russia. As regards the causes (1500-1900)

I consider that the main onus falls on England. This distinction requires some further explanation.

By 1900, having absorbed the Dutch Republics in South Africa, the British Empire was satiated. She desired only to preserve the vast possessions which she had acquired. This placed her in a defensive position, —a position which it is easy to represent as being honourable and pacific. Our own predatory period,— and it was disgraceful enough—dated from 1500 to 1900. During that period we were far more violent and untruthful than were the Germans during those fourteen years which preceded the war. Unfortunately, however, the historians of the war are bound, from lack of space, to throw the maximum emphasis upon the period when England was sitting digestive in her arm chair, and when Germany, young and hungry, was manifesting the unwisdom of adolescence. Before we blame Germany, we must first blame our own Elizabethans. The spirit was exactly the same : the Germans, however, owing to a higher state of culture and rectitude, behaved less blatantly ; and were less successful.

I should wish, therefore, that this book, which endeavours to be objective, should be read in the light of this vital qualification. The Germans, during the period which I cover, were fired by exactly the same motives and energies which illumine what we still regard as one of the most noble passages in our early history. We, for our part, were protected against all imprudence by the repletion, passivity and, I should add, the selfishness, of old age.

H. N.

November 5, 1929.

BOOK I

SPLENDID ISOLATION

I

EARLY YEARS

[1849-1879]

Birth and parentage—His early unhappiness—Admiral Sir Frederick
Nicolson—The *Britannia* and Rugby—Educational ideals in 1860—
Arthur Nicolson kidnapped and maltreated—His uncle Lord Loch—He
goes to Oxford—His studies in Switzerland and at Dresden—Entry into
the Foreign Office—Domestic difficulties—Mr. Wetherell—Private
Secretary to Lord Granville—Sent to Berlin—Germany in 1874—The
war scare of 1875—His book on the German Constitution—Transferred
to Pekin—His two years in China—His return to Germany—Bismarck,
the Berlin Congress and the Alliance with Austria—Lord Odo Russell
—Transferred to Constantinople.

(1)

THE Foreign Office List is published annually. If you
look for Lord Carnock in the current number you will
be referred to the edition of 1921. In that edition
you will find the following :

"CARNOCK OF CARNOCK (ARTHUR NICOLSON), Lord,
P.C., G.C.B., G.C.M.G., G.C.V.O., K.C.I.E., born
September 19, 1849. Was educated at Rugby, and at
Brasenose College, Oxford, of which he was elected an
honorary Fellow in 1916. Passed a competitive examination, and was appointed on probation to a Clerkship in
the Foreign Office, August 23, 1870 ; which appointment
was confirmed, February 21, 1874. Appointed Acting
3rd Secretary to the 2nd Earl Granville, Secretary of State
for Foreign Affairs, from July 2, 1872, to February 21,
1874. Appointed Acting 3rd Secretary at Berlin, February
16, 1874, and a 3rd Secretary in the Diplomatic Service,
November 30, 1874. Passed an examination in Public
Law, February 27, 1875. Promoted to be 2nd Secretary

3

at Pekin, March 27, 1876. Transferred to Berlin, August
15, 1878; and to Constantinople, June 21, 1879. Appointed Superintendent of Student Interpreters in Turkey,
July 12, 1879; appointed (with Sir C. Wilson) to inspect
Consulates in Asia Minor and Syria, October 1881.
Accompanied Lord (afterwards Marquess of) Dufferin
to Egypt in November 1882. Acting Chargé d'Affaires
at Athens from February 29, 1884, to April 25, 1885.
Promoted to be Secretary of Legation at Tehran, April 15,
1885, where he acted as Chargé d'Affaires from November
4, 1885, to April 17, 1888. Made a C.M.G., August 6,
1886; and a K.C.I.E., March 20, 1888. Received an
allowance for knowledge of Persian from August 13,
1886, to September 30, 1888. Appointed Consul-General
for Hungary, to reside at Budapest, October 1, 1888.
Promoted to be Secretary of Embassy at Constantinople,
January 1, 1893; where he acted as Chargé d'Affaires
from June 6 to October 7, 1893; and from December 9,
1893, to February 10, 1894. Appointed Agent and
Consul-General in Bulgaria, August 6, 1894. Promoted
to be Envoy Extraordinary and Minister Plenipotentiary
at Tangier, and Consul-General in Morocco, June 26,
1895. Received the Jubilee Medal, 1897. Succeeded as
11th Baronet, December 29, 1899. Made a K.C.B., July 2,
1901. Received the Coronation Medal, 1902. Made a
K.C.V.O., April 13, 1903. Promoted to be Ambassador
Extraordinary and Plenipotentiary at Madrid, January 1,
1905. Sworn a Privy Councillor, May 29, 1905. Representative at the Conference at Algeciras on affairs of
Morocco, January-April, 1906. Transferred to St.
Petersburg (now Petrograd), February 10, 1906. Made
a G.C.M.G., March 14, 1906; and a G.C.B., October 10,
1907. Appointed Permanent Under Secretary of State
for Foreign Affairs, November 23, 1910. Received the
Coronation Medal, 1911. Retired on a pension, June 20,
1916. Raised to the Peerage as Baron Carnock of Carnock,
in the County of Stirling, July 3, 1916. Has received the

Grand Cross of the Order of Charles III of Spain and the Grand Cross of the Russian Order of Alexander Nevsky, and the Grand Cross of the French Legion of Honour."

In reality, the experiences of those seventy-nine years were less categorical.

(2)

Arthur Nicolson, to the depths of his being, was a shy man. Beneath the high spirits of his early manhood, as beneath the courteous urbanity of his later years, was concealed an inner core of self-repression, diffidence and almost morbid reserve. These disabilities were due to his sufferings and humiliations as a child.

His mother died when he was scarcely two years old. The three small children were left alone in No. 15 William Street—a murky little house since absorbed by the shop of Messrs. Woollands. Their father[1] was for them either a distant legend away with his frigate in the China Seas, or else a harsh voice rasping from the dining room : a voice which wounded and alarmed. Sir Frederick Nicolson married for a second time, and

[1] The Nicolsons are supposed to derive from the Nicails of Castle Assynt in Sutherlandshire and the subsequent MacNicols of Skye. In 1570 Thomas MacNicol left Skye for Edinburgh and his immediate descendants, changing their name to Nicolson, acquired property and riches, bought and embellished the house of Carnock and the estate of Tillicoultrie, and in 1637 purchased a baronetcy of Nova Scotia. The fourth Sir Thomas Nicolson, who was also the fourth Lord Napier and Ettrick, died childless, his estates and peerage passing off into the female line, and the baronetcy devolving upon collaterals who were serving in the Scotch regiment in Holland. Sir Frederick Nicolson, father of Arthur Nicolson, succeeded as tenth baronet at the age of five, was educated on the continent and entered the Navy at an early age. He married in 1847 Mary Clementina, daughter of James Loch, M.P., and had three children : (1) Frederick, killed in the Zulu wars in 1879, (2) Arthur, the subject of this memoir, born Sept. 19, 1849, and (3) Clementina, who in 1885 married Ministerialrat Beemelmans and had one son, Friedrich, killed during the European war.

in circumstances which entailed the temporary removal of the three children from William Street. For a space of years they lived with their grandfather, James Loch, in Albemarle Street, or else at Golspie in Sutherland. It was at Golspie that Arthur first learnt his letters. He could remember trotting to the village school upon a Highland pony, while the butter from the hot roll he was munching streamed down his early morning cheeks. He could remember the sooted smell of the lace curtains in Albemarle Street, as he leant his curls against the window, watching the hats and bonnets in the street below. He remembered seeing Queen Victoria prancing on a black horse, the scarlet of her riding habit slashed by the blue of the Garter, and how the Guards, bearded from Inkerman, raised their bearskins to her upon their bayonets. He remembered talk of Alma, of Balaklava, of the China Wars : stories of his father out there bombarding forts : whispers, even, of his father having committed some error of judgment at Petropavlovsk ; of his being sent home. Fears that his father would be angry ; or killed by the Chinese ; or killed by the Russians. " Arthur," so his aunt recorded in a letter to Sir Frederick, " has no sensibility whatever. He is a famous little fellow." " Arthur," she writes in a subsequent letter, " has a pious horror of the Russians."

This prejudice was not one which remained with him in later life.

It was in 1859 that Sir Frederick Nicolson, portly, stertorous, and guilty of that error of judgment, returned from the East. The circumstances of his second marriage were not such as to commend themselves

ADMIRAL SIR FREDERICK NICOLSON 10th BART.
FATHER OF LORD CARNOCK

to Osborne. The Admiral was given no further command, but went to Woolwich for a space, and then back to 15 William Street. From here, for forty further years, he nursed a grievance against the Admiralty, interfered with the liberty and feelings of his children, dined daily at the Travellers Club, read several thousand French novels, and attended the meetings of the Thames Conservancy Board of which he eventually became the Chairman.

Arthur Nicolson, for his part, was sent to a private school at Wimbledon and then, at the age of twelve, to the *Britannia*. He passed third out of the *Britannia* and his father, for once, grunted approval. Arthur refused, however, to enter the navy and was dismissed with objurgations to Rugby. When he left that school the report furnished to Sir Frederick ran as follows : " Your boy has been an absolute failure at Rugby. We can only hope that he will be less of a failure in after life."

Even at their best, the eighteen-sixties were not a very blithe period in English social history. For Arthur Nicolson, small and motherless, they were peculiarly harsh. The rigours of the *Britannia* or of Rugby alternated with the thunderous gloom of William Street. He was taught on all sides that manliness and self-control were the highest aims of English boyhood : he was taught that all but the most material forms of intelligence were slightly effeminate : he learnt, as they all learnt, to rely upon action rather than upon ideas. Under such a system the higher sensibilities of the mind and soul were apt to become submerged if not sterilised : the furrows of Victorian habit drilled deep grooves across the brain : their theories of conduct became rigid and automatic. They believed in truth, honour, patriotism and virility : they believed in God and the British Empire and the immortality of the soul. Such were the ideals—and there may have been worse ideals—which Arthur Nicolson absorbed.

It was during his last year at Rugby that an incident occurred which had a durable effect upon his nerves and constitution. He was kidnapped one afternoon in Knightsbridge, and kept for thirty hours in some hovel in Ebury Street. A man jumped upon him, crushing him under great bruising knees ; that—before he fainted—was all that he could recollect. He recovered consciousness propped up against a lamp-post in Belgrave Square ; his body was covered with bruises and the contusions on his stomach were so serious that he was ill for months. From that date for over sixty years he was subject to recurrent spasms of indigestion. He would never in after life mention this incident. And Sir Frederick, for his part, maintained that the boy was a blackguard and had shown a precocious disposition for low life.

This affair, though at the time it shattered his nerves and wrecked his health, had one valuable outcome. His uncle, Henry Loch,[1] from the date of that incident took a special interest in his much-abused nephew, an interest which secured for Arthur a nomination for the Foreign Office and some of the happiest experiences of his earlier years. It was Henry Loch who insisted that his little nephew should be sent to Oxford. Arthur Nicolson entered Brasenose in 1867.

[1] Henry Brougham Loch was successively Governor of the Isle of Man, of Victoria, and of South Africa. He was created Baron Loch of Drylaw in 1895 ; he married Elizabeth, daughter of Edward Villiers.

(3)

The college which, fifty years later, and to his immense satisfaction, elected him an honorary fellow, did not, at their first meeting, take kindly to Arthur Nicolson. They found him indolent, undisciplined and untidy. Nicolson left Oxford without taking his degree. There were debts also, and the ensuing atmosphere in William Street was thunderous in the extreme. Arthur had, as yet, no ostensible defence. He had shirked the navy, he had failed at Rugby, he had not been successful at Brasenose. It is not surprising that Sir Frederick, a choleric and egoistic man, should have regarded his younger son with disapproval and almost with dislike.

Twenty-five years were to pass before the Admiral admitted his mistake. In the summer of 1895 Arthur Nicolson was lent Walmer Castle and invited his old father down from London. The oldest son, by then, had died in Zululand : Arthur was the heir. Sitting there on the wide bastion at Walmer, the old Admiral, softened and obese, admitted that he might have been unjust. Everybody, at that date, spoke highly of Arthur Nicolson : he was a rising man. The fat old octogenarian was pleased and proud. He sat there on the bastion at Walmer looking out to sea. His grandchildren (three singularly scrubby little boys) were climbing upon the cannons. Life adjusted itself. Sir Frederick Nicolson, as he sat there in the sun, sang a little Spanish tune which he had heard off the Barbary coast in 1839. His grandsons left their cannons and gathered round him. They asked what he was singing. He said that it was a little Spanish tune. He said that he would now sing them a song in German. He sang, a correct but bronchial voice, " Im wunderschönen Monat Mai." They were much impressed. Those few summer weeks at Walmer in 1895 redeemed the harshness of the 'sixties and 'seventies. But in those early childhood years much needless suffering was caused.

On leaving Oxford, Arthur Nicolson began to study seriously. The energy which had hitherto expressed itself only in physical exuberance was now diverted to self-education. During the year 1869 he worked fourteen hours a day. The habits of intensive industry thus formed remained with him until his death. Seldom has any man possessed a greater faculty for concentration, and, as always, this faculty was self-acquired. He went to Switzerland to learn French, and although he always spoke that language with a strong English accent, yet he mastered it in its entirety, could converse with the utmost fluency and exactitude, and write with real literary distinction.

From Switzerland he proceeded to Dresden to learn German. It was then the summer of 1870. One evening, during a concert on the Brühl'sche Terrasse, a man rushed up the steps waving a paper in his hand, leapt upon a table, and shouted out " Der Krieg ist erklärt ! " The audience rose in enthusiasm and began singing patriotic songs. Four days later, Nicolson received an urgent summons to return to London for his Foreign Office examination. He had great difficulty in reaching England but was able, owing to the kindness of a German friend, to smuggle himself into a military train proceeding to Cologne. He joined with the troops in singing the " Wacht am Rhein." The door of his compartment was chalked with the words " Nach Paris." He reached the Dutch frontier safely and two days later presented himself for his examination. He passed first into the Foreign Office, obtaining 772 marks out of a maximum 930. He was much astonished at this result and imagined that there must have been some mistake. They assured him, at the Civil Service Commission, that the figures were accurate. He was intensely relieved.

(4)

Arthur Nicolson entered the Foreign Office on August 23, 1870. He was very small and very shy. His hair was curly and his eyes blue and excited. He knew no one. He was thoroughly alarmed.

" I was appointed," he wrote subsequently in what is clearly the draft of the first chapter of some intended memoirs, " to what was then termed the French Department, and it was with extreme diffidence that I took my seat at my desk. The Department had at its head Mr. Stavely, who had passed all his life in the Office and was a master of routine. The second was Mr. Currie (afterwards Lord Currie) and in the larger room were Mr. Bertie (afterwards Lord Bertie), Mr. Kenneth Howard and myself. Our Department was next to the room of the Permanent Under Secretary, Mr. Hammond, of whom we were all in awe. Mr. Hammond (created Lord Hammond on his retirement in 1873) had been fifty years in the public service, and though suffering from gout, which rendered his temper slightly irascible, was a wonderfully quick worker and exercised a close and constant control over all the business of the Office. His experience was great, his knowledge of foreign affairs minute and exact, and he had a wonderfully retentive memory. The Foreign Office of those days was conducted on very different lines from those on which it was run when I returned to it in 1910 as Permanent Under Secretary. There were no Second Division Clerks, no typists, and practically few documents were printed for circulation. The junior clerks were employed in copying despatches, decyphering and cyphering telegrams and keeping the registers,—mostly purely mechanical work, but which occupied much time and which, owing to the war, was of a laborious nature."

Sir Frederick, in 1867, had married a third time, and this second step-mother was addicted to drink. Frederick, the elder brother, was away in India : the responsibility of coping with what was rapidly becoming a domestic, and possibly an open scandal, fell upon Arthur alone. How could he allow his sister to be taken to dances by a lady who so early in the evening showed signs of intoxication ? Frederick came home from India and the lady was moved to another house. But the mortification remained. His step-mother objected to Arthur, and there were scenes at William Street. The Admiral was only too ready to hear that his younger son was a wastrel and the friend of wastrels. There was Francis Villiers for instance or that Frank Bertie, and those week-ends at Wytham. Arthur was kept extremely short of money, was not allowed a latch-key, and if he wanted to smoke was obliged to lean forward into his bedroom fire-place, puffing up the chimney. It is not surprising that in such circumstances he should have remained friendless and reserved.

Then came Mr. T. F. Wetherell. Mr. Wetherell was Private Secretary to Lord Granville and conceived a great affection for Arthur Nicolson. He lent him books. He gave him long lists of books on moral

ARTHUR NICOLSON ON
ENTERING THE FOREIGN OFFICE

ARTHUR NICOLSON WITH
T. F. WETHERELL

philosophy and encouraged him to visit the National
Gallery and the British Museum. When they wanted
an immediate index made of the documents required
for the Alabama Convention at Geneva it was Wetherell
who suggested that Arthur Nicolson should be given
the task. He worked for three days, spreading the
papers across the carpet, crawling about the floor preparing his index. The work was well done, and he
was accorded by the Treasury a gratuity (minus income
tax) of fifty pounds. And shortly afterwards Lord
Granville required an Assistant Private Secretary.
Wetherell suggested Nicolson, who was then only
twenty-two years old. He obtained the appointment,
and thus exchanged the routine of the Department for
assiduous connection with high affairs of State.

The value to Arthur Nicolson of his two years'
intimacy with Lord Granville was immense. It gave
him increased confidence in himself. It imbued him
with a taste for the great world and for the ready and
unconventional manners of men who are at ease in it.
It assured him firm friendships in the Foreign Office,
such as his friendship with Francis Villiers, which he
might, if in an obscure position, have been too diffident
to acquire. And it compensated for that grim background of William Street, and the shames and sorrows
of his home.

Early in 1874 Lord Granville was succeeded by Lord
Derby. Arthur Nicolson, being unwilling after this
taste of wider issues to return to departmental routine,
obtained the post of acting third Secretary in Berlin.
After a short holiday in Ireland he bade farewell to the
Foreign Office. Thirty-five years passed before he
returned.

(5)

Arthur Nicolson arrived in the capital of the new German Empire in February of 1874. Berlin, at that date, was a modest little town, boasting an excellent orchestra, a fine University, a system of open drains, and an amiable population, who dined at five and who on Sundays, in prettily decorated cabs, would drive with their children in the Grünewald. German nationalism was then a somewhat gawky stripling. " It has become a joy," wrote Gustav Freytag, " to be a German." Pleasure at this thought wreathed Berlin in smiles. Prussia in 1874 was still provincial and self-contained : it was not until a decade later that she became self-conscious, envious and vulgar. The economic nationalism of Friedrich List had not, as yet, come to ruffle the gentle free-trade souls of the German economists : nor had the spirit of industrial and banking adventurism affected the then grass-grown purlieus of the Behrenstrasse. Lord Odo Russell,[1] the Ambassador, took Nicolson to a Court Ball. There was a large supper, at which, under the endless white globes of the gas-lights, the uniforms looked fine indeed. Nicolson, being small and shy, hid behind a pillar. Lord Odo noticed him, took him by the arm, propelled him into a further room, and shaking at his arm irritably, forced his attention towards a group at the far end of the green and ugly saloon. There was the Emperor William I, tall and affable ; there were von Roon and Moltke : there was the

[1] Subsequently Lord Ampthill. These notes regarding the constant changes in people's names will not be repeated. People will be called by the name by which they will most readily be recognised by the reader, irrespective of the date on which they assumed that name.

15

straight, stout figure of Bismarck. He was in a white uniform, grasping an eagled helmet. " There," said the Ambassador, " you can observe the makers of modern Germany." Nicolson observed.

It was very pleasant in Germany in 1874. The League of the Three Emperors, the Alliance, that is, between Germany, Austria, and Russia, had been concluded in August of 1872. Prince Bismarck could feel that his infant German Empire was backed by friends in the east, and on the west secured by the collapse and republicanism of France. In 1875, however, this confidence was disturbed. France was recovering too quickly from the blow of 1870, the Republic was in no way subservient, it might be a good thing to demonstrate that the League of the Three Emperors could make itself felt. The ensuing war-scare startled Germany as much as it startled Europe. For the first time people began to talk of " German chauvinism " —a malady which that acute diplomatist, Sir Robert Morier, defined as " a new and far more formidable disease than the French : instead of being spasmodic and undisciplined, it is methodical, cold-blooded and self-contained." For Arthur Nicolson the war-scare of 1875 interpreted itself in the form of increased attendance at his desk. It kept him very busy decyphering telegrams and copying despatches in the sunless cellars of the Berlin Chancery.[1] A second Franco-Prussian conflict appeared inevitable. But Gorchakow, when asked whether, in such an event, Russia would once again observe a benevolent neu-

[1] The British Embassy at Berlin was then housed in a flat at the corner of the Leipzigerstrasse where now stands the emporium of Herr Wertheim. In 1877 the British Government purchased the showy but inconvenient mansion of Herr Strussberg in the Wilhelmstrasse.

trality, showed himself to be singularly unreceptive, and in fact he joined the British Government in advising Bismarck against a second war. This led to a slight loosening of the League of the Three Emperors, which was not revived in any effective form till 1881.

It also led to acute personal rivalry between Bismarck and Gorchakow, a rivalry which was very harmful to the peace of Europe.

The crisis of 1875 passed off amid assurances. Nicolson, for his part, was able to devote much spare time to revising an ambitious work which he had then completed upon the German Constitution. This book was published by Longman & Company in 1875 under the title of *A Sketch of the German Constitution and of the Events in Germany from* 1815 *to* 1871. It was not unfavourably reviewed in England. The *Examiner*, however, launched a violent attack, describing the work as " an audacious misrepresentation of facts." Nicolson, who was then on holiday at Venice, was wounded by this assault, and replied to it in a letter which provided the *Examiner* with further cause for abuse. His holiday was thereby embittered, and his literary ambitions were thus early nipped in the bud. Other troubles assailed him. " Money," he wrote to his brother at this period, " is too painful a subject to speak of." And then he fell in love. He became, indeed, half-engaged to a lovely American lady who was visiting the Continent. Sir Frederick, on hearing of this, wrote to Lord Odo Russell summoning him to intervene. The Ambassador resented the Admiral's interference, and replied to the letter in a dignified and distant manner. At the same time he considered that it might be as well if Arthur Nicolson were to retire to some distant post. He wrote to the Foreign Office and suggested China : he made the condition, however, that after two years' absence his favourite third secretary should return to Berlin. This love affair did not therefore materialise, and early in 1876 Arthur Nicolson was appointed to Pekin.

(6)

Those two and a half years in China were not without their value. He travelled *via* America, and spent a happy few weeks in that country, where he was accorded unlimited hospitality, and learnt thereby to regard Americans with sympathy and respect. He arrived in China only a week before the signature of the Sino-British Agreement of 1876. He met Li-Hung-Chang and described him as " a tall man with a powerful head, of rollicking jovial manners, and a fearful laugh which shows huge decayed fangs." For the rest, as second secretary of Legation, Nicolson had little diplomatic work on his shoulders. His duties were confined to copying reports in his then legible handwriting and to cyphering or decyphering the endless telegraphic correspondence with the Consuls at the Treaty Ports. " The material life," he wrote, " is pleasant. An excellent house ; lots of exercise ; absolute independence ; the opportunity of wearing old clothes—this makes me dread the conventionalities of Europe. But then the petty squabbles here, and the dreary sameness of people, and the general twiddle twaddle ! " He reacted against the easy emptiness of his Pekin life by subjecting himself to a severe course of physical and mental discipline. He would awake at dawn and gallop on untrained ponies through driv-

ing sleet; at noon again he would be breaking in
other ponies in the compound : he would force himself to rise in the middle of the night, sitting in a stiff
chair, imagining in some way that to sleep all night
within a bed was effeminate and softening. These
rigours reduced to nothing the weight of that small
and wiry frame. He won several races at the Pekin
meeting, but the first twinges of rheumatism, a life-
long enemy, already assailed him at the age of twenty-
six, and the habits of insomnia which he then imposed
upon himself would return to him disastrously in later
life. He wrote to his brother in February of 1878 :

> " I have determined on and have already commenced a
> serious study of logic and philosophy. I found that
> desultory, arm-chair reading was of no great benefit, and
> as I have perfected my body I think I should put my mind
> through a course of drill also. In my profession, if one
> takes it *au sérieux*, and not as a dawdling through capitals,
> flirting and dancing, you require a critical mind. Diplo-
> matists have, I know, little power nowadays, but even
> regarding them merely as official reporters they should be
> educated to their task. Reporting accurately, finding the
> true causes, noting certain symptoms, sifting information,
> calculating chances, all these are rare gifts, or rather I
> should say rare acquirements, which require study and
> observation and experience to obtain. But this will bore
> you, and I shall appear an enthusiastic youth,—which I
> am not, but one who is appalled by his lamentable
> ignorance and incapacity."

Before these excellent intentions could be fully
executed, he was transferred from Pekin and ordered
to return to Germany. He reached Berlin in January
of 1879, and was warmly welcomed by the Odo
Russells.

(7)

Many important events had happened in Europe
during the two years that Arthur Nicolson spent in
China. The Bulgarian Revolt of 1876, the atrocities
which had accompanied its suppression, had led to the
Russo-Turkish War of 1877 and had brought the
Russian armies to the gates of Constantinople. The
ensuing Treaty of San Stefano, signed on March 3,
1878, would have placed Russia in absolute, if indirect,
control of the Balkans and of what remained of Turkey
in Europe. The Austrian and British Governments
were alarmed and insisted upon the Treaty of San
Stefano being revised by the Concert of Europe.
Russia resented this intervention, but, realising that
her communications were at the mercy of any Austro-
British combine, she had the wisdom to surrender.
A European Congress was held in Berlin in June 1878,
and the Treaty of Berlin was signed on July 13.
Lords Salisbury and Beaconsfield returned to London
bringing " peace with honour," but it was a peace
which, as this narrative will show, was fraught with
present bitterness and future complication. Austro-
Russian competition for dominant influence in the
Balkan peninsula had been emphasised in a peculiarly
categorical and blatant form. Russia, for her part,
felt cheated of her spoils ; Bulgaria and Montenegro,
who had seen their wildest dreams realised at San
Stefano, were deeply resentful ; Serbia emerged to see
Bosnia and Herzegovina given as a sop to Austria,
whereas the latter obtained only the " provisional
occupation " of these provinces in place of the Balkan
partition which she had at Reichstadt been led to

expect : Turkey lost a large part of her European
possessions ; Rumania, most ill-used of all, had been
forced to surrender Bessarabia ; and Greece had merely
obtained the vaguest of European wishes for her welfare. The Concert of Europe had established its
authority, and had prevented a European conflagration : yet Bismarck, who had presided at the Congress,
had reason to be alarmed.

The Russians imagined that they by their benevolent
neutrality had enabled Prussia to win the War of 1870,
and they therefore accused the German Chancellor of
the deepest ingratitude for not having more openly
taken the side of Russia at the Berlin Congress. Pan-
Slav publicists, such as Katkoff and Asakoff, began to
state that " the road to Constantinople leads through
the Brandenburger Tor," and there were hints even of
a Russo-French Alliance.[1] Bismarck, as usual, succeeded in drawing advantage from these disadvan-
tageous circumstances. For him the great aim, as
always, was the internal consolidation of Germany ;
for him the great nightmare, as always, was a European
coalition. France must, at any cost, be kept " in
quarantine " ; at any cost Germany must not quarrel
with Russia, Austria or England, with any two of
them, at the same time. He thus profited by the
tension between Austria and Russia to draw the former

[1] The Franco-Russian Alliance, which was first mooted as early as 1879,
only became a serious proposition when Russia began to borrow largely on
the Paris Market in 1888. In March of 1890 the French armament firms
began to supply Russia with rifles on the express condition that these weapons
would never be used against France. In 1890 came the fall of Bismarck and
the refusal of Caprivi to renew the secret Reinsurance Treaty with Russia.
The Triple Alliance was renewed in 1891, and in the same year, after the visit
of the French fleet to Cronstadt, a diplomatic arrangement was concluded
between France and Russia. It was not, however, till December 31, 1893,
that this was confirmed and supplemented by a definite military convention.

into his orbit, and after considerable difficulty with his own Emperor, he was able to sign with Austria the Dual Alliance of September 1879.[1] Feelers were concurrently stretched out to England, but the British Government were non-committal. The Austro-German Alliance was however warmly welcomed in England ; it would, they felt, increase the tension already apparent between Berlin and St. Petersburg : Lord Salisbury described it as " Good tidings of great joy."

Bismarck had once again juggled with the rivalries of the European orchestra, and once again he had emerged magnificently dominant and calm. For a decade longer Europe was to feel secure under the aegis of his violent and tortuous beneficence.

And yet Bismarck created conditions which afflicted the simple and diffident German bourgeois with a crisis of the nerves. He gave his countrymen an acute sense of power without giving them that self-reliance, or that modesty, with which alone power can be exercised with restraint. For his own purposes (for the purpose, that is, of silencing the liberals of 1848 and the socialists of 1877) he played upon the fears of Germany and on her vanity. He thus rendered his countrymen on the one hand inordinately conceited and on the other hand inordinately uneasy. He failed to educate them in those habits of self-confident and self-dependent judgment which would have provided his feeble successors with a stable basis on which to work. Hence the arrogant uncertainty which affected German policy from 1890 until 1914.

[1] Italy joined this Alliance in 1882—and it thereafter was called " The Triple Alliance."

Lord Odo Russell was the wisest as well as the most
stimulating of chiefs, and while encouraging Nicolson
to study these tendencies in high politics, he at the
same time urged him to enter into other sides of
German life, and to get into touch with circles outside
the usual round of diplomacy.   Nicolson drank quantities of white beer in the company of the younger
Reichstag deputies.   He found them over-educated
and ambitious.   He also joined several scientific
societies, and would attend their evening conver-
saziones and listen to old and young professors dis-
coursing on the current controversies of science,
anthropology and politics.   " My dear Nicolson,"
wrote Lord Odo in February 1879, " I love zeal."
" If," Nicolson wrote to his brother a few days later,
" my digestion could stand it, I should much like my
societies, but I suffer for twenty-four hours after a
supper of badly cooked veal, oceans of beer and clouds
of tobacco.   The speeches in the discussions which
follow the lectures are too long.   A German either
wanders from his subject or goes into too great detail.
The Geographical, however, really *is* interesting.   At
the last meeting I met Nachtigal, the great African
traveller."   He flung himself also into a study of
German socialism which was then passing through an
important crisis owing to the anti-socialist legislation
of 1878.   " I intend," he wrote, " to go as much into
the question as possible, as I think it one of the most
interesting studies of the century."

This was the last letter which he wrote to his brother,
who was killed shortly afterwards in the Zulu War.
And at the end of 1879 Arthur Nicolson proceeded to
Constantinople.

II

LORD DUFFERIN AND THE EGYPTIAN QUESTION

[1879–1883]

Sir Henry Layard—Visit to Damascus—Execution of the Treaty of Berlin—
Mr. Goschen—Armenian Question—Military Consuls in Asia Minor—
Lord and Lady Dufferin—Miss Rowan Hamilton—Accompanies Sir
Charles Wilson to Asia Minor—The Egyptian question—The Military
Convention and the Proclamation against Arabi—The night of Sep-
tember 15, 1882—Arthur Nicolson's marriage—Accompanies Lord
Dufferin to Egypt—The Dufferin report—Discontent with diplomacy.

(1)

" I should much like "—Arthur Nicolson had written
in 1878—" to go to Constantinople. But I do not
want Layard as a chief. I gather that he is violent and
inconsiderate."

This pessimistic forecast was not fulfilled. He went
to Constantinople, but he liked Sir Henry Layard
immensely. And Layard, who appreciated energy,
took kindly to this new secretary and at once invited
Arthur Nicolson to accompany him on a tour through
Syria. They went to Damascus. Upon the road that
leads down and up from the Lebanon to the anti-
Lebanon, upon that lovely thyme-scented road, they
were met by an escort of Druse cavalry. The men
were dressed in chain armour and waved steel axes in
their hands. Forty years before, Layard had limped
along that road obscure and penniless. He now rode
through watered orange groves to the dust of a thousand horsemen. They fired guns in his honour. The

people in the kerosene-lit cafés rose and crowded at
his approach. He was housed in a palace (since destroyed). And it was difficult for the Ambassador to
explain to all those eager acquisitive faces that his visit
was one of curiosity merely : that he had not come to
liberate. The drums beat all night. The attraction
of the East, the smell of fat frying at night-time, the
sound at night-time of dogs barking at the moon, came
to Nicolson in a dramatic form. He never forgot this
visit to Damascus.

At Constantinople things were difficult. The Congress and Treaty of Berlin had left a number of loose
ends. The African tributaries of the Sultan—Tunis,
Tripoli and Egypt—had not been dealt with. Greece
had been promised a rectification of the frontier in her
favour, and this rectification had been defined in a
protocol as including Thessaly and Epirus. Montenegro had been led to expect the districts of Gusinje
and Plava. Hitherto, however, the eyes of Europe
had been fixed on Bulgaria. It had been difficult to
delimit the frontier ; it had been even more difficult
to secure the evacuation of the Russian troops. It was
only in the first months of 1880 that the Concert of
Europe was able to devote its attention to the Greek
and Montenegrin questions, and by that date the Concert of Europe was already falling seriously out of time.

In April 1880 the elections in England led to the
second administration of Mr. Gladstone. Sir Henry
Layard was regarded by the Liberals as being too
pro-Turk ; and it was true that the arid and ungainly
qualities of the Ottoman race had twisted his judgment
into awkward shapes. He was recalled on leave of
absence. He proceeded to Venice, taking with him a

very excellent Bellini which he had obtained from the
Seraglio, and a bitter prejudice against the administration of Mr. Gladstone. The post of Ambassador
at Constantinople was given to Mr. G. J. (subsequently Viscount) Goschen, member for Ripon, whom
Mr. Gladstone had found it difficult to fit into his
Cabinet. Goschen arrived in Constantinople in May
of 1880. He was at one and the same time delighted
at being an Ambassador and disgusted at not being in
the Cabinet. This made things difficult for his staff :
he treated them exactingly : he was at one moment
over-diffident and at the next moment over-impulsive :
he got on Nicolson's nerves. The Montenegrin
problem was the first to be dealt with. Gusinje and
Plava were found to be unsuitable, and Montenegro
was therefore offered Dulcingo as compensation. It
was with great difficulty that the Sultan was induced
to agree to this concession.

The Ambassadors in Constantinople then tackled
the Greek frontier. Goschen proceeded to Berlin to
interview Bismarck. He induced him, or imagined
that he had induced him, to take the lead. " The
Concert of Europe," he wrote in triumph, " will at
last have an authoritative conductor." The idea was
to give Greece rectifications in Thessaly but to abandon
the idea of ceding Epirus and to compensate her with
Crete. This, on the whole, was a good idea and would,
if adopted, have saved much subsequent trouble. The
Ambassadors, however, were neither united nor unbiased. It was clearly unpleasant for them to impose
concessions upon the Government to which they were
accredited. Goschen, who knew that he was there for
a short time only, displayed none of these hesitations.

He advised Lord Granville to send the British Fleet to the Golden Horn. Lord Granville, for his part, knew that neither at Berlin nor at Paris were they anxious to re-open the Eastern question. Mr. Goschen then suggested that if it proved difficult to induce the Sultan to surrender Crete, Her Majesty's Government might compensate Greece by the cession of Cyprus— an island which had been filched by Lord Salisbury in 1878. Mr. Gladstone, in spite of his philhellene sentiments, feared that British public opinion, which had been shocked by Majuba and was worried about Ireland, would not at the moment support the cession of British occupied territory however questionably acquired. The Government, therefore, while refusing Cyprus, told Goschen that they " left everything to his judgment and discretion." Prince Bismarck, at the same moment, allowed it to be known that he would only accept a " pacific solution," meaning thereby that he refused to exert any pressure upon Turkey to execute the promises embodied in the Treaty and Protocol of Berlin. The result was a compromise. Turkey made cessions in Thessaly, but Greece obtained no compensation for the non-fulfilment of the promises made to her in regard to Epirus. Here, again, were sown the seeds of future trouble. Meanwhile, however, in May of 1881, Mr. Goschen returned to England and assured his constituents that he had solved the Eastern question. He was succeeded, most fortunately, by Lord Dufferin.

There was one further problem which had been mentioned in the Treaty of Berlin, but which awoke little sympathy from the Powers pledged to the execution of that instrument. Lord Salisbury had rightly

seen that the Eastern question was ultimately concerned not merely with the European, but also with
the Asiatic provinces of Turkey.   He foresaw the
Armenian question, and endeavoured to meet it by
imposing on the Sultan the obligation to introduce
reforms in his Armenian vilayets.   It was soon evident,
however, that Germany, Austria and France were not
prepared to support any policy of British supervision
in Anatolia.   Their hesitation is comprehensible.   It
was not of Article 61 that they thought but of the
secret Anglo-Turkish Convention which Lord Salisbury had imposed upon the Porte a few weeks before
the Berlin Congress.   In this Convention it was clearly
contemplated that Great Britain should establish a
protectorate over Asiatic Turkey, and the Armenian
reforms were only an item in this programme.   It is
true that Mr. Gladstone, who had bitterly dissociated
himself from any responsibilities in Asia Minor during
his Midlothian campaign, could be trusted to proceed
with Article 61 in a purely humanitarian spirit.   But
Lord Salisbury's subtlety in regard to the original
Convention had prejudiced our moral position from
the outset.   The Egyptian question, which then arose,
still further increased suspicion.   We cannot blame
either the Porte or the Powers if our Armenian schemes
were regarded with distrust.

The British Government fell back, therefore, on the
expedient of appointing " military consuls " at the
points of danger.   This policy was a mistake.   It
encouraged the Armenians to imagine that Great
Britain was in some form pledged to their assistance.
The autonomist movement was thereby stimulated,
secret societies were formed, and in the minds of many

Armenians the idea was generated that they had only
to provoke incidents to secure British intervention.
They did not realise that British benevolence is in most
cases vicarious, or that Etchmiadzin is not within
striking distance of the British fleet. The results of
our then well-intentioned but still undigested proposals was the ultimate massacre of several thousand
women and children, and a smart epigram on the part
of Lord Salisbury about our having " put our money
on the wrong horse." For the moment, however, the
intention of Her Majesty's Government was to secure,
by the appointment of these eight military consuls,
first-hand information on local conditions, and they
hoped to base upon the information thus acquired a
scheme of Anatolian reform. Sir Valentine Baker was
appointed " Inspector General of Reforms in Asia
Minor." And everybody, including Prince Bismarck,
thought this a highly amusing episode to the tiresome
business of executing the Treaty of Berlin.

(2)

Lord and Lady Dufferin arrived in Constantinople
in June of 1881. They were accompanied by Lady
Dufferin's youngest sister, Miss Catherine Rowan
Hamilton, who, although descended from one of the
most excessive of Irish rebels, was herself a gentle little
loyalist. The drawing-rooms of the Summer Embassy
glistened with Sheraton and fresh chintz. The chandeliers in the gallery tinkled as the children galloped
along the upper corridors ; the wooden shutters were
sticky with the smell of new paint ; and through their
slits the unceasing waters of the Bosphorus swung
patterns on the ceilings. They dined under the

magnolias, the candle-flames on the table swaying lightly in their large glass globes. After dinner the young men of the Chancery would come across from their house along the quayside, and there would be writing-games under the red lamp-shades, or rehearsals for those amateur theatricals with which Lady Dufferin revived the finances of the local charities. The programmes of these entertainments are still available— strange remnants of an age before self-observation had induced self-consciousness. There was " *Les Deux Aveugles.*" *Bouffonnerie musicale de J. Offenbach.* There was " *Le Printemps.*" *After the picture of that name with Gounod's song sung to it.* There was " *The Happy Pair,*" of which the principal rôles were assigned to Lady Dufferin and Mr. Nicolson. There were tableaux and picnics ; there were Dorcas sales ; there were moonlight expeditions on the Bosphorus. The caikdjis would rest on their oars smearing grease upon the rowlock-peg under a blatant Asiatic moon. Other members of the Embassy contributed to these pleasures and ordeals : we find at different dates such names as Edward Goschen and Charles Hardinge : there were Mr. Bland and Mr. Charteris and Mr. Kennedy and Mr. Block : there was the American Minister who was the author of *Ben Hur* : there was Mr. Donald Mackenzie Wallace the correspondent of *The Times.* Arthur Nicolson for his part fell in love with Catherine Rowan Hamilton. It was all rather complicated as he, in a few weeks, was due to leave on a tour in Anatolia, and she, in a few weeks, might well return to Ireland. He was diffident and said nothing. It was not till his return that they became engaged.

It was thus with an anxious heart that in August 1881

Arthur Nicolson departed on his journey through
Anatolia. He was attached to Sir Charles Wilson, a
man who, a few years later, was made the scapegoat for
Gordon's murder on the ground that he dawdled at
Metemmeh and dawdled at Gubat. In 1881, however,
Colonel Wilson was in the ascendant : he had been
specially selected to inspect the military Consulates in
Asia Minor ; he had received long private letters from
Lord Salisbury : but now that Lord Granville was
again at the Foreign Office Sir Charles Wilson em-
barked on his task with conscientious pessimism. They
visited Eneboli, Samsun, Kerasund and Trebizond.
They visited Smyrna, Beyrout, Haiffa, Jaffa, Jerusalem,
Nablus, Samaria, Latakia, Antioch, Alexandretta and
Aleppo. They returned to find that in the meanwhile
highly important events had taken place in Egypt. No
one thereafter bothered any more about the military
Consuls in Anatolia and they were gradually withdrawn. It was the Egyptian problem which from then
on filled the centre of the stage, and as this problem
exercised an important effect upon Nicolson's views
and sympathies, and became the ultimate cause of a
then undreamt-of European grouping, it is well that
the story and Nicolson's humble part in it, should in
some detail be retold.

(3)

It was in the early autumn of 1881 that Nicolson
returned to Constantinople. The Embassy had by then
moved from Therapia to where that large Italian palace
looks out through mangey cypresses upon Stamboul.
Socially the life was even more incessant and domestic
than at Therapia. The Secretaries, every evening,

were expected to call upon their Ambassadress and the dramatic entertainments became more frequent and ambitious every month. Lord Dufferin himself would attend these functions, applauding tranquilly—the two fingers of his right hand tapping tranquilly upon the palm of the left, a slow remembered smile lighting his southern face. No man has ever absorbed or distributed so much enjoyment. The brilliance of his attainments, the glamour of his parentage, the awe which he inspired, were softened by an almost feminine sensibility, by a perfect conjunction of strength and gentleness; by the fact, ultimately, that he was the kindest man that ever lived. The influence which he exercised on Arthur Nicolson was deep and durable. From Lord Granville, Nicolson had learnt that, in the larger affairs of life, fuss is the brother of inefficiency. Lord Odo Russell had taught him that inaccuracy is one of the most unpleasant symptoms of indolence. To his own temperament he owed a fanatical regard for loyalty, truth and fairness; a deep capacity for concentration. Lord Dufferin taught him that rectitude need not necessarily be disagreeable, or industry arrogant; that patience and modesty are not incompatible with a radiant rapidity of mind; that anger is not a proof of strength, nor ponderousness a sign of dignity: that the graces of the intelligence are as important as those of the body or the soul: that acidity of temperament is, after all, a very great mistake. Nicolson, gay, energetic and still curiously adolescent, responded readily to these inspiriting lessons. It must be remembered that he was essentially a late-flowering plant. His March and April growth had been retarded by the meagre soil of his early

education, by the frosts of domestic shame which had
nipped the buds. He was over thirty when he first met
Lord Dufferin, but psychologically his age was twenty-
one. The lavish radiance of Lord Dufferin's personality, the affection with which he and his wife treated
this buoyant boyish secretary, the fact that with and
through them Nicolson found at last the joys of family
and home, produced a sudden blossoming. He was
still childish and uncertain when he first reached
Constantinople. But it was as a man—happy, eager
and self-confident, that he came to co-operate so
intimately with Lord Dufferin in the Egyptian crisis
which at this stage developed.

(4)

The Egyptian situation, as Arthur Nicolson found
it on his return that autumn of 1881 from Anatolia,
was highly intricate.[1] Through insensible and invol-
untary stages the French and British Governments had
been induced by the great banking houses and other
of the Khedive's creditors to intervene in the internal
affairs of Egypt. Each step they had gingerly taken
had led them a step further ; they were by now thoroughly committed to a complicated system of controls
and responsibilities, the abandonment of which would

[1] The main dates in the Egyptian question are the following : 1863, Ismail
succeeds as Khedive. 1869, Suez Canal opened. 1875, Beaconsfield pur-
chases majority shares for British Government. 1876, Egypt, owing to
Ismail's reckless extravagance, on the verge of bankruptcy. France and
England intervene and establish Caisse de la Dette. 1877, French and English
Financial Comptrollers nominated. 1879, April, Ismail makes coup d'état
and abolishes all foreign financial control. June, France and England depose
Ismail and put Tewfik in his place. Financial controls re-established. 1881,
January, military and nationalist discontent. Movement is headed by Arabi
Pasha. September 9, 1881, Arabi organises military rising and seizes reins of
Government. It is at this stage that the main narrative begins.

cause a financial panic in London and Paris and would ruin not merely a few speculators, but a large number of perfectly honest and deserving investors. The two Governments could scarcely allow the military dictatorship of Arabi Pasha to undo the work of the last five years or to abolish the guarantees under which Egyptian finances were slowly recovering. Nor could Great Britain permit this new high-road to India to be exposed to the dangers of internal chaos. There seemed at the time little prospect of inducing Arabi, whose head had been turned by the enthusiasm of his supporters and the encouragement of that splendid eccentric, Wilfrid Scawen Blunt, to realise the facts as they stood and himself to come to some agreement with the European creditors. The two Powers decided, rightly or wrongly (probably wrongly), that Arabi was intractable and dangerous and that some form of " constitutional " government must be reimposed. They were not in the least agreed as to the means by which this should be effected. Great Britain, proceeding from the traditional theory of the integrity of the Ottoman Empire, considered that it was for the Sultan as Suzerain to re-establish the authority of the Khedive. The French Government, who had designs on Tunis and had no desire to see Turkish troops reappearing in North Africa, inclined to joint military intervention by France and England. Bismarck, for his part, was glad to encourage France in a policy which would distract her attention from Alsace Lorraine and produce inevitable friction between her and England. He urged both countries to go ahead. Italy, for the moment, and with one eye on Tripoli, remained aloof. Russia was, if anything, relieved to

c

see England beginning to envisage the Eastern question in terms, not of the Straits, but of the Suez Canal. And the Sultan oscillated between a desire to reimpose his direct authority in Egypt and a superstitious fear that Arabi might be the expected Islamic Messiah.

The play and counter play of these conflicting purposes and apprehensions produced during the next twelve months a situation of almost unexampled inconsequence. The Sultan hurriedly despatched two Turkish Commissioners to Egypt, and was at once informed by the French and British Governments that they had learnt of this mission with " surprise and regret " and trusted that the visit of the two Commissioners would be curtailed. The Commissioners were thus recalled to Constantinople. An uneasy pause ensued during which the French Government pressed for joint occupation and the British Government deferred committing themselves, hoping ardently that something would happen to render a decision unnecessary. Meanwhile the anti-foreign agitation was spreading in Egypt and Arabi Pasha was rapidly assuming the rôle of a national hero. On December 15, 1881, Gambetta suggested to the British Government that in order to reassert the Khedive's authority " the two Governments should be prepared for united and immediate action." The British Government were disinclined for action : they would agree only to a Joint Note. This Note, which was presented at Cairo on January 8, 1882, stated that the two Governments were " determined to guard by united efforts against all causes of complication external or internal which might menace the order of things established in Egypt." The Note was a mistake and its effect was lamentable. On the one hand it committed the two Powers openly and inextricably to direct responsibility for the affairs of Egypt; and on the other hand it united against them all classes of the Egyptian population, thus rendering impossible any but a forcible solution. "From the moment," writes Lord Cromer, "that the Joint Note was issued, foreign intervention became an almost unavoidable necessity."

It was at this stage, on January 31, 1882, that M. Gambetta, the protagonist of intervention, resigned. He was succeeded by M. de Freycinet, who shared M. Clemenceau's conviction that France should not for one moment allow Prince Bismarck to distract her gaze from the blue line of the Vosges. M. de Freycinet was thus opposed to Eastern adventures, and in addition he was a trustful man. He believed in the Concert of Europe; in the reasonableness of Abdul Hamid; in the Khedive Tewfik; in the pro-French sentiments of the Egyptian nationalists; in the misleading reports which emanated from the French Consul at Cairo; and in the repeated assurances that he received from England that the British Government were anxious for a pacific solution and had no desire to act alone. These latter assurances were, at the moment, passionately sincere. British statesmen are usually blind to their own tendencies but vividly aware of their own disinclinations. While not knowing what they are doing or what they want to do, they realise quite clearly what they do *not* want to do, and they are apt to grasp at this negative, and to proclaim it, in place of the very tiring calculations which any positive policy would entail. This gap between our conscious realisation of what we do *not* want to do, and our

unconscious realisation that in the end we shall have
to do it, is inevitably interpreted by foreign observers
as indicating hypocrisy or even worse. The mistake
our critics make is to state in terms of ethics a problem
which is essentially psychological. We can scarcely
expect, however, even the most intelligent and for-
bearing foreigner to regard our handling of the
Egyptian question as anything but opportunist in the
extreme.

(5)

The confusion which ensued at Constantinople developed very rapidly. Lord Dufferin found himself
in a difficult position. On the one hand he had
some sympathy for Egypt and Arabi. " All my
instincts," he wrote, " are with the national party.
First of all, I love the country." In the second place
he had a shrewd suspicion that in the end no British
Cabinet could allow Egypt either to relapse into disorder or to be occupied by a Foreign Power other than
themselves. And in the third place the issues were
still further confused by M. de Freycinet's endeavours
to combine all the advantages of all the policies which
had hitherto been propounded. An Anglo-French
fleet was sent to Alexandria to represent the policy of
joint intervention and to perpetuate the " directive "
character of Franco-British co-operation. A Conference of Ambassadors, which the Turks refused to
attend, was constituted at Constantinople, in order to
demonstrate that the Concert of Europe had also been
invoked. The French Ambassador now joined Lord
Dufferin in urging the Turks themselves to send troops
to Egypt, but under European " control." And on

June 1, 1882, M. de Freycinet startlingly assured the Chamber that in no circumstances would France herself be committed to military intervention. As a corollary to this assurance the French ships were shortly afterwards withdrawn from Alexandria leaving the British Admiral alone. M. de Freycinet has been much blamed by his countrymen for what Gambetta called this " rupture néfaste," and for behaviour which M. Reinach has characterised as " unworthy of France and the Republic." As a matter of truth, however, his policy of non-intervention reflected the desires of the majority of Frenchmen ; and when, at the eleventh hour, M. de Freycinet actually did propose to intervene in the Canal Zone he was defeated in the Chamber by 416 votes to 75. It was thus not M. de Freycinet but the French Chamber who rendered inevitable a situation in which Great Britain intervened alone.

On July 15 the Conference of Ambassadors at Constantinople agreed on a Joint Note in which the Sultan, in the name of the Concert of Europe, was invited to send troops to Egypt, but was informed that the duration and scope of this expedition must be strictly limited. The effect of this Note was somewhat diminished by the fact that four days previously, on July 11, the British fleet had already bombarded the forts at Alexandria, and that many Europeans had been massacred as a result. From that moment the direction of the Egyptian problem passed inevitably into British hands, and the Conference of Ambassadors at Constantinople met less and less frequently and in the end relapsed into embarrassed silence.

(6)

The negotiations that followed, and they were intricate and diverting, were conducted entirely by Lord
Dufferin. Nicolson accompanied him on all vital
occasions to the Sublime Porte or to Yildiz and was
a witness of the dramatic events which led to the
British occupation of Egypt, and to twenty years of
Anglo-French bitterness and distrust. Now that M.
de Freycinet had withdrawn from all co-operation, the
British Government concentrated their efforts on
securing that the operations against Arabi, henceforth
inevitable, should be of an Anglo-Turkish and not of
a purely British character. The matter was urgent.
The Europeans were fleeing from Egypt in panic. A
British Expeditionary Force under Sir Garnet Wolseley
was already on its way to Alexandria. France, and
even Italy, had been asked to co-operate but had
refused. The Sultan, for his part, was assailed by
conflicting emotions. Lord Granville had insisted
that before the British Government could " accept "
the co-operation of Turkish troops, the intentions of
the Sultan must previously be " cleared from ambiguity." This condition was necessitated by the
suspicion that Abdul Hamid might either join forces
with Arabi, or else, once the Khedive's authority had
been restored, refuse to leave the country. To meet
these dangers two documents were necessary. The
first was a Proclamation to be made by the Sultan
repudiating Arabi and all his works. The second was
a Military Convention under which the scope, duration
and conditions of the Anglo-Turkish occupation would
be defined. The Sultan hesitated to sign either of

these documents. He was afraid that if he publicly repudiated Arabi he would lose his prestige with the Islamic world. He was afraid that if he signed with Great Britain a Convention limiting his right of intervention in Egypt all hope of re-establishing his direct authority over his vassal would be gone for ever. Abdul Hamid was correct in both these apprehensions. Where he had made a mistake was in not realising that the British Government were at last determined on action, and that when once the wheels of action are set moving in England they are exceedingly difficult to stop.

It was thus not until August 7, 1882, that the Porte accepted the principle that joint intervention should be subjected to some agreed conditions. On August 9 a draft Proclamation denouncing Arabi was submitted for Lord Dufferin's approval. On August 10 Lord Dufferin accepted the draft Proclamation but found that the Sultan had gone back upon the proposed Military Convention and that he now wished for some more general agreement between Turkey and the Powers represented on the Ambassadors Conference. The Conference, for its part, was not prepared to undertake this responsibility, and on August 14 it adjourned itself indefinitely. On August 18 Said and Assim Pashas, as representing the Sultan, appeared at Therapia and for three hours discussed with Lord Dufferin the terms of a Military Convention, which they finally agreed to recommend to Abdul Hamid for his acceptance. On August 19 this draft was rejected by the Sultan and a further delay was caused by difficulties regarding the requisition of mules for the British Expeditionary Force which was at that moment assembled. On August 23 the Sultan apologised about the mules, consented to sign the Convention, but then went back upon the draft Proclamation against Arabi to which he had already agreed. During the next four days the negotiations continued incessantly, and at last on August 27 Abdul Hamid agreed to the Convention as drafted, and even appeared ready to sign the Proclamation. When once these had been signed and published the Turkish forces, which were waiting in Crete, were to proceed to Egypt and cooperate with Sir Garnet Wolseley. The Sultan still hesitated, however, to affix his final signature to either of the documents, and on September 6, in the hope of forcing Lord Dufferin's hand, he caused a wholly false version of the draft Proclamation to be published in the papers. Lord Dufferin was incensed by this " inconceivable lack of good faith " on the part of Abdul Hamid. In order to manifest his displeasure and to cool his angered brain, he proceeded to Prinkipo in his cutter. The officials at the Sublime Porte could watch from their windows the white sails of the *Lady Hermione* battling with the current round Oxeia and the Bulwer Island. They could not understand how an Ambassador, and one of unquestionable elegance, could spend his days, barefooted like a common Greek sailor, tugging at wet ropes. They could not understand how, if the situation were really as urgent as he represented, Lord Dufferin could afford to bob about the Marmora in an open sailing boat. They advised the Sultan that there was still further time for negotiation. It was thus not till the afternoon of September 15 that the Convention and Proclamation had, except for a few details, been agreed to in their final form.

At 3 p.m. on that day, September 15, 1882, Lord
Dufferin and Arthur Nicolson proceeded to Yildiz for
a final interview with Abdul Hamid. They were
received in one of the smaller pavilions. The Sultan
sat crouching over a table of ebony playing nervously
with his beads. He raised further conditions. He
suggested that these further conditions should be
negotiated with his Ministers, who clustered, troubled
and subservient, in his room beyond. Meanwhile an
urgent cypher telegram had been received at the
Embassy. Its contents were such as to necessitate its
immediate communication to Lord Dufferin. For
some inscrutable reason the head of the Chancery
omitted to send it on to Yildiz. His excuse, when
reproved later, was that he never imagined that he
would be able to catch Lord Dufferin in time. In this
he was mistaken. For five further hours Lord
Dufferin exercised all his powers of persuasion in an
attempt to induce the Ministers to agree to the Convention in the only form in which the Ambassador
could himself consent to sign it. Coffee was brought
and sweetmeats, and at nine o'clock they held a second
interview with the Sultan, who appeared to be weakening. At ten the discussions with Said and Assim
Pashas were resumed, and by midnight there was hope
of signature before the dawn. The Ministers proceeded together to the Sultan's study and Dufferin and
Nicolson remained behind. The servants in their blue
liveries stood around, their white-gloved hands clasped
upon their stomachs. The innumerable clocks struck
one a.m. and at one-fifteen the sinister figure of the
Sultan's astrologer was seen creeping across the ante-
room towards his master's study. That moment, that

scene, remained photographed upon Nicolson's memory for ever afterwards. He knew that the astrologer was in the pay of those who wished to prevent the Sultan from signing the Proclamation against Arabi. Twenty minutes later Said and Assim Pashas re-appeared. The Sultan, they said, was unable to approve the compromise agreed to, and further discussions would be required. It was now a quarter to two in the morning. Lord Dufferin refused to remain any longer at the Palace. He had already been sitting in that plush arm-chair for nearly eleven hours. They clung to his coat-tails, urging him to remain. There were only, they urged, a very few points which still required adjustment and then the agreement would be signed. Lord Dufferin insisted on entering the launch which was to take him back to Therapia. He returned to find the Summer Embassy ablaze with lights and anxiety. A secretary met him on the quay-side with the decyphered telegram in his hand. The telegram told Lord Dufferin not to sign the Convention without further instructions. It informed him also that at dawn of September 15 Sir Garnet Wolseley, after a sudden night-advance, had completely defeated Arabi at Tel-el-Kebir.

From that moment there could be no further question of Turkish co-operation in the Egyptian settlement. The same afternoon Said and Assim Pashas re-appeared at Therapia indicating that Abdul Hamid was now anxious to sign what he had rejected the night before. Lord Dufferin explained to them that it was now too late. " Your hesitation of yesterday," he said to them, " has made my reputation as a diplomatist, but has ruined it as an honest man." And it is true that there were many who believed, and who still believe, that Lord Dufferin merely played with the Sultan until Sir Garnet Wolseley had obtained a single-handed decision.

Arthur Nicolson, who was in the best position to judge, always contended that the British Government and Lord Dufferin had been sincerely anxious to secure Turkish co-operation, and that the blame for the delay rested entirely upon the Sultan. He never contended, however, that our attitude in the Egyptian question was throughout wholly defensible. When nearly thirty years later a Foreign Office official was declaiming in righteous indignation against Italy's sudden descent on Tripoli, he was startled to find himself checked by a flash of sudden wrath in the blue eyes of his Chief. " It is not for us," said Arthur Nicolson, " to cast that sort of stone."

(7)

Nicolson's private fortunes, during those months of 1882, had undergone a vital change. In February he became engaged to Catherine Rowan Hamilton, and their marriage was celebrated on April 20. It took place in the chapel of the Pera Embassy and in circumstances of the greatest diplomatic ceremony. The following notes are extracted from the *Levant Herald* of April 12 :

"The paths leading through the grounds from the Embassy to the chapel were carpeted, and on either side were drawn up the men of H.M.S. *Antelope* and *Cockatrice*. At three o'clock the bridegroom, accompanied by Mr. Maitland Sartoris, who was groomsman, entered the church, and a few minutes afterwards the marriage procession set out from the Embassy. First came the ten bridesmaids, viz. : Lady Helen Blackwood, Mlle. Novikoff, Miss d'Ehrenhoff, Mlle. Condouriotti, Mlle. de Rascon, Mlle. R. de Rascon, Miss Wyndham, the daughter of the Persian Ambassador, and the Ladies Hermione and Victoria Blackwood. The bridesmaids were dressed in cream-coloured Broussa silk, with tulle veils and wreaths of forget-me-nots. Then followed the bride—in white satin trimmed with lace, Brussels-lace veil, and real orange blossom—leaning on the arm of the Earl of Dufferin. The Countess of Dufferin, accompanied by Mrs. Wyndham and Mrs. Goschen, entered the chapel a little in advance of the procession. At the chapel porch the bridal party was met by the Chaplain and Canon Curtis in canonicals and the members of the choir in surplices. As the procession entered the chapel the organ played the nuptial chorus from Lohengrin, and the choristers, dividing right and left, the bride passed between them and took her place in the chancel, where she was met by the bridegroom, Lord Dufferin standing on her right hand, and the graceful phalanx of bridesmaids behind."

" When," continues the *Levant Herald*, " the exhortation was concluded the organ pealed forth the joyous strain of Mendelssohn's Wedding March . . . and the bride and bridegroom preceded by an officer of the household in state livery, and followed by the ten bridesmaids, returned to the Embassy on the perron of which there awaited them. . . ." The *Levant Herald* is so much excited by the event that it continues in this strain through five columns.

They drove out that spring afternoon to Therapia, where they stayed for four days in the Summer Embassy and then returned to Constantinople. From that hour the private life of Arthur Nicolson was serene with happiness. There is no more which can, or should, be said.

(8)

In October of 1882 Lord Dufferin was ordered to proceed to Egypt as High Commissioner. He invited Nicolson to accompany him. The whole party embarked on *H.M.S. Antelope* and reached Cairo on November 7. They were at first lodged in a disused palace of the Khedive and subsequently at the Villa Cattaui. Lady Dufferin at once began to organise amateur theatricals for the Egyptian charities : there was to be the play of *Catherine Cornaro, Queen of Cyprus*, by Sir Edward Malet, " with the author in the part of Fabio." Unfortunately, however, both Lady Dufferin and her sister developed typhoid. It was thus in an atmosphere of domestic anxiety and acute over-work that Lord Dufferin, assisted by Nicolson in a purely secretarial capacity, plunged into the labours of his special mission.

" Her Majesty's Government," so ran his instructions, " while desiring that the occupation should last for as short a time as possible feel bound not to withdraw from the task thus imposed upon them until the administration of affairs has been reconstructed on a basis which will afford satisfactory guarantees for the maintenance of peace, order and prosperity in Egypt ; for the stability of the Khedive's authority ; for the judicious development of self-government ; and for the fulfilment of obligations towards foreign Powers. These objects are in the real interests of Egypt, of this country, and of Europe." In other words, Lord Dufferin was expected to draw up a comprehensive scheme for the future governance of Egypt, in such a way as would combine liberal institutions with the

possibility of early evacuation. It may be supposed
that he realised the incompatibility of these ideals.
From the first he decided that his scheme of reforms
should be based on existing local conditions and not
on institutions imported from abroad. He devoted
four months to the study of these problems and during
these four months his attention was continually being
distracted by other matters. There was in the first
place the difficulty of disposing of Arabi and his supporters. It was owing to Lord Dufferin's influence
that the death penalty was commuted to one of exile
from Egypt. In the second place there was the
necessity of excluding Turkish influence and of frus-
trating the attempts of Abdul Hamid himself to dictate
to the Khedive the lines of the new regime. The
latter pleaded impotence. " Le véritable Khedive
d'Egypte," he pleaded, " c'est Lord Dufferin." The
Foreign Office displayed immense energy in asking for
interim reports on such matters as the immediate
abolition of slavery, the establishment of a police force,
the revision of the Suez Canal Convention, the Chamber of Notables, and the maintenance of the system of
dual financial control. In spite of these exacting interruptions Lord Dufferin's famous report was ready
by the end of January. Its publication was preceded
by Lord Granville's circular despatch to the Great
Powers in which he promised that Great Britain would
withdraw her troops from Egypt " so soon as the state
of the country and the organisation of proper means
for the maintenance of the Khedive's authority will
admit." These assurances were taken note of by
several Powers. The Porte were enraged but im-
potent. Bismarck, who had always smiled on isolated

British action in Egypt, was glad to feel that there was
now no prospect of a Franco-British rapprochement.
The French, for their part, sulked. When offered the
Presidency of the Debt Commission they replied that
a position of cashier was not consonant with the
dignity of France. They added significantly that
France must reserve " her liberty of action in Egypt."
" From that moment," comments Lord Cromer,
" until the Anglo-French Agreement of 1904, French
action in Egypt was more or less persistently hostile
to England."

Lord Dufferin's long report was published as a
State Paper in February 1883. Its rhetorical passages
aroused some criticism. There was the passage, for
instance, about the lips of the Egyptian fellah having
" trembled if they have not articulated " : about the
fellah himself " like his own Memnon " remaining
" not irresponsive to the beams of the new dawn." It
has been contended also that Lord Dufferin deliberately slurred over the difficulties of the future administration of Egypt ; that his picture of a self-dependent
Egypt, endowed with representative institutions drawing their ultimate authority from the village commune ;
that his picture again of a native administration
" untrammelled by external importunity, though aided,
indeed, as it must be for a time, by sympathetic advice
and assistance " ; indicated a readiness rather to provide the Liberal Administration in England with the
kind of report they desired than to disclose the realities
of the situation or the difficulties which evacuation
would encounter. Such criticism is not wholly
justified. On the one hand the more practical
recommendations of his report, those dealing with the

organisation of the army, the Courts of Justice, the
Reform of Land Assessment and Taxation, were all
admirably practical. On the other hand the report
did, even if in somewhat optimistic and indeed euphe-
mistic language, disclose the realities of what was
obviously a transitional situation. And above all,
Lord Dufferin laid it down firmly that " The valley of
the Nile could not be administered with any prospect
of success from London." Lord Dufferin's conclusions and his proposed reforms were approved by the
British Government and were promulgated in Egypt
by organic decree. This decree, for over thirty years,
remained the basis of the Egyptian Constitution.

(9)

The pressure of work during those six months in
Egypt was tremendous. The strain for Arthur
Nicolson had been increased by domestic anxiety—his
wife's typhoid and the birth of their eldest son. In
April 1883 Lady Dufferin with her sister and the children left Egypt, and for a further five weeks Lord
Dufferin and Arthur Nicolson stayed on in the glare
of an Egyptian spring, liquidating some of the endless
petty questions which still remained to be considered.
They moved to Alexandria and established themselves
in the villa of M. Antoniades. The reaction from the
wide excitements of the last year, the irksomeness of
being separated from his wife, induced in Nicolson a
mood of discontent and depression. His unceasing
clerical labours had caused, for the only time in his
life, a slight attack of writer's cramp. The absurd
contrast between this unromantic affliction and the
important events of which he had been a witness,

July 7. 1914.

Sir Edward Grey.

I hope that you will allow me to make an observation or two in regard to that portion of the conversation which P'ce Lichnowsky had with you yesterday relating to a naval understanding with Russia. He practically warned us that if we were to enter into any kind of naval arrangements with Russia certain

FACSIMILE OF NICOLSON'S HANDWRITING

brought home to him the limitations of diplomatic life, its incessant trivialities, its constant interruptions, and the cruel claims that it makes upon one's social and intellectual liberty. " My brain," he wrote, " heaves and works, I fear, unceasingly. I feel I have endless wells into which I shall never dip. For I am becoming coated over with a thick layer of official mud. I know it is right to do one's duty in the line of life one has chosen and I do try to fulfill it, but I do long to be free of all the trammels and dull unending labour of official life. I shall—*some day*. But only when my brain can make but one or two feeble throbs an hour, and when my energy will be confined to hobbling along a verandah." To his wife he poured out these veerings of depression and hope. A characteristic letter is dated from Alexandria at the end of April 1883. " I am so discontented when I think of the narrowness of my own life—only large and wide on the side of its love for you. But so wee and cramped over small and trivial matters. Opportunity is everything. I do not think I have ever missed any."

And further opportunities were soon to come.

III

ATHENS AND PERSIA

[1884-1888]

Appointed to take charge in Athens—Debts and loneliness—Yachting—
Views on diplomacy—M. Tricoupis—the Gendarme Incident—
Nicolson demands reparation—Indignation of Greek Government and
public opinion—He leaves Athens—Transferred to Persia—His journey
to Tehran—Views on Middle Eastern Question—The Panjdeh incident
—Nasr-ed-Din Shah—Views on Russian influence in Persia—Nicolson's
desire to secure German co-operation—Nasr-ed-Din Shah offers to place
himself under British protection—Mission of Prince Dolgorouki—
Escape of Sirdar Ayoub Khan—Critical situation in Tehran—Arrival of
Sir H. Drummond Wolff—Nicolson returns to England—Unfriendly
reception by Foreign Office—Appointed to Buda Pest.

(1)

THE summer of 1883 was spent at Therapia. They
rented a wooden house looking down upon the harbour, and their eldest son, protected by mosquito
netting, would dream the days through under the
magnolias of the Embassy. Arthur Nicolson spent
his afternoons training horses on the Buyukdere
meadows, while his wife sat sewing in the garden.
This happy existence was not of long duration. A
few months later Arthur Nicolson received instructions
from the Foreign Office to proceed to Athens to take
temporary charge of the Legation. He arrived in
Greece in March of 1884.

This, his first independent mission, was not auspicious. The charm of the Hellenic character can in
general be apprehended only by those who have a wide
classical education or who have resided in the country

for several years. Nicolson did not understand the
Greeks, and his sojourn in Athens began with irritation
and ended in disaster. In the first place there was
M. Tricoupis, Prime Minister and virtual dictator,
who, though he subsequently proved himself the
wisest Greek statesman of the pre-Venizelos period,
was at that date an uncertain and immoderate nationalist with whom it was difficult to deal. In the second
place Nicolson tried to run the Legation on the pay
of a first secretary. And in the third place, after the
birth of their second son, his wife returned for the
summer months to Ireland, leaving him alone in
Athens and already in debt.

Nicolson was bored and lonely. He removed from
the Legation, dismissed the servants, and took a bedroom at the hotel. He was discontented with his
career. " The desire," he wrote to his wife, " for a
quiet cottage grows on me. I should be so thoroughly
contented with my family and books. Parliament is
my real ambition, but that seems out of the question.
Oh dear ! how I hate hum-drum official work ! "
" I wish," he wrote again, " I could get a good berth
in the Colonial Service. It would be more interesting
administering new countries than scribbling rubbish
about old ones." " Do you know," he wrote a
week later, " that I feel sure I should have been
a literary man if my lines had fallen otherwise ?
From my early boyhood I always had an inclination
to scribble and I am sure my editorship of the
journal at Oxford increased this desire. But I
fell into dreary diplomatic life and all desire
dribbled out of me. Until I married you I had lived
with stupid little people and amongst books which I

did not read as I should have done. Let us hope one of our boys will take to letters." He was worried also by debts, and tried to be optimistic about them. " I don't care two straws," he assured his wife, " for financial difficulties so long as we are together. A few pounds are not going to spoil my happiness." Nor were these his only preoccupations : he was much distressed by the shallowness of human intercourse, by the trivial vulgarity of diplomatic society. " When," he confessed, " I live amongst those who have no thought for the morrow, there comes over me a great big tightening of the heart. I feel that the world is wrong and that society is doing far more harm than is thought. . . . Nothing will justify a lie even at the expense of causing pain to others. This is, I think, the true honest course, and we will bring up our boys never to swerve from the strictest truth, no matter what are the consequences to themselves or others. For truthfulness is the basis of all education and character, I mean truthfulness to the very smallest point—no exaggerations, no veiling—it must be bare naked truth. Truth and a strong religious faith are the two essentials. . . . I thank God that I *did* go through a period of doubt since it has only strengthened my faith. I hold to it that the great salvation of England is the deep-rooted religious feeling of the people. What has saved us from the loose immoral mode of thought so pre-valent among the Latin races is the great power exercised among us by the Church, whether Anglican or Nonconformist." These principles appear, at that period, to have influenced his attitude even towards his official colleagues. The following is a description of a dinner at the Russian Legation. " Afterwards I had dinner with the Bakhmetieffs and was quite disgusted. After dinner they amused themselves by reading out *horribly* improper passages from Diderot to the delight of Madame P. . . . I could hardly prevent myself from making some remarks. What made me unhappy was poor Mrs. H. . . . , who I know dislikes such converse and yet to avoid appearing unsociable and stupid she made clumsy and unwilling attempts to be interested. . . . A person who lives on such food must in time lose all knowledge of what is right, and all means of judging between what is healthy and what unwholesome. I hope our boys will never develop a taste in that direction." In later life his attitude towards such matters became far more civilised : but to the end he would, by the instinctive reserve of his nature, impose silence upon the prurient.

To relieve his boredom, as a contrast to " pounding up and down dusty roads," he joined with Sir Brooke Boothby, the secretary of the Legation, in hiring a sailing boat. On successive week-ends they went to Nauplia and Sunium, to Hydra, Zea and Paros, to Epidaurus and Aegina. A love of the sea was one of the few indulgences which remained to him in his poverty and subsequent ill-health, and he manifests in his letters a shy enthusiasm for the beauty of the Aegean. " Some of the boats had deep orange sails, a wonderful effect against the blue seas and purple hills." " But," he adds characteristically, " I am becoming aesthetic." Sir Brooke Boothby, who was a valetudinarian, was not moreover the ideal companion for such expeditions. " He is," wrote Nicolson, " a great bore on board. He will sit up till one a.m. and then go clattering to bed. He is always

bothering the men for absurd little comforts and is in
every way quite unfitted for this kind of life. He
spoils half my pleasure and is always grumbling. If
I only had Charlie Hardinge with me how different
things would be ! B. bores me as I have never been
bored before." But in the autumn the family were
re-united and the Legation was again opened for their
reception.

(2)

The somewhat conventional opinions held by
Arthur Nicolson on the moral problems of his age
did not extend to his views upon his own profession.
Unlike so many diplomatists of that now distant period
he did not imagine that he belonged to a caste apart,
or that the activities of his professional life were in
general anything but trivial, vulgar, and ridiculous.
His sympathies were wider than those of many of his
contemporaries : we have already recorded his early
interest in Socialism : his attitude towards commerce
was scarcely less revolutionary and advanced. There
is a passage in one of his letters of this period in which
he makes the startling discovery that business men,
that is the more successful among them, are not really
uninteresting. " I like," he wrote, " our upper mer-
cantile men. There is so much energy and sense about
them. I think they are the very marrow of England."
Nor was he blind to what, in essence, is the main
temptation of the professional diplomatist. " Most
diplomatists," such was his opinion in 1884, " write
rosy accounts to make themselves popular. I could
rattle the windows of Ford and Egerton with stones
for having given far too sanguine a view of affairs in

this country." For his part, he proceeded to write a devastating report upon the economic and financial consequences of M. Tricoupis. This report was unfortunately published in the Board of Trade Journal. The Greek Prime Minister was furious. He was unable to contradict Nicolson's assertions, but he considered them unfriendly and ill-timed. By the end of 1884 the relations between them were already somewhat cold. At the beginning of 1885 these relations were exposed to a test which they were unable to withstand.

The incident of January 16, 1885, was not one on which, in after years, Nicolson would dwell with any pleasure. It arose from the fact that the Municipality had decided to plant some little pine-trees on the Lycabettus, and that the Gendarme Calpouzos, who had been detailed to prevent people throwing cigarette-ends among the trees, was suffering from cerebral inflammation which later developed into homicidal mania. Nicolson, who was unaware of either of these circumstances, as also of the Greek language, decided on that afternoon to take his wife along the path which ascends the mountain and, from the summit to admire that indeed remarkable view. They were stopped by Calpouzos, who seized Nicolson by the arm and struck him over the shoulder with a stick. Astonished at this onslaught, Nicolson explained in the demotic tongue that he was the British Chargé d'Affaires. The gendarme at once struck him again, and this time violently, upon the back of the neck. Nicolson " proceeded to descend " the path, and on the high-road met two Greek gentlemen, whom he requested to explain to the gendarme the enormity of the outrage committed and

to obtain his name and number. They endeavoured
to do so, but Calpouzos " pushed them on one side and
told them to be off. They obeyed his orders, and I
remained on the high road. He suddenly rushed at
me, struck me a third violent blow, and as I retreated,
threw several stones at me." Enraged at this indignity
Nicolson at once visited M. Tricoupis, and in a few
hours the offending gendarme was brought under
escort to the Legation and was identified as the
assailant. An official Note of apology was tendered
by the Greek Government and the King sent his Aide-
de-camp to express regret. The offending gendarme,
they assured him, would at once be dismissed. Nicolson himself was prepared to accept this solution but
Herr Brincken, the German Minister, assured him that
the reparation offered was not sufficient and that more
public expiation must be afforded. Nicolson insisted
therefore that Calpouzos should be publicly dismissed
and that an Order of the Day should be read to the
assembled gendarmes stating the reasons for dismissal.
To this M. Tricoupis also agreed and Nicolson expressed himself as satisfied. Unfortunately, however,
the Order of the Day when drafted appeared to place
the blame on Nicolson and in fact furnished an incorrect version of the outrage. It was this version
which M. Tricoupis published in the Government
paper. The British Chargé d'Affaires then lost his
temper. He addressed a Note to M. Tricoupis in
which he insisted upon a new Order of the Day being
drafted and published. This new Order, when approved, was to be read out to the gendarmes, not, as
previously arranged, in the Barrack Square, but in the
Place de la Constitution. Moreover, at the close of

the ceremony, the band was to play *God Save the Queen* in the presence of the British Consul. The Greek Cabinet met and after a lengthy sitting they decided to capitulate. The ceremony passed off without incident. The Foreign Office at home, somewhat coldly, approved Nicolson's attitude. The German Minister was delighted : he wrote to Nicolson asking him to accept " my very sincere congratulations " for the " firmness and circumspection " he had shown. But Nicolson himself was troubled. His anxiety was increased when next day a violent press attack was opened, and there followed a debate in the Boulé which lasted for five days. " I am very sorry," he wrote to Lord Granville, " for the whole affair, and especially for Tricoupis whom I like and admire. But why did he play me that Oriental trick ? " A report of the dispute reached England and criticisms were made in Parliament and in the press. Fortunately the news of the fall of Khartoum and the murder of Gordon arrived at the same moment to divert attention.

Arthur Nicolson felt thoroughly ashamed of himself. " It has," he wrote to Francis Villiers, then Private Secretary to Lord Granville, " been a very painful and distressing incident to me. I hope none of you consider me a hasty, testy, and sensitive man. With all my faults, I am far from being that." " My dear Boy," replied Mr. Villiers, " the telegram sent you will have set your mind at ease as showing that none of your proceedings were disapproved. To tell you the whole truth, however, we think that the assembly in the Square and the playing of the National Anthem went a little beyond what was quite necessary. There now, I have played the part of the candid friend, which is always an ungrateful task." M. Tricoupis, for his part, was less conciliatory. Nicolson wrote privately to him on February 9 asking that the gendarme might now be released and pardoned. "I trust," he wrote, " and indeed I feel sure, that you will accept my proposal in the friendly spirit in which it is offered, and that it will assist towards obliterating an incident which has caused to no one more pain than myself." M. Tricoupis' reply was not encouraging. It ran as follows :

February 11, 1885.

"DEAR MR. NICOLSON,
        I am sorry I cannot see that your proposal is likely to assist towards obliterating the painful incident you allude to.

Yours sincerely,
TRICOUPIS."

A few months later the gendarme Calpouzos committed a murder and was found to be insane. But by that date Nicolson had already been recalled from Athens.

Twenty-two years later Nicolson accompanied King Edward on a visit to the Emperor of Russia at Reval. The Queen of the Hellenes happened at that moment to be visiting her Russian relations and was invited to luncheon on board the *Victoria and Albert*. " I think you know," said King Edward, " my Ambassador in St. Petersburg ? " The Queen drew herself up unbendingly. " There is no Greek," she answered in icy tones, " who has not reason to remember M. Nicolson."

King Edward, on hearing the whole story from Nicolson, was considerably amused.

(3)

In the spring of 1885 Arthur Nicolson was appointed
to Persia as first secretary of Legation. Sir Ronald
Thomson, the Minister at Tehran, was shortly returning
to Europe : his successor had not yet been chosen :
there was every prospect that Nicolson would be left in
charge for several months. Fate decreed, however,
that he should remain as Chargé d'Affaires for the
unprecedented period of two and a half years. The
opportunity which fortune thus accorded marked the
turning point of his career. He acquired a sense of
responsibility and a firm basis of self-confidence. He
restored his shattered finances. He came to understand the complexity of the external problems by which
the Government of India are menaced. And above
all, he absorbed certain deep convictions regarding the
Middle Eastern question which profoundly influenced,
and indeed directed, his subsequent judgment. He
learnt, for instance, that the advance of Russia towards
the Indian Frontier was no mere Cossack adventurism
but some slow tidal movement, imponderable and dis-
continuous. He learnt, that is, that the policy of
supporting the independence and integrity of Persia
and Afghanistan was little more than an expedient,
and even, as such, an expedient which might tempt us
to assume responsibilities which we could not execute
or to encourage hopes which we should be unable to
fulfil. He saw that this policy exposed Great Britain
and Russia to constant local friction, and to the ever
present menace of hostilities in Central Asia. He
passed through various phases. At one stage he advocated our withdrawing to a more defensible line,

abandoning northern and central Persia to Russian influence and consolidating our position in Fars and on the Gulf. At a later stage he urged that the situation in Persia should be internationalised, and that Germany should be induced by commercial concessions to share our interest in the maintenance of Persian independence. At one moment he toyed cautiously with the suggestion that Great Britain should enter into a form of alliance with Persia and should offer that country some stable guarantees. But in the end he came to the conclusion that the solution of the Central Asian problem lay in St. Petersburg; that if Great Britain desired to avoid a war with Russia on the Middle Eastern plateaux she must, at any sacrifice, come to some comprehensive understanding with her rival; and that any such convention must embrace Anglo-Russian interests not in Central Asia only, but also in Europe and the Far East. These apprehensions and convictions were somewhat premature. A few years later the Russian tide set suddenly, and at German instigation, towards the Far East; the acute pressure on the Indian frontier was for almost two decades relieved. But it was the experience acquired in Tehran that guided Nicolson's negotiation of the Anglo-Russian Convention of 1907. And it is for this reason that his sojourn in Persia—the realisation which he then acquired of the instability of all Asiatic affairs—must be recorded in some detail and explained.

(4)

His appointment to Tehran, which ended in triumphant success, began with difficulties and dismay. He had been warned that it would be madness to take his

two babies to Persia during the summer months. He
disregarded this advice. Accompanied by an English
nurse, they travelled via Constantinople and Trebizond
to Batoum. The nurse and children nearly died of
sea-sickness. On reaching Batoum Arthur Nicolson
and his wife sat upon the beach doing accounts : they
came to the conclusion that they were too poor to
continue in diplomacy and must exchange at once into
the Consular Service. From Batoum they proceeded in
the August heat to Tiflis and Baku. They crossed the
Caspian : the mountains of Persia were hidden in the
steam which rose from the rice-fields. They travelled
up from Resht by caravan, moving by night only and
resting in muddied caravanserais by day. The women
and children were carried in litters slung over the backs
of mules—a wooden coffin on each side of the mule
in which the traveller lay on cushions. On the third
day the English nurse could stand it no longer. Looking over the edge of her litter she had seen, a hundred
feet sheer below her, the seething yellow waters of the
Sefid Rud. She scrambled out of her coffin and asked
to be taken home at once to Littlehampton. Nicolson
forced her back into the litter with threats of violence.
She remained angry for over three years. On the fifth
day, worn with anxiety and exhaustion, they reached
Kasvin. The younger baby was teething and developed convulsions. Nicolson lanced the child's gums
with a rusted penknife. On the seventh day (the children still howling in their litters) they reached the
capital and rode in under the plane-trees of the Legation
compound. Nicolson, on entering his drawing-room,
flung himself with relief into the first arm-chair. It
collapsed, as is the way with Tehran chairs, beneath

him. On the next day the family proceeded to the cooler altitude of Gulahek. In a few weeks Sir Ronald Thomson took his departure and Nicolson assumed command.

(5)

The Middle Eastern Question at that date was just emerging from a highly critical stage. The Russians, having established themselves, by a process which they called " spontaneous infiltration," in Khiva, Bokhara and Samarkand, had in February of 1884 occupied the Merv oasis, and advanced along the Oxus until they came in contact with the frontier of Afghanistan. The latter country had entrusted her foreign relations to Great Britain in return for a guarantee of her independence and integrity, a guarantee which Her Majesty's Government devoutly hoped they would never be called upon to honour. A mixed commission was appointed with the task of fixing a line which the Russians would accept as the definitive frontier of Afghanistan and beyond which they would agree not to penetrate. In March of 1885, however, the Russians claimed the Panjdeh valley, which was indubitably Afghan territory, and then proceeded to occupy it by force. The Amir Abdurrahman was at that moment visiting Lord Dufferin, the new Viceroy, at Rawal Pindi ; and the latter was in honour bound to offer him assistance in recovering Panjdeh. For a week it seemed that an Anglo-Russian war was inevitable ; patriotic cartoons appeared in the pages of *Punch* ; the European Governments were agog with excitement. To the surprise and relief of all concerned the Amir, who did not wish for war, generously

released us from our difficulty by stating that he did
not care about the Panjdeh valley in the least. The
Frontier Commission was thus able to continue its
labours, but it was not until July of 1887 that the
delimitation protocol was actually signed. Throughout the period of Nicolson's sojourn in Persia Anglo-
Russian relations were thus in an inflamed condition,
and serious friction was to be expected in the event of
any internal or external disturbance arising either in
Persia or Afghanistan.

Nicolson proceeded therefore with great caution.
The first conflict which arose was in regard to the
construction of roads linking Tehran with the Caspian
and the Persian Gulf. Sir Ronald Thomson had
argued that a road from Resht to the capital would
place the Shah at the mercy of Russia and had advocated that all proposals for road construction should
therefore be opposed. Nicolson disagreed with this
view. He contended that, if it came to physical force,
the Government at Tehran were in any case at the
mercy of Russia, and that the slight advantage which
would accrue to Russia from the construction of a road
to the Caspian would be balanced by the commercial
benefits which would be reaped by British trade if good
communications could concurrently be opened in the
south. He applied therefore for a concession for the
navigation of the Karun river, and for the construction
of a southern trade route linking Mohammerah, via
Shustar, Khoremabad and Burujird with Tehran. The
Russians countered this by pressing for a road concession in Khorasan. "We are limited," wrote
Nicolson, "to persuasion and good counsel, which is
writing on water, while the Russians use brusquer and

stronger methods. Even if it were desirable, we could not, as far as I can see, adopt the latter method of pressure." It was thus only after years of persuasion and patience that the road concessions were obtained.

Meanwhile Nicolson exerted all his efforts to winning the confidence of the Persians themselves. " I intend," he wrote, " to lay myself out to be on intimate and friendly terms with the Persians, in which direction the Russians have gained a considerable advantage over us. Although the Legation has a good position, relations are a little chilly and formal." The Persians, for their part, rapidly responded to these advances ; and after twelve months of residence Nicolson succeeded also, and to an almost embarrassing extent, in winning the confidence of the Shah.

The King of Kings, Nasr-ed-Din Shah, was then in his fifty-eighth year and had been on the throne for thirty-seven years. The anti-British feelings which he had cherished since we turned him out of Herat in 1857, had been diminished by his visits to Europe in 1873 and 1875, and had by now given place to a mild regret that England was not more actively helpful in enabling him to resist the continuous demands of Russia. He was delighted with the new British representative ; liking his gay ways and cheerful friendliness ; appreciating the sympathy with which he listened to the tale of Persian woe. They met frequently ; they corresponded directly ; and twelve months after Nicolson's arrival the Shah pledged his word of honour that he would not enter into any secret agreement with Russia without first " consulting " Her Majesty's Government. This interview took place in a garden : the Shah,

grunting enormous under his diamond aigrette, twirl-
ing his huge moustaches, sat on one side of a little
stream under a bower of jasmine. Nicolson, on the
other side of the stream, was shaded by a pine tree.
It was in such idyllic circumstances that the pact was
made. Nasr-ed-Din Shah, who was a man of honour,
maintained his promise in the spirit and the letter.
The Foreign Office were delighted. On July 31 of
1886 Nicolson was accorded the C.M.G.

The Chargé d'Affaires did not, however, exaggerate
the security of the position. " I sometimes," he wrote
to Lord Dufferin, " have a little qualm as to my
Padishah. All is so very tortuous here that few can
walk straight." Something more, he felt, was necessary if Persia were permanently to be preserved.
" Unless," he recorded, " we are prepared to offer some
kind of guarantee to Persia (which personally, in view
of the condition of the country, I consider out of the
question) we should not waste our energies in endeavouring to counteract Russian influence on the
Central Government at Tehran. This part of the
world is lost to us and we should devote the modicum
of attention which we seem disposed to give to Persia
to the South alone. If we could persuade some other
Power, say Germany, to join us in some definite
assurances . . . well and good. But failing this we
could not single-handed undertake so serious a responsibility as any definite commitment." A few weeks
later we find him again writing to the Foreign Office.
" There is only one country whom we could invite
into partnership and that is Germany. The doubt in
my mind is whether Germany would be willing to
join with us. To her it would seem a one-sided

E

arrangement. Perhaps some commercial inducements
could be found to attract her."

Such, therefore, were the general lines of his advice.
To avoid all conflict with Russia in the north : to consolidate our position in the south, and for this purpose
to open trade routes and to secure the friendship of the
Zil-es-Sultan who ruled as an independent Satrap at
Ispahan ; to endeavour to internationalise the situation
at Tehran by interesting Germany in Persian integrity
and independence : and meanwhile to win the confidence of the Shah and his people without, however,
encouraging them to hope for support which in the
last resort would not be forthcoming. Nor did Arthur
Nicolson fully share the Anglo-Indian obsession regarding Russia. " You must not think," he wrote to Lord
Dufferin, " that I am one of those who see the hand of
Russia in everything : for I believe that we frequently
give her credit or discredit for far more activity and
intrigue than she actually exercises." " I do not
think," he wrote to Lord Iddesleigh in September 1886,
" that Russia will be desirous of raising a Persian
question by any demands for annexation of Persian
territory. But I do think she will insist upon obtaining certain engagements from the Shah which will
enable her to enjoy all the advantages of complete
subserviency on the part of Persia without openly
attacking the principle of Persian integrity." This
particular danger he was able to conjure owing to the
close relations which he had established with the Shah.
He saw, however, that such relations were precarious,
and indeed that all expedients were but a postponement
and not a solution of the problem. When asked, in
later years, why he was so convinced of the necessity of

an Anglo-Russian Convention, he replied unhesitatingly
" From what I saw in Persia in 1886." And already
in February of that year he had written tentatively to
Sir Philip Currie : " Of course if we could come to
a mutual understanding with Russia on the integrity
question—that would be the best solution of all."

The Russians, early in 1887, became alarmed at the
position which Nicolson had created for himself at
Tehran. Their Minister was recalled and Prince
Dolgorouki, who was understood to possess the special
confidence of the Tsar, was sent on a special mission
to Persia. Nasr-ed-Din felt anxious. He sent at once
for the British Chargé d'Affaires. He said that the
moment had arrived " for opening his mind without
reserve to Her Majesty's Government."

" He was desirous "—the quotation which follows is
from Nicolson's despatch to Lord Salisbury of July 5,
1887—" of improving his country and of making her
strong, prosperous and independent. But for years the
incubus of Russian proximity had weighed him down and
it was becoming more and more oppressive. He now
turned to his only friend, England, to whom he opened
his mind candidly and frankly. If England would protect
him from the consequences and if she would give him
strength to resist the demands of Russia, which he was
convinced would be impossible and exacting . . . he
would do all that Her Majesty's Government desired. He
would be guided absolutely and entirely by us and place
himself with confidence in our hands. But without such
support, alone and unaided, he could not face the consequences."

Nicolson was somewhat embarrassed by this appeal.
He explained to His Majesty that the British Government could only enter into foreign commitments if

supported by British public opinion : that the latter did not as yet understand the importance to British interests of the integrity and independence of Persia ; that the British public thought in terms of trade and progress : and that only if the Shah opened the southern trade routes and introduced democratic reforms would British opinion become sufficiently interested in Persia to enable the Government to assume any responsibilities in regard to the future of that country.

It was with some perturbation that he reported this conversation to the Foreign Office. The reply which reached him three months later was not discouraging. His language was entirely approved. For long he had been urging that some man of position and influence should be sent out to succeed him in order to counteract the dreaded machinations of Dolgorouki. The Foreign Office were pleased by the modesty and objectivity of this suggestion and stated that " a person of prominence " would be selected to continue the work that Nicolson had so daringly initiated. They selected for the purpose Sir Henry Drummond Wolff, a politician whose membership of the fourth party had rendered his name familiar to the British public. Nicolson was relieved. But at that very moment there arose a crisis which threatened to revive the whole Middle Eastern Question and to undo the good work of the last two years.

(6)

It will be known to some that Sirdar Mahommed Ayoub Khan, who had routed the British army at Maiwand, had since that event been himself defeated, firstly by Lord Roberts and secondly by his own cousin,

Abdurrahman Khan, Amir of Afghanistan. The latter victory had been the more crushing of the two, and Ayoub had been obliged thereafter to escape with some fifteen hundred followers into Persian territory. A large number of these Afghan refugees remained in the vicinity of Meshed, but Ayoub and his immediate supporters proceeded to Tehran, where he was received with great honour by the Shah of Persia, who placed a palace at his disposal. The position, as Nicolson found it on assuming charge in 1885, was, to say the least, ill-defined. Moslem tradition, on the one hand, obliged the Shah and his Government to treat these unwelcome and disorderly refugees as guests. British policy, on the other, necessitated their being regarded as potential dangers. An arrangement was come to whereby Ayoub Khan and his followers should continue to enjoy the hospitality of the Shah, while the Government of India should pay the cost. The implication of this arrangement was that the Persian Government should see to it that Ayoub Khan did not escape into Afghanistan, where, owing to his victory over the British forces, he continued to enjoy a highly embarrassing prestige. Until the summer of 1887 all went well. " Ayoub," Nicolson repeatedly assured the Viceroy, " although sulky, seems contented." " I give you my word," so the Shah repeatedly assured Nicolson, " that Ayoub Khan is under surveillance." In spite of this, however, everybody, including the British Chargé d'Affaires, was uneasy. In the spring of 1887 the Ghilzai tribes in the south of Afghanistan revolted against the Amir Abdurrahman, and the garrison of Herat burst forth into open mutiny. In July of that year the Chargé d'Affaires learnt by chance that

Ayoub had left his palace in Tehran and had proceeded with his family to a villa in the vicinity of Gulahek. Nicolson expressed his disquiet to the Foreign Minister. The latter assured him that Ayoub had merely made the change for the needs of his health ; that he was in a humble and indeed contrite mood ; that he was about to open negotiations with the British authorities for the grant of a final asylum in India. Nicolson solicited, and obtained, authority to conduct these negotiations. He had several conversations, during the first weeks of August, with Yahia Khan, the Minister of Foreign Affairs. And yet, on the afternoon of August 16, 1887, Colonel Wells, the Director of the Indo-European Telegraph Company, came to inform him that the line to Meshed was being cut stage by stage and that a party of Afghans were galloping down the route snipping the wire as they went. " This looks," Nicolson noted in his diary, " as if someone were escaping." He at once informed the Foreign Minister, the Prefect of Police, the British Agent at Meshed, and the Government of India. The Foreign Minister was full of reassuring evidence. He produced letters signed with the seal of Ayoub Khan which had that very day been given him by the Khan's chief doctor, stating that Ayoub, to his great regret, was unable to call in person since he was confined to his anderoon, or harem, by an attack of fever. Nicolson's suspicions were fired by this information. He sent a woman, who was in the habit of bringing apricots to the wives of Ayoub, to penetrate into the anderoon and to report whether Ayoub was really there. She was driven away by blows and objurgations. Again he visited the Foreign Minister and insisted that he should at any cost himself have a sight of Ayoub Khan. His Excellency produced more letters which he had that very morning received from Ayoub signed with his name and seal. Nicolson was not convinced, and in the end Yahia agreed to send one of his own eunuchs to penetrate into the anderoon of Sirdar Ayoub Khan. The result of these investigations was conveyed to the Chargé d'Affaires in the morning of August 22 in a note of great breathlessness.

> " Mon cher ami," wrote the Foreign Minister, " Le Sirdar a en effet parti. Est parmi les fuyards. Mes gens et les siens viennent de me le confirmer. Je ne suis qu'étonné. Votre tout devoué. Yahia."

Ayoub had by then had five and a half days' start. The wires buzzed. The Foreign Minister became seriously alarmed, and sent off endless orders to the Governor of Khorassan and the frontier authorities to the effect that at any cost Ayoub Khan should be prevented from crossing into his own country. Nicolson, for his part, despatched a messenger post-haste to the Shah. The messenger came upon His Majesty shooting partridges among the pleasant uplands of To-Tchal. Nasr-ed-Din, as Nicolson recorded in his diary, cast from him with a gesture of fury the shot-gun which Messrs. Cogswell & Harrison had inlaid with gold. He returned in a fury to Tehran. And Yahia Khan was instantly and furiously dismissed.

The Shah, the Chargé d'Affaires, the Agent at Meshed, Lord Salisbury, and above all the Government of India, waited in an agony of suspense expecting daily to hear that Ayoub in triumph had entered Herat and set Afghanistan flaming into civil war. The frontiers

were scoured by horsemen ; the villages of Qaf, of
Khorassan, of Seistan and of Qain, were searched for
news ; the houses and family of Ayoub at Tehran were
watched day and night by secret agents. Ayoub was
meanwhile hiding in a little house next door to the
British Agency at Meshed. His adventures, since that
summer night when he had slipped, armed with a
Martini and a wire-cutter, over the garden wall at
Gulahek, had not been without their romantic element.
He had left his seal with his doctor instructing him to
address daily letters to the Minister of Foreign Affairs.
His women had been told to play backgammon noisily
in the anteroom indicating thereby the presence of their
master. And off he had galloped, past the wall of the
British Legation, and on under the summer stars to
that pale road which leads to Samarkand. The Afghan
boundary had been crossed at Ghurian on September 2,
and on the next day they had been met by two regiments of Afghan cavalry who had been sent out to
patrol the frontier. Ayoub and his followers were by
then exhausted with fatigue. They endeavoured to
seduce the two Herat regiments and the Colonels came
and kissed Ayoub's hand while begging him not to
persist. The night descended and the little party
decided to disperse. Ayoub and one of his generals
took the only two horses which were capable of
travelling and then stole across the plain. His companions were captured by the Afghans and subsequently beheaded. Ayoub himself, his horse having
died, chewed bullets to slake his thirst. On the third
day he saw the black tents of some nomad shepherds
and was given milk and a guide. He returned in the
guise of a shepherd to Persia, and crept into Meshed

where he remained in hiding for five weeks. He then disclosed his presence to his neighbour, the Agent for the Government of India, and arranged his capitulation. He was given honourable terms on the condition that he would agree to live in India on a pension from the British Government. He consented. That was the end of Sirdar Ayoub Khan.

Meanwhile the uncertainty of his fate had produced a crisis at Tehran, where his remaining followers, some 800 strong, provoked a situation of the greatest delicacy. Nicolson had induced the Persian Government immediately to arrest the leaders of the Afghan refugees who remained at the capital. " These arrests," he records with characteristic frankness, " were a mistake and should not have been made." The remaining Afghans at once took sanctuary in the Shah's mosque, from where they began to threaten the Government with violence. That very day Nicolson received an urgent summons to proceed to the Palace in Tehran, and on entering the capital he was surprised to see the road lined with military, and his carriage surrounded on passing through the gate by a clattering escort of mounted police. On reaching the Palace he found the whole Cabinet assembled. He enquired in his optimistic manner why he had been arrested. They informed him that the moment was not one for merriment ; that the mob sided with the Afghans ; that the military were not to be relied on ; that the refugees in sanctuary had published a list of impending assassinations, on which list his own name stood first. " The Shah," Nicolson records, " I am sorry to say, at this moment completely lost his head, and shut himself up in his palace, while the streets of the town were patrolled by the military, a foolish measure which aroused popular excitement very unnecessarily." Nicolson, like all old diplomatists, believed in the value of time. The Cabinet begged him at once to allow them to release the imprisoned leaders. He replied that they must wait eight days for his answer ; he returned to Gulahek, leaving them uncertain and disturbed. He then let it be known that Ayoub had been defeated by troops loyal to the Amir of Afghanistan ; he did not let it be known that no one at that moment had the slightest idea where Ayoub really was ; but he indicated at the same time that any of the refugees who found their sanctuary uncomfortable would be granted a free passage to India. By twos and threes during the next eight days they came to him. The news of these desertions, as they occurred, was spread through the bazaars ; the crisis passed ; and so soon as the capitulation of Ayoub himself was brought home to his followers, the danger melted away.

It was many a long month, however, before the final terms of settlement were drawn up with Ayoub Khan and before that admirable adventurer was safely on the road to India. He passed close to Tehran on his return journey and sent the Chargé d'Affaires his signed photograph and a message of esteem. The Shah was more than appreciative, and produced for Nicolson an oval snuff-box richly encrusted in diamonds bearing His Majesty's portrait in the centre. " I know," he said, " that you English are not allowed to receive foreign decorations. My highest decoration is the Imtiaz, which is my portrait in brilliants. I give it you in the form of a little box." Lord Salisbury, when consulted, decreed that this present should be accepted. And on March 16, 1888, the following entry occurs in Nicolson's diary : " Received telegram from Dufferin saying I had been appointed K.C.I.E." The next entry is for March 23 : " Ayoub Khan crossed into Turkish territory."

There are no further entries in the Persian diary.

(7)

Sir Henry Drummond Wolff, a convivial politician, was about to arrive. The new Minister disembarked at Enzeli with his wife and a huge St. Bernard dog. Nicolson handed over the reins of office with a pleasant sense of relief. A few weeks later, while peach and judas trees stained the valleys of the Elburz with pink and purple, he descended with his family (there were now three children) to the rice fields of Gilan. They spent a night at Resht. The Governor-General came round after dinner, and there was tea and caviare. The next day Nicolson embarked on the Russian steamer for Baku. He crossed the Caspian, that orphaned sea, with feelings of regret and anticipation.

Those three years in Persia had been years of great happiness. The beauty of the country, the gentle charm of the Persians, the stimulus of hard work in such conditions and in so buoyant a climate, had combined to expand his intelligence and fortify his energies. He had liked and understood the Persians, respecting their distinction and culture, viewing their failings with affectionate disregard. " Of all Orientals," he wrote later, " they were those with whom I felt the most sympathy and with whom one could make real friends. There is something very taking in their view of life and affairs, and they lie so peacefully that one has to be very stern to resist their blandishments." His finances also, though only temporarily, had recovered. He had been successful. " I must congratulate you," wrote Lord Dufferin, " upon the great step you have taken in the estimation of the initiated both here and at home. You are now, my dear Arthur, one of the marked men of the service."

The service, it appears, thought otherwise. Nicolson, on returning to London, found that Lord Salisbury and the Foreign Office did not welcome him with that enthusiasm which he had been led to expect. For the next twelve years a slight prejudice existed against him in Downing Street, the causes of which are difficult to fathom. It is held by some that Lord Salisbury had been much alarmed by the escape of Ayoub, and visited upon Nicolson his resentment at this gratuitous anxiety. Others again contend that Lord Salisbury's principal Private Secretary, Sir Eric Barrington, who was peculiarly sensitive to social elegance, felt that the Nicolsons were too poor and too dowdy to shine in any of the more decorative posts. The fact remains that until 1904 Nicolson was not treated with any indulgence by his superiors. Lord Dufferin, who on leaving India had obtained the Embassy in Rome, requested that Arthur Nicolson should be appointed Counsellor in that capital. The Foreign Office refused to accede to this request. They did not, they said, approve of " family Embassies." And meanwhile, before the appointment of Sir Henry Drummond Wolff, certain influential journals in London had suggested that Nicolson should himself be raised to the rank of Minister in Persia. The Foreign Office were naturally annoyed. Their irritation was increased when the suggestion was warmly supported by those circles in the city who were interested in the Persian trade. The Foreign Office excused themselves on the ground of Nicolson's extreme youth (he was entering his fortieth year) and inexperience. Moreover, he had obtained the K.C.I.E.—an Indian Order conferred upon him by his brother-in-law. Surely he should rest content with that ?

Thus, after some delay, Arthur Nicolson was appointed Consul-General at Buda Pest.

IV

THE NEAR EAST

[1888-1895]

(1)

THE four years which Nicolson spent in Hungary were
four years of boredom. They stand in no important
relation to the main lines of his political education and
can thus, unlike his experiences in Persia or during the
Egyptian crisis, be dismissed in a few paragraphs.
The Consulate-General at Buda Pest was subordinate
to the Embassy in Vienna and it was to the Ambassador
that Nicolson had to address his reports. After nearly
three autonomous years in Persia this restriction was
irritating in the extreme. The stupidity of the Magyar
aristocracy got on his nerves. Their arrogance disgusted him. " I should," he wrote to his wife, " be
a Socialist of the deepest magenta were I a workman
here." He wrote to Lord Rosebery :

" The young magnate in general is not to be compared
with his father. The latter with all his eccentricities and

peculiarities was a fine specimen of manhood. The youth
of the present day in many instances are poor pallid
representatives of the race. The energy and activity for
which the fathers were distinguished are not cultivated by
the sons, who spend their nights card playing and listening
to gipsy music, pasting £5 and £10 notes on the fore-
heads of their favourite musicians. The vigour of the
race will be preserved chiefly in what are called the gentry
here—or what we should call the squirearchy—and
though these are mostly ruined they have the grit
and determination so characteristic of the Magyar and
which have pulled the country through so many
difficulties."

For the rest Nicolson spent his time discussing the
Eastern question with Professor Vambéry ; discussing
Austrian history with General Pejascevic ; writing
trade reports ; and on occasions taking a holiday in
the mountains, or in the hospitable castles of Princess
Batthyanyi—a delightful Jewess. For one summer he
stayed at Fiume at the Villa Hoyos. A second was
spent at Stübing in the company of Sir Richard and
Lady Burton who had come up from Trieste. Burton
would play amicably with the three Nicolson children,
thrusting his dark face into theirs, shouting at the
youngest baby, " Hallo, little Tehran ! " The child
yelled : the memory of those questing panther eyes
remained with this infant as a thrill of terror and
delight.

In one direction only did Arthur Nicolson's appointment to Buda Pest prove of subsequent value. He
devoted much time to the minority problem, and made
an extended tour in Croatia and Transylvania, studying
the subject nationalities on the spot. He thus carried
away from Hungary a deep distrust of Hungarian and

indeed of Austro-Hungarian policy—an instinctive fear
that the Hapsburg Empire was an element not of
stability but of disintegration and decay. This feeling
became intensified with the passage of time. His
judgment in this respect, though based upon what
history has shown to have been a correct apprehension,
was perhaps coloured by his personal antipathy to the
shallow rigidity of the Austro-Hungarian system. A
letter to his wife reflects this antipathy in a characteristic manner : " Official dinner at Körmend. Poor
Princess and I smothered by uniforms and so stiff and
funny. All the juniors in fear, and my little Major
trembling before the Inspector. What asses we
humans are ! Oh dear me, what does this all matter,
and why can't we be natural and not try each of us to
rise on tip-toe an inch above his neighbour ? I would
give my head (my least valuable part) to throw off
official clothes and plant cabbages with my little wife
in the country. I am getting so tired of all scrambling
and envy and shoving and pushing."

On October 22 of 1892 he was appointed Secretary
of Embassy at Constantinople. " I am delighted," he
wrote, " the more I think of it." On October 31 he
was travelling back from Vienna and was lunching in
the restaurant car with Count Szapary, the Hungarian
Prime Minister. In the middle of the luncheon there
was a sudden ping upon the window and something
whistled between them. A rifle bullet had pierced the
plate glass leaving a little round hole. It buried itself
in the wood-work opposite. Count Szapary continued
his luncheon undismayed.

(2)

November and December of 1892 were spent on leave. He stayed with friends in Ireland, and at the end of the year he travelled alone to Constantinople. His wife and family were deposited at Folkestone. He was again in debt and it was necessary to economise. He took a cheap steamer from Marseilles, and on leaving Smyrna the ship was caught by a blizzard and for four days took refuge under the lee of Lesbos. His family, at Folkestone, became alarmed. It was only on the fifth day that he was able to telegraph from Chanak that he had not after all been drowned.

He arrived at Constantinople to find a situation of some delicacy. In March of 1892 Sir William White, an ex-Consul and the greatest of British Ambassadors since Stratford Canning, had been succeeded by Sir Clare Ford. The latter was an amiable diplomatist, but not one who was very adapted to the conduct of Eastern policy. The Foreign Office had heard rumours of his lack of energy, and had instructed Nicolson to inform them directly and privately whether Sir Clare was in fact as ill-suited to an Oriental post as they had been given to understand. Nicolson did not relish this rôle of informant, and his distaste for his task was increased when he realised that the very worst that had been said about Sir Clare Ford was more than true. He concentrated upon his chief's amiability ; never, so he informed Lord Rosebery, had any man been so amiable and indeed so lovable as Sir Clare. The latter, in February 1894, was transferred to Rome, where his charm and intelligence proved of real value. He was eventually succeeded at Constantinople by Sir Philip

Currie. Meanwhile, however, the execution of British policy in the Near East fell mainly upon Nicolson's shoulders. It was not an easy task. For the Eastern question was by then already assuming a different form. On March 15, 1890, Prince Bismarck had been dismissed. The specialised diet which that great practitioner had prescribed for his adolescent country was neither understood nor followed by his successors. Caprivi, though well-intentioned, lacked authority. Marschall von Bieberstein, the Foreign Secretary, displayed an elephantine insensitiveness to the difference between strength and force. The young Emperor, a singularly gifted person, was mystically inclined : he came to represent the emotions of his people rather than their thoughts. The conduct of Foreign Affairs fell into the hands of Herr von Holstein, a secretive civil servant, whose views on public, and indeed on private, affairs were meticulous but inverted. The Emperor, with the best intentions, personified and encouraged the self-dramatisation of the German people, their acute self-consciousness, their moods of envy, self-pity and self-glorification ; their love of quantity and size. Holstein, on the other hand, represented the disordered suspiciousness of the Slav-Teutonic race, their love of intricacy, their conception of foreign affairs as some elaborately shifting pattern rather than as the development of perfectly simple and ascertainable probabilities. In addition Holstein was a little mad.

The main tenour of Bismarck's policy had been defensive. His axiom was the isolation of France. He believed, and rightly, in the French desire for revenge. This axiom entailed certain corollaries.

Germany must keep on good terms with Austria, Russia and England. The immediate difficulty was the Eastern question. Bismarck allied himself both with Petersburg and Vienna, hoping, in this way, that when the crisis arose he would be able to play the part of " honest broker " and partition the Balkans between the two. Holstein, for his part, did not share Bismarck's terror of European coalitions. He failed to renew the re-insurance treaty with Russia. He was convinced that the rivalry between England and France and England and Russia was so profound and durable that any agreement between these countries was absolutely impossible. Upon this basic and erroneous conviction he constructed the policy of the " free hand," by which Germany was to keep the balance between her Eastern and Western neighbours. This policy was perfectly logical and might well have proved advantageous had not Holstein gone a step further and added thereto the policy of " two irons in the fire." This also might have proved compatible with the needs of Germany had not a third slogan been added—that of " compensations." Holstein's idea was that Germany, by exploiting her central position between the rival Powers, might extract material profit from their differences. Had he been governed by any consistent or even simple principles he might have been able to exercise his mediatory position to the great advantage of Germany and Europe. His mind, however, was small, intricate and diseased. His every thought was a stratagem, and the sequence of stratagems which came to represent his policy affected Europe with bewilderment, irritation, and distrust. His intentions, on the whole, were pacific and bene-

ficent ; but in aiming at the momentary rather than at
the ultimate advantage of his country, in scheming
unceasingly for little immediate things, he rendered it
inevitable that the rivals of Germany should sooner or
later combine together to resist the blackmail which
he imposed.

It must be remembered also that the German people
during these years were passing through a complicated
spiritual crisis. The amazing expansion, between 1870
and 1890, of German wealth and population, had
induced a corresponding expansion of ambition. The
German people were no longer content with being
merely European : they desired to become a World
Power. Their sense of national identity, their consciousness of national vigour, had not, however, as
with older countries, been acquired through centuries
of experience. They possessed none of our own tradition of past blunders and intemperance wherewith
to moderate the vigour of their youth. The con-
genital diffidence of the German people, their over-
sensitive pride, came in this way to assume jerky forms
of envy and self-assertiveness. The earlier phase of
this neurosis (which even Bismarck failed to still) had
coincided with the most discreditable period of modern
history. The last two decades of the nineteenth
century were marred by the " scramble for Africa,"
during which Great Britain (and to a lesser extent
France, Belgium and Italy) behaved like beasts of prey.
The German people were justly incensed at seeing the
older countries give full vent to their predatory instincts, while treating Germany's requests for consideration with pained and patronising surprise.
Great Britain was particularly arrogant and selfish in

dealing with German requirements. Our great mistake was our failure to realise that Germany's desire
for expansion was perfectly legitimate. It was our
patronising obtuseness in this respect which drove
Germany to the unfortunate conclusion that she would
not be treated as an equal until she was able to inspire
fear. We behaved with greed and discourtesy in the
matter of Walfisch Bay. We behaved with equal tact-
lessness in regard to South West Africa. The Germans
countered by allowing Nachtigal to commit sharp
practices in Togoland and the Cameroons. It was only
then that Her Majesty's Government modified their
attitude and behaved decently to Karl Peters in East
Africa. The impression had, however, been conveyed
that we were stingy and hostile ; that we were ungrateful for Germany's support in the Egyptian
question ; and that the only way to secure the assistance of England was not to be polite to England, but
very rude indeed. This impression had not been
dispersed by the friendly exchange of views which took
place between Bismarck and Lord Salisbury in 1887
and again in 1889—nor yet by the cession of Heligo-
land in 1890. German opinion required something
wider if not more tangible, and the Emperor, sensitive
as he was to the superficial currents of his country's
emotions, desirous as he was of improving on Bismarck's policy of caution, turned his restless eyes
towards the East. By January 1893 the Drang nach
Osten had already begun. This protracted and highly
unsuccessful adventure produced undesirable results.
It diverted Russian attention to the Far East and created
circumstances which led to the Russo-Japanese War.
It earned for Germany the suspicion, not of Russia

only, but also of England. It encouraged Austria in
her Balkan ambitions. It destroyed what remained of
the Concert of Europe. And it damaged the high
moral prestige of William II. by identifying him with
Abdul Hamid. Such compensations as Germany
obtained in return were neither proportionate nor
durable.

For the moment, however, in those early months of
1893, British opinion was still inclined to look upon
France and Russia as our natural rivals and upon
Germany as our natural if unimportant friend. The
readiness with which British statesmen at that date
assumed that Germany in all circumstances would support British interests was touching but wholly unfortunate. Their premises were correct enough.
They knew that the two countries were racially, and
even psychologically, akin : that they were dynastically
connected. They realised that Germany's position as
between France and Russia rendered it axiomatic that
she should keep on good terms with the British
Empire. They thought that Germany would also
realise the force of these assumptions, and they thus,
most regrettably, took Germany for granted. The
German people, fired as they were with magnificent
energy, conceit and adolescence, did not relish being
taken for granted. The framers of British policy
imagined with curious thick-headedness that there was
no quarter of the globe in which Anglo-German
interests were not in harmony. They looked forward
to a situation in which the peace of Europe would be
safeguarded by the German army and the British navy.
They knew that Bismarck had rejected M. Herbette's
suggestions that Germany should join France in

making difficulties for us in Egypt. They knew that
Bismarck cared little either for a navy or for overseas
possessions ; that he had proclaimed the Near East as
not worth the bones of a Pomeranian Grenadier.
They thought that Caprivi would be inspired by similar
convictions. But Caprivi, desirous as he was to
" bring Germany back to everyday life," was not
inspired. All he did was to bring Germany back to
the Emperor William and to Herr von Holstein. The
Emperor's judgment was distorted by the desire to
provide his country with something so exciting that
they would forget the dismissal of Bismarck. He
provided them with the Drang nach Osten and the
High Seas Fleet. This entailed the hostility of Russia
and England. Baron von Holstein, for his part, was
concerned with rendering the conduct of German
foreign policy so intricate and tortuous that no one
but himself would be able to unravel the skein. In
this he succeeded to perfection. " We cannot hide
from ourselves," writes Theodor Wolff,[1] " what it cost
us to own such an eccentric."

(3)

It is interesting to trace in Nicolson's letters and
despatches during these early months of 1893, the
stages by which he adjusted himself to the thus altered
proportions of the Eastern question. The first shock
was to discover how seriously, since 1883, British influence at Constantinople had declined. The tradition
of Anglo-Turkish friendship which dated from the
Crimean War and beyond, had been snapped on that
" memorable night " when he attended Lord Dufferin

[1] Theodor Wolff's *Vorspiel*, p. 199.

at Yildiz. "The Sultan," he wrote to Mr. Villiers a
month after his arrival, "is strongly anti-English, and
I am not surprised." And yet the Egyptian question
was not at the moment an acute cause of controversy.
"I always rely," Nicolson wrote, "on the Sultan never
taking any decisive action in regard to Egypt; he has
. gone splashing about from bog-hole to bog-hole and
will never be able to haul himself up on dry ground.
With his machinations and his schemes and intrigues,
he has got the Egyptian question into such a hopeless
tangle in his brain (and busy fingers are always twisting
and twining the mesh) that he will never be able to
unravel the skein." That at least was something to
the good, and yet the very degeneracy and hopelessness
of Abdul Hamid and his surroundings constituted a
source of disquiet. "Venice," wrote Nicolson, "in
its darkest days was light and freedom compared to
the Stamboul of to-day." The Sultan himself was
incapable of all but the most panic-stricken or tortuous
decisions. "The whole system," Nicolson complained
despairingly to Lord Rosebery, "is rotten to the core.
The Sultan wandering from room to room during the
night; snatching an hour or two on this and that
divan; calling up his Sheikhs, astrologers and atten-
dants at all hours to try and get some solace and con-
solation from some new terror which seizes him; this
is the sad picture of the terrible life he leads. The
ex-Sultan Murad, soused in raki, plentifully supplied
by his affectionate brother, sits slobbering and dazed,
while his palace is the haunt of all that is despicable
and depraved." It would appear indeed that during
this year 1893 Abdul Hamid was already succumbing
to that peculiar form of mental derangement which

developed into homicidal mania and caused the Armenian massacres of 1895. In Nicolson's private letters of this period there are many references to the progress of His Majesty's disease. "We dined"—so he writes to Mr. Villiers :

"We dined at the Palace yesterday. I found the Sultan looking much aged since I saw him 10 years ago, tho', as he ate a big dinner, he belied the rumours as to his weak health. A solemn dreary entertainment, a farewell to Ford and in honour of Max Müller and a General Kent whom Ford had presented as 'one of our most distinguished generals'—a good old lady, but not likely to enhance our warlike reputation as far as appearance and abilities go. The Sultan was in good spirits and 'gracious,' but all these Yildiz entertainments with their tawdry splendour and courtiers practically crawling about on all fours have a rather comic though saddening effect. We don't see the real Palace—the Sheikhs, and the astrologers and the hole and corner intrigue, and all the dark doings and sayings. We are only, alas ! treated to a pièce montée."

A few days later Nicolson again wrote to Mr. Villiers as follows :

"The Padishah is in a fume and has passed a thoroughly bad week. He had a great scare. When he went to pay his annual devotions to the Prophet's relics in Stamboul (the only occasion on which he goes any distance from his palace), a series of most unfortunate accidents occurred, and Testa, who went to see him next day, found him in a state of collapse and terror. First an A.D.C.'s carriage horses bolted, and the A.D.C. banged his head against the kerb and died : then a baby was run over on the bridge ; then while the Sultan was still in Stamboul, a launch with the royal scullions on board was run into and sunk, drowning 20 people. This so alarmed the Sultan that he gave orders to his carriage to go back by another route at full speed—consequently more people were run over, and the quaking sovereign returned to Yildiz, overcome with terror.   He was convinced that all these untoward accidents were in some way, known only to his fearsome mind, connected with plots against his life, and he became panic-stricken.   Then there is the Armenian question ; then the latest Egyptian papers which have been published, over which he is gnashing his teeth.   I suppose he will calm down shortly, but we must be prepared, while he is in this frame of mind, for some folly, and we shall have to watch carefully the manœuvres of Cambon."

Clearly all dealings with such a maniac were impossible, and yet it was not merely the personality and eccentricities of Abdul Hamid which were to blame.   The younger generation of Turks were not as amenable to British advice as their forebears.   Nicolson wrote as follows to Mr. Villiers on February 27, 1893 :

" We should not forget that now we have to deal with very different Turks from the Turks of Ld. Stratford de Redcliffe for instance.   The men we deal with and who are now the instruments of the Sultan are not the old Turks, but are the products of a vitiated French education overlying the old stock.   Young Turkey may have forefathers, but they approach closely on many sides to the corrupt wily Levantine, with a good dose of fanaticism underneath, and a craze for money making and speculation. The old Turk understood us, and you had a man to tackle. The present men's training and habits of thought are largely influenced by French ideas, not of the highest order, and widely opposite to anything Anglo-Saxon. With the old ruling classes we could get into touch and sympathy, and exercise some influence over them.   To the present entourage of the Sultan, England and English modes of thought and habits are antipathetic."

These Parisian tendencies on the part of the younger

Pashas were warmly encouraged by the French Ambassador, Monsieur Paul Cambon [1]—who in fact did
everything in his power to destroy the last vestiges of
British influence and to rub salt into the Egyptian
wound. The respect which Arthur Nicolson came in
later years to feel for M. Cambon was not based on any
very early affection. " I had," he writes to Francis
Villiers, " a long talk with Cambon the other day.
Very sharp, very much Monsieur le Préfet—till he sees
you are not overawed and then he becomes human
again. He is pining for a diplomatic success of some
kind. He is very agreeable but, I believe, a great
intriguant." With the German Ambassador, Prince
Radolin, and with his Austrian partner, Baron Calice,
Nicolson's relations were very intimate indeed.
" Radolin," he writes, " tells me that there is a scheme
on foot on the part of Cambon to reorganise the whole
Ottoman Bank and get rid of Edgar Vincent.[2] He
asked me whether that would not be a great blow to
our influence. The Ottoman Bank is not much help
to British interests, in fact of late they have rather
supported French projects—so we should not suffer
much. But I did not tell Radolin this. I merely said
it would be a pity if we lost so pleasant a man as
Vincent, with so charming a wife." This evasion was
tactful and necessary ; from the first Nicolson had
noted a tendency on the part of the German Ambassador to assume that the British Embassy were

---

[1] It is well to differentiate the two Cambon brothers from the outset.
M. Paul Cambon, at that date French Ambassador in Constantinople, was
shortly afterwards transferred to London, where he served as Ambassador
for over twenty years. His younger brother, M. Jules Cambon, was French
Ambassador in Madrid and subsequently, and until 1914, in Berlin.

[2] Now Lord D'Abernon.

incapable of resisting French influence at the Porte. Sir Clare Ford had perhaps given some grounds for this assumption—and after all, what did it matter? " I think," he wrote, " that Radolin is a little too keen to take us in tow and he tells us that we cannot possibly do without his support. Personally I don't mind this, and if he is going to god-father us here let us hope he will be responsible for all our omissions. Calice, who in manner and appearance is like an old family coach-horse, ambles peacefully along with us and the Italian completes the happy family."

Within a few weeks, however, this domestic harmony was disturbed.

(4)

Early in 1893 an acute controversy arose between the several Embassies in Constantinople regarding railway concessions in Asia Minor. The incident deserves to be recorded in some detail. In the first place it is curiously illustrative of the atmosphere in which the old diplomacy pursued its activities. In the second place it was from this very seed that grew the later wrangles about the Baghdad Railway. And in the third place it was through this incident that Arthur Nicolson first came face to face with the methods of Baron von Holstein.

Her Majesty's Government assumed, in their complacent way, that British interests possessed some sort of prescriptive right over all railway construction in Asia Minor. It was true that so long ago as 1856 a certain Sir Francis Chesney had obtained some sort of option over a railway from Alexandretta to Baghdad. Sir Francis had, however, been unable to raise the

capital necessary for his enterprise, and the option had
lapsed. Since then another British Company had constructed a line from Smyrna to Aidin with important
branch connections, and further British Companies
held concessions for the line from Mersina to Adana,
as well as for that from Smyrna via Kassaba to Alashir.
The nucleus of what in after years became the Baghdad
Railway was at that date represented by the line from
Haidar Pasha, opposite Constantinople, to Ismidt.
This small section of 91 kilometres had been constructed by the German engineer, von Pressel, in 1871,
and had in 1880 been conceded to a British group.
In 1888 this group had been bought out by the
Deutsche Bank, who had at the same time obtained
from the Porte a concession entitling them to extend
the line to Angora. On March 16, 1889, the Deutsche
Bank had joined with the Bank of Württemberg in
founding the Anatolian Railway Company, of which
Herr von Kühlmann, father of the subsequent Foreign
Secretary, was appointed managing director. On
February 15, 1893, this company, acting through Herr
Kaulla, obtained from the Porte an Imperial iradé,
which gave them the right to construct a line from
Eski Shehr to Konia and to extend the Angora line via
Caesarea, Sivas and Diarbekir, to Baghdad. The latter
alignment proved too difficult and was eventually
abandoned in favour of a more southerly trace through
the Taurus and thus to Nisibin and Mosul. The final
conventions entrusting the Baghdad Railway to the
Anatolian Railway Company date from 1899 and 1902.
The concession of 1893 was, however, the nucleus of
the whole scheme, and it was this concession which
caused Nicolson such acute distress.

The British groups had at that date, scenting expansion, tendered for the concession. The first was
the Smyrna-Aidin Railway, the oldest and most reliable
of railway enterprises in Turkey : the second was a
group represented by Mr. Staniforth, who desired to
build a line from Alexandretta via Biridjik to Baghdad.
French interests were at the same time pressing for
railway concessions in Syria. The terms offered by
the British groups were more favourable than those
advanced by the Anatolian Railway Company, but the
latter, to Nicolson's pained exasperation, were receiving from the Berlin Government strong and even
violent diplomatic support. Sir Clare Ford, for his
part, was at first cynical and aloof. " Yesterday,"
Nicolson wrote on January 12, 1893, " an affair
occurred which would have made Layard or Dufferin
or White bring out their heavy artillery. Ford takes
it as a matter of no concern. The Germans are pushing to extend their railway in Asia Minor in a way to
throttle and ruin our two lines, and to completely
monopolise all future enterprise on our part. This
German concession is being pushed even by the
Emperor William." The French Government meanwhile had succeeded in inducing the Turkish Government to transfer to French control the Smyrna-Kassaba
Railway, which till then had been owned by a British
group. " All yesterday," wrote Nicolson, " I was
trying to push Ford into a little activity about the
railways, but without much success. His légèreté is
appalling, and he does not care twopence about the
work. The French and Germans will monopolise the
whole of Asiatic Turkey and we shall be completely
shut out both politically and commercially. Ford

treats it all rather as a joke. It is hopeless ; and yet he is so cheery and so kind that it is difficult to be cross with him." In his perplexity Nicolson went to call upon the Austrian Ambassador. " Had a long talk," he notes, " with Calice. He said that he viewed with despair the rivalry between us and the Germans about the railway. It seemed to him as if the good understanding which had been built up so laboriously was being destroyed. However, I soothed him on this point." To Nicolson, at that date, the obvious solution of such a difficulty was to go shares with the Deutsche Bank. Sir Edgar Vincent thought differently. " Vincent is in great despair about our position here and is for cracking the whip loudly. I don't think we should as yet. It would look like irritation and we should be complacently indifferent : watchful, and very patient and silent." Sir Clare Ford, for his part, tended in a feeble way to agree with Sir Edgar Vincent and Sir Vincent Caillard. A certain divergence of action is at this stage observable between the Ambassador and his Counsellor. Nicolson was already in negotiations with the German Embassy. " I am afraid," he wrote privately to the Foreign Office, " that Ford has muddled the railway affair by not going in with the Germans. I flatter myself, however, that I have put things straight here with Radolin." The dual control which the Foreign Office had deliberately established in the Embassy in Constantinople was detrimental to British interests. Sir Clare Ford made representations to the Porte asking that the firman to the German group should be deferred until British financiers could be consulted. At the same time he encouraged the Ottoman Public Debt

Administration and the Bank to raise obstructions. This policy was a mistake. The German Emperor was already telegraphing to the Sultan insisting on the acceptance of the Kaulla contract. The Wilhelm-strasse were already aware that the concession was being blocked by British intervention. Herr von Holstein acted rapidly. He at once telegraphed to Baron Leyden, German representative at Cairo, in-structing him to notify Lord Cromer that " in view of the aggressively hostile attitude of the British Embassy in Constantinople " the German Government would be compelled to withdraw the consent they had already given to certain administrative reforms which we desired in Egypt.[1] Lord Cromer, on receipt of this intimation, was furious and alarmed. He urged capi-tulation. On February 22, 1893, Lord Rosebery tele-graphed to Sir Clare Ford as follows : " Do what you properly can, without compromising your position, to remove obstacles which Germans complain are being unnecessarily interposed by Caillard in way of the Kaulla concessions." These obstacles were at once removed. Sir Clare Ford was shortly afterwards re-called. The Germans obtained the Baghdad Railway without British participation. And Nicolson learnt that the methods of Herr von Holstein were very different from the methods which, in 1874, had obtained in Berlin. He was quick to make his peace with the German Embassy. Good relations were re-established. And on July 14 of the same year Holstein, in writing to Count Hatzfeldt in London was able to say that " von Nicolson's Tätigkeit in Konstantinopel hört man viel gutes." [2] That was all very well. But

---

[1] G.P., vol. viii, p. 185, No. 1816.   [2] G.P., vol. viii, p. 210.

from that moment Nicolson came to look upon the
Wilhelmstrasse with a wary eye.

(5)

Nicolson was also distressed at not receiving from
the German Embassy the support that he expected
in the question of Armenia. In the second chapter
of this biography reference was made to Lord Salisbury's endeavours to improve the condition of the
Armenians in Turkey. In March of 1891 the Sultan
Abdul Hamid formed his bands of authorised Kurdish
brigands which he called the "Hamidieh Cavalry."
In the following month many Armenians were
arrested at Erzeroum. In March of 1892 Sir Clare
Ford reached Constantinople with instructions not
to insist upon the execution of Article 61 of the
Treaty of Berlin but to bring isolated incidents to the
notice of the Porte. A period of nagging followed,
which exasperated the Turks and kept the pro-
Armenian societies in Great Britain busy compiling
statistics of oppression. At the end of the year the
Sultan promised reluctantly to send a commission to
Kurdistan to report on conditions. This commission
failed to materialise, and on March 21, 1893, Lord
Rosebery began to threaten. "Her Majesty's Government," he telegraphed, "will have to institute an
enquiry of their own if prompt action be not taken by
the Turkish Government." The Grand Vizier replied
that the reports had been much exaggerated but admitted that many Armenians had been arrested for
distributing seditious leaflets. The preparation of
these leaflets was traced to the American College at
Marsovan, which possessed a hectograph machine,

G

In April of 1893 two Armenian professors of the
College, Professor Thoumaian and Professor Kayaian,
were arrested, loaded with chains, and sent for trial
in Angora. When the news reached England and
America great indignation was aroused. Sir Clare
Ford had at that date departed and the responsibility
fell on Nicolson alone. The United States Minister
was of little assistance. The following passage occurs
in a private letter to Lord Rosebery :

> " I am sorry to say that the U.S. Minister, who is a
> rugged, rough-hewn Texas judge, has been nobbed by the
> Sultan, I think only temporarily. But the wily Caliph,
> hearing that the Transatlantic Press was becoming
> troublesome in regard to American missionaries and
> Armenian matters, had the idea of inviting Mr., Mrs. and
> Miss Terrell to dinner, set the young lady down with his
> son (who is always produced on such occasions), decorated
> her with the order of merit, a Chefakat, the same to her
> Mama, and listened for an hour patiently to Judge Terrell,
> who delivered an oration on the art of Government,
> informing H.M. that he was a ' plain man, unused to
> Courts, but confident that truth was a commodity that
> rarely reached the ears of Kings or Sultans.' Terrell told
> me the Sultan hung his head and sighed and he thought
> he had hit the mark. All this comedy has, however,
> persuaded this hitherto uncorrupted minister that the
> Sultan is the best man that ever breathed and only his
> agents are vile."

The Tribunal at Angora had meanwhile condemned
the two professors to death. Lord Rosebery sent the
strongest instructions. " Her Majesty's Government," he telegraphed on June 27, " cannot conceal
their disappointment at the procedure adopted at the
trial and its result, nor can they attempt to control the

indignation it has caused in this country." On June
28 Nicolson visited the Grand Vizier and spoke earnestly to him on the subject. Said Pasha (" a sleek and
portly Turk, with drooping eyelids, from under which
he gives little sly glances ") mumbled something about
a right of appeal to the Court of Cassation. Arthur
Nicolson replied that British confidence in Turkish
Courts, whether of appeal or other, had been shaken.
" This remark," he records, " nettled His Highness
and a somewhat warm discussion ensued." The
Grand Vizier stated that a spirit of what he might be
allowed to call fanaticism was being shown in England.
" I replied," so Nicolson reports to Lord Rosebery,
" that there was no doubt fanaticism in England for
justice and fair dealing and that I personally associated
myself with that fanaticism." The Turks continued,
however, to evade the issue by stating that the case
must come before the Court of Appeal and that the
Government could not interfere with the prescribed
course of justice. Lord Rosebery was firm. Nicolson
was instructed to inform the Porte bluntly that " Her
Majesty's Government cannot wait for the result of
the proceedings of the Cour de Cassation." The
Turks were furious but alarmed. On July 4 the two
professors were pardoned, and on July 11 Nicolson
had the pleasure of telegraphing as follows : " Professors Thoumaian and Kayaian left for Brindisi
yesterday afternoon by Austrian Lloyd." Lord Rosebery and the *Daily News* were delighted. They both
expressed themselves as highly satisfied with Nicolson's
activity. The fact remained however that the whole
odium of protecting these two professors had fallen
upon the British Embassy. Prince Radolin and Baron

Calice, in spite of Nicolson's appeals to the Treaty of
Berlin, had remained aloof. M. Cambon had diplayed
every sympathy with the Porte at this further instance
of British interference with the internal affairs of
Turkey. M. Nelidoff, the Russian Ambassador, was
delighted at the increasing unpopularity of his British
colleague. The Khedive of Egypt chose this moment
to visit his Suzerain at Constantinople. It was an
awkward visit, but Abdul Hamid fortunately displayed
his usual incapacity for taking decisions. No harm
was done.

The Armenian question, however, was by no means
settled. Petitions flowed in from Armenian prisoners
in Sivas and Samsun. There were disturbances at
Yuzgat. In February of 1894 Sir Philip Currie arrived
in Constantinople. In July of 1894 Nicolson was
appointed Agent and Consul-General in Bulgaria. It
was only after his departure that the full fruit of the
Armenian problem was gathered. In October of that
year the Hamidieh Cavalry indulged in a wholesale
massacre in the Sassoun district. Women and children were herded into a church and burnt alive. Lord
Rosebery spoke of " horrors unutterable and unim-
aginable." He instructed Sir Philip Currie to demand
an enquiry and to insist on the punishment of those
responsible. Abdul Hamid, realising that the Powers
were not united, returned a vague answer in which he
stated that he would conduct his own enquiry into
" the criminal conduct of the Armenian brigands."
Joint representations were then made and a joint commission was appointed. The enquiry disclosed that
the Kurds had been alone responsible, and that the
negligence of the Turkish authorities had been culpable

in the extreme. The Powers then proceeded to discuss how such outrages could be prevented in the future. A joint scheme of reforms was elaborated and France and Russia at last joined with us in urging the acceptance of this scheme upon the Sultan. Abdul Hamid appealed at this stage to Germany. Lord Kimberley became impatient. He informed the Porte that if the Sultan did not give way Her Majesty's Government " would employ their own measures of restraint." This alarmed the Russians, who proceeded to withdraw their support. Abdul Hamid thereupon accepted our scheme of reforms and proceeded to institute the wholesale massacre of 1895. The Powers took this calmly. Prince Lobanoff announced that " he saw nothing to destroy his confidence in the goodwill of the Sultan." Thus encouraged, Abdul Hamid proceeded to massacre the Armenians in Constantinople itself. Six to seven thousand Armenians were butchered in broad daylight under the very eyes of the Ambassadors. The streets of the capital were littered with men, women, and children whose heads had been battered by the clubs of the Kurds. The six Ambassadors thereupon presented a joint Note. In England, however, the indignation was deep and absolutely sincere. The British public regarded Abdul Hamid as a homicidal maniac, and would have been prepared to depose him by force. It was then remembered that the Emperor William had visited Abdul Hamid in 1889, and when in 1898 he visited him again under dramatic circumstances British opinion was disturbed. This second visit was certainly a most unfortunate incident in the Drang nach Osten.

(6)

During the summer of 1894, at the very height of
the Armenian crisis, Nicolson had been dangerously
ill. He left one Saturday for a yachting expedition to
the Gulf of Ismidt. Two days later his family were
startled to see the *Imogen* at anchor under the very
windows of the Therapia Embassy and a stretcher
being lowered into the gig. He was carried into a
ground-floor room suffering from ptomaine poisoning.
The danger was acute, and the illness was succeeded by
a prolonged attack of gout. For six weeks he was unable to put his foot to the ground, and for three months
he was on crutches. He emerged from this ordeal
with shoulders prematurely rounded and bowed, and
the persistent arthritis which thereafter developed gave
to his small frame an increasingly crippled appearance.
It was thus in circumstances of great physical suffering
and debility that he had to cope with the dangers which
threatened Professor Thoumaian. The Turkish Ministers would visit him at Therapia. He would dress
himself and be carried into the next room. Propped
in a chair, his face in perspiration from the agony of
his limbs, he would sit there arguing with Said Pasha
or the timorous Artim. He would then return exhausted to his fomentations. The experiences of those
four months aged him by many years. He was glad
in the autumn to reach the comparative quiet of his
new post at Sofia—at that date a sleepy little Balkan
village cowering under the massif of Mount Vitosh.
He did not remain at Sofia for more than ten months,
but they were ten months of great importance to the
history of Bulgaria.

(7)

The Powers who at the Congress of Berlin had created the tiny Principality of Bulgaria, and had thereafter selected Prince Alexander of Battenberg as its ruler, had been under the impression that this new Balkan State would be little more than a protectorate of Russia. The Russian Government shared this illusion, and in fact flooded the country with their own soldiers and officials. Prince Alexander, a wholly sympathetic figure, though at first subservient to the dictation of St. Petersburg, gradually fell in love with his adopted country, and when in 1885 he was forced into proclaiming the unions of Bulgaria and Rumelia, and thereafter conducted a successful campaign against the Serbs, he was universally hailed as a national hero and regarded as the protagonist of Bulgarian independence. The revenge of Russia was summary and immediate. A military conspiracy was organised at Sofia and Prince Alexander was kidnapped and forced to abdicate. The Government of St. Petersburg thereafter announced that it would boycott Bulgaria, hoping doubtless that the country would relapse into chaos and would end by placing itself unreservedly in Russian hands. M. de Giers had not, however, foreseen the emergence of Stambouloff. This rugged and ruthless patriot immediately assumed control of affairs, summoned the Grand Sobranye, nominated a Council of Regency, and proceeded to select a ruler to replace the admirable but exiled Alexander. The choice eventually fell on Prince Ferdinand of Coburg, who arrived in Sofia in 1887. Prince Ferdinand was subtle and ambitious : he was also patient. For seven years he lay low in his palace, leaving the conduct of affairs to Stambouloff, fully aware that that powerful man would reap all the odium inseparable from strong, and in this case violent, government. Ferdinand bided his time. He had been pronounced an usurper by Russia, and the other Powers had only accorded him half-hearted recognition. He was well aware that he could only establish his position by making terms with St. Petersburg. But he was prepared to wait. When in 1894 the news came of the death of Alexander III. of Russia, Prince Ferdinand decided that the moment had come to strike. Stambouloff was dismissed. M. Stoiloff, a creature of the pro-Russian party, was appointed Prime Minister. The conduct of foreign policy was openly assumed by Ferdinand himself. Overtures were immediately made at St. Petersburg. It was arranged that a Bulgarian Mission should be sent to Russia to re-establish relations. It was at this juncture that Nicolson arrived.

He had an audience with Prince Ferdinand, who devoted two hours to abusing Stambouloff. He had several interviews with M. Stoiloff, who was also at pains to prejudice the British Agent against the late dictator. Nicolson, with the help of Mr. Bourchier of *The Times*, then made great friends with Stambouloff himself. The latter spoke with appreciation and sympathy of Prince Ferdinand. He was in no sense pessimistic about the future of Bulgaria : he assured Nicolson that there was no danger of Bulgaria again becoming a Russian protectorate : that the mission to St. Petersburg was an excellent idea ; that M. Stoiloff, in difficult circumstances, was really doing very well. Nicolson appreciated such impersonal generosity :

Stambouloff was just the sort of man he admired and liked. He saw, however, that there was no prospect of making peace between Prince Ferdinand and the creator of the new Bulgaria. And Prince Ferdinand was annoyed when he learnt that Nicolson would once a week dine openly with Stambouloff at the Sofia Club.

In the early months of 1895 the Bulgarian Government embarked on a system of persecution against Stambouloff and his followers. In January it was reported that the ex-dictator was to be arrested, and Nicolson warned M. Stoiloff that such action would be badly interpreted in the British Press. In February and again in April Stambouloff informed Nicolson that the attitude of the Prince and M. Stoiloff " placed a great strain on his party's loyalty to the throne." The persecutions continued, and summonses were issued against Stambouloff and his colleague Petkoff for misappropriation of public funds. Stambouloff countered by fusing with the party of Radoslavoff, thus constituting a united Liberal opposition. On May 25 Stambouloff applied for permission to proceed, on the advice of his doctor, to Carlsbad. His application was refused on the ground that he was about to be impeached. On July 13 the Government newspaper, the *Mir*, published an article denouncing Stambouloff and Petkoff and urging their " removal." Prince Ferdinand, for his part, was absent in Austria. Two days later, on July 15, Nicolson looked in at the club before dinner. Stambouloff and Petkoff were talking together and the former offered to drive Nicolson home. He refused the offer, saying that his own carriage was waiting. A few minutes later, at 7.50 p.m., Stambouloff and Petkoff also left the club and called a passing cab. Stambouloff's body-servant climbed on to the box. At the corner of the next street a shot rang out and Stambouloff leapt into the roadway. Petkoff, observing that his chief was being assailed by three men armed with swords, called wildly to two gendarmes who were posted at the opposite corner. They paid no attention. Stambouloff's servant, who had noticed a senior police officer stationed fifty yards further on, ran to him for assistance. He was at once arrested and disarmed by two further policemen who were hiding round the corner. Meanwhile Stambouloff's three assailants were hacking at him with their yatagans. He put up his hands to protect his head. His fingers were severed and dropped upon the pavement. He himself collapsed upon the roadway in a pool of blood. He was taken to his house and died there three days later. While still conscious he forbade his wife to have any further dealings with Prince Ferdinand, or to answer the telegram of condolence which the latter would assuredly despatch.

British public opinion was deeply shocked by the assassination of Stambouloff. Queen Victoria instructed Nicolson personally to place a wreath upon the coffin, and to attend the funeral as her representative. The funeral took place on July 20. When passing the scene of the assassination, the procession paused and Petkoff began to deliver an oration on the merits of his murdered chief. His opening words were interrupted by a volley of rifle-shots, and mounted police, debouching from two side streets, charged at the procession with drawn swords. A stampede followed. The roadway was littered with wreaths, umbrellas, and top-hats. Nicolson lost his temper.

Escaping down a side-street he proceeded at once and on foot to the house of M. Stoiloff. He found some difficulty in gaining admittance. The door eventually was half-opened by the Prime Minister himself, who held a revolver in his hand. Nicolson, for a space of twenty minutes, was able to tell M. Stoiloff exactly what he thought. Ten days later, on his appointment as Minister in Morocco, he left Sofia for England.

In the following year Nicolson was invited to a garden party at Buckingham Palace. At a turn of the path he came face to face with the Prince and Princess of Bulgaria. The former failed to recognise him and the Princess stopped for a moment, placed her hand upon her husband's arm, and said " Tiens, voici Sir Nicolson." " Notre chemin," replied Prince Ferdinand, turning in the opposite direction, " est par ici." Fourteen years later, at St. Petersburg, they met again. On that occasion, as will be recounted, King Ferdinand was very affable indeed.

V

MOROCCO

[1895-1901]

(1)

THE summer of 1895 was spent at Walmer Castle. Lord Dufferin, who had been appointed Warden of the Cinque Ports in 1891, was completing his last months as Ambassador in Paris. He was pleased to lend Walmer to his brother-in-law, and Nicolson was thus able to revive forgotten memories of Lord Granville, and to entertain his father and other relations in that historic and unhealthy mansion. At the end of September he embarked with his wife and youngest son for Gibraltar. The two elder boys were already at school at Folkestone. His daughter had not yet been born. For three days they stayed at the Convent where Sir Robert Biddulph, Governor of Gibraltar, entertained them with banquets for the garrison officers. On October 3 they crossed in H.M.S. *Bellona* to Tangier.

The guns boomed a welcome. The new Minister was received by the Moorish population and by the European colony with unwonted enthusiasm. A severe epidemic of cholera had for weeks been decimating the town, and the arrival (the apparently gratuitous arrival) of a new Minister with wife and child cheered their drooping spirits. They interpreted Nicolson's advent as a sign that the cholera was not so serious as they imagined. The epidemic, however, increased. The Legation garden was separated from the Moorish cemetery by a low rubble wall covered with convolvulus. The youngest son of Arthur Nicolson was able, by standing on a tub, to watch the funerals in progress in the field below. All day long the high funeral chant echoed across the garden. *La ilaha illa Allah. Mohammed Rasul Allah. All—ah.* The child from that moment conceived a marked distaste for cholera. It remained with him in after life.

Arthur Nicolson was curiously indifferent to the dangers of the body. He flung himself unperturbed into a study of the history and present conditions of Morocco. It was not a very cheerful study. Morocco, in that year 1895, shared with Abyssinia the honour of being the only profitable country in Africa which had maintained its independence. England, being already satiated, desired only to safeguard her commercial superiority and that *status quo* which secured for her complete control of the Straits of Gibraltar. The French, till 1901, confined themselves to nibbling at those portions of the country which lay south of the Atlas. The Spaniards, who were about to embark on a singularly unsuccessful war with America, hung on by

their eyelids to the garrisons at Ceuta and Melilla. And
Germany, who was only too delighted that Morocco
should divert French attention from the blue line of the
Vosges, adopted an attitude of " stillschweigendes
Abwarten "—of Sphinx-like expectancy.

Shortly after Nicolson's arrival, his German colleague, Count Tattenbach (of whom much will be
heard hereafter) was succeeded by Baron Schenk von
Schweinsberg. The latter was described by Nicolson
as " an old friend of mine and a great improvement on
his hot-headed predecessor. He is mild and conciliatory." The withdrawal of Count Tattenbach left
Nicolson as the only important Minister who took a
direct interest in the maintenance of Moorish integrity
and independence. M. Victor Bérard, in his book
entitled *L'Affaire Marocaine*, has misinterpreted the
situation which then arose. " Les missions," he writes,
" de M. de Schweinsberg et de M. de Mentzingen
furent une période d'acquiescement complet de l'Allemagne aux projets de l'Angleterre. Grâce à cet
acquiescement, le Ministre anglais, M. Nicholson (*sic*)
régna à Tanger." It is true that, almost from the day of
his arrival, Nicolson found himself in a position of
undesired dominance in Moorish affairs. It is not true
(and in saying so M. Bérard displays the wonted silli-
ness of French publicists) that the British Foreign Office
had any " projets " at all. They were profoundly bored
with Morocco, and their only desire was that the
country should not be added to the long list of international complications. The new Minister was quick
to realise the dangers of his embarrassing popularity,
and the misunderstandings to which it might lead. On
December 7, 1895, barely eight weeks after his arrival,

he wrote as follows to Kaid Maclean, the British
Officer commanding the Sultan's army :

> " I do not know whether it would be desirable for us to
> obtain a very intimate and powerful footing at Court.
> We should thereby incur certain responsibilities which I
> think it would be wiser to avoid.   The future is very
> uncertain in this country, and I should like our hands to
> be quite free and not to encourage these people to imagine
> that we were their sole support and advisers.   I do not
> think this would be fair as they might expect more than
> we should probably perform.   I am anxious to be on the
> most friendly terms and do what I can to help them, but
> not to strive for a specially predominant position.   The
> consequences might be awkward."

" *I do not think this would be fair* " : it is from phrases
such as these, and not from M. Bérard's conclusions,
that the motives which inspired Arthur Nicolson can be
gauged.

(2)

The southern frontier between Morocco and Algeria
had never, even in 1845, been accurately delimitated.
The territory claimed by the Sultan contained certain
oases essential to the communications between Algeria
and Equatorial Africa.   One of such oases was Tuat
and from time to time the Sultan or the Governor
General of Algeria would make attempts to establish
their authority in the Tuat area.   The Sultan appealed
to the British Minister.   The French, he said, were
again about to occupy both Tuat and Tafilet and what
on earth were the Shereefian Government to do ?
Nicolson advised them " to take no action which would
be likely to induce the French authorities to raise the
question in a form which might have unpleasant

consequences." [1]   All this, however, was merely
beating the air.   He must know more about Morocco
before he could feel justified in giving advice to the
Moorish Government.   The whole future, to his mind,
turned upon the internal situation, upon the capacity of
the boy Sultan and his Government to introduce
internal order and reforms.   It was impossible, from
Tangier, to judge of what was really happening at Fez
or Marakesh.   Nicolson determined therefore to proceed to the Court and see for himself what hopes there
were of Morocco being able to stand alone.

The prospects were not inspiring.   Muley Hassan,
one of the strongest Sultans whom Morocco had ever
possessed, had died in 1894.   He was succeeded by
Abd-ul-Aziz, a boy of fourteen years of age, who was
completely under the domination of Bu-Ahmed, the
Grand Vizier.   Even in the best days of Muley Hassan's
supremacy, Morocco had been divided between the
Blad-el-Maghzen or the territory which recognised the
Sultan's authority, and the Blad-es-Saba, or the territory
which was in open and avowed revolt.   The Blad-el-
Maghzen had been much restricted since Muley
Hassan's death.   Insecurity was on the increase and
during the first weeks of his sojourn in Tangier
Nicolson received complaints from British merchants
of goods looted by Riff pirates, of merchandise raided
even in the warehouses at Saffi.   " I consider," he
wrote to the Foreign Office on December 2, 1895,
" that Persia is a rich and prosperous country in com-
parison with this loose agglomeration of turbulent
tribes, corrupt Governors, and general poverty and
distress."   It was thus with no undue optimism that he

[1] A.N. to Lord Salisbury, No. 10, January 23, 1896.

embarked in the spring of 1896 upon his first mission to the Sultan.

He sailed in H.M.S. *Arethusa* to Mogador. " On landing," he wrote, " there was a great crowd with many ragamuffin soldiers and an excruciating band. It was difficult to make an imposing landing balancing oneself along a slippery plank. We walked up solemnly to the Consulate—I tried to look like a Bashador." He spent two days at Mogador and was able to intervene with the Governor on behalf of the Jewish community who were cruelly restricted within the confines of the insanitary Mellah or ghetto. He obtained for them permission to extend the area of their pale. From Mogador he journeyed by slow stages to Marakesh, camping by night in the Arghan forest, riding in a continuous procession during the day. He recorded his progress in daily letters to his wife :

> " A man with a great silken standard rides in front of me, and I have a special escort of 12 who never leave me ; —rather a bore. It amuses me at night to hear the different guards calling to each other to keep themselves awake— ' Ismail, is that you ? ' ' Yes, how are you, Mahmut ? ' and so on. Harris [1] says it is no use saying ' hush ' as the following will take place. The guard at the tent will whisper awestruck to the next one, ' The Bashador is awake and is speaking.' ' What is he saying ? ' ' I do not know, it is in English.' ' Peradventure he is ill, let us get someone,' and then they will wake up the whole camp and troops of anxious inquirers will appear and thoroughly disturb me."

On April 9, a Friday, they camped outside Morocco City but were obliged to defer their entry until the

---

[1] Mr. W. B. Harris, correspondent of *The Times*, who accompanied Nicolson on his mission.

following day. Kaid Maclean came out to visit the
Minister in camp. This was Nicolson's first meeting
with the little Scotchman who was to be a keen if
embarrassing coadjutor in the years that followed.
Kaid Maclean had at that date been some twenty years
in Moorish service. He had left his regiment as a
subaltern and had been employed by Muley Hassan,
first as instructor, and later as Commander-in-Chief of
the Moorish army. He was small and round, with a
clean little white beard, and the gayest eyes that ever
shone above a bagpipe. Arrayed in a turban and a
white bernous he would stride along the garden paths
blowing into his bagpipes. " The Banks of Loch
Lomond " would squeal out into the African sunshine.
He was indeed a simple and an honest soul. Nicolson
took to him from the first. The Kaid had brought a
magnificent black stallion on which the Minister, a
frail but expert jockey, was to make his formal entry
into the capital. The entry was exhausting but successful. He described it to his wife as follows :

" It was a perfectly heavenly day—not a cloud—and the
air cool and the ground free from dust after the rain. The
whole snowy range of the Atlas stood out clear-cut :
magnificent. We were ready to start at 8 a.m., I on a very
showy big black horse lent me by Kaid Maclean. After
about ¼hrs. solemn ride we came near the long line of
troops—which lined the road 4½ miles from the city. Here
I was met by masters of ceremonies—not bluecoated
stockinged individuals—but creatures in huge turbans and
wideflowing white garments and prancing steeds and with
velvet saddles all the colours of the rainbow. On one side
of the line were horsemen from all the tribes, with their
banners drawn up in a line either one or two deep—there
were about 8,000 of them. On the other side was the line

of soldiers, some in blue, others in mauve or red or green
—a brilliant mass of colours—a band struck up—a
general salute and cries of ' Welcome oh Bashador ' from
all the people. I then rode slowly down, accompanied by
Minister of War, Governor of Town and a huge escort.
There were heaps of townspeople about, and the sight was
one of the most striking I have ever seen. My tail
swelled and swelled as I advanced till I led a whole army,
for as I passed the lines the men forming them closed in on
my rear. The march down took an hour, and I began to
get very hot as my steed curvetted about in the most
approved fashion. We suddenly dived into a gate in to
the town wall and found ourselves in the most lovely
garden—our own—a mass of large orange trees with the
fruit and the blossom on them—huge olive trees—shady
walks—birds singing and a most delicious perfume—a
real paradise of rest and coolness after the glare outside."

(3)

There was but little specific business which Arthur
Nicolson desired to conduct with the Moorish Government. He was able within a few days to settle such
outstanding British claims as he considered justifiable.
He obtained from the Government an undertaking to
improve the condition of Moorish prisons ; to restrict
the public sale of slaves ; to consent to the establishment of a Christian cemetery at Marakesh ; to agree in
principle to the construction of a new pier at Tangier.
The Maghzen, for their part, expressed a wish to send
a diplomatic mission to London. Nicolson was able to
evade this awkward proposal by stating that by the
time the mission arrived the rulers of England would
" have departed to their summer residences." He
succeeded even in inducing them to reduce the export
duty on coriander seed. On the practical side his

mission was in every way a success. He was warmly congratulated by Lord Salisbury. The main purpose of his visit had been, however, to get into touch with the boy Sultan and his Grand Vizier. His impressions of these people were qualified by certain reservations.

The first interview was purely formal. He described it in a letter to his wife :

" Linares [1] and the French Commandant have just called. They have both, I am told, been spreading all kind of reports as to my sternness and duplicity, and warning the Moors against me. They are very foolish people—as they gain nothing by these tactics. To-day was *the* day— and the great event came off very successfully. We were all ready by 8.45 a.m. having sent on the gun and all the presents. We looked very smart. A Master of Cere- monies came to fetch us and we rode solemnly down a series of horribly smelling streets till we came to a closed door. After a little thumping this was opened and I found myself in a huge square. All round the square were soldiers two deep in their varied costumes ; behind them were squatting on their haunches the Kaids of all the tribes. There were various other picturesque groups, but I had hardly time to notice them, for, arriving at the centre, I dismounted and almost simultaneously a bugle announced the approach of the Sultan. A green door was thrown open. First came troops, then 6 led horses beautifully caparisoned, then an old green brougham, and then the Sultan on his horse, umbrella and all. He rode slowly up to me and wished me welcome. I gave him the letter ; made my speech (without reading it) ; then Irwin read the translation—very nervous ; then the Sultan replied, but terrible to say Irwin said he could not hear a word and didn't understand a word. I told him to go on saying anything to me and pretend he was interpreting, while I bowed and smiled as if he was. I thought the Sultan

[1] Linares was the French agent attached to the Court.

spoke very low but very clearly. Having got thro' this farce, I presented each of the staff—a bow and the affair was over. The Sultan sat bolt upright and looked straight ahead of him without moving a muscle—almost apathetic. He is not bad looking, but podgy and puffy : good features and good clear eyes. He didn't look unhealthy, but like a boy who ate too much. We were then taken into the garden, but I was so hot in my big dress that I left for home before long where we were photographed. I am so cross about Irwin and it was noticed, as the Vizier sent directly afterwards to say he saw the Interpreter had not understood the Sultan and so he would send me a copy of the Speech. The sight was very pretty, but I could not see much as I was obliged to be talking or appearing to listen and so could not look about."

Two days later Nicolson was accorded a private audience, at which he presented to the boy Sultan the maxim gun which had been sent from England :

"Yesterday morning we went off to our private audience. I was shown into a summer room, where the Sultan was sitting on a kind of throne. I sat on a chair by him while the Vizier and Irwin stood up—the rest were left outside. We had a conversation of some 10 minutes and the boy behaved very well. He has a pleasant smile and by no means an unintelligent face. We then went to a square to fire off the maxim. He was a little nervous when it first began to fire—then became interested. He fired off a good many rounds himself and was delighted. He amused me by biting his lips to prevent breaking out into a broad grin of delight. He is so pleased with it that we are to go quite privately on Sunday and practise at bottles. He wants to have a ' happy morning.' "

These audiences were repeated. " When," Nicolson recorded, " I have an audience of the Sultan, the Master of Ceremonies shouts out, ' Here is the British

Minister. May God bless the life of the Lord.' Till
within very few years he used to add, ' May God forgive
me for bringing him here ! ' Then one sensitive
Bashador had this stopped—but it indicates their
feelings towards us."

Regarding these feelings Nicolson had no illusions.
Nor, at this first meeting, did he obtain a very hopeful
impression of the Sultan. In a letter to Sir A. Bigge
(Lord Stamfordham) he described His Majesty as
follows :

" He is still a mere boy and entirely under the influence
of his Grand Vizier, who is in reality a Maire du Palais.
Kaid Maclean says that it is curious to see the way business
is transacted at Court, the Sultan amusing himself with his
picture books and mechanical toys, while the Grand
Vizier sits on the floor in front of him working with his
Secretaries outside."

A puffy, over-fed youth, with bright eyes. That was
all the impression he retained. Behind this school boy
stood Bu Ahmed, a reactionary scoundrel ; and beyond,
across thyme-scented hills, stretched tribes and governors and the whole shoddy corruption of the Moorish
system. Nicolson was appalled by the internal condition thus disclosed. He recorded his opinions in a
letter to the Permanent Under Secretary, Sir Thomas
Sanderson :

" The more I have seen of the members of the Government, the more hopeless seems any prospect of reform or
progress. The main policy and occupation of the Government is to set the tribes by the ears, to support one side,
then wring money out of the beaten one, and then later
to extort money out of the victors for assistance rendered.
They wish to ruin the tribes, leaving them but the barest

necessaries, so that they may be harmless. Their idea is
that if a tribe becomes quiet and orderly it becomes rich
(relatively) and that they will purchase arms and munitions
and shake off subjection to the Government. No wonder
that with this system the country is going backward and
backward and commerce languishing, and that merchants
find it impossible to collect debts. It is rapacity, treachery,
intrigue and misgovernment. I have been in most
Oriental countries, but I have never seen such complete
darkness as reigns here. The ignorance of the men I have
met is simply incredible. It will all jog on thus till some
move is made from outside, but once the rickety edifice
gets the slightest push, all will come down. From what
I hear the Moors would welcome any European invader.
They are tired to death of this grinding system of government and their much talked of fanaticism, which exists
chiefly I believe in the towns, would not prevent their
joyfully receiving any change."

Such criticism was purely negative. Nicolson was
too human, and too alive to the charm of Moorish
muddle-headedness, not to wish to make some more
constructive effort to remedy the existing ills. On his
return to Tangier he addressed to Kaid Maclean an
exhortation of a prophetic nature. He wrote in
September 1896 :

" There is little doubt that the country is rapidly getting
into the condition when the people in despair would open
their arms to anyone. The only way out would be for the
Moorish Government to change their policy in toto, and
open up the country to the investment of foreign capital
in railways, roads, etc. If they continue as they now do,
it is only a question of time and opportunity when they
will lose all or a greater part of what they have. I wish we
could drill into their thick obstinate skulls that the longer
they delay improving their country, the more hopeless

becomes the future. . . . The Moors should understand
that if they remain in their present condition (an annoyance
and weariness to all who have dealings with them) no one
will take any interest in their continuance as a nation."

Such advice was excellent but of little avail. The
policy pursued by Nicolson in Morocco was throughout a negative policy. A less modest or less prudent
man might have been tempted to exploit his personal
ascendancy in directions inimical to the true interests
of England, of Morocco, and of the peace of Europe.
Nicolson's great achievement during the nine years he
ruled at Tangier was that he did nothing. It was only
at the end of his life, when he had witnessed the great
work of humanity and civilisation performed by
Lyautey, that he recognised how right he had been.
For many years he wondered whether he should not
have been more assertive and more adventurous. His
acute sense of fairness was, however, justified by the
event.

(4)

Meanwhile, on his return from Marakesh, he concentrated his energies on an endeavour to remedy the
more crying abuses which he had observed. He did
much, in those years, to mitigate the system of the
public sale of slaves, although he contended that
domestic slavery as practised in Morocco was on the
whole, and given the circumstances, a benefit rather
than an abuse. He became known throughout the
country as the protector of ill-treated slaves—and the
Legation garden was often filled with battered creatures
who had managed to escape. He would treat such
people with firm gentleness and would ignore the

protests which his continued interference evoked from
the Moorish slave-owners. The prisons, also, were his
special care. " I don't think," he wrote to Kaid
Maclean, " that it would be a bad thing if you let the
Grand Vizier know that the treatment of prisoners
shocks and horrifies us all, especially the tortures. It
is lucky for them that Europe is so busy elsewhere, but
this method of Government will certainly alienate all
sympathies." This hint appears to have produced but
little effect. A month later he wrote again to Kaid
Maclean instructing him to deliver the following
personal message to Bu Ahmed : " As a friend I exhort
him to take immediate steps to alter the whole treatment of prisoners and thoroughly to reorganise the
prisons. All prisoners, no matter what their crime,
should be treated humanely, and how many innocents
are imprisoned by this Government ! Pray speak
earnestly to him on these subjects." His energy was
directed also towards less obvious scandals. He
inspired the Tangier Sanitary Council to renewed
efforts in dealing with the drainage and other hygienic
requirements of the town. He would spend hours
riding across the neighbouring hills in an endeavour to
decide what steps could be taken to check the deforesta-
tion of the charcoal-burners. The fact that the hills
round Tangier are not to-day an arid waste is largely
due to Nicolson's efforts and insistence during the nine
years that his influence was the main civilising element
in the country. He had no illusions, moreover, as to
the abuses practised by the smaller Powers in extending
their protection to persons who could in no sense be
called their immediate servants. The Brazilian Consulate in particular (there was at that time an honorary

Brazilian Consulate) was suspected of selling protection rights to the richer natives. Such rights carried with them exemption from taxation and immunity from seizure. Nicolson objected to the system in its entirety. " I am almost appalled," he wrote to Kaid Maclean on November 27, 1895, " by the iniquities of the protection system when it is pushed to the extreme to which in many cases it is. One can lay many evils and short-comings to the door of the Moorish Government, but it seems to me that the history of European diplomacy in its dealings with this unfortunate country has a few chapters which might well be dispensed with."

Inevitably he was hampered by the jealousy and suspicion of others. In the end, he was able, by the sheer integrity of his nature, to still all misgivings, even those of the French. It was unfortunate, however, that he should have been faced at the outset by a singularly unsavoury incident for which he was in no way responsible. In 1897 a group of financiers styling themselves " The Globe Venture Syndicate " were anxious to obtain certain trading and mining concessions in Southern Morocco. Their agent, Major Spilsbury, visited Nicolson at Tangier, and indicated that the best method of obtaining these concessions was to purchase them from the chieftains of the local Sous tribes. He contended that the Sousi at that date were only nominally under the control of the Sultan and were sufficiently autonomous to grant these concessions without reference to the Central Government. Nicolson (who did not take to Major Spilsbury) informed him that, on the contrary, it would be madness to disembark in the Sous districts without first having obtained the Sultan's permission and favour. Major

Spilsbury implied that he knew better, and Nicolson
was so disturbed by the interview that he informed the
Foreign Office, adding that he was not without suspicion that the whole venture was no legitimate trading
enterprise but an attempt at gun-running. In September of 1897 Major Spilsbury appeared suddenly at
Mogador, from where he got into touch with the Sousi
leaders and signed with them some form of contract or
engagement. The Moorish Government on hearing
of this, requested that Major Spilsbury should be
instructed not to return to Morocco, and the Directors
of the Globe Venture Syndicate were thereupon
informed by the Foreign Office that before proceeding
further they must obtain the formal consent of the
Sultan and his Ministers. They ignored this intimation.
In December of 1897 the British Consul-General at
Antwerp notified the Foreign Office that the yacht
Tourmaline, the property of a certain Major Spilsbury,
was shipping large quantities of rifles at that port.
Nicolson sent an express to Fez to warn the Sultan of
what was impending, and the Moorish gun-boat, the
Hassanieh, was despatched under the command of a
German captain to patrol the Sous coast. On January
13 she sighted the *Tourmaline* landing rifles on the beach
at Arksis. Five of Major Spilsbury's companions (four
of whom were British subjects) were already on the
beach supervising the disembarkation. Only one case
of 80 rifles had at that stage been landed. The Major
himself remained on board. On seeing that the
Hassanieh meant business, he fired one shot at her, and
then made off towards the Canaries and eventually to
the River Thames. His five companions took to the
hills and hid in a cave. Next day they were captured by

the local Moorish authorities and sent in chains to Mogador. It was with the greatest difficulty, and in return for a promise that they would all be prosecuted under British law, that the Moorish authorities were induced to hand them over. They were lodged in the British Consulate in Tangier and were there charged with " having fired on the officials of the Sultan of Morocco in his territorial waters while these officials were discharging their official duty." They were condemned to light sentences. The Foreign Office meanwhile, having a certain sympathy for the five unfortunates who had been abandoned on the beach at Arksis, were anxious to impose reparation upon the Directors of the Globe Venture Syndicate and upon Major Spilsbury, the responsible authors of the incident. They consulted the Law Officers of the Crown. It was found that no case could lie against the Directors but that a warrant could be issued against Major Spilsbury for " riot and assault." He was arrested in August and tried at Gibraltar. He was there acquitted amidst the cheers of the crowd, who saw in him a victim of bureaucratic persecution.

The Moorish Government did not understand these acquittals. They imagined that the British Government had shown bad faith, and they lent a ready ear to the suggestion that Major Spilsbury had throughout been acting with the tacit approval of the Legation. " It is annoying," wrote Nicolson to Sir Thomas Sanderson, " that this wretched Government should now have a grievance, and a legitimate grievance, against us. Further, as we have been unable to carry out all they expect, our good faith will be impugned and our authority weakened." Nor was it the Moors only who regarded the *Tourmaline* venture as an unsuccessful but deliberate gesture of British Imperialism. The German Emperor spoke strongly on the matter to Sir Frank Lascelles. The latter, on February 2, 1898, reported the conversation to Lord Salisbury. " His Majesty said that it seemed to be a repetition of the Jameson raid. He made a sarcastic remark about a trade which supplied the Sous tribes with rifles and ammunition."

The whole incident was one which left Nicolson angered and distressed.

(5)

The years passed : 1895, 1896, 1897, 1898, 1899. From the backwater of Tangier Nicolson was able to watch the main stream of international politics eddying and changing—its waters becoming more turbulent and muddied as the years progressed. The Franco-Russian Alliance became an accomplished fact in 1895 ; the Triple Alliance between Germany, Austria and Italy was renewed for six years in May of 1891. In the summer of 1895 the Emperor William paid a regrettable visit to Cowes. He annoyed the Committee of the Royal Yacht Squadron by criticising their handicaps. He annoyed Lord Salisbury by scolding him for being late. He annoyed the Prince of Wales, his uncle, by calling him " an old peacock." By such undeft touches he antagonised just those circles in England which at that date were politically and socially the most authoritative. In 1894 Germany had shown a protective interest in the Transvaal ; in 1895 this interest had been confirmed and advertised by an exchange of highly indiscreet speeches between President Kruger and the

German Consul at Pretoria : on January 3, 1896, the
Emperor William was persuaded by his advisers, and
against his better judgment, to address to President
Kruger a telegram of congratulation upon the failure of
the Jameson raid. This telegram created in England a
prejudice against the German Emperor which, though
unfair, was persistent. The Cretan crisis of 1897, the
support which Germany was by then pledged to give
to Turkey, led to a further estrangement. Germany
retired from the Concert of Europe ; in Prince Bülow's
phrase, " she laid her flute upon the table." The same
year she seized Kiao-chau, the event being advertised
by the Emperor William in a speech about the " mailed
fist." In June of 1897 Admiral Tirpitz was appointed
Chief of the German Admiralty ; and in November of
that year he introduced his first Navy Bill which
created the German High Seas Fleet. Less than a year
later the Emperor proclaimed that the future of
Germany lay upon the water. Public opinion in
England became alarmed. The British Press, from
that moment, behaved with constant irresponsibility.

Our relations with France were even more unfriendly.
We quarrelled about the New Hebrides in 1887, about
Bizerta in 1890, about Siam in 1893. Egypt was a
constant source of friction, and this standing grievance
was now embittered by disputes about the Upper Nile
and by the rejection by the two Governments of the
compromise negotiated between Lord Dufferin and M.
Hanotaux in 1894. In September of 1896 we occupied
Dongola. In July of 1898 Colonel Marchand hoisted
the French flag at Fashoda, and on September 2 of that
year Sir Herbert Kitchener defeated the Mahdi at
Omdurman. The enthusiasm aroused in England by

this massacre was increased to fever point when it was learnt that the sturdy hero of Khartoum was advancing upon Fashoda to turn out Colonel Marchand. Had it not been for M. Delcassé war might well have ensued. Colonel Marchand was recalled. It is only fair to add that British public opinion, having obtained its triumph, had the decency to feel ashamed. It was our remorse for Fashoda which was one of the earliest elements of our Entente with France.

For the moment, however, the Fashoda incident led to a détente with Germany. Compared with France and Russia the Germans had behaved with friendliness over Egypt and the Sudan. Conversations were opened between Lord Salisbury and Count Hatzfeldt, the German Ambassador in London. The former was not very enthusiastic, and Count Hatzfeldt considered it more profitable to continue the conversations through Mr. Joseph Chamberlain, who was quite willing to go further than his Chief. The Colonial Secretary, indeed, went so far as to propose an Anglo-German alliance. The Germans replied that a secret Treaty would be at the mercy of our party system, whereas a Public Treaty would endanger their own relations with Russia or France. The negotiations thus reached a deadlock. The British overtures were, as the Emperor informed the Tsar, " by my commands coolly and dilatorily answered in a colourless manner." Sufficient advance was made, however, to enable the two Governments to sign the secret Agreement of October 1898 providing for the eventual partition of the Portuguese Colonies. Unfortunately, however, the British Government in 1899 also signed a secret Treaty with Portugal (incorrectly called " The Treaty of Windsor "), under which

they in effect guaranteed that country against the operation of the Anglo-German Agreement of the year
before. The Germans came to know of this second
Treaty and regarded it as an act of unexampled perfidy.
Holstein in particular was incensed. " With these
people," he exclaimed to one of his secretaries, " it is
impossible to enter into any engagement." [1]

On October 11, 1899, Great Britain declared war
upon the Transvaal. It was only then that the full
effects of Lord Salisbury's policy of splendid isolation
could be gauged. Great Britain woke up infamous.
British opinion was shocked to discover over-night
how much we were disliked. The South African War,
however, was one of the most salutary events that ever
happened to the British Empire.

Nicolson, at this moment, was summoned suddenly
to London by the death of his father. The old man, up
to the last moment, had read his daily French novel,
and had dined every evening at the Travellers, by
preference off partridges and champagne. He died
suddenly, the day before the century ended, at the age
of eighty-four. It was a sad and apprehensive London
to which Nicolson returned. The following letter to
his wife reflects the general atmosphere. It is dated
January 8, 1900 :

" I was talking with a group (de Vesci, Portsmouth,
Tweedmouth, Fitz, B. Mitford, and A. Yorke) this
morning at the Club. It is no longer a positive ' we must
win in the end '—but an interrogative ' shall we win in the
end ? ' I am most sad. The gloom of the weather, the
deep gnawing anxiety, the suppressed rage against
Chamberlain, has made all of us most unhappy. The

[1] Information supplied verbally by Herr von Rosen.

ineptitude of our generals is incredible. I can't write about private matters. One is too absorbed and anxious for I feel we have the Empire at stake, and all risked for personal greedy ambition. Oh my dear little wife, it will be heartbreaking if our Empire is endangered for *such* a cause."

A few days later the ineptitude of war was brought home to him by a more personal tragedy. Lord Ava, the Dufferins' eldest son, was wounded at Ladysmith and died a few days later. Nicolson hurried across to Clandeboye to see his sister-in-law and Lord Dufferin. He found there an atmosphere of dignified despair. It was under the shadow of such sorrows and humiliations that he returned, early in 1900, to Morocco.

Things were going badly. The French, encouraged by our disastrous preoccupations in the Transvaal, were manifesting renewed activity in Southern Morocco. The internal situation was worse than ever. He wrote to the Foreign Office on February 25, 1900 :

" I do not believe that it is possible to reform this country from within. The necessary native elements to work with are absolutely wanting and it is a mere delusion to imagine that the Vizier or any man in power here would assist in any reform. Self-interest is the only motive and the sole object of the governing classes, and any real reform would necessarily run counter to that. A powerful and active neighbour like France will undoubtedly make progress, and rapid progress, in the debatable ground to the South. It is almost a law of nature that she should."

Writing two days later to Kaid Maclean :

" It is sad," he said, " to admit it ; but I fear that the country is doomed."

I

For the moment Nicolson was able to evade the embarrassing appeals which reached him from the Moorish Government. As always he counselled patience, as always he begged them not to rely too much on England and above all to do nothing provocative as regards the French. As the months passed these appeals became more and more insistent. In September he proceeded on leave to England but was caught before his departure by an autograph letter from the Sultan to Queen Victoria which he was asked to deliver personally. The letter, which was dated September 10, 1900, suggested that Queen Victoria should induce the French Government finally to fix a frontier between Algeria and Morocco beyond which they would agree not to advance. On receipt of this letter the British Government did, as a matter of fact, institute discreet enquiries in Paris. M. Delcassé assured the British Ambassador that the French Government had no intention of attacking Morocco and repudiated all rumours of "any underhand or unacknowledged projects" against that country. These assurances were communicated to the Sultan, who expressed his warmest thanks. In October Nicolson visited Queen Victoria at Balmoral. He found her frail and uncertain. With a trembling hand she inscribed for him a copy of *Leaves from Our Journal in the Highlands*. He left Balmoral with the conviction that he would not see his small and terrifying Sovereign again.

(6)

The storm of Anglophobia aroused on the Continent by the South African War, the delight manifested by foreign opinion at our successive defeats, convinced

the British Government that the policy of splendid
isolation could no longer be pursued. They turned,
once again, to Germany. The Emperor William, on
November 19, 1899, had with courageous disregard of
his own public opinion, paid an official visit to London.
Mr. Chamberlain, in his speech at Leicester ten days
later, expressed our gratitude for this inspired courtesy
by stating that "it must have appeared evident to
everybody that the natural alliance is between ourselves
and the great German Empire." The effect of these
gestures was diminished by Prince Bülow's speech of
December 11. "The times," he said, "of our political
anaemia and economic and political humility must not
recur. In the coming century the German people will
be either the hammer or the anvil." A few weeks later
the German steamer *Bundesrath* was seized by British
men-of-war on the charge of taking contraband to the
Transvaal. The German Navy League exploited this
incident to their advantage, and the German Navy Bill
of 1900 doubled the 1898 programme and created a
large High Seas Fleet. The German Government,
however, and the Emperor in particular, were unwilling
to join Russia and France in enforcing mediation
between us and the South African Republics. President Kruger, on his triumphal visit to Europe, was
received by M. Delcassé : he was not received at
Potsdam. The Emperor finally obliterated all recollec-
tions of the Kruger telegram by his sympathetic
behaviour on the death of Queen Victoria. It was thus
early in 1901 that negotiations for an alliance with
Germany were reopened. Mr. Chamberlain was more
than frank. Great Britain, he explained, could no
longer afford the luxury of splendid isolation. She

would prefer an alliance with Germany, but failing that she would turn to France and Russia. Herr von Holstein, true to his convictions, was irritated by this threat of an alternative. He described it as a " vollständiger Schwindel," [1] a complete piece of humbug. Prince Bülow for his part dismissed it as a mere bogey —as a " Schreckgespenst." [2] In March of 1901 the negotiations reached a precise stage. The Germans were ready to guarantee the integrity of the British Empire provided that Great Britain, bringing Japan with her, would join the Triple Alliance. Lord Lansdowne, who by that date had succeeded Lord Salisbury, was patient and persevering. He suggested that perhaps an agreement might be reached by taking separately the actual causes of difference between the two countries. Holstein replied that Germany must first receive a guarantee of British assistance in the event, not only of being herself attacked by more than one Power, but of her being compelled to support one of her own allies. Lord Lansdowne asked for a definite statement in writing. Holstein hesitated to supply it. " If the people in Berlin," said Lord Lansdowne, " are so short-sighted, there is no help." It was only a few months after this that Baron Eckardstein, the officious counsellor of the German Embassy in London, observed Mr. Joseph Chamberlain talking earnestly to M. Cambon at a dinner party at Buckingham Palace. " There can be no more talk," Chamberlain said to

[1] *G.P.*, vol. 17, p. 22, No. 4984.

[2] Prince Bülow imagined that Mr. Chamberlain's offer was designed to separate Germany from Russia (*see* Theodor Wolff's admirable *Vorspiel*, p. 95). Bülow was also obsessed by Bismarck's dictum, " In any alliance into which Germany entered she must constitute the stronger half " (*see* Bülow, *Deutsche Politik* : *Volksausgabe*, p. 25).

him on leaving the Palace, " of co-operation with Germany."

Professor Brandenburg [1] in his admirable work on German foreign policy, entitled *From Bismarck to the World War*, has contended that the failure of these 1901 conversations marks the point from which affairs drifted towards the catastrophe of 1914. This may well be true. It is difficult, however, to apportion blame to either side. It is questionable whether at that date British opinion would have ratified any alliance which committed us to the defence of Austria. It is even more questionable whether German opinion would, especially at the height of the South African War, have allowed Prince Bülow on any terms to guarantee the British Empire. A formal and extended alliance was in fact out of the question. Where we made a mistake was in not realising that no price was too great to pay if we were to exorcise the growing menace of Anglo-German rivalry. Where they made a mistake was in discounting the possibility of our making terms with France and Russia, and in trusting too confidently to the chance that in a year or so, weakened and humiliated, we should come to them in the guise of suppliants. Holstein has been blamed also for not responding more readily to Lord Lansdowne's suggestion that before discussing any general alliance it might be well to reach agreement on specific points of difference. Holstein's hesitation is, however, comprehensible. He had been tricked once by a British Minister over the Portuguese colonies : he was determined never to be tricked again.

[1] Erich Brandenburg, *Von Bismarck zum Weltkriege*, Chapter 7 *passim*.

BOOK II
THE ANGLO-FRENCH ENTENTE

VI

THE LANSDOWNE-CAMBON AGREEMENTS

[1901-1905]

M. Cambon's first hints of a Morocco Agreement—The Menebhi Mission to
London—Nicolson's warnings against undue optimism—Menebhi's
arrival and reception by King Edward—Nicolson's conversation with
Baron von Eckardstein—The Ben Sliman Mission to Paris—Franco-
Moorish friction—Arrest of Menebhi—British advisers at the Sultan's
Court—Nicolson proceeds to Rabat—Franco-Spanish negotiations—
Disorder in Morocco—Capture of Mr. Harris by Raisuli—Signature of
Lansdowne-Cambon Agreements—Effect of this in Morocco—Capture
of Mr. Perdicaris—Nicolson appointed to Spain—Herr von Holstein
and the Morocco question—German mistakes—Herr von Kühlmann's
warning—The Emperor's visit to Tangier—Resignation of M. Delcassé
—Rouvier-Rosen negotiations—The Emperor William and Bjorkoe—
Conclusion of Rosen-Rouvier negotiations.

(1)

FROM 1901 onwards Morocco ceased to be a backwater
in European diplomacy; it became one of the main
channels through which, with ever-increasing speed
and volume, the waters of policy poured towards the
cataract.   Already, in his first tentative conversations
with Lord Salisbury, as in his more detailed negotiations with Mr. Joseph Chamberlain, Count Hatzfeldt
had mentioned Morocco as a possible area for Anglo-
German co-operation.   Lord Salisbury had smiled
and murmured—in French—"Divisons, divisons!"
Mr. Chamberlain, for his part, actually suggested that
Great Britain might take Tangier and give Germany a
port or ports on the Atlantic coast.   The French, who
suspected that something was pending, decided that the
moment had come to anticipate any Anglo-German

solution of the Moorish problem. On January 15, 1901, M. Cambon hinted to Lord Lansdowne that " one of these days " an agreement might be necessary in regard to " boundaries which are still undecided." A few weeks later renewed activity was manifested at Tuat. The Moorish Government appealed to Great Britain and Germany and their appeals (described by M. Révoil, as " ces démarches diplomatiques d'une si singulière incorrection ") [1] convinced the Quai d'Orsay that there was little time to lose. Bu Ahmed, the Grand Vizier, died in May of 1900. Increased chaos was apprehended. The Sultan was falling more and more under British influence, and the new Minister of War, Menebhi, was known as an opponent of French penetration. The French Government decided that the moment had arrived when they must stake their claim.

They were confirmed in this opinion by the fact that in the summer of 1901 the Sultan despatched Menebhi on a diplomatic Mission to London and Berlin. Nicolson was at pains to discount from the outset both the hopes and the suspicions which this action might arouse. On March 29, 1901, he wrote privately to the Foreign Office :

" Personally I do not quite see what the Sultan can do alone and unsupported to resist the French advance. I doubt whether any Power would care to uphold the integrity of Morocco, and if the crash were in sight, the interested Powers would I presume content themselves with securing those portions of the Empire which they might think useful and which the others would permit them to acquire. Moreover on broad grounds of general welfare I question whether it would be easy to justify the

---

[1] *Livre Jaune*, 1901-1905, No. 11, p. 8.

maintenance of this Government unless the Sultan really
reforms his administration."

To Kaid Maclean he wrote on April 20 :

" To my mind it would be undesirable that any possible
cause should be given for the impression that there was a
disposition on the part of the Sultan to treat the French
Government with any suspicion or want of courtesy or
regard. You may tell His Majesty the above from me."

A few weeks later he wrote again to the Kaid as
follows :

" If the Sultan asks my advice on matters affecting the
development or improvement of this country I am always
ready and glad to give it to the best of my ability and to
afford him all the assistance I properly can. I do so out of
a strong personal regard for His Majesty and from an
earnest desire to see some progress and some enlighten-
ment introduced into this country. I do not understand
how anyone, British, French, or of any other Nation, can
live for some years amid all this oppression, misgovernment and general misery, without being anxious to do
something to better matters. On the other hand I am
anxious not to cause embarrassment to the Sultan or to
place him in a false position. It is with that desire that I
do not wish to give the slightest cause for unnecessary
jealousy or suspicion."

That passage epitomises the directive principles of
Nicolson's policy in Morocco. The hints conveyed to
the Sultan had at least the effect of deciding him to send
a concurrent Mission under Ben Sliman to Paris.
Meanwhile Nicolson left for London to prepare for the
arrival of Menebhi.

(2)

Sid Menebhi el Meheddi, a young and intelligent patrician, arrived at Plymouth on June 22 of 1901. He was dashed up to London in a special express of the Great Western Railway. It was the first time that he had experienced any means of locomotion faster than an ambling mule. He sat there in the saloon, ducking his head whenever the train roared through a tunnel or flashed under a bridge. Nicolson much admired his fortitude and self-control. A few days later they were received in audience by King Edward and Queen Alexandra. The Moorish Mission was introduced by Nicolson and accompanied by Kaid Maclean, who immediately became a popular figure with the London crowds. A private audience and investiture was held a few days later. Nicolson wrote to his wife on June 28 :

" All went off most successfully yesterday. We were shown into the Throne room and chairs were put on the right of the King for Sanderson, Menebhi and myself. We sat there like Christy minstrels. The King talked with the Envoy and then gave him a letter for the Sultan, and also a parcel containing His Majesty's G.C.B. He then put the collar of the G.C.M.G. round Menebhi, who bowed very prettily and behaved very well. Then came my turn. I had to trot into the next room and appear again with two gentlemen on either side of me as if I were paying a surprise visit. I then knelt on a cushion, and the equerry with a great flourish drew his sword and handed it to the King. I thought Menebhi would imagine that my last hour had come and would throw himself on his knees to intercede for my life. The King accolated me on each shoulder, slipped the ribbon over my head, pinned on the star—I kissed hands—I returned to my seat."

THE RECEPTION OF MENEBHI BY KING EDWARD

From the painting by Seymour Lucas in His Majesty's collection.

The presence of Menebhi in London was not exploited by the British Government for any exclusive political or commercial advantage. The Moorish Plenipotentiary was induced to agree in principle to the construction of roads and bridges ; to the engagement of European technicians in sanitation and engineering ; to facilities for the coastal trade ; to the improvement of the ports and harbours ; and to the construction of a telegraph line from Tangier to Mogador. Nicolson was anxious that this latter concession should be taken over by the Germans. He mentioned this desire to Baron Eckardstein of the German Embassy. The Baron, a friendly but impulsive man, appears to have misunderstood him. All that Nicolson intended was to interest Germany commercially in the impending modernisation of Morocco so that Great Britain should not have to withstand French competition single-handed. He could not, as the Baron implies in his memoirs,[1] have gone so far as to suggest joint political penetration in Morocco accompanied by an Anglo-German agreement regarding spheres of influence. The Baron's memory of this incident is almost certainly at fault. He mentions, for instance, having sent " long cypher telegrams " to his Government reporting this conversation. No trace of any such telegrams can be found in the archives of the German Foreign Office.[2] It is possible, of course, that they were addressed direct to Herr von Holstein. The whole incident, as it figures in Eckardstein's *Memoirs*, is mysterious and unconvincing. It is fairly safe to assume, however, that he misunderstood the scope and purport of

[1] Baron von Eckardstein, *Lebenserrinerungen*, vol. ii., p. 358.

[2] *G.P.*, vol. xvii., p. 333 note.

Nicolson's visit and proposals. There is no single word in any of Nicolson's letters or diaries of any such overtures : it is merely stated that he begged Eckardstein to interest his Government in the Mogador cable.

Lord Lansdowne communicated to the French Ambassador the text of our arrangement with Menebhi. M. Cambon expressed himself as satisfied. The French Ambassador " spoke very highly of Sir Arthur Nicolson but added that his predecessors had not all of them been so tactful or so prudent." [1] Menebhi thereupon proceeded to Berlin, where he was given much the same advice as he had been given in London : to improve the internal condition of the country, and not to provoke the French. Ben Sliman, in Paris, fared less successfully. He was able to negotiate a Convention with the French Government providing for the joint policing of the Morocco-Algeria frontier. He did not, however, succeed in obtaining from them any very definite or complete undertaking that that frontier should in its entirety be delimitated. The French contended, and not without justice, that to define a frontier in a nomad locality was " incompatible with the very nature of the district and the character of its inhabitants." They also made it perfectly clear to Ben Sliman that they considered France to possess preferential rights in Morocco, and that it would be unfortunate for the Sultan were he to look to any other Power for assistance. This intimation was conveyed in even more explicit terms in the instructions addressed by M. Delcassé on July 20, 1901, to M. Saint-René Taillandier, who was succeeding M. Révoil as French Minister at Tangier. The latter

[1] Lord Lansdowne to Sir E. Monson, July 3, 1901.

was to explain the position to the Moorish Government in the following terms : " Nous ne pouvons être pour le Makhzen—et à son choix—que le plus rassurant des amis ou l'ennemi le plus redoutable. ...."[1]

The South African War meanwhile was drawing to its close. Nicolson had been surprised to observe in London the general indifference to the later stages of that struggle—a welcome contrast to the gloomy anxieties of 1899. " People here," he wrote to his wife on June 19, 1901, " seem quite tired of the war, and you hardly ever hear it mentioned. I do so thoroughly loathe and detest this war—and feel that it has done irreparable injury to our reputation. I can hardly bear to think of it ! "

(3)

In July of 1901 Nicolson returned to Tangier. The prospect for the moment was encouraging. The Mission of Menebhi to London and Berlin had, so it appeared, done much to stimulate British and German interest in the Moorish question. The Mission of Ben Sliman to Paris appeared at first likely to result in the delimitation of the Algerian frontier and the consequent removal of the main cause of Franco-Moorish friction. Above all, Morocco had at last produced in the person of Menebhi a statesman—young, active and enlightened —who would have the fortitude to cope with the corruptions and incompetence which was leading his country into chaos. These hopes proved illusory. The interest aroused on behalf of Morocco in London and Berlin rapidly degenerated into mere concession-hunting. The Ben Sliman Mission, as has been stated,

[1] *Livre Jaune*, 1901-05, p. 20.

induced the French to claim a special position in Morocco. And Menebhi, on returning to his country, was placed under arrest. The protests addressed to the Sultan by the British and German Governments induced him within a few weeks to restore Menebhi to favour, but the latter's position remained precarious and he was unable to enforce the extensive reforms which he had planned. Those summer months of 1901 were the last opportunity accorded to Morocco to reform herself from within, while relying for her external protection upon the balance of French, Spanish, German and British interests. The opportunity was missed.

One of the main obstacles to French penetration was the marked predilection displayed by the Sultan and Menebhi for British surroundings and advice. The French announced their intention of breaking the " English ring " around the Court, and Nicolson, realising that His Majesty's Government would in the last resort leave Morocco in the lurch, decided himself to visit the Court and to clear the atmosphere. Accompanied by a large staff, which included his cousin Lord Loch and his old Oxford friend Fitzpatrick (Lord Castletown) he embarked on H.M.S. *Illustrious* and reached Rabat on January 22, 1902. He at once recognised that the French had good cause for their suspicions. Not merely did the Sultan take no action without the knowledge of Kaid Maclean, but he had gradually surrounded himself with a somewhat mixed group of English cronies, consisting of grooms, gardeners, electricians, plumbers, cinema operators, commission agents, and the man who repaired his bicycles. " These men," Nicolson wrote, " do not render any service to British interests, while their employment causes irritation among those who reproach the Sultan for his alleged English proclivities." The real defect of these people was that they led the young Sultan into useless extravagances. They would show him photographs in *Black and White* or the *Illustrated London News* of such things as lawn-mowers, house-boats, cigarette-lighters, and gala coaches ; they would induce His Majesty to order such objects from London. These commissions were profitable to no one but themselves. " Be assured," Nicolson wrote to Kaid Maclean on returning to Tangier, " that it is wise in the interests of the Sultan to limit the number of Englishmen employed at Court. I am perfectly aware of what might be done if we had only ourselves to think of, and there is much that I should *like* to see done. But it would be impolitic and unfair to land the Sultan in an embarrassing position and then leave him to fight his own way out of it."

At Rabat, meanwhile, he had had a long interview with the Sultan. He recorded it in a private letter to Lord Lansdowne :

" It was a quaint proceeding. He received me in a small wooden shed built up against the wall of the palace. There was only a billiard table in it and a few kitchen chairs. Outside, a white deal table, a packing case or two, a cage with a young leopard, and a rubbish heap within ten yards. Nothing could have been more squalid. His Majesty was most affable, but I fear he is of very weak character. The way he clung to my hand and coat-tails and pleaded tearfully for advice was pathetic. In short I was disappointed with him."

This disappointment was presumably mutual. The

advice which Nicolson gave to Abdul Aziz can scarcely
have been welcome :

> " I replied that it was essential that His Majesty should
> not give the slightest cause for complaint on the part of
> the French Authorities. He should be as courteous and
> amiable as possible, as His Majesty should remember that
> the French were powerful neighbours and would find
> many opportunities of rendering themselves inconvenient
> without necessarily raising any international question.
> His Majesty should give no undue preference to any
> individual country, but should seek to satisfy all and adopt
> measures which were of general interest and to the
> advantage of his own country and of all other nations."

He returned to Tangier in a mood of depression.
" I wish indeed "—so he had written to the Foreign
Office in August of 1901, " that we could all work
together towards introducing some order and progress
into this wretched country. I do not see why we should
not. Personally I should gladly welcome French or
German co-operation." He knew now that this ideal
of international co-operation was impossible, that the
Moorish Government would continue to misgovern
internally, and externally to play off one Power against
the other. He had now been nearly seven years in
Morocco, and was fifty-three years of age. Much as he
loved the country—the view of Spain stretching before
one from Trafalgar to Europa Point, those rides
through fields of iris and narcissus, the pungent hubbub
of the little market place—yet he yearned from now on
to devote his activities to some less negative task. He
wrote to his wife on April 17, 1902 :

> " I really do not mind one more year here as I am keen
> to set this old machine going better, and without vanity

I think I can be of more use than an entirely new man. Morocco is, I am sure, at the turning of the ways, and I want to do my best to lead it in the right one. I somehow should feel selfish and not loyal to the young Sultan if I left just now. One is so beastly selfish really."

Nicolson, as events turned out, remained on in Morocco till 1905, but the above letter marks the final gleam of optimism.

(4)

The French, in 1902, opened direct negotiations with the Spaniards for the partition of Morocco. Señor Silvela replied that he could not consider such an arrangement unless England were also consulted. On August 6 of 1902 M. Cambon suggested to Lord Lansdowne that the moment had arrived to discuss what would happen " in the event of Morocco passing into liquidation." Lord Lansdowne answered that any attempt to deal prematurely with the " liquidation " of Morocco would lead to serious complications. An exaggerated version of this conversation reached the Sultan, who despatched Kaid Maclean to London with a personal letter to King Edward asking Great Britain to guarantee the integrity of Morocco, failing which the Shereefian Government would apply to Berlin. A loan was also asked for. The Foreign Office replied that no arrangement had been come to between France and Great Britain and that the loan must be shared with Germany. Kaid Maclean insisted on a more definite answer. " My dear Nicolo," wrote Sir Thomas Sanderson, " Kaid Maclean is rapidly developing into a perfectly phenomenal bore." The attention of the Sultan was at this moment distracted by internal events of serious importance. A pretender, Bu Hamara, raised his standard in the Taza district and by the end of the year was threatening Fez. The capital was saved by Menebhi's victory of January 29, 1903, but in the meantime the Riff had also risen in revolt. Communications between Arzila and Tangier were in May cut by the local brigand Raisuli, who in June was threatening Tetuan. On the 16th of that month, Mr. W. B. Harris, *Times* correspondent at Tangier, was kidnapped and taken to Zenaat. Nicolson at once decided that the only hope of saving his highly entertaining compatriot was to conduct the negotiations himself. The terms which Raisuli demanded were onerous in the extreme. Nicolson had some difficulty in securing their acceptance by the Sultan's representative :

> " Mohammed Torres behaved like an old brute : said that Harris was in the hands of the Lord. I said he was not, but in the hands of a devil. When I went away, I said, ' I have been over thirty years in uncivilised countries but I have never met a man with so cruel a heart as you have or who so thoroughly disgraces the position he so unfortunately holds.' I then left him without saying good-bye. I must say I *boil* to have to humiliate myself and negotiate with these miserable brigands within three hours of Gibraltar."

These representations had their effect. Mr. Harris, " thin and rather subdued," was released on July 6.

While the internal condition of Morocco was thus relapsing into almost complete anarchy, its external destiny was being shaped by forces equally beyond the Sultan's control. In the spring of 1903 King Edward paid his historic visit to Paris. This visit was returned by President Loubet and M. Delcassé in July. The latter informed Lord Lansdowne that France could not regard with indifference the prevalence of chronic disorder in Morocco, " or admit that it was the business of any other Power but France to undertake the task of regenerating the country." Lord Lansdowne replied that it was unlikely that Great Britain would desire any such task, but that we could not remain indifferent to the fate of Morocco, particularly of Tangier and the neighbouring coast. There were also British commercial interests to consider, as well as the position of Spain. M. Delcassé replied that he foresaw no difficulty either as regards Tangier, Spain, or the principle of the open door. The negotiations were continued by M. Cambon. Lord Lansdowne indicated that British interests in Egypt must also be brought into the discussion, and M. Cambon replied that in that event France would require from us in respect of Morocco assurances " moins hypothétiques " than those hitherto suggested. Lord Lansdowne enquired what attitude Germany would adopt. M. Cambon replied that " nothing had recently been heard of German designs in Morocco." Towards the end of 1903 Nicolson was informed of the progress of these negotiations. " A great end," he replied to Sir Thomas Sanderson, "·will have been achieved if they come to a successful issue." The Anglo-French agreement [1] was signed on April 8 of 1904. It was accompanied by a secret convention [2] of the same date. The effect of the two instruments (besides settling points at issue

---

[1] *See* Appendix I.

[2] This Secret Convention was a great mistake, as the Germans got it into their heads that it contained a clause regarding the Rhine frontier (*see* Bülow to Metternich, June 4, 1904). The secret clauses were published by the *Temps* in November, 1911.

regarding Siam, the Newfoundland fisheries, West
Africa, Madagascar and the New Hebrides) was to give
France a free hand in Morocco and ourselves a free
hand in Egypt.

An Anglo-French Entente from that moment became a possibility. The Morocco problem was not,
however, disposed of by this agreement.

(5)

The Sultan, the Moorish Government, and the
British Morocco merchants were incensed by the conclusion of the Anglo-French agreement. They complained of abandonment and betrayal. Nicolson,
who for nearly nine years had been regarded as a
bulwark of Moorish independence, found his position
under these altered circumstances one of embarrassment. The Sultan wrote to him stating that French
assistance could only be accepted if Great Britain would
guarantee that after the introduction of the desired
reforms all French advisers would leave. His Majesty
added that, however badly Great Britain might have
behaved, Germany remained his friend. Nicolson
recommended the Sultan to meet the offers of the
French Government in a conciliatory spirit. He at the
same time warned the Foreign Office that the Moors
had not as yet realised that "French advice and
assistance would be effective and permanent." He
wrote also to Menebhi, who was then on a pilgrimage
to Mecca, advising him to make his peace with M.
Delcassé. He foresaw, indeed, that the Sultan would
visit upon Menebhi his resentment at the Anglo-
French convention. These forebodings were fulfilled.
On returning to Morocco, Menebhi was placed under

arrest, his property was confiscated and his life was in danger. Nicolson, after consulting with his French colleague, took Menebhi openly under British protection. A compromise was reached whereby the fallen Minister was allowed to retain half his property and to reside unmolested at Tangier. In October Nicolson passed through Paris, and personally enlisted M. Delcassé's sympathies on Menebhi's behalf. He was gratified at having thus assured the future of a man who might, had he not been abandoned by his master and his friends, have proved the regenerator of his country. In May of 1904 Nicolson was due to return home on long leave of absence. Two days before his departure an incident occurred which was not without importance in the history of the Moorish question.

A mile or two from Tangier stands the villa and garden of " Aidonia "—" the place of nightingales." A comfortable house with green shutters, an open fore-court, red candles on the dining table, a large telescope on the terrace, and groves of myrtle, roses and arbutus falling to the sea. This house was owned by Mr. Perdicaris, a wealthy American citizen of some sixty years and more. He lived a cultured and retired life with his wife, his stepson Mr. Varley, his daughter-in-law Mrs. Varley, some grandchildren, some tame pheasants, a demoiselle crane, and several monkeys. Mr. Perdicaris spent his time in painting huge symbolical pictures of Virtue pursuing Vice through what were quite recognisably the cork-woods around Aidonia. On that evening of May 18, the family were dining in the fore-court, drinking their coffee under the heavy clusters of the wistaria. A clamour was raised from the back quarters. Shots were fired. Mr. Varley

rose and hurried into the house. He was followed by
Mr. Perdicaris in his dinner jacket. Further shouts
arose. The elderly Mrs. Perdicaris, the anxious Mrs.
Varley, rose in their turn and crept cautiously towards
the servants' wing. The servants had been bound and
gagged. Mr. Perdicaris and Mr. Varley, with their
hands tied behind their backs, were being lifted on
to the backs of mules. Brown men in brown *jelaabs*
stood around holding martini rifles. Mrs. Varley ran
to her husband. She was knocked down and lay there.
Mrs. Perdicaris screamed. They saw their husbands
jogging off under the cork-trees into the night. It was
shortly after this that Mrs. Varley telephoned to Arthur
Nicolson.

The British Minister established immediate communication with his American colleague. They went
together early next morning to interview the Sultan's
representative. Raisuli's terms were not long in coming. He demanded, as conditions for the release of the
prisoners, the dismissal of the Governor of Tangier,
the withdrawal of the Government troops from " his "
territory, the arrest of certain of his personal enemies
and the release of certain of his personal friends, the
cession to him of some fifteen villages, and a ransom of
ten thousand pounds. These terms were granted.
After five weeks' imprisonment, Mr. Perdicaris, immensely improved in health, returned with Mr. Varley
to Tangier. Shortly afterwards he left Morocco
and bought a pleasant little property at Tunbridge
Wells.

The capture of these innocuous American and British
citizens (for Mr. Varley for some odd reason was
of British nationality), caused a panic in Tangier.

English and American men-of-war were at once
ordered to the harbour. The Admirals telegraphed
that they could not guarantee that the two Ministers
might not also be kidnapped. " This Legation,"
Nicolson assured an anxious Foreign Office, " is, I
really think, the safest house in Tangier." The Moorish Government poured troops into the town. And,
what was far more important, public opinion in Europe
and above all in America, realised that the condition of
Morocco was one of chaos. That trade would suffer
if order were not rapidly restored.

Nicolson left for England on leave of absence. He
returned in the autumn having meanwhile been appointed Ambassador to Spain. It was in the last days
of January, 1905, that he left Morocco for ever.

(6)

His mission to Madrid was not of long duration. In
October of the same year he was appointed Ambassador
to Russia. From January to April of 1906 he served as
British Delegate at the Algeciras Conference. The
eleven months he spent in Spain were not, however,
devoid of interest.

The Embassy, in those days, was housed in the old
Palace of Cardinal Ximenez in the Calle Torrijos. From
the corner boudoir on the upper floor there was a view
of mountains, but the other rooms looked on the street
or upon a courtyard heavy with the smell of stables.
The reception rooms were hung in red damask. The
chandeliers tinkled when the cabs rattled by outside.
The house was dark. There were no bathrooms, and
the electric light was apt to fuse. Nicolson, in his
optimistic way, found the Embassy delightful. He

could not understand why his predecessors had been so full of complaints.

On February 7 he presented his letters to King Alfonso. He drove to the palace in a coach of crystal and gold surrounded by detachments of Horse Guards and Halberdiers. The King stood high upon the throne, slim and dignified, his hand resting upon the gilded lion of Castille, the ribbon of the Garter under the heavy chain of the Golden Fleece. Around him were grouped the Chamberlains, the Members of the Cabinet, the Dukes of Granada, Luna, Bejar, Tamames and Arion—grandees of Spain. Nicolson read his speech. The King read his reply. The Ambassador, in bowing backwards towards the exit, stumbled over a stool, and fell flat upon the carpet. Not a muscle moved on the face of King Alfonso. It was only when the great doors had closed behind him that Nicolson heard from the throne-room peal upon peal of school-boy laughter. His admiring affection for King Alfonso dated from that moment.

" During my residence in Madrid," Nicolson recorded afterwards, " I was largely occupied with matters concerned with the future royal wedding. I hardly think it would be decorous to record what passed between the Spanish Royal Family and myself and others in regard to the royal matrimonial projects." This reticence must be respected. The negotiations were important to Nicolson if only because they brought him into intimate touch with King Edward. In June of 1905 he accompanied King Alfonso to England. The whole incident was dismissed with a charming Victorian phrase : " I had left Madrid before the nuptials took place."

Meanwhile the question of the moment was Morocco, and in that question Nicolson was intensely and continuously involved.

(7)

The Morocco crisis at this stage provoked by Bülow and Holstein marks a turning point in international relations. It led directly to what Germans call the " policy of encirclement "—a policy known to British historians as " the strengthening of the Entente." On Nicolson himself its effects were even more immediate. Until that date he had regarded Germany with confidence and friendship. Writing to his wife on June 1, 1902, he expressed the view that " the hatred of Germany displayed by *The Times* and its people is very regrettable and very foolish." His attitude towards Germany was profoundly modified by the violence and inconsistency displayed by Herr von Holstein during 1905. It is important, therefore, to examine in some detail the methods and purposes of the Wilhelmstrasse during this vital period. Unless some digression is made at this stage the reader will, with justice, ask himself " But what was it all about ? "

Before approaching this intricate and disputed problem it is necessary to sound a note of caution. That admirable compilation of German State Documents known as *Die Grosse Politik* does not throw any convincing light on the real intentions of the German Foreign Office. It does not, for instance, reproduce the private instructions which Herr von Holstein was only too apt to address to German Representatives abroad. Nor does it reveal the fact that the Emperor and his Advisers were often at cross purposes. Every

endeavour has been made to render the following
account accurate and unbiassed. It is recognised,
however, that certain gaps in the story have to be filled
by a process of guesswork. Nor is the intuitive method
necessarily misleading : the other Powers, owing to
the Sphinx-like reticence of the Wilhelmstrasse, were
also obliged to guess : it was their impressions, and not
their certainties, which determined the crisis. They
may well, as is argued by German publicists, have been
too suspicious. The fault lies, however, not with
them, but with the Delphic conduct of the German
Foreign Office.

The position, subject to the above reservation, was
as follows. The German Government had never been
seriously disturbed by the Franco-Russian Alliance.
They put their faith in the autocratic nature of the
Tsarist régime. It was only with the conclusion of the
Anglo-French Entente that they began to ask themselves whether Bismarck's " nightmare of coalitions "
might not after all become a reality. It was natural that
they should fear that a ring might be formed around
them : it was inevitable that they should try to dislocate
the coalition before it was too late. Unfortunately,
however, they did not possess either Bismarck's
certainty of diagnosis, nor yet his certainty of handling.
Their vision was distorted, and their fingers fumbled.

They possessed at the outset two assets of great value.
In the first place they possessed, as against France, an
overwhelming superiority of force. Russia, preoccupied with her war in the Far East, could be of no
assistance to her ally : the Entente with England had
not as yet thrown its roots : and France herself,
politically and militarily, was unprepared. In the

second place they possessed, in the Morocco question, an undoubted right of intervention. Germany, as signatory of the Madrid Convention of 1880, and as having acquired important commercial interests in Morocco, had the right to be consulted in regard to any alteration of the *status quo*. M. Delcassé had informed Germany of the Anglo-French Convention, but he had not asked for her recognition of France's special position in Morocco. This error on the part of M. Delcassé gave Germany a legitimate grievance and one which, in principle, would be recognised as such by the public opinion of the world. " German intervention," recorded Nicolson, " cannot be said to have been without justification, though the methods by which it was exercised may be open to criticism." Had Bülow proceeded with moderation and skill, he could have exploited these two assets to great advantage. As it was, he was so obsessed by his premises that he forgot critically to examine his conclusions.

The errors committed by the German Foreign Office can be divided under two headings of errors of diagnosis and errors of treatment. Their diagnosis was vitiated by two fallacies. In the first place they imagined that Great Britain would not risk the bones of a British Grenadier for the sake of France. " We can," wrote Holstein, " take it for granted that British diplomatic support, as provided by Article 9 of the (Anglo-French) Agreement, will remain platonic." [1] The Emperor, who in contrast to Bülow and Holstein had a real, if intermittent, comprehension of the English character, did not fully agree with this assumption. He realised that England would go to

[1] *G.P.*, 20 A, p. 207.

great lengths to support France so long as that policy contributed to the balance of power. He joined with his advisers, however, in adopting their second fallacy : in imagining that France could be induced by force to enter with Germany into a continental alliance. Their mistake was seriously to underestimate the strength of the French desire for revenge. They concentrated their efforts on proving to France that the English Entente was no substitute for the collapse of the Russian alliance—hoping that the sense of isolation thus induced would oblige France to come to Berlin on trembling knees.

These errors of diagnosis were supplemented by elaborate errors of treatment. " German policy," writes Professor Brandenburg, " was considered incalculable and impenetrable. In reality it was merely uncertain, empirical and petty." [1] This is not, however, a complete explanation. The failure of German diplomacy in 1905 and 1906 was due rather to two fundamental misconceptions. In the first place, as I have indicated, they believed in force as a method of policy. In the second place they were unduly affected by considerations of national prestige, by what Prince Bülow called " our dignity and our recently acquired authority as a World Power." [2] It was the interaction of these two misconceptions which clouded their judgment.

They had two objectives, the one strategical, the other tactical. Their strategical objective was to detach France from England and to incorporate her, together with Russia, in a continental alliance. Their tactical

[1] Erich Brandenburg, *From Bismarck to the World War*, p. 182.
[2] Bülow, *Deutsche Politik*, *Volksausgabe*, p. 88.

objective was to exploit the Morocco question as a means towards this end. Unfortunately, however, they were never clear in their own minds as to what was strategy and what tactics. They thus expended upon the Morocco question a degree of violence which should have been reserved for wider operations. They became so blinded by their own anger, by their thoughts of national dignity, that they confused the means with the end. And thus, while obtaining, more or less, their empty and ephemeral triumph over M. Delcassé, they failed entirely to secure the strategical objectives which they had, or ought to have had, in view. Their position, after the diplomatic campaign of 1905 and 1906, was infinitely worse than it had been before. It remains to record, through Nicolson's eyes, the details and reverses of that campaign.

(8)

The numerous papers and private letters which Nicolson left behind him are, from this stage onwards, supplemented by a record of political events from 1904 to 1914 which he compiled after his retirement. This record, which consists of four bound volumes of typescript, he called his " Diplomatic Narrative." It will frequently be quoted under that title in the pages that follow. It is in this Narrative and not in any of his despatches or private letters, that mention is first made of Germany's initial *caveat* against the Anglo-French Agreement :

> " In the autumn of 1904, while I was at Tangier, I received one morning a visit from the German Chargé d'Affaires, Herr von Kühlmann, who mentioned to me in the course of conversation that his Government did not

consider that the Anglo-French Agreement had any official existence : it had not been officially communicated to the German Government, and had not consequently been officially accepted by them. France and Great Britain were of course at liberty to settle their own differences, but these were matters between those two countries alone, and in no wise affected the rights and interests of third parties. I cannot recollect (and I can find no papers bearing on this conversation) whether I reminded him that Prince Bülow had in the Reichstag publicly given his blessing to the Agreement ; but in any case I considered Herr von Kühlmann's warning of sufficient importance to cause me to lose no time in acquainting my French colleague with what had been said. It was evident that Germany would not remain quiescent while France took Morocco in hand and that she expected that France would enter into negotiations for the purpose of obtaining her concurrence. On my informing my French colleague of what had passed and expressing my opinion that it foreshadowed German interference with French projects, he remarked, after a moment's hesitation—' Nous sommes parfaitement tranquilles du côté de Berlin.' Future developments showed that this confidence had no sound foundation. It was clearly an oversight on the part of France to have taken the consent of Germany for granted and not to have conversed with Berlin.''

Here was the first heavy rain-drop that fell from the thunderous silence of the Wilhelmstrasse. The French, however, were not alarmed. They proceeded to consolidate their gains under the Anglo-French Agreement. M. de St. Aulaire was despatched to Fez as " éclaireur," and in June of 1904 an advance of twenty-two million francs was accorded to the Sultan by a French Consortium, who obtained in return certain liens on future loans. Negotiations were at the same time opened with Spain, and an agreement was signed on October 3 of 1904 providing for respective spheres of influence. Not a word, meanwhile, was said to Berlin. At the beginning of 1905 Prince Bülow considered that the moment had come to make himself felt. He suggested that the Emperor should visit Tangier. His Majesty raised objections to this proposal, contending that, given the local conditions, such a visit would be undignified and unsafe. Prince Bülow thereupon inserted an announcement of the visit in the German Press, and informed the Emperor that it was impossible, now that his intention had been published, to withdraw. Such a retreat, they said, would be interpreted as a sign of weakness. The Emperor capitulated. Apprehensive and distressed, he landed at Tangier on March 31, 1905. He received the Moorish representatives, the diplomatic body, and the foreign colonies. He announced that his visit was a deliberate recognition of the Sultan's independence. The world was aghast.

The Emperor William's visit to Tangier was one of the most ill-considered acts in history. So dramatic a gesture could not but be interpreted as a challenge by France and England. In the former country it rallied all parties in favour of France's Morocco policy ; from that moment Morocco became for the nationalists a symbol of revenge. English public opinion, which had hitherto regarded the Anglo-French Agreement merely as a settlement of outstanding differences, was by this histrionic challenge aroused to a new conception of the Entente ;—to the idea that it was something which must be defended against German pressure. The Sultan was encouraged to expect from Germany a degree of support which the latter could only afford him at the price of a European war. And Germany found herself in a position from which it proved impossible to retreat without sacrificing that " national dignity " which it had been her intention to affirm.

Having committed Germany to a dramatic rôle in regard to Morocco, having from the outset confused the means with the end, Prince Bülow proceeded with great activity to exploit the disadvantages thus acquired. He announced at Washington that Germany was aiming only at the policy of the open door. He told the Italian Government that Germany was aiming at a Conference and expected Italian support. He told Abdul Hamid that Germany was justifying her rôle as the protector of Islam. He despatched to Fez the most violent of German diplomatists, Count Tattenbach, with instructions to prevent the Sultan accepting French assistance. And he endeavoured to induce Spain to repudiate the Franco-Spanish Agreement. He adopted, for this particular seduction, the methods of cajolery and menace. Nicolson, writing privately from Madrid on April 8, 1905, described these proceedings as follows :

" The Germans have during the last few days been endeavouring to win over Spain by two methods. The Emperor has been exceedingly courteous and gracious and despatched effusive telegrams to King Alfonso, while his Ambassador (Herr von Radowitz) has adopted another method by assuming a threatening and overbearing attitude. He was exceedingly active with the King, the Queen-Mother, the Prime Minister and the Foreign Minister, and they were all, at least the first two and the last, offended and surprised by his unnecessarily violent

demeanour.   The King told M. Cambon [1] that M. de
Radowitz had hinted, not darkly, that he might have to
ask for his passports.   The storm lasted for a few days and
now M. de Radowitz has subsided into peace and calm,
having gained nothing, but having merely caused ill
feeling and offence. . . .   Now all is right, but the incident
was curious and significant."

Nicolson did his best, by personal persuasion, to
encourage Spain to resist these efforts.   The British
Government were becoming alarmed.   They could not
believe that all this activity on the part of Germany
proceeded solely from a desire for the open door (to
which France was pledged in any case) or was based
solely on questions of prestige.   They imagined (with
some justification) that Germany wished to obtain a
port on the Atlantic coast of Morocco.   They assured
M. Delcassé that they would give him " all the support
in their power " to resist any such attempt on the part
of Germany.   A distorted version of these assurances
reached Berlin, where it was believed that Great Britain
had offered France " an offensive and defensive alliance
against Germany " and that this offer had been rejected
by M. Delcassé.[2]   This false information, while it
increased their desire to dislocate the Entente before it
was too late, also convinced them that France was too
frightened to make resistance.   Prince Bülow therefore
instructed Prince Radolin, German Ambassador in
Paris, to make it quite clear to the French Prime Minister
" that so long as M. Delcassé remains in office there is
no possibility of an improvement in Franco-German
relations."   Prince Radolin was, at the same time, to

[1] This is of course M. Jules Cambon, French Ambassador to Spain.
[2] B.D., vol. iii., pp. 72-87.

indicate to M. Rouvier how dangerous it would be for
France if M. Delcassé remained on as Minister for
Foreign Affairs.¹ The French Cabinet was alarmed at
this menace. M. Delcassé begged his colleagues to
allow him to accept the British offer of assistance. They
refused to do so. On June 6, 1905, M. Delcassé
resigned.

No one believed thereafter that so violent an interest
in the Morocco question could be wholly disinterested.
Germany's moral position, which at the outset had been
unassailable, was thus weakened. And the British
public opinion, who felt that France had been humiliated, was determined that she should not be humiliated
again.

M. Rouvier, who had no great faith either in British
armed assistance or in the capacity of the French Army
to resist a German invasion, immediately offered Prince
Bülow a comprehensive settlement of outstanding
Franco-German questions. He felt that it was better
to buy Germany off. This offer placed Prince Bülow
in an awkward position. Having loudly advertised
himself as the Protector of Moorish integrity and
independence, he could scarcely accept immediate
compensations for abandoning Morocco to France.
He decided therefore to shift the responsibility for this
abandonment to wider shoulders, and he proposed the
immediate summoning of a Conference of the Powers
signatory to the Madrid Convention of 1880. M.
Rouvier resisted this proposal. The German Ambassador informed him that " Germany stood behind
Morocco with all her forces." M. Rouvier yielded :
he accepted the proposal for a Conference. Prince

¹ Bülow to Radolin, May 30, 1905.

Bülow then stated that he was now prepared to discuss such matters as the Baghdad Railway, the cession of Fernando Po, and the frontier of the Kameroon. M. Rouvier was at last on firm ground : he turned upon Prince Bülow : he pointed out to him that it was now too late to speak of direct compensations payable by France or Spain to Germany. The latter had insisted on internationalising the Morocco question. Well and good. But having obtained her desires in this respect, she could not now claim the compensation which would have been payable in the event of a direct Franco-German deal. The logic of the French attitude was unassailable and Prince Bülow was obliged to confine the forthcoming discussions, which were conducted on the French side by M. Révoil and on the German side by Herr von Rosen, to an agreement regarding the main points of the Conference programme. He had tried to get both compensations and a Conference, and was now left with only the Conference upon his hands. He was confident, however, that this Conference would secure that diplomatic victory which he desired. America, for one, was wholly with him. President Roosevelt, after congratulating him on having got rid of that " unbelievable scamp," M. Delcassé, had assured him that he shared Germany's views on the Morocco question.[1] Austria and Italy, his partners in the Triple Alliance, would be certain to accord him support. The smaller Powers would rally to the policy of the open door. Russia was weak and well-disposed : and Spain, scenting the isolation of France, would adhere to the majority. There was England, of course, but then British support of France,

[1] G.P., 21 A, Nos. 6896, 6897.

as Holstein agreed, would be merely platonic. Prince
Bülow, with his accustomed empiricism, looked forward therefore to the forthcoming Conference with
assurance. It is significant, indeed, that he and Holstein
concealed from the Emperor William M. Rouvier's
offer of a direct Franco-German agreement. They felt
that His Majesty, who was no very sound supporter of
their Morocco policy, might jump at this opportunity
of enticing France into a Continental alliance. In this
interpretation of their Master's probable attitude they
were correct. Several years later the Emperor came to
learn of M. Rouvier's overtures and of their rejection
by Prince Bülow. " If," he wrote, " I had been told
about this, I should have gone into it thoroughly and
that idiotic Conference would never have taken place."

(9)

The Emperor William was in truth haunted by
desires wider and more mystic than those aroused in
his advisers by the Morocco question. It is only
possible to interpret the impulses of this wayward and
intelligent monarch by referring them to the strange
psychic abscess produced by his love-hate for England.
This obsession was assuredly pathological : the pupil
of Freud could doubtless recognise in its main symptoms, above all in its naval symptom, all manner of
diverse complexes—Oedipus : Electra : he might add
Patroclus. As some torturing nemesis the curse of this
emotion clouded his soul, impelling him blindly into
blind actions. He dreamt of uniting the nations of
Europe into one community under his own direction :
he saw himself, in his day-dream, laying at the feet of
England the eagles of Germany, Russia and Austria,

the crescent of Islam, and the silken standards of Italy and France. He would prove to England that she owed her continued existence solely to his own Imperial chivalry and love.

One hesitates to quote against this unhappy, upright, and frequently brilliant man the devastating evidence of his own letters to the Emperor of Russia, or the barrack-room jocosity, the incredible levity, of the marginal comments with which he defaced the despatches of his own Ambassadors. The letters were in many cases drafted for him by Bülow or by Holstein ; the unfortunate style of the minutes was due to a desire to emulate the marginal comments of Frederick the Great. It is essential, however, to record the strange endeavours which he made, during 1904 and 1905, to isolate England, since it is only in the light of these endeavours that what for years remained the mystery of the Wilhelmstrasse can be explained.

The Emperor William in his private correspondence with the Emperor Nicolas had for long been endeavouring to sow suspicion between Russia and England. Believing that Russia " must and will win " in her war with Japan, he had strained German neutrality by coaling Russian ships, and had exploited, in a singularly unscrupulous manner, the Dogger Bank incident of October 1904. The Emperor of Russia suggested a treaty. The Emperor William immediately prepared a draft : " Nobody knows anything about it, not even my Foreign Office. The work was done by me and Bülow personally." There was some uncertainty, of course, about France, " that Republic of miserable civilians." The Emperor of Russia wished to consult his ally beforehand : his German colleague stated that this would be fatal. Meanwhile Port Arthur fell on January 1, 1905, and in May of that year the defeat of Russia was sealed by the battle of Tsushima. It was in July of 1905 that the two Emperors met " as simple tourists " at Björkoe in Finland. The Emperor William had brought with him a treaty of alliance which he had drafted in confabulation with Prince Bülow. This draft provided for mutual assistance in the event of either party being attacked. It also provided that Russia was to obtain the adherence of France. The Emperor William hustled his cousin into the cabin of the *Polar Star* and flung the Treaty before him. The Tsar, never a very strong man, agreed to sign the Treaty on condition that the words " in Europe " were inserted after the words " will assist each other." The Emperor William, blinded by excitement, agreed to this fatal insertion. The Treaty of Björkoe, a document written on a single sheet of foolscap in a boyish handwriting, was signed on July 24/11, 1905. " This," triumphed the Emperor William, " should cool down British self-assertion and impertinence." He telegraphed to Prince Bülow in terms of hysterical self-glorification. The latter, on reading the text of the Treaty, observed that the insertion of the two words " in Europe " destroyed its whole effect. Germany assumed immense obligations for the defence of the Russian frontier in Europe. Russia was released from the obligation of taking any action in Asia—the sole region where, as against England, her co-operation would be really effective. Prince Bülow, dismayed at this blunder on the part of his Emperor, threatened to resign. The Emperor replied that if he did so, then he, the Emperor, would have a nervous breakdown, and might even commit suicide. No less unfavourable was the reception accorded to the Treaty by Count Lamsdorff, the Russian Minister for Foreign Affairs. He pointed out to his master that the Treaty might well be interpreted in Paris as inconsistent with the spirit of the Franco-Russian Alliance. The Tsar then endeavoured to induce the Emperor William so to modify the Treaty as to exclude from its operation a war between Germany and France. The German Emperor was enraged. " What was signed," he wrote, " was signed. And God was our witness." The only other witnesses had been Herr von Tschirschky, who had not read the Treaty, and the deaf old Vice-Admiral Birileff, who had not understood it. The Treaty of Björkoe was thus still-born. Its sole result was a distinct chill in the relations between Berlin and St. Petersburg. But, from the historical point of view, it justifies the apprehensions of those who imagined that the Emperor William was aiming at a Continental block.

Meanwhile the negotiations in Paris between Herr von Rosen and M. Révoil had led to an agreement which was signed on September 23, 1905. Under this agreement Germany recognised the right of France and Spain to organise the Moorish police in the districts adjoining their frontiers, and France undertook that the question of who was to control the police in other parts of Morocco would be for the Conference to decide. It was agreed also that a State Bank should be created in which the interested Powers should participate. The site of the Conference was to be Algeciras. Both the French and German Missions were in the meanwhile to leave Fez.

The Conference opened in January of 1906.

VII

THE ALGECIRAS CONFERENCE

[1906]

Departure for Algeciras—The Reina Cristina—Sir Donald Mackenzie Wallace—Opening of the Conference—The various delegates—Alma-dovar—Visconti Venosta—Radowitz—Tattenbach—Révoil—Cassini—Mr. Henry White—Portrait of Nicolson at Algeciras—Liberal Government in England—Sir E. Grey continues Lord Lansdowne's policy of support of France—His instructions to Nicolson—Instructions received by German delegates—Attitude of Bülow and Holstein—Franco-British military conversations—Early stages of Algeciras Conference—The police question—German appeals to America—Count Tattenbach's attempt to suborn Nicolson—The Wolff communiqué—Renewed appeals to President Roosevelt and to Italy and Russia—Deadlock over police question—The vote of March 3—Germany isolated—She makes conciliatory offer which is rejected by French—The Inspector General question—M. Rouvier's Government falls—Renewed German pressure at Algeciras—German misrepresentations abroad—American eleventh-hour intervention—German evasions thereof—End of Algeciras Conference—Its results.

(1)

NICOLSON left Madrid on January 12. At Cordova he observed Madame Melba struggling on the platform ; he invited her into his saloon and gave her tea ; they chatted together for several hours until the train reached Bobadilla. Nicolson himself travelled direct to Gibraltar, where he stayed for two nights with the Governor. On Monday the 15th he crossed the bay to Algeciras and established himself with his staff in the villa of Mr. P. & O. Smith—a comfortable house with English furniture, and a garden full of orange blossoms, freesias, and white broom. From his study, through open French windows, he could see the crouching mass of Gibraltar, grey and granite between the pink geraniums. The other delegates were less fortunately housed. They were herded into the Reina Cristina Hotel—a low-storied, bow-windowed structure, under Scotch management. The place buzzed with diplomatists, experts, concession-hunters and journalists. The congestion in the Reina Cristina was highly irksome. People kept on over-hearing other people through open windows, or at luncheon tables, or behind the mimosa bushes and bamboos. Nicolson, in his villa, was isolated and immune. " I see," he wrote to his wife, " that the *Daily Mail* says that even the boldest correspondent would not have the temerity to button-hole me. I am glad that they are in this righteous frame of mind." With one correspondent, however, he remained in the closest contact. This was Sir Donald Mackenzie Wallace of *The Times*, an old friend of Constantinople days, and a great coadjutor in the years to follow. " I am very glad," wrote Nicolson, " that Mackenzie Wallace is here. I talk most freely to him, feeling absolute confidence in his discretion. He has a cool head and his opinion is worth having." The Wilhelmstrasse, for some obscure reason, imagined that Mackenzie Wallace had been despatched to Algeciras to keep an eye on Nicolson. The Emperor described him as " Very intelligent ; a friend of King Edward's ; a Jew naturally," and in a marginal comment upon a subsequent despatch reporting some concession on the part of the British delegate—" Wallace," he wrote, " is beginning to make himself felt."

The Conference was formally opened in the Town Hall of Algeciras on January 16, 1906. The Ayuntamiento had been cleaned for the occasion : there were

red carpets on the staircase and in the patio ; there
were rows of flower-pots down the steps ; the long
table in the council chamber had been covered in green
baize ; there were ink-stands, and racks with note-
paper, and trays for pens.

White hunched figures against the red walls or under
the hard electric globes—the Moorish Delegation
grouped themselves around the bowed figure of Sid
Mohammed Torres, octogenarian, pitiable and indignant. The presidential chair was occupied by the
Spanish Foreign Minister, the Duke of Almadovar—
an Arabian face, flashing Arabian eyes, challenging but
empty—retreating when in difficulty behind the barrier
of breeding : becoming grandee. The Italian representative was Marchese Visconti Venosta, a hero of
the *risorgimento*, the Foreign Minister of Cavour, dominating, experienced, raised above them all by the
glamour of his seventy-six years, by the glamour of
what was already history. He possessed a fine face,
fine eyes, and slim cheek-bones above and below a
startling white fire of whiskers and hair. Herr von
Radowitz, the first German delegate, was gently arrogant, menacingly gentle, a diplomatist by profession
and even by instinct, but a soldier in the twirl of his
moustache and mind. Count Tattenbach, the second
German delegate, was a serjeant-major in face and
voice, cracking rude jokes—waves of Deutsch-
National anger flushing the scalp under his upright
stubble hair. Mr. Henry White, the United States
representative, was conciliatory, ignorant and charming ; Mr. White was so full of charm that there was
room for little else. M. Révoil, the first delegate of
France, was a small man, his waxed moustache curling

downwards, smiling always, smiling at the brilliance of the epigrams which he dared not make, smiling admirably at all the smaller Powers. Count Cassini, representative of Russia, was sociable, insinuating, uncertain—obviously anxious to play some historic part. The minor Powers, Holland, Portugal, Belgium, Sweden, were there also. Two delegates for each. Wishing to acquit themselves nobly, terribly desirous to agree, with an appearance of initiative, with the majority. Arthur Nicolson was sole representative of the British Empire. Already bent with rheumatism and arthritis, he would bend even lower over his papers. A shy person, one would say—a small, frail figure with a finely shaped forehead. Diffident, apparently, and enragingly honest. Suddenly he would raise his eyes—those blue and piercing eyes—from his papers. In fluent Oxford French he would state his case : fact upon fact : moderately, calmly and with an authoritative certainty which hushed all interruptions. He had about him a sense of control which was something more than self-control. They did not accost him when he left, small and smiling, for his villa. It was as follows that M. Galtier, correspondent of the *Temps*, described Nicolson at Algeciras :

" Petit, le dos un peu voûté, la figure rose et osseuse, les moustaches coupées courtes à l'anglaise, les cheveux légèrement bouclés sur les côtés, l'Ambassadeur d'Angleterre, Sir Arthur Nicolson, fait une impression fort sympathique. J'ai rarement vu des yeux aussi pétillants de vie, d'humour. Il expose les questions avec une netteté, une précision et une fermeté qui en imposent. Je vous assure que cet homme sait ce qu'il veut et qu'on s'en apercevra à la Conférence. Il ne se perd pas dans les détails, et il ne s'écarte de la ligne droite (qui convient à son esprit) que pour quelques arabesques de l'ironie ; mais vite il rentre dans le chemin qu'il entend suivre."

(2)

In December of 1905 the Conservative Government in England had been replaced by a Liberal Administration under Sir Henry Campbell-Bannerman. This change of government had been confirmed by the large Liberal majority returned by the electorate in January, 1906. Sir Edward Grey succeeded Lord Lansdowne as Foreign Secretary. " I am pleased," Nicolson wrote to his wife, " with the elections. I think it is ridiculous to be alarmed because some 40 or even 50 Labour members out of 670 are elected. I have no fear of our working-classes ever becoming Socialists of a dangerous type—it is not in our character and it is well that labour should be represented. What delights me is that protection should again have been buried. . . ."

The instructions already provisionally furnished him by Lord Lansdowne were more specifically confirmed by Sir Edward Grey. Nicolson was in all loyalty to support France to the extent provided by the Anglo-French Agreement. The Liberal Government interpreted this Agreement in the spirit as well as in the letter. " Tell us," King Edward had remarked to Paul Cambon, " what you wish on each point and we will support you without restriction or reserves." [1] This statement in no sense exceeded the intentions and wishes of the Cabinet. By Article II. of the Anglo-French Declaration we were bound to give France a free hand in establishing order in Morocco, and by

[1] Sir Sidney Lee, *Life of King Edward*, vol. ii., p. 361.

Article IX. of the same instrument we were also bound to support her diplomatically in achieving this object. Sir Edward Grey was perfectly frank in telling the German Ambassador that we should abide by these commitments. " What," he added, " made a nation most likely to take part in war was not policy or interest, but sentiment." On December 21, 1905, he had written privately to Nicolson as follows :

> " The Morocco Conference is going to be difficult if not critical. As far as I can discover the Germans will refuse altogether to concede to France the special position in Morocco which we have promised France not only to concede to her but to help her by diplomatic methods to obtain. If she can succeed in getting this with our help it will be a great success for the Anglo-French Entente. If she fails the prestige of the Entente will suffer and its vitality will be diminished. Our main object therefore must be to help France to carry her point at the Con-ference."

The instructions received from his Government by Herr von Radowitz were less categorical. " Our main object," Prince Bülow had written on November 23, 1905, " must of course be to secure that we are not placed in a position of isolation. If in any question on which we have once taken a stand we find all the others, or a majority of them, against us, then neither forcefulness nor threats will be of any use, as our position, after all that has passed, would be rather ridiculous." [1] Their secondary object was to prevent France achieving anything in the nature of a diplomatic triumph. Prince Radolin was instructed to make it clear to the French Government that Germany was not

[1] *G.P.*, 21 A, No. 6900.

bluffing and that in the last resort she would go to war.[1] Finally it was explained to the German delegates that, as the Emperor had assured the King of Spain at Vigo that he desired nothing but the open door, Germany was precluded from claiming any territorial gains for herself; they must press only for equality of economic opportunity and the independence and integrity of Morocco. The Police question, they added, would constitute the crux of the whole dispute. If France obtained the sole mandate for the organisation of the Police throughout Morocco, then Tunisification would set in. Germany did not want the Police for herself. All she wanted was control at some Atlantic port opening into the interior.[2] To the world, Prince Bülow announced that he desired that the Conference should terminate without there being either " victors or vanquished." He was further encouraged by the moderation displayed by M. Révoil at the opening meeting.[3] These meetings had dealt with non-controversial questions such as the prevention of arms traffic. He felt that this showed that France realised that she could not rely on British support. He was fortified also by the early reports received from Herr von Radowitz regarding the pro-German attitude of Marchese Venosta and Mr. White. And above all he was heartened by the results of the British elections. So was Holstein. " The French," wrote the latter in a Minute of February 22, " will only entertain the idea of closer relations with Germany when they have come to realise that British friendship (which since the recent elections can only be platonic) is not sufficient to secure

[1] G.P., 21 A, No. 6916.   [2] G.P., 21 A, No. 6922.
[3] G.P., 21 A, No. 6950.

to them German consent to their taking Morocco." [1]
Herr von Holstein was always consistent to his premises. The unfortunate thing about these premises
was that they were not correct. The optimism of the
Wilhelmstrasse would have been clouded had they then
known of what took place between M. Paul Cambon
and Sir Edward Grey on January 31. The British
Foreign Minister had, on that occasion, agreed to
" solely provisional and non-committal " communications between General Grierson of the War Office
and the French Military Attaché. These communications were to provide for military co-operation in the
event of an attack by Germany. Similar " enquiries "
were to be made of the Belgian General Staff by the
British Military Attaché in Brussels. Naval conversations were also opened. M. Cambon, knowing the
hesitations of his Government and their disbelief in
British good-faith, asked for something more. Sir
Edward Grey replied that he had already told the
German Ambassador that a German attack on France
would not find England neutral, but that any assurance
to support France in all circumstances would amount
to a defensive alliance and that this could only be under-
taken with the consent of Parliament. The Germans,
being a race of military tradition and attaching thereby
great importance to the General Staff, considered, when
they eventually heard of these things, that Grey had
behaved with cynical duplicity. They did not understand that this perfected type of British parliamentarian
did not attribute any but a purely technical and conditional importance to such conversations as soldiers
or sailors might hold. These conversations, to his

[1] *G.P.*, 21 A, No. 7034.

M

mind, were mere matters of routine which could be reversed with a stroke of the pen. They possessed, to his mind, no more importance than discussions between the London Fire Brigade and the Westminster Water Works. It cannot be expected that anyone not deeply imbued with the doctrines of British parliamentary liberalism will understand this point of view.

For the moment, however, and for many years the German Government did not know of General Grierson. Nor, it must be admitted, did the French themselves take the General and his conversations very seriously. The eyes of the world were centred on Algeciras. For nearly three months the Conference, through thirty sittings, plenary and other, swung from crisis to crisis, punctuated by weeks of excruciating delay. It would be superfluous to record in any detail the discussions at Algeciras. They bore on technical points and the decisions come to were not very durable. Behind the Morocco question loomed the essential problem of the balance of power. It is from this aspect, and in outline only, that the Conference will be described.

(3)

The Conference of Algeciras falls into two distinct periods, separated from each other by what is known as " The Vote of March 3." During the first period Germany assumed the offensive, imagining that she could obtain her desire by force. The vote of March 3 convinced her that she was isolated. During the second period she retreated slowly, desiring only to save what remained of her prestige. These two main periods are in their turn subdivided into successive

phases of local and general actions. For a week or so
Germany would concentrate on intensive activity at
Algeciras itself. There would then be silence ; and
minor offensives would be launched at Paris, Washington, St. Petersburg and Rome.

There were two main channels, the Police and the
State Bank, through which France might hope to
establish her predominance in Morocco. Were she to
succeed in obtaining from the Conference a mandate
to control either the finances of Morocco or the only
organised force in the country, it would only be a
question of time before the whole Sheereefian Empire
fell under her protection. The French Government
were from the first prepared to open the Bank to some
degree of internationalisation. They were not, however, prepared that the Police should be internationalised in any form which would prove completely
exclusive of French influence. It was thus on the
Police question that the fiercest combats ensued. The
story of the Conference can best be told by keeping this
Police controversy continuously in the foreground.

The first battle of the campaign lasted from January
19 to February 6. M. Révoil made a skilful move at
the outset by remarking to his Italian and United States
colleagues that France would prefer the continuance of
the *status quo* to any Police Force inimical to French
influence. The *status quo* meant the continuance of
that chaos which had recently been dramatically de-
monstrated by the capture of Mr. Perdicaris. Mr.
White and Marchese Visconti were distressed by this
alternative. Nicolson assured the latter that he for his
part " would leave the Conference with a heavy heart
if nothing had been done to remedy the perfectly

intolerable situation which now exists." He begged
the Italian delegate to use his influence with his colleagues of the Triple Alliance, to urge upon them " a
sense of responsibility which they would assume " by
obstructive methods. At the same time he advised
M. Révoil to get into direct touch with Herr von
Radowitz. A meeting took place between the two
protagonists on January 25, but the German delegation
refused to show their hand. Nicolson then urged M.
Révoil, "in view of the cloud of dust which hangs over
the real intentions of Germany," to lay his cards upon
the table, to say exactly what France wanted and to ask
for a definite expression of German views. M. Révoil
did not respond to this suggestion.

Prince Bülow, meanwhile, instructed Herr von
Radowitz not to encourage England to execute a
mediatory rôle, " as Germany had no interest in
strengthening the Entente." The position of mediator,
in the opinion of the Wilhelmstrasse, should be assumed by President Roosevelt, who had excellent views
upon the policy of the open door. They did not
realise that the President would not be allowed by the
Senate or by American opinion to play any very dramatic or leading part at Algeciras. They put all their
money on Washington, and here again they made a
damaging mistake. Their first move was an endeavour
to induce President Roosevelt to sponsor a scheme,
known as the " De Lanessan Scheme," under which
the Sultan should select his own Police Instructors
from different nationalities. They informed the United
States Government that the Austrians and Italians
agreed to this scheme, and that the Russians also approved the German attitude. At the same time they

suggested at Madrid that the Police should be entrusted
to Spain alone, and at Rome that it should be the
Italians who should undertake the task. Nicolson
wrote to his wife as follows :

> " I don't at all like the look of things. The Spaniards
> will not run straight, I fear. Germany is playing a double
> game, false, and contradictory. She says one thing at
> Berlin, another at Washington, another at St. Petersburg,
> another at Rome and Madrid. And Radowitz says different
> things from all these and different things to every person
> he talks to. The reason is that Germany does not know
> what she wants."

The German Government appear at this stage to have
been optimistic regarding the success of their " smoke-
cloud " policy. Herr von Radowitz reported on
January 26 that there was now no danger of Germany
being isolated. Even Arthur Nicolson was becoming
more " tractable." Prince Bülow, on February 7,
takes this success as assured. " Now," he writes,
" that we need no longer fear isolation."

Meanwhile Count Tattenbach had been so much
encouraged by the polite assurances received from
Madrid and Rome that he thought the moment had
come for a direct attempt to suborn the British
representative. He visited Nicolson on February 3.
The latter reported this interview to Sir Edward Grey
in his telegram No. 29 of February 4 :

> " Count Tattenbach paid me a long visit yesterday
> evening. Following is a summary of the most important
> and significant portions of the conversation :
> " His object was evidently to try to detach me from my
> French colleague and to induce me to urge the latter to
> make concessions to the satisfaction of Germany.

" He told me that the commercial interests of Germany and England were endangered by French predominance in Morocco, and that it would be well if I joined forces with the German Delegates to secure full guarantees for the open door. He observed that the situation had completely changed since the Conference had been agreed upon and that now vis-à-vis to France I was exactly in the same position as the other delegates. He continued that if I urged my French colleague to make all required concessions on the Police question, my words would be decisive ; while if I declined to say those words, I should practically be encouraging my French colleague to resist ; and he hinted that if the Conference fell through a great deal of the responsibility would fall on me.

" I replied that I had not the least fear that British commercial interests were in any danger and that he knew that ample guarantees were being offered and would be given as to the open door. For me, the situation had in no wise changed since the Conference opened and I was not at all in the same position vis-à-vis to France as the other Delegates : that we had special engagements with France which both my Government and myself intended to observe loyally and honourably. It was not for me to urge concessions upon my French colleague ; it would be most disloyal were I to do so, while I should certainly not encourage him to resist. I said my French colleague had shown throughout the Conference the most conciliatory disposition and the greatest moderation and that I intended to stand firmly by him."

Nicolson was perhaps unduly incensed by this tampering with his honour. " Tattenbach," he wrote to his wife, " nearly made me lose my temper. I felt really insulted and really furious. I was quite calm outwardly, but the idea that I was on the level of Ojeda and that I could be disloyal to Révoil stirred me so that I could eat nothing afterwards. I was ill and upset. He is really a horrid fellow, blustering, rude and mendacious. The worst type of German I have ever met." To Sir Edward Grey, in a private letter of February 8, he described the second German delegate as follows : " A rasping, disagreeable man, not straightforward or truthful, and he evidently has to exercise much effort to control his temper." [1]

Meanwhile, through Wolff's agency, the Germans published a completely false account of the negotiations which had been proceeding. This account was contradicted by the French via Havas, who went so far as to describe the German version as " a lie." Herr von Radowitz was disconcerted by this direct challenge : he explained away the statements published by Wolff on the ground of " a telegraphic error." The expression was well chosen. The incident left, however, a bad impression on the delegates at Algeciras. They discovered, in the course of private conversation, that they had all individually received different versions and different promises from the German delegation. M. Révoil, smiling, conciliatory, mild and so amusing, had told them the truth. Sympathies began to shift at Algeciras towards the side of the French.

Under the smoke-cloud thus created, Germany, during the second half of February, launched a combined attack on Washington, St. Petersburg and Rome.

(4)

In the second week of February the Wilhelmstrasse renewed their efforts to induce Mr. Roosevelt to take

---

[1] The following description of Count von Tattenbach figures in Theodor Wolff's *Vorspiel* : " He was the type of those grenadier-guard diplomatists who are gaily convinced that one can force the solution of any problem by giving the other man a kick in the stomach " (*Vorspiel*, p. 160).

some initiative. They wished him to propose that the
Sultan should entrust the reorganisation of his Police
to officers from the neutral Powers. Nicolson, fortified by his long experience of Moorish conditions,
pointed out to Mr. White that a mixed force of this
nature would not possess sufficient unity of direction
or efficiency of execution. What was required above
all was some hyphen between the foreign inspectors
and the Moorish rank and file. This hyphen could
only be provided by non-commissioned officers of
similar race, language and religion, capable of adjusting
themselves to the difficult relation between European
officers and native troops. Such trained instructors
could be obtained from Algeria, and possibly from the
Spanish garrisons in Africa, but from nowhere else.
Any other scheme would render impossible the establishment of trade and good order in the Sheereefian
Empire. Mr. White advised his Government that a
mixed force under the Sultan would not effect the
objects desired : he begged them to appeal to Berlin
to accept French instructors for a limited period.

The German Government, at the same time,
addressed a peremptory reminder to the Italian
Government to the effect that the Italian representative was not to take the side of France. The Con-
sulta were in an awkward position. On the one
hand they were bound by their obligations under their
Alliance with Germany and Austria. On the other
hand they were bound by a secret Treaty concluded
with France in 1902 whereby they had agreed to the
latter having a free hand in Morocco provided that
Italy might eventually have a similarly free hand in
Tripoli. Moreover, they were alarmed by England,

and alarmed by the prestige of their own delegate. The latter from the first took an independent line. The German Ambassador at Rome explained to his Government that Marchese Visconti " was not so much a francophil as a realist. For him the attitude of Sir A. Nicolson was the decisive factor." [1]

The attitude of the Russian Government was also unsatisfactory. Count Witte, whose anglophobia was considered an asset by the Wilhelmstrasse, had just returned to St. Petersburg after concluding peace with Japan. He wrote to his German friends warning them that Russia was in urgent need of a foreign loan, and would be unable to obtain that loan if a breakdown occurred at Algeciras. He told them that European opinion was beginning to credit them with a desire merely to humiliate France, that they would be unable to dislocate the Anglo-French Agreement, and that their best course was to woo France with concessions. The Germans replied to Count Witte that if he desired a peaceful outcome of the Conference he should induce the French Government to yield. " We do not want," they wrote, " the Conference to break up, but the Emperor cannot render himself ridiculous or allow himself to be humiliated." [2]

Having obtained no definite reply from Washington, Herr von Radowitz, on February 13, proposed to M. Révoil a scheme whereby the Sultan should entrust the Police to " foreign officers " who would be under the supervision of an Inspector General chosen by the diplomatic body at Tangier. M. Révoil replied that he would agree to this provided that the said " foreign officers " were French and Spanish. The question of

[1] G.P., 21, No. 7028.   [2] G.P., 21, No. 7141.

the Inspector General could be left for the Conference
to decide. This proposal was supported by Marchese
Visconti and Mr. White. It was categorically rejected
by the German delegates. A deadlock ensued.

The tension thus produced had a bad effect on
Nicolson's nerves. Hitherto he had been calm and
cautious. From time to time he would dash across to
Gibraltar and obtain a respite from the strain. In
forty-six days he had written eighty telegrams and sixty
despatches, apart from sessions and interviews. This
activity was welcome to him. " I find the Conference," he wrote to his wife, " *most* interesting. The
Government leave me entirely alone. I work along
happy and untrammelled. I am very well, and sleep-
ing excellently." His staff meanwhile had collapsed.
Two of them took to their beds. It was characteristic
of Nicolson that he did not ask the Foreign Office to
have them replaced. His spirits and his health always
soared upwards under the pressure of fevered occupation. It was the deadlock which extended from
February 13 to March 1 which told upon his temper.
His letters during those weeks lack their usual
moderation :

" We sadly need a strong and active Chairman. Not a
weak and lazy man like Almadovar. I very often nearly
lose my temper the way that business drags on."

" I think that we are close on a rupture as the Germans
have behaved in a most disgraceful way. Their mendacity
has been beyond words, and I would not have thought
Radowitz capable of such unblushing lying and double-
dealing. As matters stand at present, I do not think
there is a chance of agreement, and I am not at all sure
that the Germans do not want the Conference to break
down."

" Even Révoil I find changeable—sometimes firm and
positive, at other times weak and vacillating. I miss Jules
Cambon dreadfully. Révoil is most childish and irritating
with his formulas and ' artifices de rédaction ' as if the
Germans were asses enough to be deceived by a cloud of
words. Révoil's is an odd mind. Far too subtle. But I
admit that he has done very well—far better than I
expected."

Meanwhile, at the end of February, the Germans
allowed it to be known that France was about to yield.
Even Nicolson was deceived by this manoeuvre. " I
don't care two straws," he wrote to his wife, " whether
they yield or not. What I do care is that they led us
to believe that they would not yield, and consequently
induced us to back them up and thus, quite unnecessarily, to embitter our relations with Germany." The
theory was that France was about to accept a Spanish
proposal whereby the Police were to be purely native,
paid by the State Bank but provided with no foreign
officers at all. M. Révoil was unable to assure Nicolson whether or no his Government would accept this
proposal. On March 1, however, he told him that
the Quai d'Orsay had decided to reject the Spanish
scheme even at the risk of breaking the Conference.
This meant action, and Nicolson pulled himself together. " This next week," he wrote to his wife,
" will be intensely interesting. I must be prudent and
cautious."

The Germans, meanwhile, had realised that the
Police question did not now constitute the firm ground
which they expected. What the Powers desired was
the re-establishment of order, and they had been much
impressed by the contention that an efficient Police

Force could only be constituted with the help of Moslem non-commissioned officers. Moreover, the Germans had lost the favour of the Conference by their policy of mystification and by certain suggestions that they might demand the control of the ports of Mogador or of Casablanca for themselves. They decided therefore that it would be better to drop the Police question for the moment and bring into the foreground the question of the Bank. By this, at least, the appetite of the other Powers would be stimulated. There could be no appearance in this matter of a desire to humiliate France. They announced their intention of shelving the Police question while the Conference discussed that of the Bank.

Nicolson and Révoil were opposed to this adjournment. The French did not wish to make concessions on the Bank question before they had obtained an agreement regarding the Police. Nor could they allow to grow cold the sympathies which had been won for them by the truculence of Germany on the latter problem. If the Conference had to break down, let it collapse over the Police, a matter in which world opinion considered Germany to have been unduly obstructive. A rupture on the Bank would not be understood by public opinion.

On February 29 Nicolson crossed to Gibraltar to think things over. The Atlantic and Mediterranean Fleets had the very day before effected a conjunction. They lay there—thirty battleships, innumerable cruisers, countless destroyers. He dined with Lord Charles Beresford upon the flag-ship. Those great grey shapes lay around him under the great grey rock. *Illustrious, Indefatigable, Implacable, Indomitable.* Clearly

SIR A. NICOLSON AT COWES, AUGUST 1909

there was no reason to be frightened of Count
Tattenbach.

Nicolson decided that at the very next meeting he
would put things to the vote.

(5)

This decision entailed risks. In the first place the
Conference could only vote on points of procedure;
it would be difficult to find a point of procedure of
sufficient weight and breadth to justify us in placing
Germany in the minority. In the second place, although by now the sympathies of the Conference were
veering towards France, it was by no means certain
that the neutral delegates would consent to record a
vote which might expose their Governments to re-
criminations from Berlin. It was with some anxiety,
therefore, that on the 3rd of March, Nicolson drove
to the Ayuntamiento. Fate, and a false move on the
part of Herr von Radowitz, played into his hands.

The scene which followed has been well described
by M. André Tardieu in his comprehensive work upon
the Conference.[1] " Monday morning," he writes—(it
was Saturday morning, but we can let that pass)—
" Monday morning, the third of March. Noon. For
two hours a discussion had been continuing about the
Bank. Ten draft articles have been adjourned."
The brilliant André Tardieu then proceeds to recount how Marchese Visconti and Herr von Radowitz
suggested that, as it would take some days for the
financial experts to reach agreement on these ten
articles, the Conference should suspend its sittings.
Arthur Nicolson, seizing this providential opportunity

[1] André Tardieu, *La Conférence d'Algésiras*, p. 276 ff.

intervened. The remarks, he said, of his German and
Italian colleagues had made it clear that all discussion
on the Bank question would in any case have to be
postponed for several days. Would it not be possible,
during that interval, to continue in full Conference the
discussion of the Police? " At once," continues M.
Tardieu, " Count Cassini approves this proposal.
M. Révoil does likewise. M. de Radowitz, with
obvious displeasure and embarrassment, suggests that
it would be preferable to finish the Bank question
before advancing further. Sir Arthur Nicolson, with
some vivacity, points out that the Conference has done
nothing for a whole week and cannot remain permanently inactive. The President then states that in
view of this difference of opinion the decision of the
Conference must be taken by vote. Too late M. de
Radowitz sees his danger. The hour has come for
that vote which he had done everything to avoid."
The vote was taken. The Moors, the Austrians and
the Germans voted against the proposal. The French,
the Russians, and the British in its favour. The representatives of Holland, Belgium, Sweden and Portugal
stated that they would range themselves with the
majority. Mr. White, when consulted, replied that he
was not in favour of any further suspension of the
Conference. The Spanish delegation were of the same
opinion. Marchese Visconti Venosta, to the horror
of his Allies, expressed his view in favour of the
majority. Germany found herself isolated by a vote
of ten to three.

Prince Bülow, whose one object had been to avoid
any overt humiliation, was enraged. He at once forbade Herr von Holstein to deal any further with the

Morocco question, and took the whole Algeciras dossier into his own hands. The disgrace of Holstein was reflected in the relations between the two German delegates at the Conference. Hitherto Herr von Radowitz had scarcely dared to control Count Tatten-bach who was known to be one of Holstein's special favourites. More moderate counsels now prevailed. On March 6 Prince Bülow informed the Austrian Government that he would be prepared to accept a compromise on the Police question, by which France and Spain should share the Police between them at the several ports with the exception of Casablanca. The instruction of the Police at the latter port was to be entrusted to a Dutch or Swiss national who should at the same time act as Inspector General of all the other detachments. Prince Bülow suggested that the Austrian representative might propose this compromise as his own. He did so on March 8. "The Germans," wrote Nicolson, "have been wonderfully conciliatory." He urged his French colleague to accept at once. M. Révoil refused. Nicolson poured out his indignation in a letter to his wife : "Having been unnecessarily yielding on many other points, he suddenly becomes obstinate on a point on which he might be conciliatory. Like all weak men, he is weak when he ought to be strong, and obstinate when he ought to yield. A tiresome man to work with."

M. Révoil, as a matter of fact, was in the right. He had been privately informed by the Prince of Monaco that the vote of March 3 had produced in Berlin an impression amounting to panic. The Germans, apparently, were in full retreat. Where M. Révoil made a mistake was in not confiding fully to Nicolson the

nature and sources of his information. He merely
asked Nicolson to oppose, to take the initiative in
opposing, the suggestion regarding Casablanca and
the Inspector General. Nicolson was indignant :
" This is the third time," he wrote to his wife, " that
I have raised his banner and on each occasion he has
hid behind a bush and only come out when the
fighting was over. He is so dreadfully weak and
irresolute that he put me in a false position and gives
ground for the charge that the Germans are always
bringing against me that I am more French than the
French."

Somewhat sulkily Nicolson agreed (for after all he
was bound by his instructions) to sponsor this objection which he did not approve. He pointed out to
the Conference that the prestige of the Inspector
General would be diminished if he concurrently possessed the same rank and the same functions at Casablanca as those of the other Instructors whom he was
supposed to supervise. Besides, who was to inspect
the detachment of the Inspector General ? These
criticisms were not ill received. " The sitting,"
Nicolson wrote, " was particularly friendly and har-
monious. There were clear signs of a disposition on
the part of the German delegates and of others to come
to an amicable arrangement with as little delay as
possible." That evening he visited his German colleagues at their hotel. He told Herr von Radowitz that
" he had come on an errand and wished to speak frankly
and as to an old friend." He asked him whether he
could not give way to the French about the Inspector
General. Herr von Radowitz assured him on his word
of honour that he had made his last concessions and

could retreat no further. Nicolson was convinced that his German colleague was speaking the truth, and indeed Herr von Radowitz honestly under-estimated the length to which Prince Bülow was now prepared to go. " The Germans," Nicolson wrote, " have made great concessions and will be wounded if the French don't respond." But M. Révoil was obdurate. The information which he had received from the Prince of Monaco was more accurate than that possessed either by Nicolson or M. de Radowitz. Unfortunately at that very moment an event occurred which led the Wilhelmstrasse to revert suddenly to the violent tactics of Herr von Holstein.

On March 7 M. Rouvier had been defeated in the Chamber on an internal question. The French Government resigned. The intensity of the parliamentary crisis which then arose in France tempted the German Government to undertake a final campaign of violence and misrepresentation. " Tattenbach," Nicolson wrote, " is talking again of war. He says in his usual graceful style that Germany does not want to fight, but that if she is obliged to ' nous les écraserons comme des punaises.' " Prince Bülow, at the same time, addressed to his Ambassadors at the several capitals a telegram informing them that all the representatives at Algeciras, including Arthur Nicolson, were convinced that the French were in the wrong. Russia, he added, was also inclining to the German point of view. This telegram produced great confusion. M. Clemenceau visited the British Ambassador in Paris and informed him that the French Government suspected England of having some secret agreement with Germany and that " Nicolson's advice

to Révoil about Casablanca" confirmed their suspicions. M. Clemenceau himself attributed Nicolson's
behaviour to mere clumsiness. Nicolson denied that
he had ever given any indication to the Germans that
he was weakening in his support of France. Similar
denials were received from Rome and St. Petersburg.
The final attempt of Germany to sow dissension mis-
carried.[1] On March 13 M. Léon Bourgeois succeeded
M. Rouvier in the Sarrien Cabinet. Unity of direction
was re-established. On March 17 Herr von Radowitz
begged Nicolson to give M. Révoil " des conseils de
sagesse." Nicolson replied that he was not in the
position to give his French colleague advice, although
he was always ready to accord him support. On
March 18 Herr von Radowitz stated that his Government were in a "conciliatory mood" and would
yield on the Police question if given compensations
elsewhere. From that moment the success of the
Conference was assured.

At the eleventh hour President Roosevelt decided
to respond to the persistent, though by now out-dated,
efforts of Germany to evoke his intervention. He
expressed the view that to divide the Morocco ports
between France and Spain would savour of partition.
It would be much better if French and Spanish instructors were to operate together in each individual
port. The Germans were appalled by this suggestion,
which would clearly prove unworkable in practice and
could in no case be accepted by the Conference. All
that the Wilhelmstrasse desired at this stage was to
hush up the Algeciras Conference as rapidly as possible.

[1] This curious incident is dealt with at length in Grey's *Twenty-Five Years*,
vol. i., pp. 105-112.

President Roosevelt's belated brain-wave threatened to revive the whole business. The minutes written at the time are illustrative of the false position into which Prince Bülow had drifted. Vienna had suggested to Berlin that it would perhaps be best to ignore the President's inconvenient proposal. Prince Bülow's comment on this suggestion is as follows :

" I entirely agree. We must see to it that Roosevelt doesn't think that it is we who have countered his precious plan. Please submit at once a draft telegram to Washington on these lines."

Here follows a minute by Tschirschky : " I have repeated to Sternberg (German Ambassador at Washington) Radowitz's telegram No. 125, in which he reports that Nicolson, France and even Spain are opposing the American proposal. This should meet your Highness's point." [1]

It is significant that neither Herr von Radowitz's telegram No. 125 nor the instructions addressed thereon to the German Ambassador at Washington are printed in the *Grosse Politik*. All we have is the Ambassador's reply. It runs as follows :

" I have just communicated to the President the contents of your telegram of March 23. President summoned Secretary of State and stated that he would protest emphatically against the refusal of England, France and Spain. The President was particularly sharp in his criticism of the conduct of the British Delegate, and is of opinion that England is backing France up and causing the main difficulties." [2]

The Washington Government, in view of the fact that they were not directly interested in Morocco, did not

[1] *G.P.*, 21, No. 7127 note.   [2] *Ibid.*

press their proposal. All hope of American intervention was abandoned. The final stages of the Algeciras Conference went with a rush.

(6)

Three further concessions were then made by Germany. They agreed that the Inspector General should reside, without any detachment of his own, at Tangier. Casablanca was handed over to the French. They agreed, after a sharp struggle, that the Inspector General should merely report to the Diplomatic Body and should not be directly under their orders. They agreed finally that he should be of Swiss and not of Dutch nationality. By March 31 everything had been concluded. The Bank question had meanwhile been settled on a basis of joint participation. The Final Act of Algeciras was prepared so rapidly that it contained erasures in manuscript. Nicolson, although he was anxious to accept an invitation to join King Edward at Biarritz, was irritated by this unseemly scramble at the last moment. " I hate," he wrote, " slipshod work." The signature took place on April 2.[1]

Congratulations poured in upon him. A telegram from the Government. A more personal letter from the Prime Minister. The official thanks of the Government of France. A warm letter from King Edward. Eulogies in both Houses of Parliament. A G.C.M.G. " Between ourselves," he wrote to his wife regarding the latter decoration, " I don't want it in the slightest. I have quite enough stars and I wanted to keep my old C.M.G.—my first Order. Do you remember when I received it ? Dear me ! It is a long time ago ! How

[1] For Summary of the Act of Algeciras see Appendix II.

young and pleased we were ! " He was not, however, indifferent to all this applause. " I feel," he wrote, " like a school-boy who has done well and had a prize. People are very good to me, aren't they ? And sometimes I feel I am a humbug." " You know," he wrote the next day, " that I am not conceited. But I really do think this Conference has increased my reputation at home and will give me authority if I have to do any negotiations at St. Petersburg." On the final departure he was able to record a tribute which gave him even greater pleasure. " Radowitz," he wrote, " said that he must say that I was a most loyal friend and a most honest adversary. Very pretty and civil of him."

Nicolson spent his last day at Algeciras visiting the lunatic asylum.

There were other rewards and departures. Herr von Holstein, on April 4, was dismissed.[1] Count Welsersheimb, the Austrian Plenipotentiary, was, on the other hand, accorded by the Emperor William the Grand Cross of the Red Eagle for his services " as a brilliant second." This invidious eulogy much offended the pride of Austria. Mr. White, on returning to Rome, informed his German colleague that Arthur Nicolson, " who was by no means rabidly anti-German," had expressed the hope that the outcome of the Conference would be better relations between England and Germany.[2] Prince Bülow was pleased

---

[1] The end of Holstein cannot but awake our sympathy. He lingered on in his squalid little rooms in the Grossbehrenstrasse till May of 1909 : he was very poor, having lost all his money speculating on the Exchange : he was very vindictive : at night he would creep from his flat and walk down to the Wilhelmstrasse, glaring through strong pince-nez at the windows of the room which had once been his : Prince Bülow, from time to time, would come to visit him : but essentially, except for a bullying housekeeper, Holstein died alone.

[2] *G.P.*, 21, No. 7147.

by this remark. He went out of his way to express
to the British Ambassador in Berlin his appreciation
of the " tact and courtesy with which Sir Arthur
Nicolson had performed his duties." He added that
" the manner in which Sir Arthur had performed his
task had earned for him the personal appreciation of
his German colleagues." [1]

This was all very well. The outcome of the Conference had not in reality left a favourable impression
on the Wilhelmstrasse.

(7)

" L'Allemagne," writes Tardieu, " croyait pouvoir
forcer la fortune. La fortune lui résista." The Conference proved, in fact, a misfortune, not for Germany
only but for the world. Its effect upon Morocco can
be discounted : that, at any rate, was not the main
issue involved. Germany had endeavoured, under
the cover of the Morocco question, to isolate France.
She had an excellent case, and, had she handled it
correctly, the opinion of the world would have been
upon her side. She did not handle it correctly. Uncertain, or unwilling, to declare what she really wanted,
she resorted to mystification and menace : the con-
genital diffidence of the German race expressed itself,
as always, in paroxysms of bullying, in weaker phases
of untruth. She lost the confidence of Europe : what
was even more important to her, she also lost the confidence of America. She obtained no compensations.
She did not even succeed in humiliating France. The
open door remained an aspiration. Her protection of
Islam appeared to be mere rhetoric. France and Spain,

[1] Sir F. Lascelles to Sir E. Grey, No. 141, May 17.

England and Russia, had drawn closer together. The nakedness of the Triple Alliance had, with Italy's defection, been exposed to public gaze. And above all the Anglo-French Entente had assumed an entirely new character. From that moment it became essential for Germany to recover her prestige by some diplomatic victory elsewhere. " If," writes Tardieu, " one wished to define the change that took place, one could say that at Algeciras the Entente passed from a static to a dynamic state. Its force increased from the speed thereby acquired." All this was very bad for Europe.

Mr. White, on his return to Rome, expressed to his German colleague the view that " The victor at the Conference is England." The Emperor minuted the despatch which reported this conversation with the single word, " Correct ! "

This undesired triumph was very bad for England.

BOOK III

THE ANGLO-RUSSIAN ENTENTE

VIII

RUSSIA IN 1906

(1)

ON May 25, 1906, Nicolson left London for St. Petersburg. The Nord Express lumbered around Berlin, disclosing suburbs and other ostentations which had not existed in 1878. There were tenement houses in the Jugendstil ; there were parks and Exhibition buildings ; there were a great many new statues. Sir Frank Lascelles, a little out of breath, came to the Railway Station. A few words were exchanged before the train swung on into the night.

The next evening, shortly after dark, they reached the Russian frontier. The engine chunked across the little bridge between Wirballen and Eydtkühnen. They were received by Russian officials in green uniforms, who saluted in a curious manner, bending their heads downwards to meet the uprising hand. The sentries stood there with fixed bayonets presenting arms. The imperial waiting rooms were opened for them—red silk curtains draped heavily over high walnut doors—an eikon flickering in the top right hand corner. In the middle of this airless ante-chamber stood a table set for dinner. There was a huge brass candelabra with red candle-shades. They were given gelinottes and bortsch and small buttered pies. They sat there, as people sit in waiting rooms, with bags upon their knees. An hour later, the officials came to say that the train was ready. They passed out onto the other platform—Nicolson, a bowed and smiling figure, saying " gracias " (he always spoke Spanish when in Russia) to the station master : his wife, train-sick and shy : Fräulein Herbst, the German governess : his daughter Gwendolen, at that time a singularly pert child of ten : a Dachshund dog : a valet : a maid : luggage. The special car was waiting for them. Half an hour later the platform echoed with the feet of other passengers, finding their wagon-lits.

On May 28, after thirty hours of saddened conifers passing sadly past their windows, they arrived at St. Petersburg. The representatives of the Russian Government, the staff of the Embassy, met them on the platform. A row of top hats. Cecil Spring Rice, the Chargé d'Affaires, made the introductions. Colonel Napier, the Military Attaché, Captain Stanley, the Naval Attaché, Mr. Norman, Lord Errington, Lord Cranley. The top hats were raised and hands were shaken. The Dachshund tugged at its leash. They drove through that slip-shod and tragic capital to their home.

The British Embassy was an immense though low-storied house, washed in blood red. It stood at the corner of the Troitzky bridge, and the trams would ring their bells wildly as the horses galloped up the incline. The reception rooms were on the top floor, and the staircase (scarlet and white) ran up to them through a series of pile-carpeted landings graced with Empire statues. The bedrooms were in the mezzanine. The saloons above were large and hung with red, blue, and yellow damask. There was a large white ballroom, and a large oval dining-room in which the candles were swathed in mauve. Outside, the Neva rushed with twisted waters : beyond, the fortress of St. Peter and St. Paul thrust a slim gold pencil into the sky. The bridge cut the view diagonally ; it was decorated with cast-iron eagles painted green, and pylons of polished granite. When the windows were opened, the smell of Russia—that strange smell of leather and fish-oil— would puff into the silken drawing-room as if the scent of blood.

The servants had already arrived. Mr. Sale, the Steward, efficient and intimidating. Mr. Perry, the Groom of the Chambers. M. Zamboni, the really admirable Chef. Footmen, coachmen, porters, house-maids, moujiks. The Chasseur wore a green uniform with a large cocked hat fluttering with green cock-feathers : he carried a sword, the hilt of which was a lion in ivory and gold. The porter, for his part, was known to be a spy. Dinner was served that first evening as if they had always been there. There was coffee afterwards in the Ambassador's study. A large room, with white bookcases and dark red walls, from which the portraits of former Ambassadors glowered upon the vast Sheraton writing table and the leather arm-chairs. A fire, although it was late in May, was burning in the grate. Next morning Nicolson settled down to his task.

(2)

It was not an easy task. The idea of an Anglo-
Russian understanding had, it is true, for long been in
the air. In the autumn of 1903 tentative conversations
had taken place between King Edward, Lord Lans-
downe and Count Benckendorff. In April of 1904
King Edward had spoken at length on the subject to
M. Iswolsky, then Russian Minister at Copenhagen.
In May of that year Sir Charles Hardinge was sent as
Ambassador to St. Petersburg. With admirable
patience and dignity he succeeded, in spite of the ill
feeling created by our alliance with Japan and by the
Dogger Bank incident, in laying the foundations for the
Convention which followed. In February, 1906, Sir
Charles Hardinge was appointed Permanent Under
Secretary at the Foreign Office. It was of immense
advantage for Nicolson to have in Downing Street a
man who not merely shared his views and endeavours,
but who was at the same time an intimate and trusted
friend. Contact had also, during those early months
of 1906, been established with leading members of the
Liberal Cabinet. There is a record of a dinner party in
Queen Anne's Gate in April. It was at that dinner that
the future programme was discussed with Haldane,
Morley, Grey and Asquith. For four hours they sat
there discussing possibilities. Nicolson was not
optimistic. He told them that he would do his best but
that it would take time. They promised him their
confidence, encouragement and support.

" I undertook the post," he records in his Narrative :

" with great diffidence and considerable misgivings.
Personally I was most anxious to see removed all causes of

difference between us and Russia. I considered that many
of these differences were caused by simple misunderstanding of each other, and because each country attributed to
the other plans and projects which in reality were not
entertained. I feared that I might find insurmountable
difficulties and irreconcilable opposition, and I knew that
abortive negotiations would leave matters in a far worse
position than if none had been initiated. I did not know
whether I should not find among the majority of Russians
the old traditional feeling of mistrust and dislike of Great
Britain. Moreover in England the feeling towards
Russia cannot be described as being at all sympathetic.
Among the official classes there existed in flourishing
vigour the old antipathy to Russia, mingled with some
contempt for her since the campaign in Manchuria. In
large sections, Russia was regarded as a ruthless and bar-
barous autocratic State, denying all liberties to her subjects
and employing the most cruel methods in the suppression
of freedom of speech and indeed of thought. I mention
these currents of feeling in England as indicating that
during the course of the coming negotiations it would
be possible that some event might arouse public
opinion in England against the continuance of any
discussions.

" The above considerations dictated the advisability of
restricting the discussions to a matter-of-fact treatment of
the respective British and Russian interests in certain
specific regions. The proceedings, it was evident, must
be thoroughly business-like, and the field in which they
were to operate must be strictly defined."

Nicolson was thus under no illusion that his task
would be an easy one. Even with a Government which
was both friendly and stable, negotiations of this nature
would necessarily be delicate. The Russian Government of 1906 did not, however, fulfil either of these two
requirements.

In the first palce there existed in ruling circles a strong prejudice against Great Britain and a deep suspicion of her politics and intentions. Japan, they felt, would never have dared to challenge Russia had she not been encouraged by her English ally. The hereditary enemy remained the hereditary enemy and her present overtures were merely attempts to win concessions from a Russia crushed by defeat and racked by revolution. France also, during those early months of 1906, was unpopular in St. Petersburg. She had not, during the Japanese war, manifested that benevolent neutrality expected from an ally : her own weakness had been exposed by her capitulation to England over Fashoda and to Germany over Morocco : moreover she was governed by atheists and republicans, and the Press of Paris vied with that of London in encouraging the Duma and the revolutionaries and in decrying the sacred rights of Russian autocracy. Inevitably their eyes turned towards Berlin with admiration, gratitude and hope. There at least you had strength, order, religion, efficiency and sound reactionary principles. Moreover Germany alone of the Great Powers had assisted Russia during the Far Eastern war. " My own opinion," wrote Nicolson,[1] " is that if the Emperor and the Russian Government were free from any other political ties they would gladly form an intimate alliance with Germany. . . . German influence to-day is predominant both in the Court and in Government circles. . . . The alternate hectoring and cajolery, which are a distinctive feature of German diplomacy in other countries, are not employed here. A suave conciliatory attitude and a gentle solicitude are

---

[1] B.D., vol. iv., No. 243.

characteristics of German diplomacy in this capital."
The prospect, therefore, was far from promising. Not
only were the rulers of Russia hostile and suspicious,
they were also unstable. It is necessary, before
recording Nicolson's first tentative overtures, to
describe the impression, the almost despairing impression, which he obtained from his first examination
of the Russian internal situation.

(3)

The Russo-Japanese War, with its unbroken series
of military and naval disasters, lasted from February
1904 to October 1905 ; the first phase of the Russian
revolution extends from January 1905 to December of
that year—from that " bloody Sunday " of January 22
when Gapon's followers were shot down outside the
Winter Palace to the suppression of the December
rising in Moscow. The general strike of August and
September, the increasing acts of terrorism, the fears of
a general uprising of the peasants after the harvest, had
induced the Emperor and his Advisers to publish the
manifesto of October 30, 1905, promising the widest
constitutional reform. With the collapse of the general
strike and the suppression of the Moscow rising they
regained a portion of their confidence and repudiated
most of the promises of the October manifesto. The
Duma, it is true, was constituted by an Imperial ukase
of March 7, 1906. But its representative character was
diminished by an elaborate electoral law, and its
functions were curtailed by withdrawing from its
competence what were called the " Fundamental Laws
of the Empire." On May 2, 1906, Count Witte
resigned office. On May 9 these " Fundamental Laws "

o

were published ; it was found that the Emperor had
withdrawn from the competence of the Duma all
matters affecting his own autocratic privileges. A
storm of indignation was aroused. On May 10 a new
Cabinet was constituted under M. Gorémykin. M.
Iswolsky was made Foreign Minister, and the ex-
Governor of Saratoff, Peter Arcadevich Stolypin,
succeeded M. Dournovo as Minister of the Interior.
On the same day the First Duma was opened by the
Emperor. The deputies at once manifested their
independence and resentment. They demanded a
reform of the electoral law, universal primary education, full liberty of speech and meeting, a general
amnesty for political offences, and above all agrarian
reforms based on the expropriation of the large estates.
M. Gorémykin refused all these concessions. An
almost complete rupture of relations between the
Government and the Duma then ensued. It was at this
moment, on May 28, that Nicolson arrived. In one of
the first reports which he forwarded to the Foreign
Office the situation was painted in dark colours : " the
outlook becomes blacker day by day and there are few
competent observers who think that a cataclysm can
long be averted." The cataclysm was none the less
averted for over ten years.

For the moment, however, the situation was obscure,
and menacing. A mist hung over the marshes and at
every step the earth yielded treacherously. There was
no firm ground and no certain landmarks. The Duma
indulged in hysterics and rhetoric. The Government
appeared paralysed. The Emperor, down at Peterhof,
was invisible and silent. Nicolson visited M. Gorémykin, the Prime Minister, and was appalled. He

found him " reclining on a sofa surrounded by French
novels." " An elderly man," he recorded in his diary,
" with a sleepy face and Piccadilly whiskers.   He
treated the Duma with the greatest disdain : ' Let them
babble,' he said, ' the Government alone knows the
country.' He was very indignant with the tone of *The
Times* and the *Daily Telegraph* in regard to the Jews,
whom he characterised as the vilest of people, anarch-
ists, extortioners and usurers. I went away with a sad
heart : the Russian bureaucracy is incorrigible." The
views of his foreign colleagues, whom he next visited,
were not of a nature to dispel this pessimism. M.
Bompard, the French Ambassador, was afraid of a
complete collapse and of the consequent impoverish-
ment of millions of French investors.   Herr von
Schoen, the German Ambassador, was gentle and
discreet. Baron von Aehrenthal, the Representative
of Austria-Hungary, expatiated on the complete para-
lysis of will which was destroying the Russian body
politic.   " An amiable and chatty man," Nicolson
recorded in his diary, " but not brilliant." The British
correspondents, the members of the British colony,
could only speak of murder, arson and pillage. The
leaders of Russian society were either sullen or
indifferent.   " This country," Nicolson recorded, " is
passing through a period of transition, and it is impossible to estimate what forces are working within her
or to predict in what direction they may impel this vast
Empire, with all its heterogeneous elements, its conflicting interests, and with its great inarticulate mass of
many millions—half civilised, wholly uneducated, but
with a hidden strength, which may work for great evil
or for great good." " One fact," he wrote somewhat

later, " has been borne in upon me, and that is the absence of any patriotism in the general public. There seems to be an increasing tendency among the rising generation of intellectuals to discard the sense of any love of their country as being but a narrow selfish ideal and to feel that for the future the great idea of humanity should alone animate their minds and contain their aspirations."

Such wide and mist-laden horizons were to him unknown. He wisely decided to deal with the facts of the situation, with the few dim landmarks which emerged from the surrounding fog. He also, and with equal wisdom, decided to summon expert assistance. He sent for his friend Sir Donald Mackenzie Wallace, a recognised authority upon Russian history, conditions, and psychology. For nearly seven months this scholarly publicist resided at the British Embassy, obtaining information from sources generally closed to diplomatists, puffing huge cigars into the red-silk curtains of his bedroom, reading revolutionary pamphlets, visiting Witte, Milioukoff, and the reactionaries, attending secret conclaves of the Social Democrats. The young men in the chancery would refer disrespectfully to Sir Donald Mackenzie Wallace under the name of " Mordekai the Jew." But the Ambassador, for his part, benefited immensely from his knowledge and advice. For among his many virtues and attainments Sir Donald had the advantage of an intimate acquaintance with the Emperor Nicolas. He had been attached to the Imperial suite when the Emperor as Tsarevitch had visited India. It was thus through Sir Donald's eyes that the fluctuating figure of Nicolas II acquired for Nicolson a certain precision of outline.

This gentle but uneducated Emperor (endowed, as
Nicolson again and again asserts, " with many amiable
and virtuous qualities ") was afflicted with the misfortune of being weak on every point except his own
autocracy. He would agree with everyone on everything except the introduction of constitutional reform.
" He considered," Nicolson records, " that his autocratic power had been handed down to him as a sacred
heritage and that it would be unworthy of him to
betray such a trust. In these views he was encouraged
by the Empress. On several occasions it was unfortunate that he should have been guided by these
considerations. The Emperor was liable to be
influenced not so much by persons as by outside events,
without being able to appreciate their true importance
and bearing. It would not be easy to deny that the
acts of the Emperor were on occasions disappointing,
ill-judged and inopportune. Criticism, however,
should not be hard on a man placed in so dangerous a
situation. The Emperor had a conscientious sense of
duty towards his own position and towards his country.
I am afraid that on occasions it was difficult to reconcile
the two ; and that the former became the governing
factor." On one point, however, Nicolson would
always defend the Emperor Nicolas with absolute
conviction. He considered him " quite incapable of
any duplicity." There are many who will question this
assertion. It is true, indeed, that the Emperor was
frequently landing himself in false positions out of
mere affability. It is true also that his reserve amounted
at moments to secretiveness if not to concealment. It
is probable indeed that the truth has been best recorded
by his cousin William II. This particular apophthegm

of the German Emperor can be found as a marginal minute to a despatch from Herr von Schoen in which the latter, reporting on some audience at Peterhof, adds that his remarks evidently produced upon the Tsar a profound impression. " Yes," writes William II, " until Iswolsky, or Martens, or Nicolson delete that impression. The Tsar is not treacherous but he is weak. Weakness is not treachery, but it fulfils all its functions." [1]

It was unfortunate that a man so forceless and so all-powerful should be constantly exposed to influences which increased his mystic faith in its own mission. The Empress, even at that date, was dabbling in spiritualism. There are references in Nicolson's letters to the influence of the Montenegrin Grand Duchesses or to " M. Philippe the medium,"—an adventurer whose real name was Nizier Vachol, and who had been a butcher-boy at Lyons. The immediate advisers of the Emperor were not able to counteract these influences. There were the Court officials such as Baron Friedrickz and General Trepoff, whose sole desire was to cause pleasure. There were a few elderly bureaucrats. And there were the Grand Dukes. The latter were of small importance :

" Iswolsky," Nicolson wrote home, " spoke to me privately the other day as to the ultra-conservative views of the Empress and the Grand Duchess Serge. . . . He said that he was sorry to observe how reactionary were the Empress and the Grand Duchess and he feared that their spiritualistic tendencies did not create a very invigorating atmosphere at Peterhof." " Apart," Nicolson records in his Narrative, " from these immediate influences the

---

[1] G.P., 23 A, p. 161, No. 7877.

Court Circle was of little importance, the Grand Dukes especially being of little account. With two or three exceptions they were not men of any intelligence or character, and they played no part either socially or politically. In regard to society, the Grand Duke Vladimir and his wife were prominent people. The Grand Dukes Constantine and Nicolas Mikhailovitch were intelligent and occupied themselves with literary pursuits. The others were not conspicuous. The Grand Duke Nicolas Nicolaievitch was a man with spasmodic periods of varied emotions. One week he was a stern disciplinarian ; the next week he would be absorbed in religious devotions ; and the third week he would spend quietly in the country engaged in field sports. His nerves had been shaken by the recent attempt on his life during firing exercises at the camp and he had no continuity of purpose."

On May 29, 1905, Nicolson paid his first visit to the Foreign Minister. He informed him that he had been instructed to " exchange views on several important matters." M. Iswolsky was affable but reserved. Nicolson made it clear that the British Government had " no desire to forge a weapon against others " and that no questions would be discussed which affected the interests of any third Power. M. Iswolsky showed evident relief. " I think it well," Nicolson wrote to Sir Edward Grey, " to put a ring-fence around our discussions, but I do not feel sure that Iswolsky will not take the German Ambassador into his confidence as the negotiations proceed." On the same day he made the following entry in his diary. " May 29. First interview with Iswolsky. Overtures well received, but evidently one eye on Berlin. Discretion promised, but will not be observed. Tiresome."

On June 5 Nicolson proceeded to Peterhof to present

his letters of credence to the Emperor. The ceremony was short and formal. Outside, the Gulf of Finland was wrapped in mists : the rain poured in a deluge upon the fountains and cascades. " Emperor," noted Nicolson in his diary, " in excellent spirits and looking in robust health. Empress with an anxious look, and a little *guindée*." The usual amicable assurances were exchanged. Nicolson returned to the capital and the next day opened serious negotiations with M. Iswolsky.

(4)

Alexander Iswolsky, who scarcely a month before had succeeded the epicene Count Lamsdorff as Minister for Foreign Affairs, was at that date exactly fifty years of age. One's first impression was not favourable. He was obviously a vain man, and he strutted on little lacquered feet. His clothes, which came from Savile Row, were moulded tightly upon a plump but still gainly frame. He held himself rigidly with stiff shoulders. He wore a pearl pin, an eyeglass, white spats, a white slip to his waistcoat. His face was well cared for, but pasty and fattening, with loose and surly lips. His hair and moustache were carefully parted ; he had a way of turning his short Russian neck stiffly above his high white collar, glancing sideways, as so often with Russians, away from the person with whom he was shaking hands. His voice was at once cultured and rasping. He left behind him, as he passed onwards, a slight scent of *violette de Parme*.

The close intimacy which Nicolson thereafter established with M. Iswolsky enabled him to modify his first impression. The following description of the Russian Foreign Minister figures in his Narrative:

" I can confidently say that he always acted towards me loyally and honestly, and that during our long intercourse no serious cloud ever arose between us. He was earnestly desirous to conclude a satisfactory arrangement with us ; he had a great admiration for English institutions, a marvellously intimate acquaintance with English literature and history, and a perfect knowledge of the English language. His intelligence was alert, quick and subtle ; but I must add that like all human beings he had his defects. I do not think that he ever quite understood the minds and feelings of his own countrymen, and on one or two occasions this misapprehension led him into serious difficulties. Again he was nervous and timorous, and was exceedingly sensitive to public criticism. This necessarily led to some want of continuity in his foreign policy and somewhat weakened the confidence with which one could depend on him. He was much impressed with the power and might of Germany, and was always anxious lest by any mischance he should give offence to her. He was also a little too eager to play a part in society, and he was exceedingly open to the influences of the fashionable world."

On June 6, 1906, Nicolson opened formal negotiations. He began with the question of Thibet. He imagined that, of the three main subjects of discussion, the Thibetan problem was the one which would be the least likely to lead to controversy. The first stage of his negotiation was not auspicious. It forms, however, a useful illustration and specimen of the kind of difficulty with which Nicolson had to cope.

The Thibetan problem, in itself, was simple enough. The monastic kingdom had for long been a source of irritation and disquiet to the Government of India : the Thibetans refused not only to recognise existing agreements but even to negotiate for the re-establishment of trade relations. In 1903 Sir Francis Younghusband was sent on an armed mission, and on September 7, 1904, he secured a Convention under which the Thibetan authorities undertook to open the trade routes, and not to enter into relations with any Power other than Great Britain. An indemnity was at the same time imposed upon them, and as security for its payment British troops were to remain in occupation of the Chumbi Valley. The Russians complained at the time that this Convention implied a British protectorate over Thibet and as such constituted a violation of the pledges which we had previously given. On April 27, 1906, a further Convention, known as the " Adhesion Agreement," was signed between Great Britain and China, under which the latter, as suzerain of Thibet, adhered to the Younghusband Convention, while Great Britain for her part undertook not to annex Thibetan territory or to interfere with the domestic affairs of that country. The Dalai Lama, in the meanwhile, had escaped to Urga, where he was hospitably entertained by the Princes of Mongolia. The Government of India were alarmed lest he should return to Lhassa and continue to act in an anti-British sense. Their anxiety was increased when on April 10, 1906, the Emperor Nicolas addressed to the Dalai Lama a telegram of compliments and friendly assurances. Nicolson was instructed to obtain from the Russian Government, firstly an assurance that they would join with us in recognising China's suzerainty over Thibet and would abstain from any interference in Thibetan affairs ; secondly a recognition that Great Britain possessed " a special interest in seeing that the external relations of Thibet are not disturbed by any other Power " ; and thirdly a

self-denying clause under which neither Great Britain
nor Russia would send representatives to Lhassa or seek
for any concessions in Thibetan territory. In other
words we wished to keep Thibet as a buffer state
immune from penetration by either Power : we were
prepared to abandon the position implied in the Younghusband Convention, if Russia would agree to regard
Thibet as a zone forbidden to her agents and her
infiltration.

Nicolson began by communicating to M. Iswolsky
the texts of the Younghusband Convention and of the
subsequent Adhesion Agreement with China. He then
submitted to him the substance of the instructions
summarised above. M. Iswolsky was not receptive.
He asked what was meant by the expression " disturbed
by any other Power." He spoke of the high esteem in
which the Dalai Lama was held by the Russian buddhists, of the important spiritual relations maintained
between the Lhassa monasteries and the Buriats. " I
was careful," Nicolson recorded in his diary, " to let
him talk. I want to reach the back of his mind. It
would be fatal to force the pace, as they would only
become suspicious. I must walk warily and show no
impatience."

Nicolson was not by nature a patient man. In the
small affairs of life he would fidget at a momentary
block in the traffic, at the slightest hesitation or stum-
bling in a person addressed. In public affairs, however,
his patience was phenomenal. It was put to a severe
test in the year that followed. For the internal situation
at this moment deteriorated so rapidly that all further
progress with his negotiations was out of the question.

(5)

The Imperial Duma had not since its inception displayed any great intelligence. Most of the deputies were in fact almost illiterate and the intellectuals who led the several parties regarded the tribune of the Tauride Chamber as a vehicle of propaganda rather than as the workshop of constructive statesmanship. They made proposals and speeches which they well knew bore no practical relation to the possibilities or even the needs of the time. On the few occasions when M. Gorémykin appeared before them they merely booed at the foolish old man. He ceased to appear before them. Stolypin alone, cold, dignified and impressive, inspired them with a certain respect. M. Milioukoff, the leader of the Kadets, whose election had been quashed owing to some technical irregularity, fussed about the lobbies inspiring his followers with noble but obstructive ideals. The leaders of the Octobrists, Heydn and Stakhovitch, were equally doctrinaire. Professor Kovalevsky, who made some attempt to form a centre party of parliamentary co-operation, was only a professor. The Duma listened with more willing ears to the intoxicating rhetoric of Aladyin, the leader of the so-called Labour group. The Social Democrats gloated over the obvious fiasco of a consultative chamber. The Socialist Revolutionaries had boycotted the whole business. M. Gorémykin continued to read his French novels; and meanwhile the flames of anarchy, stilled for a moment at the meeting of the Duma, began once more to crackle in the far-flung provinces and in the capital itself.

The number of provincial Governors and officials

murdered by the terrorists between February of 1905
and May of 1909 totalled 1,421. By June the average
of assassination began to rise. The peasants were also
threatening trouble, and it was feared that a general
agrarian rising would take place in the autumn. The
Black Band, a reactionary organisation, was also busy,
and a serious massacre of Jews took place at Biyelostock. The Jewish Societies in Great Britain became
active in Downing Street. Nicolson was instructed to
make representations to the Russian Government on
behalf of their co-religionaries. M. Iswolsky received
these representations " with exceeding stiffness." On
June 22 there occurred at St.Petersburg a serious mutiny
in the Preobrajensky regiment of Guards. " The near
future," Nicolson reported, " will produce some
startling and terrible development."

The development, when it came, was startling, but
it was not terrible. M. Iswolsky has recounted in his
memoirs how, on the night of July 21 he dined at the
British Embassy, and stood there upon the balcony
gazing sadly at the sunset in the midnight sky. The
impending dawn, he knew, was fraught with terrible
possibilities. For on July 22 the Duma was dissolved,
a state of martial law was proclaimed, and the forma-
tion of a new Cabinet was entrusted to the hands of
Stolypin. St. Petersburg was taken by surprise. The
deputies, on reaching the Tauride Palace, found the
gates closed against them. The Kadets and Octobrists
rushed off to Viborg in Finland from where they issued
a manifesto of protest urging passive resistance.
Mutinies broke out at Kronstadt and Sveaborg but
were immediately repressed. A general strike was
decreed for August 3, but petered out after two days.

The Government, to the astonishment of all observers, had triumphed.

Meanwhile, however, the dissolution of the Duma produced in England an outburst of self-righteous indignation which was prejudicial to an Anglo-Russian Convention. The strained relations existing between the Russian Government and the Chamber had already led to sharp criticism in the British House of Commons and the British Cabinet had thought it wiser to cancel the proposed visit of the Channel Fleet to Russian waters. The Biyelostock massacre had also been ill received. The eager hearts of British politicians were wrung by the indignities imposed upon their colleagues of the Tauride Palace. Sir Henry Campbell-Bannerman made a speech in which, amid applause, he exclaimed, " La Douma est morte, vive la Douma ! " These words, and the admonitions of the British Press, produced much irritation in Russia.

Nicolson found his task immensely complicated. He notes in his diary for August 6 : " An angry article in *The Times* abusing the Tsar. The attitude of our Press is most unfortunate, and they have completely misunderstood the position. On top of this comes the speech of the P.M. Iswolsky's former eagerness has been replaced by silence and apparent indifference. The Emperor is wounded. Two months ago there was every hope, and now very little. When I mentioned to Iswolsky that I should like to have some outline of his views on Persia, he looked blankly at me and said that he had no views at all." What made it all so irritating was that Nicolson himself realised that the Duma bore little relation to the facts of the position. " The only people who matter," he wrote, " are the

Government on the one side and the Revolutionaries
on the other. If only the Kadets would have the sense
to realise this they might be less conceited and futile."
" The future," he reported, " really lies in the hands of
the peasants. Should the peasantry, excited by socialist
and anarchist agitators, be led on whither the latter
desire to draw them, and should the working classes
simultaneously rise in the towns, there will be a
catastrophe such as history has rarely witnessed." [1]
" The revolutionaries," he wrote again, " care nothing
for Constitutions or Dumas or reforms. Their sole aim
is, by a course of relentless terrorism, to endeavour to
render all government impossible and to pave the way
for a socialist republic of the most advanced type." [2]
It is no wonder that, seeing as he did below the surface
of parliamentary sentimentalism, he should believe
more in Stolypin than in Milioukoff. The effect of these
events on public opinion in England had, however, to
be taken into account. Sir Edward Grey wrote to him
that the negotiations had better be suspended. Sir
Charles Hardinge repeated this opinion. Nicolson
replied to the latter on July 29 as follows :

" I think that there is little doubt that either the present
dynasty and present Government will last, or that there
will be a general upheaval which will sweep away dynasty,
Government, and much else. I cannot tell you with
certainty which is the more probable alternative. Personally I should be disposed to favour the former, but I
do not wish to attach weight to conjectures. . . . To my
mind it would be prudent to continue discussions on the
assumption that we are dealing with a stable Government.
Should our assumption be falsified, nothing will be lost :

[1] Despatch to Sir E. Grey, No. 491, July 31, 1906.
[2] Despatch to Sir E. Grey, No. 554, Aug. 26, 1906.

as when the wreckage had been cleared away we should most assuredly have to deal with an entirely new set of conditions, which would render it necessary to reconsider the whole scope, basis and aims of our negotiations. . . . If, on the other hand, the Government remain, we . . . should lose in three ways. We should have given the Russian Government ground for believing that we doubted in their stability. If the Government remain and we only assumed seriously our negotiations when we were sure of the fact, we might find them more self-reliant, more confident and more exacting. We should afford time for German policy to develop itself in Persia, and for Germany to establish a footing there. She would then, as she did in Morocco, insist on having a voice in the settlement in regard to Persia."

" My observations," Nicolson records in his Narrative, " had some result. The negotiations were not abandoned, though they proceeded very slowly."

(6)

" Sir Arthur Nicolson," reported the German Chargé d'Affaires, " at first flung himself wholly to the left : later he was induced by his friend Mackenzie Wallace to adopt an attitude of greater reserve." [1] This interpretation of Nicolson's political development during his first months in Russia is incomplete rather than inaccurate. It is true that he was by conviction a British Liberal, that his instinctive sympathies were on the side of the Duma, and that his early interview with M. Gorémykin had filled him with disgust. It is true also that Mackenzie Wallace, with his expert knowledge of past conditions and events, subsequently convinced him that Russia could only be reformed gradually and

[1] *G.P.*, vol. xxv., No. 8535.

from above. It is true again that as the weeks passed he
came to despise the Duma doctrinaires—to realise that
the issue was social rather than political, and that the
only combatants who mattered were the Government,
the revolutionaries and the peasants. Incontestably,
also, any enthusiasm which he may have had for
representative institutions in Russia was chilled by the
ignorance and sentimentality of his fellow-liberals of
the London Press and Parliament. His sympathy for
the Jews was also somewhat damped by a closer study
of the question. He realised, moreover, that the too
open expression of liberal sentiments was not welcomed
at Peterhof : his French colleague, M. Bompard, had
displayed an indiscreet interest in the Kadet party—his
removal was demanded and obtained. For this reason
alone " an attitude of greater reserve " was incumbent.
It was better in all such matters to work through
Mackenzie Wallace. Yet it was something far more
important than mere discretion which turned Nicolson's sympathies away from the Kadets. It was the
personality of P. A. Stolypin.

    " Stolypin," Nicolson recorded in his Narrative, " was
a great man. He was, in my opinion, the most notable
figure in Europe. His task as Minister of the Interior, and
subsequently as Prime Minister was a gigantic one. He
had to deal with a situation which threatened the existence
of the Empire. I had always the most intimate relations
with him and knew him well. He was not a man of a very
high order of intelligence, but he possessed, what was far
more important, great courage, great determination, an
ardent love for his country, and a most earnest desire to
steer her safely through the troubles and difficulties by
which she was surrounded. He was anxious to develop
her great resources and lead her progressively to a higher

level. He considered that the elements which were so active in 1906 were really anarchic and revolutionary, and that it was essential to crush the revolutionary movement which, if successful, would have disintegrated the whole Empire and brought the country to ruin. He was equally determined when the revolutionary movement had been suppressed, to introduce reforms generally, and to satisfy, as far as was possible and prudent, all the legitimate demands of the people. Had not his life been cut short by the hand of an assassin,[1] I think that he would have achieved great things."

Stolypin, at that date, was forty-three years of age. A tall stiff man with a dead white face and a dead black beard. He entered a room stiffly, carrying a top hat and kid gloves, looking straight in front of him, bowing like an automaton over the hand of his hostess, passing rigidly from guest to guest. His frock-coat had been made by the best tailor in Saratoff. He spoke in a cold and even voice, as cold as the clasp of his white hand. Unlike most Russians, he looked one straight in the face with firm and honest eyes. He smiled but rarely, and his habitual gesture was to pass his fingers lightly along the under side of his moustache. The ends of this moustache twirled upwards. He gave one no impression of ferocity. He left an impression only of cold gentleness, of icy compassion, of saddened self-control.

From the outset Arthur Nicolson was immensely impressed by Stolypin. At their first meeting on July 2 the then Minister of the Interior had spoken to him in dispassionate but convincing tones of the tragic malady from which Russia was suffering. It would, he said,

---

[1] M. Stolypin was murdered by the Jew Mordka Bogrov in the stalls of the Kieff Theatre on Sept. 14, 1911.

take three full years to eradicate the poison which was
infecting the country. He was in favour of wide
reforms but the immediate objective was health and
order. The lack of common sense displayed by the
Duma was both a disappointment and a problem.
" His own ideal," Nicolson reported, " was the British
Constitution, but it was impossible to cast Russia at
once into that mould. In some years she might
possibly reach that goal, but sudden or impetuous
changes would work ruin." Meanwhile further acts of
terrorism must be expected. Stolypin had himself
warned the Emperor to have duplicate Ministers ready
to fill the places of those who might be murdered. The
Socialist Revolutionaries cared nothing for democratic
reforms. All that they were aiming at was disorder.
The Kadets were incapable of grasping the opportunity
offered to them. " For the moment," Stolypin concluded, " the Government must govern."

The Socialist Revolutionaries, for their part, were
not slow to recognise that the cold force of Stolypin's
personality represented the main obstacle to their desires. On the afternoon of August 25 they despatched
three of their number disguised as gendarmes to
the villa which the Prime Minister occupied on the
Apothecary's island. The party arrived in a hired
landau and ran up the steps into the hall. They
endeavoured to penetrate into the ante-room beyond,
but were stopped by an aide-de-camp. One of their
number thereupon flung upon the marble floor the
portfolio which he was carrying and which was packed
with bombs. The explosion which followed soared
across the river and out into the suburbs beyond.
Twenty-five people were killed and thirty wounded.

The whole front of the house collapsed, burying in its
ruins Stolypin's two children who were playing in the
balcony above.   His daughter of fifteen had both her
legs crushed and his infant son was also severely
wounded.   Both the nurses who were with them were
killed.   The hand of the aide-de-camp was found in a
tree some fifty yards distant.   M. Stolypin himself,
who was in his study at the back of the house, was
flung to the ground but remained unhurt.   The
assassins were blown to atoms.   The Prime Minister
searched anxiously among the heaps of rubble for his
children.

Nicolson was informed of what had happened.   He
told his youngest son to drive to the Apothecary's
island with the Embassy chasseur.   They were allowed
to pass through the police cordon and to approach the
scene of the disaster.   The dust of the explosion still
hung upon the air, and the figures of the stretcher-
bearers, passing and repassing over heaps of rubble,
were blurred in mist.   The trees fringing the little quay
had been snapped at the trunk ; they hung over the
quay-side with seared leaves : through their branches
were twisted the lace curtains which had been blown
outwards from the upper bedrooms.   In the roadway
lay the stark remains of a landau and two horses.   A
silence shrouded the surrounding gardens broken only
by the staccato orders of the ambulance officials.
Silently the great red-cross motors swept away.

(7)

The outrage on the Prime Minister led to sterner
measures of repression.   Authority was given to the
local officials to hold drum-head courts martial in the

event of terrorist attacks. Nicolson expressed the fear
lest " grave abuses might arise " from this power of
life and death given to the police and military authorities. " What we should all wish," he wrote, " is for a
moderate, sensible Duma with a good sound constitutional majority, who would keep the Government up
to their promises, and insist on their proceeding
steadily on the path of reforms." He was under no
delusion, however, as to the danger of any weakening
of executive control :

> " The authors," he wrote, " of the crime (of August 25)
> are the extreme section of the Socialist Revolutionaries,
> who term themselves ' maximalists,' as they assert that
> they undertake ' maximal ' acts. M. Stolypin doubts
> whether they are more than forty or fifty in number,
> but he confesses that the police are unable to trace them or
> to find a clue to their whereabouts. They probably
> frequently move their domicile, and very probably pass to
> and fro between Russia and abroad, which, notwith-
> standing all passport regulations, is not difficult to effect."[1]
> " The views," he wrote later, " of a determined minority
> usually carry the day among Russian working classes,
> who, when the decisive moment arrives, meekly obey the
> orders of the dominant few. . . . It must be remembered
> that the thorough-going Socialist Revolutionaries have
> little sympathy with such a ' bourgeois ' institution as a
> Duma. It is not by constitutional means, or benevolent
> legislation_that they hope to reach the establishment of the
> Socialist Republic. Their aims are to render all Govern-
> ment impossible and to create such a condition of affairs
> as will pave the way to a general revolution. It is im-
> possible to estimate their numbers or resources, but it is
> clear that they have numerous devoted adherents, and be
> they few or many, they undoubtedly exercise a terrorising

[1] Despatch to F.O., No. 591, September 6, 1906.

influence over Russian society. I do not think that repressive measures have any effect upon the Socialist Revolutionaries, who seem to pursue their methods with calm, cold-blooded, precision." [1]

For reasons such as these Nicolson was in no sense carried away by the wave of optimism which thereafter began to sweep over Russian reactionary circles. The people, they all said, were tired of agitation : the revolutionaries were losing ground : the Duma had been discredited : the Government had gained in prestige : the peasants, though easily misled, retained for the Emperor their old religious veneration. The August outbreaks were in fact followed by a lull. Stolypin himself assured Nicolson in October that things were going better, that the revolutionaries had lost the sympathy of the people, that the elections to the second Duma would produce a counter-attraction, that the peasants were settling down. The Ambassador was not convinced. He knew that somewhere in that wide and melancholy Empire there existed a handful of extremists, possessed of unknown resources, organised with terrifying secrecy, directed by some hidden intelligence, and fired by a fanatical determination to destroy the old at any cost, and at any cost to build the new. In his despatch No. 2 of January 1, 1907, he informed the Foreign Office that the internal situation had improved enormously since the preceding July. " I do not," he wrote, " believe that, as conditions exist at present, a general revolution is possible for some time to come." At the same time he warned them against the " sanguine optimism " which had been aroused in St. Petersburg by the acquiescence of

[1] Despatch to F.O., No. 22, January 9, 1907.

Russian opinion in the dissolution of the first Duma.
" I do not," he wrote, " for one moment imagine that
the repressive measures now being adopted will
effectually stamp out the revolutionary agitation, at
least among the determined revolutionaries. . . . The
great dangers to my mind at present are over-confidence
on the part of the Government and the revival of
reaction." He expressed his doubts whether Stolypin
was prepared to deal with the Jewish question in a
really liberal spirit. " It is for the above reasons," he
concluded, " that I feel myself unable fully to share the
optimism which is prevailing in many quarters, as I do
not regard the existing comparative tranquillity, or the
momentary disorganisation of some opposition parties,
as indicating a real and permanent improvement."

IX

THE ANGLO-RUSSIAN CONVENTION

[1907]

M. Iswolsky's visits to Paris and Berlin—The scope and purpose of the
Anglo-Russian negotiations—The question of "encirclement" of
Germany—Nicolson's own views on that point—Justifications for
German uneasiness—Progress of the negotiations—Thibet—Afghanis-
tan—The Persian problem—The defence of India—The two " self-
denying zones "—British promises to consider the Straits question—
Nicolson's daily occupations—His social life—Dissolution of the Second
Duma—A spy story—Criticisms in England of the Anglo-Russian
negotiations—Agreement reached on Persian zones—Question of the
Persian Gulf—Eleventh-hour difficulties—Signature of the Convention
—Lord Curzon's attack—Reception of the Convention in France and
Germany.

(1)

IN spite of his fundamental scepticism regarding any
deep or durable improvement in Russian internal conditions, Nicolson considered that the time had come
when he could safely resume his interrupted negotiations for an Anglo-Russian Convention. M. Iswolsky,
in October of 1906, had visited France and Germany.
He had gone to Berlin for the purpose of sounding
Prince Bülow as to the projected Anglo-Russian conversations and " in order to avoid a repetition by
Germany of her attitude in the Morocco question and
Russia being placed in the dilemma of France." [1] He
was assured by the Wilhelmstrasse that Germany would
welcome the agreement so long as it did not affect
her own interests. He returned to St. Petersburg
much fortified by this encouragement. Nicolson was

[1] B.D., vol. iv. No. 230.

sceptical. He warned the Foreign Office that "a similar charitable disposition had been shown by the German Government in the early days of the Anglo-French Agreement, and subsequently a change of attitude had ensued." [1] It appears indeed that the indifference of the Wilhelmstrasse was not as cordial as M. Iswolsky contended. M. Clemenceau informed Sir F. Bertie that he knew for a fact that M. Iswolsky had been forbidden by Prince Bülow to visit London. And the next year M. Iswolsky himself confessed at Marienbad to Sir E. Goschen that " it had required all the patience at his command to withstand the continual ' hammering ' to which he had been subjected from Berlin." [2] Meanwhile, however, the road was clear for the resumption of negotiations. Nicolson was encouraged by a despatch from Sir F. Lascelles, in which the latter reported a conversation which he had held with the Russian Foreign Minister during the latter's passage through Berlin. M. Iswolsky on that occasion had spoken highly of Nicolson and expressed his admiration for the rapidity with which he had grasped the Russian problem. He referred to him as " indeed the right man in the right place," and stated that Nicolson's " clear and sound judgment would be of the greatest utility in carrying on these complicated negotiations." [3]

The negotiations were indeed so complicated that it would be outside the scope of this monograph to record their several phases in any detail. It is important, however, if we are to see the Anglo-Russian Convention in its right proportions, clearly to define the

[1] B.D., vol. iv. No. 247.   [2] B.D., vol. iv. No. 523.
[3] B.D., vol. iv. No. 234.

objectives which the two Governments had in view. Propagandists both in England and in Germany have obscured the issue by insisting on extreme interpretations : by arguing on the one side that the Anglo-Russian Convention was a purely Asiatic agreement, by contending on the other side that its sole purpose was the encirclement of Germany. The truth lies somewhere between these two extremes. It is a fact that the negotiations were strictly confined to those points of friction which caused Anglo-Russian " rivalry " in Central Asia, and that they in no way affected the interests of other European Powers. The immediate objective of the British Government was to facilitate the defence of India by creating sanitary cordons against the " spontaneous infiltration " of Russian influence into Thibet, Afghanistan and Persia. It would be untruthful, however, to contend that the British Government were not also guided by considerations of wider scope. Inevitably they were alarmed by the prospect of a Russo-German Alliance, and of a subsequent European coalition into which France would be incorporated almost by force. We know to-day that their fears were justified. Inevitably also they realised that the only country to benefit by Anglo-French or Anglo-Russian friction was the German Empire. It may be said even that the fear of Germany was one of the main motives inspiring the agreement. But it can in all certitude be affirmed that the Anglo-Russian Convention was part of no deliberate or conscious programme of encirclement, and that the British Government desired only to re-adjust, by such defensive precautions, the balance of power. It was not a question of getting Russia to join England

against Germany : it was solely a question of preventing Russia from joining Germany against England.

In his Diplomatic Narrative (which, it must be
recollected, was dictated at the height of the European
War during the winter of 1916-1917) Nicolson, looking
back over this period, assesses as follows the motives
inspiring the several Governments :

"The position at this epoch (1906) was as follows.
Russia needed some years of peace and quietude to recuperate and reorganise ; her ally, France, at a critical
moment, had shown that she was not able to resist German
dictation and had only succeeded in regaining some lost
ground and in recovering some firmness of character when
she felt that she could rely on British assistance. If Russia,
therefore, desired that a counterpoise should be created
against German domination, it was evident that a good
understanding with Great Britain was desirable.

"There was no question of ' encircling ' Germany.
There were no secret agreements with France, and there
would certainly be none with Russia, which contemplated
any combination or menace against Germany. With
France, it is true, there had been certain conversations
between the General Staffs as to possible measures in the
event of a German attack, but these were but natural
measures of precaution for defence and not for aggression.
I do not pretend that it was considered likely that an
Anglo-Russian understanding would be pleasing to
Germany. Such an understanding was regarded in Berlin
as an even more unlikely event than an agreement between
England and France : its conclusion would perforce be
proportionately displeasing to Berlin. A cardinal point of
German policy had always been to cultivate and maintain
the closest relations with Russia and to be content that
fundamental divergencies of views and of policy should
continue to exist between Russia and Great Britain. I do
not see anything Machiavellian in such a policy on the part

of Germany. It appears to me to have been, from her
point of view, sound and reasonable. It was conditioned
by her aspiration—I may say by her determination—to be
the predominating factor in Europe. It was inevitable,
perhaps even natural, that she should work to achieve such
a position. She was conscious of her strength and of her
great vitality, and the vast progress which she had made
in the brief period of one generation might well inspire
her with the belief that her expansion would continue
until she was securely established in a commanding
situation.

" At the same time she should have appreciated that too
manifest an exhibition of these aspirations and a too
premature application to others of the effects of a German
hegemony would create some apprehension. Notwithstanding the fact that, in dealing both with France and
Russia, we had honestly no other object than to place our
relations on a safer and more secure basis in the general
interests of peace, yet the subconscious feeling did exist
that thereby we were securing some defensive guarantees
against the overbearing domination of one Power. We
were trending towards a regrouping of the States of
Europe. The dispersal of the clouds between us and
France and Russia, and our consequent though perhaps
imperceptible adhesion to a new combination, restored to
us our liberty of action and strengthened the position of
all three countries.

" It is not an uninteresting question to examine whether
the new situation did or did not promote the interests of
peace. It can safely be postulated and admitted that
neither France nor Russia nor Great Britain had the
remotest desire to disturb the peace or to impair the
relations between themselves and Germany, Austria and
Italy. It can be asserted with absolute truth that there was
not an aggressive or bellicose feeling or aim existing
among members of what came to be called the Triple
Entente. The three Powers forming this Entente desired

nothing more than to work out peacefully their respective
destinies, without giving offence or causing injury to any
party of the Triple Alliance.   Had Germany appreciated
this, and had she reciprocated these amicable sentiments,
and recognised that the creation of the Triple Entente had
nothing minatory in character, there should have been no
reason why these two European groups should not have
existed side by side, and should not have, when required,
coalesced to stamp out the sparks in those regions of
Europe where conflagrations are engendered.   I am by
no means overstating the case for the Triple Entente when
I assert that unless the Powers composing it were exposed
to aggression, or to a wilful invasion of cherished interests
and rights, they were resolved that peace should be
maintained throughout Europe.   It was indeed their hope,
though not perhaps their expectation, that, as time
proceeded, a general unity of all the Great Powers might
eventually be attained.

"Germany, however, was persuaded that the Triple
Entente was established with a jealous intention of cir-
cumscribing her progressive activity and was misled by
information that secret agreements to that end existed
between France, Russia, and Great Britain ; while the
rivalry and eventual antagonism between Russia and
Austria Hungary in regard to Balkan affairs, introduced
fresh elements of discord and distrust."

This statement has been quoted at length since it
represents a fair opinion of the purposes and scope of
the Triple Entente.   It is indeed true that the German
Government were much misled by their Secret Service
and that their particular spy in the Russian Embassy
in London provided them with information of the
most alarmist nature.   It is probable also that M.
Iswolsky's own aim in negotiating an Asiatic Agreement with England was not merely to secure his flank

but to assure himself British diplomatic support in
Europe.[1]   Many Russians imagined also that the
Convention was desired in England simply and solely
as a weapon of defence against Germany.   Even the
Germans themselves do not contend that the Ententes
possessed any specifically aggressive character.   " You
may," writes Bethmann Hollweg, " call it ' encirclement,' ' balance of power,' or what you will, but the
object aimed at and eventually attained was no other
than the welding of a serried and supreme combination
of states for obstructing Germany, by diplomatic
means at least, in the full development of her growing
power." [2]   It is difficult to contradict, but easy to
qualify, this statement.

(2)

The instructions which Nicolson had received from
the Cabinet were definite enough.   He was to remove
from Anglo-Russian relations the three points of friction represented by Persia, Thibet and Afghanistan.
As regards Persia, he was to secure the formal recognition by Russia of the principle of Persian independence and integrity and a definition of the spheres in
which Great Britain and Russia were respectively to
formulate self-denying clauses.   With respect to
Afghanistan, his instructions were to secure a formal
acknowledgment on the part of Russia that that
country was of special interest to Great Britain ; that
no Russian agents were to penetrate into the dominions
of the Amir ; and that Great Britain should be the

[1] But not to the degree implied in Taube's *Politique Russe d'avant guerre*,
p. 140.

[2] Bethmann Hollweg, *Reflections on the World War*, p. 12.   English edition.

sole intermediary through which the external affairs of
Afghanistan should be conducted. As to Thibet, he
was, as we have already seen, to obtain a full recognition of our predominant position and an engagement
on the part of Russia to abstain from any interference,
direct or indirect, in the affairs of that country. He
secured all these objectives.

The negotiations lasted, with but few intermissions,
for fifteen months, from June of 1906 to August of
1907. Nicolson adopted the methods of a humane
and highly skilled dentist dealing with three painful
teeth. He would work for a bit on Afghanistan,
proceeding delicately but firmly ; at the first wince of
pain, he would close the cavity with anodynes, cotton
wool and gutta percha, and proceed, at the next sitting,
with Thibet. He was enabled by these methods to win
the entire confidence of M. Iswolsky, and gradually to
bring his three tasks to a simultaneous state of readiness
without at any moment having jabbed the nerve.

The Thibetan negotiations lasted from June 7 of
1906 to January 15 of 1907, by which date they reached
a stage where only a few final touches were required.
Three main difficulties arose. The Russians were unwilling to accept our formula by which we claimed a
predominant position in regard to the external relations
of the country. They were unwilling also to renounce
the right of sending Buddhist pilgrims and scientific
missions to Lhassa. And they objected to the British
occupation of the Chumbi Valley. These difficulties
were met in a conciliatory spirit and the reluctant
compromise was embodied in a Convention which is
a masterpiece of drafting.[1]

[1] *See* Appendix III.

The Thibetan negotiations proved the simplest, and indeed the most durable, of the three subjects of discussion. The early stages of the Afghanistan negotiations proceeded with equal facility. Almost from the first the Russian Government recognised that Afghanistan " lay outside the Russian sphere of influence," and their efforts were concentrated on obtaining from the British Government assurances of non-intervention in Afghan affairs. It was difficult to formulate these assurances in such a way as not unduly to tie the hands of the Government of India in the event of frontier disturbances. The Afghanistan negotiations were dropped for the moment while Nicolson and Iswolsky applied themselves to the far more complicated question of Persia.

For more than thirty years the Government of India had been obsessed by two menaces. The first was that Russia might establish herself on the Persian Gulf, and the second that Russian influence might penetrate to the province of Seistan—the eastern province of Persia contiguous to the Indian frontier. Lord Curzon, in his famous despatch of September 21, 1899, had laid it down as an axiom that " the Government of India could not contemplate without dismay the prospect of Russian neighbourhood in Eastern and Southern Persia." There were, according to Lord Curzon, only two means open by which this danger could be exorcised. The first was Anglo-Russian co-operation in re-organising Persia as an independent State. " We cannot rely," Lord Curzon commented, " on written pledges to safeguard the future of Persia. . . . Russia is interested not in the reform of Persia but in her decay. In the background of her ambitions is the

vision of a country and a people falling from inherent
debility into her grasp." There remained, therefore,
as the second alternative, the division of Persia into
spheres of interest. This policy would also have its
disadvantages. In any such delimitation the northern
zone, including the capital, would " become a Russian
proconsulate." Nor would such an agreement regarding Persia prevent Russia from pressing onwards
to Baghdad—" an issue which we should regard with
scarcely inferior repugnance." In spite of these dangers, however, Lord Curzon recommended that the
experiment was worth trying.

Nicolson approached the Persian problem therefore
solely from the point of view of the defence of India.
He explained his attitude in a characteristically frank
and lucid passage in his Narrative :

" The point which I desired to have specifically settled
before I opened the negotiations was what were to be the
limits of the prospective British sphere in Persia. This
was a matter of political and military importance and one
which principally concerned India. So far as I understood
the question it would be necessary to obtain the recognition by Russia of a certain specified area in Persia in which
she engaged to have no concern and which she abandoned
entirely to British influence and enterprise. From our
point of view we desired to define a sphere which would
protect the vulnerable portion of India from any Russian
aggression or encroachment. Such a region would
naturally remain a portion of Persian territory under the
sovereignty of the Shah, and all that we desired was that
Russia should recognise our special and exclusive interest
in it. This was a perfectly legitimate desire, and it did not
in any way impair or modify the sovereign rights of
Persia. . . . Our Indian authorities were of opinion that it

would be advisable to restrict our share to an area which, in case of necessity, we should be in a position to defend; and that it would be unwise to extend our obligations over too great a stretch of country, the defence of which would, in certain possible eventualities, place an undue strain upon our military resources. I desire to mention this point, as in subsequent criticisms of the final arrangement certain complaints were made that we had contented ourselves with too modest and circumscribed an area, and had been too generous to Russia in our concessions to her. We secured all that our competent authorities considered it necessary or prudent to secure : neither more nor less. It is quite possible that had we asked for a wider area in constituting our sphere, Russia would have raised no difficulties : but we considered, and I venture to think rightly considered, that we obtained all that was necessary for the proper protection of the Indian frontiers in that region."

An opportunity for defining the British zone was afforded in September of 1906 in connection with a joint Anglo-Russian loan which was then being made to Persia. Nicolson said something to M. Iswolsky about a line from Birjand to Bunder Abbas. The Russian Foreign Minister showed some irritation : he stated quite frankly that the military party in Russia would be disinclined to surrender so important a strategical asset as Seistan without substantial compensations. "I am afraid," Nicolson reported, "that if we insist on a preliminary and immediate recognition of the Birjand-Bunder Abbas line, we may frighten him off the whole question." It was agreed, therefore, to drop Persia for the moment and to proceed with other subjects of discussion.

It was clear that some lubricant would be required if the wheels were not to be clogged by the opposition of the Russian General Staff and other critics of M. Iswolsky's policy. "In our negotiations with France," Nicolson explained, "we had something substantial to surrender, and which she eagerly desired, namely our position in Morocco. In the present case we are not in a position, either in Persia, Afghanistan or Thibet to make any great concessions, or, as our hostile critics say, any concessions at all." It was for this reason that in November of 1906 some hope was held out to the Russians that we might be prepared to consider widening the scope of the negotiations so as to include the Near and Far East. On November 28 Sir Charles Hardinge informed M. Poklewsky, Counsellor of the Russian Embassy, that even as regards the Dardanelles "we should be glad to consider any proposals that Russia might submit." Nicolson found M. Iswolsky "beaming with pleasure" over this intimation. He described it as "a great evolution in our relations and a historical event." The atmosphere from that moment became more favourable. The opposition of the Russian Staff diminished. An amicable and expectant pause ensued from November to February, during which M. Iswolsky proceeded with his negotiations with Japan supplementary to the Treaty of Portsmouth. Nicolson was not wholly satisfied by this delay. "Iswolsky," he wrote on December 5, "keeps his eye constantly fixed on the Berlin thermometer and will carefully note any change in the temperature." The interval was employed by the Ambassador in getting into touch with every section of Russian society and in combating the prejudices which still survived.

(3)

He was fully occupied. The following extracts, taken at random from his diary, illustrate the variety of his interests and occupations :

" *November* 10, 1906. Received King's birthday visits. Called on Schwanenbach who is still hopeful and confident. *Daily News* correspondent came to see me with information he had received from a man in the Ministry that Iswolsky was discussing with Berlin some arrangement regarding Poland, the Balkans, and the *status quo* in the Far East, to act as a counterpoise to the possible Anglo-Russian understanding. I think it is quite possible that something of this nature may be contemplated. It would fall in very well with Austrian and German views and ease Iswolsky's fears as to our discussions. I have always thought that Iswolsky will later suggest some ' compensatory advantages ' for Russia outside the questions we are treating. I think I must try to ascertain from him whether he did not discuss above-mentioned questions at Berlin. The correspondent was too stupid to see the bearing of the information he had received, but it gives me a line which I might follow up."

" *November* 11. A gloomy snowy day. Floating ice on the Neva. Big luncheon at Schoen's to bid Aehrenthal farewell. Met General Jacobi there,—a pleasant man. Then on to the Club, the usual old fogies, generals and Grand Dukes,—very useless and dull. Had a long visit from Japanese Minister. He tells me that Iswolsky declared at Berlin and Paris that Russia intended to abide by and recognise the consequences created by the late war. We discussed the possible revival of the Dreikaiserbund. Aehrenthal has had exceptional honours heaped upon him by the Emperor, who had a long private conversation with him of over an hour. I expect they chiefly discussed Poland and the Balkans."

" *November* 12. Saw Iswolsky, who had nothing to give me. He lamented difficulties he was having with Japanese over the fisheries question. Prince Dolgorouki called, my old Tehran friend. He has a high position at Court, and talked freely as to the excellent organisation of the Revolutionaries. He was of opinion that the movement was by no means checked or modified, and he was emphatic in asserting that the revolution was not political but social. This is quite true. He is of opinion that the Emperor should take the risk and come up for the winter. Altogether he was a little pessimistic and not enthusiastic about Stolypin."

" *November* 13. Wallace had a long talk with Witte, but chiefly on the past. Witte considered that the real revolution existed during October, November and December of 1905, and collapsed in the latter month owing to the failure of the Moscow rising. He explained that the troops at the disposal of the Government were insufficient and that they could not get troops back from Siberia owing to the railway strike and dislocation. The Government were bewildered and feeble, and the public had gone ' mad.' He doubted whether such a situation would easily arise again. He lamented reactionary and mystical spirit of Empress, who had a bad influence on the Tsar. We had many Russians to dinner ; they were agitated and pessimistic. Persian reformers are making difficulties about our loan."

Amid all thse politics, Nicolson was careful not to neglect the social obligations which formed so absurd an element in the old diplomacy. Night after night the porter would don a gold-laced uniform and a huge beadle hat. He would thump with a golden mace upon the floor as the guests arrived. They would stream up the scarlet staircase between a double row of hired footmen standing like zanies in their powder and state liveries. The guests themselves were only a degree less gorgeously arrayed. The women carried tiaras on their heads and were dressed by Worth and Paquin. The men wore diamond stars upon their breasts, and their shirtfronts were slashed by blue or scarlet ribbons affixed invisibly but magnificently to their braces. There would be orchids and printed menu cards stamped with the royal arms in gold ; and much expensive food and much expensive wine and a discreet hum of affable conversation. Nicolson himself was curiously gay and simple at such functions. He had none of the strut and swagger which so often affects small men when they are feeling grand. His one anxiety was lest the guests might overstay their welcome. As eleven o'clock approached he would flip the air with a silk handkerchief as a signal for them to leave. They found this eccentricity engaging. Only on very formal occasions were the guests allowed to stay after 11.45. The following figures in Nicolson's diary for June 1, 1907 : " Grand Duke Vladimir and Grand Duchess dined here. Forty people. They played bridge till well after midnight. Otherwise a pleasant evening."

The Nicolsons, as the years passed, became extremely popular in Russian society. He was so gay, they felt, and she so gentle and so unpretentious. The food was the best in St. Petersburg, and one could leave there early after dinner and go on to somewhere amusing. Moreover, the Ambassador displayed such evident liking for them all, had succumbed so completely to that attractive form of charlatanism known as " le charme slav." He appreciated, even, the frequency and readiness with which Russians become overtly insane. " The Grand Duke Constantine," he wrote to his wife during one of her rare absences, " the nice one, has gone cracky—a pity—the result of being a poet without a poet's brain. Do you remember that curly-headed Princess S. . . . with a husband whose eyelids drooped in an unpleasant manner ? He has gone mad too. I am still sane."

The internal situation meanwhile was becoming comparatively normal. The second Duma assembled on March 5 of 1907, and its members were, as Stolypin informed Nicolson, " of an even lower intellectual level than their predecessors." On May 24 the Prime Minister made to the Duma an important statement on agrarian policy, in which he sketched a scheme by which the peasants would be enfranchised from the tyranny of the village commune and would be enabled to acquire portions of the State and appanage lands. The Duma did not understand or appreciate the importance of these proposals. It was clear that if a workable representative body was to be secured the electoral law would have to be drastically amended. On June 16 the second Duma was dissolved and a new electoral law, which gave predominance to the landowners and middle classes, was promulgated by Imperial decree. " I trust," Nicolson wrote, " that this is not going to be the prelude to any reactionary measures." His fears were not entirely unjustified. M. Stolypin, who had many enemies at Court, was obliged to make concessions to autocracy. The great gain, however, was that order was being re-established. The following extract is from Nicolson's diary for August 16, 1907 :

"*August* 16. Called on Stolypin. Found him in his zareba : the garden is surrounded by a high palissade and

triple rows of barbed wire entanglements, besides armies
of mounted and foot gendarmes. He was in capital
health and more hopeful as to the future than I have ever
seen him before. He considered what he termed ' the
revolution ' was rapidly spending its forces, and that the
great mass of the people were tired of politics and
agitation."

M. Stolypin, as events proved, was right. Outrages diminished. People began to work. Nicolson
during that summer of 1907, would walk on to his
balcony and look across with satisfaction to where the
chimneys of the Putiloff Works streamed their smoke
across the Neva. Things were improving. And yet,
in that summer air, there hung above the capital a
sense of oppression. Policemen would peep cautiously around the corner of the Winter Palace. An
atmosphere of fear, suspicion and delation brooded
over the saddened town, straining the nerves of all but
the indifferent, giving to the very cabs the sound of
tumbrils.

It may well have been this hidden unhealthiness,
this constantly imagined inflammation, that induced
the Ambassador's youngest son (at that time an under-
graduate) to behave that August in a most unfortunate
manner. There had been much talk in the Chancery
of spies and midnight burglars, and the gummed slips
which would be affixed overnight to the official cup-
boards were morning after morning found to have
been broken. The Ambassador's son woke one night
at the sound of some sharp instrument passing and
repassing across the door which led from his bedroom
into the archive-room. He turned on the light and
listened. There could be no mistake ; someone with

a chisel was feeling very carefully along the outer side of the door. He crept from his room, and passed silently through his father's dressing-room with the purpose of arousing one of the secretaries who lived on the other side of the house. The Ambassador, who was a light sleeper, woke and asked what was the matter. He was delighted by the prospect of an adventure, and instructed his son to creep round the back quarters to the secretaries' rooms, while he himself (a frail figure in a dressing gown) kept guard at the staircase exit to the Chancery. " In this way," he said, " we shall catch the fellow between two fires." It took some ten minutes, however, before the under-graduate was able to navigate the back quarters and rouse the resident secretary. Mr. Neville Henderson, at that time Attaché to the Embassy, was a young man of courage, beauty and immense muscular development. He seized his life-preserver and crept towards the waiting-room which preceded the Chancery. Unfor-tunately, however, the Ambassador, who was (as has been said) an impatient man in little things, had got bored waiting on the staircase and had determined to investigate for himself. He also, therefore, in complete darkness crept towards the waiting-room. There was a shout, a crash, a gurgle. " Animal," yelled Neville Henderson, " je vous tiens." The undergraduate, who had remained behind, rushed to the switch and turned it on. He observed his father struggling violently in the hands of Neville Henderson, who had grabbed him by the throat. There followed an embarrassed and somewhat perfunctory examination of the Chancery and adjoining archive-room. It was found that a large brown cat had been locked into the latter room and was trying to get out by the outer door. Next evening Nicolson, somewhat inconsiderately, told the story to his Austrian colleague. In a few hours it was known all over St. Petersburg and beyond. Neville Henderson, who was a shy young man and had an affection for his chief, was much embarrassed. And it was years before the undergraduate could recollect the incident without the colour flaming to his cheeks.

(4)

Undeterred, although somewhat shaken, by this accident, Nicolson embarked upon the final stages of his negotiations. Our apparent willingness to meet Russian desires in regard to the Straits and the Near East had done much to silence the opposition to M. Iswolsky's policy, and even Count Witte informed Nicolson in February that " the foreign policy of Germany was so erratic, so impulsive and so eminently selfish " that Russia must be careful not to be " cajoled by the allurements which emanate from Berlin." [1] " While admitting," Nicolson reported, " that many motives impel the Emperor and his Government to draw nearer to Germany and to accept as an unfortunate necessity the alliance with France, it seems to me that more powerful factors than personal sympathy will counteract the tendency to drift too much into the German orbit." These factors he defined as the determination of the Russian Government no longer to be inveigled by German prompting into further adventures in the Far East, and as their " desire to husband their resources and keep their hands free for recovering their position as a European Power."

[1] B.D., vol. iv. No. 251.

British public opinion also was becoming reconciled to the idea of an Anglo-Russian understanding. It is true that a few intelligent and instructed critics urged upon Sir Edward Grey the danger of trusting to Russian good faith. The most effective of these critics was Earl Percy, and Sir Edward wrote privately to Nicolson informing him of the warnings he had received. Nicolson replied in a private letter of May 8 :

> " I do not share Percy's views. Once we have come to an agreement with Russia I do not consider it likely that she will disown her engagements. . . . If we regard Russia as incurably smitten with bad faith, it would, I admit, be useless to make any agreements with her and we should have to resign ourselves to a continuance of the former unsatisfactory relations. But looking at the circumstances present and future I think it wise to come to an agreement."

The negotiations therefore continued. It was decided not to enlarge their scope beyond the original three subjects in order not to touch the interests of third Powers. In this way all formulas regarding the Straits and the Far East were postponed to a later date. The controversy centred, during those early months of 1907, upon Persia and Afghanistan.

By April 2 agreement had been reached as to the delimitation of the respective spheres of influence in Persia, and the Russians had consented to Seistan, and indeed the whole region covering the Perso-Afghan, as well as the Indo-Persian, frontier, being included in the British sphere. The British Government, on the other hand, had been obliged to abandon to Russia the whole northern zone including not only Tehran itself but the important trade route from Khanikin to Kasvin as well as the towns of Ispahan and Yezd. The Persian Government had meanwhile got wind of the negotiations and became seriously alarmed. Sir Cecil Spring Rice, who on leaving Russia had been appointed Minister to Tehran, warned the Foreign Office of the " fear and indignation " which would be aroused by what would " simply be regarded as a Treaty of partition." The Foreign Office replied in pained reproof that the Treaty provided for the independence and integrity of Persia and was in fact merely a self-denying ordinance by which Persia could only benefit. The Persians, who for generations had maintained themselves by playing on the rivalry between Russia and Great Britain, were not in the least solaced by this explanation.

The next problem was that of the Persian Gulf. The development of this question is best recorded in Nicolson's own words. He writes in his Narrative as follows :

" We were anxious that in the Convention an article should be inserted by which Russia would recognise our special interests in the maintenance of the *status quo* in the Persian Gulf. On this point I wrote on June 19, 1907, to Sir Charles Hardinge : ' There is one point which may cause difficulty, and that is the Gulf. In the first place I have no doubt that Iswolsky would require to be informed as to the precise meaning which we attach to the phrase *status quo*. There is, however, a more serious difficulty which he may raise. He is, as you know, exceedingly anxious to avoid giving offence to Germany, and he assured Berlin that our negotiations would not touch upon the Baghdad Railway, and he will have seen from our memorandum that the Railway might, if entirely in German hands, be considered a disturbance of the *status quo* in the Gulf. He would then, I feel pretty sure, consider that if he were to subscribe to an acknowledgment of our special interests in the maintenance of the *status quo*, he would indirectly bind himself to opposing the Baghdad Railway on the ground that British interests were imperilled. He would consequently expose himself to reproaches from Berlin for not having kept his word, and for having assented to a principle which in present circumstances Germany might assert was in reality directed against her railway project. We must be exceedingly careful with Iswolsky just now and not alarm him. Our accord with Spain and our views in regard to the Baghdad Railway have disturbed his mind : and he fears, I think, that we are weaving webs and forging rings round Germany, and he will not allow himself to be drawn into any combinations, or place his signature to any document, which might, in his opinion, be aimed, however indirectly, against Germany.'

" I endeavoured, however, to induce M. Iswolsky to agree to the insertion of the article I have mentioned, but without success. On July 4, 1907, I wrote : ' It would be impossible to induce Iswolsky to put his signature to any document which he considered would cause umbrage at Berlin. Both the personal and official factors in the case weigh heavily with him. As to the personal factor, he has always as a warning before him the fate of M. Delcassé ; and you will see that in his aide memoire he naïvely indicated that. As to the official factor he takes as the bed-rock of his policy to take no step which might in any way cause any friction in the relations between Russia and Germany. M. Iswolsky thought we were leading him on to delicate and dangerous ground, and he shrank from taking any step in the direction which we had indicated. I am quite sure that I should not have overcome his objections. If France had intervened that would have increased his apprehensions, as he would have thought that we were both endeavouring to induce him to enter into some combinations, especially at a time when he was disturbed by the Spanish agreement, and by our views as to the Baghdad Railway.' This question of the *status quo* in the Gulf was eventually settled by Sir Edward Grey writing me an official despatch on the subject, which was appended to the Convention and published with it."

By such " artifices de rédaction " the Gulf question was turned. At the end of July Nicolson paid a flying visit to London in order personally to discuss the questions which were still in suspense. He returned in August and the several Conventions were put into final form. On August 25 all seemed ready. The consent of the Emperor had been obtained subject to the unanimous approval of the Council of Ministers. At the last moment, however, a hitch occurred. The meeting of the Cabinet lasted till 2 a.m. and unexpected opposition developed. A majority of the Ministers objected to M. Iswolsky having agreed to the suppression of a clause in the Afghanistan agreement in which Great Britain undertook not to interfere in the internal affairs of Afghanistan or to annex or occupy Afghan territory. This opposition was due largely to the suspicions instilled into the mind of the Emperor by the tendencious rumours forwarded to him by William II. Nicolson replied that His Majesty's Government would only consent to the insertion of this clause if Russia consented to omit the clause which then figured as Article V. by which both parties agreed, in the event of any modification occurring in the political status of Afghanistan, " to enter into a friendly exchange of views with the object of ensuring the maintenance of the equilibrium in Central Asia."

Somewhat to his surprise, the Russian Government accepted this compromise, and the whole Convention was signed at the Russian Foreign Office at 4 p.m. on August 31.

(5)

The strain of the last few weeks had been tremendous. "How I hate politics," he wrote to his wife, "yet how I love them." Certain members of the Chancery fell ill. "My poor Chancery," he wrote, "is very over-worked. They are very busy, but very good. The way young men tumble down nowadays surprises me. They seem to have no go, and collapse when they snuffle. Ichabod for England." In writing to thank Sir Edward Grey for his "unfailing support and consideration," Nicolson reviewed the results with satisfaction :

> "I do not think that the opponents can knock many holes in the Convention, and if it be loyally executed a great improvement should come over our relations with Russia. I wish that M. Iswolsky would still his heart and stiffen his back against Press criticisms. At present he is over-anxious to propitiate the *Novoe Vremya*. He has acted most loyally to us throughout and I have not detected the slightest attempt to take an unfair advantage. The game has been played most fairly. I was pleased that you sent him a kindly message. He was much gratified."

Congratulations poured in. King Edward wrote that these negotiations and the part he had played at Algeciras "placed him in the front rank of our diplomatists." Sir Edward Grey was even more enthusiastic. "Since I have been at the F.O.," he wrote, "I can say without qualification that in everything in which you have been engaged you have made

a success. I wish that you could be multiplied at will
so as to be available at once in every place where there
were difficulties." Lord Morley wrote as follows :
" For patience, resource and tenacity the sight of your
work has been a liberal education to me. I should
guess that this is one of the most skilful performances
in the records of British diplomacy. . . . We owe you
a great debt—I mean the country."

Nicolson's own conception of his achievement was
more modest. He wrote to his wife directly after
signature. " We signed this evening. I telegraphed
the fact to the King, and have just had his reply. Very
civil. The chef arrived back yesterday and I am glad
to say that the new footman has entered on his duties.
The porter's wife has had a little girl—she was moved
to the hospital . . ." " I can say without conceit,"
he wrote the next day, " at least I can say so to you—
that I have had a considerable part in framing these
agreements. I hope that they are of real benefit to the
country. It is a great responsibility taking even a
minor part in arrangements of this magnitude and I
confess that occasionally, when examining the things
from *all* points of view, I have some qualms. They
do not keep me awake at night. I am sure that the
best has been done in the circumstances and the only
alternative was no agreement at all. We shall be well
pelted with criticisms, but this we can bear."

The Convention was not published till September
and the full blast of criticism only burst in February
of 1908. It was on February 6 that Lord Curzon
launched a full-dress attack upon the Convention in
the House of Lords. He called it " the most far-
reaching and the most important Treaty which had

been concluded by the British Government during the past fifty years." He stated that we had obtained nothing in Afghanistan and that the Thibetan Convention was a surrender. In Persia he contended that " we had thrown away the efforts of our diplomacy and our trade for more than a century." We had handed over to Russia not only the trade route from Baghdad but also the important marts of Ispahan and Yezd. We had not safeguarded our position in the Gulf : and we had exposed ourselves to bitter criticism in the Islamic world. Similar strictures were made in the House of Commons. The Treaty was, however, ratified and entered into force. It was faithfully observed by Great Britain. It was not faithfully observed by Russia. And the Amir of Afghanistan, to say nothing of the Persian Government, refused for one moment to recognise the instrument as applicable to their countries.

The French, for their part, were delighted. The Germans adopted an attitude of reserve. Prince Bülow instructed the Press to treat the matter calmly. " No one," commented the German representative in St. Petersburg, " will reproach England for such a policy : one can only admire the skill with which she has carried out her plans. These plans need not necessarily be ascribed to any anti-German tendency, yet Germany is the country which is most affected by the Agreement." The Emperor William minuted this despatch as follows : " Yes, when taken all round, it is aimed at us." [1]

But by that time M. Iswolsky was taking a cure at Marienbad, and Nicolson was enjoying a damper holiday in Ireland.

[1] *G.P.* vol. xxv., No. 8537.

X

THE BOSNIAN CRISIS

[1907-1908]

Europe in 1907—Interpretation of the Near Eastern Crisis—Artificial nature
of the Anglo-Russian Convention—M. Iswolsky's policy—His miscon-
ceptions—The Baltic and North Sea Agreements, 1907—Freiherr von
Aehrenthal—Macedonian reforms, 1907-1908—The Sandjak Railway—
Russian indignation—The Reval visit, June 1908—Sir C. Hardinge and
M. Iswolsky—Effect of the Reval visit—German apprehensions—
Secret Austro-Russian negotiations—The Young Turk revolution—
The Buchlau visit, September 15, 1908—The annexation of Bosnia and
Herzegovina, October 6, 1908—German attitude—Effect on M. Iswol-
sky's position—Proposals for a Conference—Iswolsky's encouragement
of the Serbs—Nicolson's audience with the Tsar—His increased distrust
of Germany.

(1)

THE War of 1914-1918 was caused by a false conception of international values. In every European State
the generations which succeeded each other from 1850
onwards were taught that national egoism was an
honourable, and indeed a necessary thing. It was
considered " patriotic " to desire that one's country
should be larger, richer, and above all more powerful
than any other country. It was not considered patriotic to desire that one's own country should on every
occasion set an example of unselfishness, humanity and
intelligence. It thus came about that all but a small
minority of scientists and intellectuals approached the
problem of civilisation in a competitive and not in a
co-operative spirit. In organised communities this
competitive spirit can be controlled by the authority
of law. The European community of nations was not

an organised community, and for them the ultimate appeal was not to law but to force.

The Bosnian crisis of 1907-1909 affords a unique " specimen " for the study of this uncivilised state of mind. Not only does it constitute an almost exact parallel to the conditions which repeated themselves in 1914, but each protagonist in the drama conducted himself with consistent fidelity to type. The competitive instinct was throughout the dominant factor. Throughout the crisis the dominant appeal was an appeal to force. The ostensible causes of the controversy—whether or no Austria should annex two Slav provinces which she already occupied—whether or no she should crush Serbia's resistance to this procedure by a " preventative " war—were of small importance compared to the essential issues. Those issues can be summarised as follows. The Austro-Hungarian Empire, which contained a large number of Slav subjects, was threatened with disruption. The Slav minorities were receiving encouragement from their kinsmen in Serbia, and the Serbians looked for support to Russia. The latter, having failed disastrously as an Asiatic Imperialist, was now anxious to regain her shattered prestige by coming forward as a European Liberator, by emerging once more as the protector of Slav and Orthodox elements in the Balkan peninsula, and thus indirectly of the Slav and Orthodox populations subject to Austro-Hungarian rule. The Austrian Government considered it essential to nip this dangerous theory in the bud. They determined, before it was too late, to demonstrate to the Slavs that Russia would not, when it came to the point, be strong enough to assist them. In its essence, therefore, the

Near Eastern crisis was provoked by an attempt on the part of Austria to contest the claim of Russia to protect the Southern Slavs.

Certain further aspects should also be noted. The German Government, had they been wise, would have foreseen that this conflict between Slav and Teuton would eventually drive Russia into the arms of the Western Powers. Their policy was based on two misconceptions. They were in the first place unduly alarmed lest Austria might desert them and join the Triple Entente. They were in the second place obsessed by the idea that by a display of force they could frighten France and Russia out of their new friendship with England. It was owing to these misconceptions that they encouraged Austria and drove her to her doom.

(2)

The signature of the Anglo-Russian Convention did not, by any means, imply the conclusion of an Anglo-Russian understanding. The Convention was regarded by M. Iswolsky as a purely negative insurance and one which should not be allowed to affect his relations with the Central Powers. " If matters," Nicolson recorded in his Narrative, " had been more tactfully handled by Germany and Austria I have little doubt that the general trend of Russian policy would have been most benevolent and intimate towards Berlin and Vienna and that Russia would not gradually have drifted into a position which forced her to lean upon France and Great Britain and which eventually prevented any close or intimate understanding between her and the Triple Alliance."

Even as an Asiatic Agreement the Anglo-Russian Convention was a feeble and artificial growth. It was popular neither in England nor in Russia. It was cordially disliked by the Government of India as well as by all the Russian and British officials on the spot. It proved unworkable and damaging in Persia, and it was never recognised by the Amir of Afghanistan. It was in essence an attempt to reconcile two fundamentally divergent attitudes—to reconcile the Slav tendency towards disintegration with the Anglo-Saxon tendency towards preservation—to combine the British policy of creating a chain of self-supporting and independent States on the borders of India with the Russian policy of " spontaneous infiltration." It was a regrettable alliance between the sand-dune and the sea.

Had the Anglo-Russian Convention remained confined to Asia (as many desired it to remain confined) it would unquestionably have led to a permanent estrangement between England and Russia. It was the violent attitude adopted by Austria and Germany in the Bosnian crisis which transformed what was a negative arrangement applicable only to Asia into a positive understanding applicable mainly to Europe. Even as the Anglo-French understanding had been quickened into life by the mistakes of German diplomacy at Algeciras, so also was the Anglo-Russian understanding vitalised by the mistakes of Austro-German diplomacy in the Near Eastern crisis.

Nicolson was himself well aware of the artificial nature of the Convention which he had concluded. He warned the Foreign Office that it was " not the natural result of ordinary evolution." " Until," he wrote, " the material as well as the political interests of the two Powers are closely connected, I do not consider that the foundations of an understanding are firmly or solidly laid." [1] In a private letter to Sir Edward Grey he was even more explicit : " The understanding with Russia is in its early infancy and will require, for reasons which I need not explain, careful nurture and treatment. Any serious check to this infant growth may kill it before it has advanced in years, and its disappearance would doubtless eventually react upon our relations with France." [2]

(3)

Alexander Iswolsky, realising that the Anglo-Russian Convention was not very popular in St. Petersburg, determined to establish his social and political position by winning diplomatic victories in other fields. His restless eye fixed upon the two questions of the Aland Islands and the Straits as those which would assure for himself the title of Count and for his country increased prestige among the Powers of Europe. Both these questions were ill chosen.

By the Convention annexed to the Treaty of Paris of March 30, 1856, Russia was not allowed to fortify the Aland archipelago off the coast of Sweden. On October 26, 1905, Norway had declared herself independent of Sweden, and this rupture of the union between the two countries affected the international agreements governing the *status quo* in the Baltic.

---

[1] Annual report for 1908.

[2] Private letter to Sir E. Grey of July 19, 1908.

M. Iswolsky determined to take advantage of this fresh
deal to secure for Russia the abrogation of the servitudes imposed upon her in regard to the Aland Islands.
On August 3, 1907, a meeting took place between the
Russian and German Emperors at Swinemünde. M.
Iswolsky on that occasion handed Prince Bülow a
secret protocol by which he hoped, in return for
rendering the Baltic a *mare clausum* to all but the
riverain States, to obtain Germany's support in inducing Sweden to accept the abrogation of the Aland
servitudes. He suggested slyly to Prince Bülow that
such an agreement might be " franchement désagréable
aux Anglais." [1] Prince Bülow (who never seems to
have taken very warmly to M. Iswolsky) replied that
he would give the matter every consideration. On
August 30, 1907 (on the very day before the signature
of the Anglo-Russian Convention) M. Iswolsky received from Prince Bülow a revised draft which, while
providing for a Russo-German guarantee of the *status
quo* in the Baltic, expressly excluded the Aland Islands
from the scope of the negotiations. The Germans at
the same time allowed it to be known in Paris and
London that these secret discussions were in progress.
M. Iswolsky became alarmed, and in order to render
the whole business more respectable he suggested that
Sweden and Norway should be admitted to the negotiations. Prince Bülow agreed. The Swedish Government for their part refused absolutely to discuss the
Aland question, and M. Iswolsky was thus obliged to
rest content with a perfectly meaningless document
guaranteeing the Baltic *status quo*. " Iswolsky "—so

---

[1] For the only clear account of these obscure negotiations *see* Taube, *La
politique Russe d'avant guerre*, pp. 123 ff.

wrote Hardinge to Nicolson—" did not tell you or Bompard about the Baltic agreement until after Metternich had informed us. Consequently the French are angry." M. Iswolsky's first attempt at laurel-gathering was not, therefore, successful : his second attempt was disastrous.

Article 63 of the Treaty of Berlin of July 13, 1878, had confirmed the stipulations of the former Treaties of London (1871) and Paris (1856) under which the Straits of the Dardanelles and Bosphorus were closed to vessels of war. M. Iswolsky determined to secure the cancellation of these provisions. In giving effect to this conclusion he laboured under two misconceptions.

In the first place he misunderstood the ideas and ideals of his own countrymen. As a young man he had lived much in Pan-Slav circles and had then absorbed the doctrine that the white soul of Russia yearned only after Constantinople. He had for so long been absent from his country that he failed to realise that Russian opinion, in the interval, had changed. The emotions of Russia were no longer centred upon the Church of St. Sophia or upon the revival of the old Byzantine Empire. They were centred upon the Slav races in the Balkans and upon the protection of these races against the oncoming tide of Teutonism. The problem had become one of nationalism rather than one of mysticism ; it had ceased to be religious and had become ethnical. People cared a great deal about the Serbs and very little about Constantinople and the Straits. Iswolsky failed to appreciate this change of attitude.

In the second place M. Iswolsky, as indeed most of

his contemporaries, had never thought out clearly what was meant by this " Freedom of the Straits." Did it mean, not only that Russian ships of war should be allowed out of the Black Sea, but that other ships of war should be allowed in ? Or did it mean that the Russian fleet could go out and in as they chose, whereas the Straits remained firmly barred to all foreign intruders ? His lack of definition on this point was, as we shall see, a further cause of misunderstanding.

His approach to the Straits question was thus obscured from the outset by the mists of imprecision. It was unfortunate for him that his first steps upon this dark and slippery path should have brought him face to face with an antagonist who envisaged his own objectives with the utmost clarity.

(4)

Freiherr von Aehrenthal—an unwieldy man, with heavy hapless jaws, a stubble head of hair, and sad turbot eyes—had been appointed Austrian Minister for Foreign Affairs on October 24, 1906. He was regarded as an authority on Russia.[1] He knew at least that Russia was for the moment incapable of waging war. He determined to exploit this fact for the furtherance of his own position, the prestige of the Dual Empire, and the humiliation of M. Iswolsky. For the moment, he was eminently and lamentably successful.

Sir Edward Grey, who had been much alarmed by

[1] Baron von Aehrenthal was then 54 years of age. He had been Secretary of the Austro-Hungarian Embassy in St. Petersburg from 1878-1883, and 1888-1894, and Ambassador from 1902-1906. He died of pernicious anæmia on February 17, 1912.

the continued disorders in Macedonia,[1] had used every endeavour to induce the Concert of Europe to co-operate in enforcing reforms of an administrative, financial, and judicial character upon the Ottoman Government. His efforts had been frustrated, partly owing to the unwillingness of the German Government to do anything which might offend Abdul Hamid, and partly by the endeavours of Baron von Aehrenthal to create a block of what he termed " the conservative Powers." The Austrian Foreign Minister had in fact made secret attempts to induce Germany, Russia and France to act separately in Macedonia to the exclusion of Great Britain and Italy.[2] The Russian Government informed their British friends of what was being planned, with the result that protests were addressed to Vienna. Baron von Aehrenthal hotly denied that he had ever cherished any such intentions, and at the same time he confessed to the German Ambassador that the " indiscretions " of the Russian Government had placed him in a " most unpleasant

[1] The following are the important dates in the Macedonian question. In June, 1902, the Porte asked the Powers to oblige Bulgaria to dissolve its Macedonian Committee. Russia and Austria, who since the secret Agreement of 1897, had pledged themselves to co-operate in Balkan affairs, replied that reforms must first be introduced. The Sultan promised reforms and appointed Hilmi Pasha as Inspector General. This was insufficient and the two Powers therefore drew up a joint programme of reforms known as the " February programme." In July of 1903 an insurrection broke out in Macedonia which was suppressed in September. The Powers were convinced that the February programme was not enough, and in October, 1903, Austria and Russia drew up the " Muerzsteg programme," the main point of which was the organisation of a gendarmerie under foreign officers. The Sultan evaded most of the items of the Muerzsteg programme and Lord Lansdowne pressed for financial and administrative reforms. Germany was, however, unwilling to join the Concert of Europe in pressing further concessions on the Turkish Government. In 1907 a renewed outburst of comitadji activity again faced the Concert with a crisis. Sir E. Grey pressed for further reforms. It is at this point that the main narrative continues.

[2] G.P., vol. xxii., No. 7676.

position." [1]   He determined therefore to have his revenge.

On January 27, 1908, he informed the Delegations [2] that he had applied to the Porte for sanction to build a railway from Sarajewo through the Sandjak of Novi Bazar to Mitrovitsa.[3]   Such an application was unwise and dishonourable from two points of view.   In the first place it was disloyal to the Concert of Europe to ask for favours from the Porte at a moment when the Powers were endeavouring to exert joint pressure. And in the second place it was disloyal to Russia who relied on the Muerzsteg Agreement[4] to secure that Austria would do nothing of a nature to upset the balance of power in the Balkans.   The Sandjak Railway, which would establish direct communication between Sarajewo and Salonika, was considered, in the words of the *Novoe Vremya*, as aiming at " the Germanisation of the Near East."   In any case it represented an undoubted violation of the spirit of the Muerzsteg Agreement by which, by implication, the Balkans were to be partitioned into zones of Austrian and Russian influence.

M. Iswolsky was personally incensed.   He complained bitterly of Baron von Aehrenthal " having sprung upon him the Sandjak Railway without any warning whatever—a proceeding which had seriously

---

[1] *G.P.*, vol. xxii., No. 7677.

[2] The Delegations, under the constitution of the former Austro-Hungarian Empire, were a deliberative body of the dual monarchy which met annually to discuss matters of high policy affecting both countries.   They represented a sort of " Imperial Conference " of the Austro-Hungarian Empire.

[3] The Iradé sanctioning construction was issued by the Sultan in February, 1908.

[4] *See* note 1 on previous page.

disturbed the *status quo* in the Balkans and shaken all confidence in Austrian policy." " It was clear," M. Iswolsky protested, " that in spite of Baron von Aehrenthal having spent seventeen years in Russia he had not grasped the real feeling towards the Slav populations in the Balkans, since he imagined that there would be a short flare-up in the Russian Press and that Austro-Russian relations would then return once more to their former groove. In this he was entirely mistaken, since the relations between Austria and Russia in connexion with affairs in the Balkans could not be the same again." [1] " His vexation," Nicolson reported, " will doubtless pass away : but his confidence has been shaken : and what is galling to a man of some vanity he feels that he has been in a measure duped." [2] The Emperor Nicolas was even more indignant. Had he not conferred upon the Austrian Foreign Minister the St. Andrew in brilliants ? He received Nicolson in a private audience and launched into a diatribe against the Austrian Foreign Minister :

> " His Majesty knew Baron Aehrenthal very well and had always considered him to be a straightforward gentleman anxious to act in accord with Russia in all Balkan matters. The tortuous course which he had pursued of late showed His Excellency in a different light and it was strange that advent to a high and responsible office should have altered an estimable character." [3]

The Iradé which Baron von Aehrenthal thus obtained for his Sandjak Railway was of no value to him. The

[1] *B.D.*, vol. v., No. 193.
[2] A. N. to Sir E. Grey, Private, February 26, 1908.
[3] *B.D.*, vol. v., No. 217.

Russians countered with a demand for a line from the
Danube to the Adriatic, and in the end the Young
Turk Revolution of July, 1908, disposed for ever not
only of the railway question but also of the question
of Macedonian reform. Baron von Aehrenthal's conduct had, however, far-reaching consequences. M.
Iswolsky informed Count Berchtold, the Austrian
Ambassador in St. Petersburg, that the Sandjak concession was a death-blow to all hopes of Austro-
Russian co-operation in the Balkans. An atmosphere
of suspicion and personal resentment was thus created
from the outset. It was in such an atmosphere that
a meeting was arranged between the Emperor of
Russia and the King of England.

(5)

On Saturday, June 6, 1908, the *Victoria and Albert*,
escorted by the *Minotaur* and the *Achilles*, steamed out
from Portsmouth into an angry sea. It was only when
they reached Kiel that the company was able to
assemble. There were the King and Queen and
Princess Victoria : there were Sir Charles Hardinge,
Sir John French, Sir John Fisher and Arthur Nicolson :
there were the ladies and gentlemen in attendance—
Lady Antrim, Miss Charlotte Knollys, Lord Howe,
Lord Hamilton of Dalziell, Sir Seymour Fortescue :
there was the Chevalier de Martino—" His Majesty's
Marine Painter in Ordinary " ; there was an immense
amount of food. At Kiel they were received by
Prince and Princess Henry of Prussia, and were escorted
by a division of German torpedo boats which turned
and twisted in front of them to the great admiration
of the officers of the Royal Yacht. At 11 a.m. on

Tuesday, June 9, they anchored in the small but tense roadstead of Reval. The Emperor, the Empress, the Dowager Empress, the Tsarevitch, the Grand Duchesses had arrived by train : M. Iswolsky and Stolypin were also present : so was the Queen of the Hellenes. The English and the Russian flags were saluted by a thunder of artillery. King Edward donned the uniform of the Kieff Dragoons. He summoned Arthur Nicolson to his cabin. There were photographs in silver frames, a pot of *lilium speciosum*, and a strong smell of expensive cigars. King Edward, ill at ease in his tight uniform, reclined in a chintz arm-chair. He asked Nicolson to sit down. He then asked him to explain the present nature and purposes of Russian policy ; the exact names and past records of the Tsar's staff ; the prospects of agriculture in Russia ; the personal relations between M. Iswolsky and M. Stolypin, as well as the personal relations between them and the Empress ; the exact provisions and scope of the Anglo-Russian Convention and what relation, if any, it bore to the Anglo-French Convention and the Franco-Russian Alliance ; whether the Emperor would wear the uniform of the Scots Greys or whether he would appear dressed as a Russian Admiral : what decorations he would wear and in what order : what about the Russian Railways ? whether M. Stolypin spoke French, or German, or even English : what exactly were the present relations between the Government and the Duma ; was the Duma a thing one should mention ? Or not ? The state of Russian finances : the conditions in the army and navy : the progress in education : the names of some of the leading Russian writers, musicians and scientists. Would the Emperor

talk about the Japanese Alliance ? If so, what was the
best thing to say ? Was it a thing to mention ? Or
not ? Would the speeches be at luncheon or at
dinner ? Would Baron Frederickz be content with a
K.C.V.O. ?

Nicolson answered these questions as best he could.
Towards the end of the audience he observed that His
Majesty's eye returned with angered insistence to the
same spot. That spot was the point where (for
Nicolson was also in full uniform) the badge of the
Nova Scotia Baronetcy dangled from his throat.
" What," grumbled King Edward, " is that bauble ? "
Nicolson with some pride explained that was the only
hereditary Order in England. It had been conferred
on his ancestors in 1637. The King contended that
it should not carry precedence over the Bath. Nicolson was obstinate and not in the least conciliatory.
He said that in his opinion it should carry precedence
over any non-hereditary Order. King Edward, at
that, presented him with a large silver inkstand. A
man came to say that the Imperial barge was approaching the *Victoria and Albert*. King Edward placed his
hand on Nicolson's shoulder. " Never," he said,
" wear that bauble again." Nicolson thereafter always
wore that peculiar, and indeed lovely, decoration at
his throat.

The guns boomed again. The Tsar, his wife and
family boarded the *Victoria and Albert*. Everybody
kissed everybody else. The Emperor was gay and at
his ease. Even the Empress, a shy and sulky woman,
inclined to unbend. She walked across the carpeted
deck with that stooping movement adopted by affectionate women who are much taller than their husbands ;

the whites of her eyes were yellow with prolonged dyspepsia : she pointed at things and people with a lace sun-shade. The Tsarevitch went off somewhere and played with Derevenko, his sailor-friend who never left him. The Grand Duchesses, in English school-girl clothes, simpered like English school-girls. The band played national anthems. The officers stood at the salute. King Edward spoke to Stolypin and Iswolsky about the nature and purposes of Russian policy ; the prospects of agriculture ; the pacific aims of the Anglo-Russian Convention ; the marvellous progress made in the Russian railway system ; the improved relations between Russia and Germany ; the gratifying collaboration between the Government and the Duma ; the flourishing state of Russian finances ; the amazing reforms introduced into the army and navy ; all that Stolypin had done for his country at Saratoff ; all that Iswolsky had done for his country at Copenhagen (how well he remembered their conversation there—how often he had thought of it since!); how magnificent the Emperor looked in his uniform of the Scots Greys ; how gratified he was, how really gratified, to meet them.

There was a luncheon that day upon the *Polar Star*, the yacht of the Dowager Empress. There was a banquet that evening upon the *Standart*, the yacht of the Emperor of Russia. The food was bad. They were serenaded afterwards by certain carefully chosen inhabitants of Reval who appeared in a tug. King Edward, who only cared for Puccini, was bored : he fiddled in an abstract manner with the gold bracelet on his left wrist. There were friendly speeches, and each monarch made the other an Admiral of his fleet.

GROUP TAKEN AT REVAL

Figures from left to right: Front row: Lord Howe, Sir Charles Hardinge,
Queen Alexandra, King Edward, Lady Antrim, Miss Knollys, Sir J. Fisher,
Sir Arthur Nicolson, Chevalier de Martino.

At the back: Sir J. French and Count Benckendorff.

On June 10 there was a large luncheon on the *Standart*.
Stolypin expressed to Nicolson his amazement at the
grasp which King Edward had shown of Russian
external and internal policy. " On voit bien," he said,
" que c'est un homme d'état." Nicolson agreed that
he was. On June 11 at 3 a.m. they left for England.
On June 14, a Sunday, they arrived at Port Victoria.
At 10 a.m. there was divine service on board. They
thereafter entered a special train for London.

Sir Charles Hardinge, during that historic meeting,
had held certain conversations with the Russian
Ministers. M. Iswolsky, as usual, had discoursed at
length on the duplicity of Baron von Aehrenthal. He
had stated that it was " imperative that Russia should
act with the greatest prudence towards Germany and
give the latter no cause for complaint, that the improvement of relations between Russia and England
had entailed a corresponding deterioration of the relations between Russia and Germany." They had
spoken vaguely about Macedonia. M. Iswolsky had
said that the two Powers must have a joint railway
policy in Persia. Sir Charles Hardinge had replied
that a junction of the Russian and Indian railway
systems appeared to him somewhat premature. That,
in effect, was all that passed at Reval.[1]

[1] Baron Taube in his interesting book, *La politique Russe d'avant guerre*,
states that M. Iswolsky returned from Reval under the impression that he had
received assurances from the British visitors regarding the Straits. There is
no mention in the official British record of this matter having been raised.
What probably happened was that M. Iswolsky mentioned the Straits and that
Sir Charles Hardinge replied that we were always prepared to discuss that
question in an amicable spirit. By the " Straits," however, Hardinge and
Iswolsky each meant something different. Hardinge meant that the Straits
might be open to everybody : Iswolsky meant that they should be open to
Russia only. Lord Hardinge, who has been consulted on this point, assures
the author that the above is probably a correct interpretation of how the
misunderstanding arose.

And yet (such was the inflammation of international feeling) the German Government were convinced that the Royal meeting represented some important re-grouping of what they were already beginning to call " our adversaries." The following comment occurs in Nicolson's Narrative :

" The German Press has often attributed great political importance to that visit, and has wished to have it believed that secret arrangements were reached which had for their object the ' encircling ' and isolation of Germany. There is no truth in this. The two Sovereigns did not discuss politics at all, and their meeting, with their respective families, was a strictly family reunion. Sir Charles Hardinge and M. Iswolsky had some conversations regarding Macedonia and other matters, but they were merely an interchange of views, and nothing definite was concluded."

This is all very well. It is perfectly true that no agreements whatsoever were concluded at Reval ; but it is also true that the presence of Stolypin and Iswol-sky, the presence of French, Fisher, Hardinge and Nicolson created the inevitable suspicion that there was something more in the visit than a family re-union. The Germans, moreover, were justifiably apprehensive of the effect upon the Emperor Nicolas of King Edward's tact. They had hitherto relied upon the dynastic relation with Russia to keep open the wire between Berlin and St. Petersburg. They had an un-easy suspicion that the Emperor William was a little apt to bother his Russian cousin and to patronise him. There had already been signs of irritation and revolt at Peterhof. King Edward managed these things better. He did not patronise the Tsar : he treated him as a highly successful nephew. The mere fact that he avoided all political questions inspired the timid little autocrat with confidence, gratitude and relief. Stolypin and Iswolsky were also reassured by the circumstance that no awkward questions had been asked, that their British visitors had shown infinite discretion. The Tsar had returned from Bjorkoe and Swinemünde frightened and humiliated : he returned from Reval flattered and reassured. The greatest diplomatic victories are gained by doing nothing : and King Edward, although too superficial to be a statesman, was a supreme diplomatist.

It is not surprising therefore that the Germans, who had taken the Anglo-Russian Convention with comparative calm, were alarmed by the Reval meeting. Even so cautious and unbiased a historian as Erich Brandenburg fixes upon Reval as a turning-point in European diplomacy. The Emperor William was indignant. A few days after the Reval visit he reviewed the Cavalry Guard at Doeberitz and burst out into one of the least fortunate of his allocutions. " It seems," he said, " that they wish to encircle and provoke us." He threatened to break the ring. The speech was reported to London, Paris and St. Petersburg, where it aroused much anxious questioning. Why should an improvement of the relations between Russia and England be regarded as a provocation to Germany ? Why should the German Emperor threaten to break our understanding ? To many people the Emperor William's words came as confirmation of the fear that Germany wished to maintain France and Russia in a position of continental weakness and subservience. These suspicions (and as always with suspicions they were largely unjustified) were strengthened by the events which then ensued.

(6)

In the month of May M. Iswolsky had swallowed his acute mortification regarding the Sandjak Railway, and had reverted to his original idea of a secret arrangement between Russia and Austria whereby the Treaty of Berlin would be modified to their common advantage. Austria was to obtain Bosnia and Herzegovina : Russia was to obtain the freedom of the Straits.[1] Immediately on his return from Reval he resumed his interrupted negotiations, and in a memorandum of June 19 he informed the Austrian Government that although neither of these two questions could be settled without the consent of the Powers signatory of the Treaty of Berlin, yet he was prepared to discuss matters " in a spirit of friendly reciprocity." The Austrian reply to this intimation was contained in their secret memorandum of August 27. In this important document it was suggested that if Austria, " bowing to imperious necessity," were constrained to

---

[1] By Article XXV of the Treaty of Berlin the two Jugoslav provinces of Bosnia and Herzegovina were to be " occupied and administered " by Austria while remaining nominally under Turkish suzerainty. Aehrenthal's object in transforming a *de facto* into a *de iure* situation was " to deal a deathblow at Serbian irredentism " (Aehrenthal to Bülow, February 20, 1909, *G.P.*, xxvi, 9386). Under the Secret Treaty of 1897 Russia had recognised Austria's right to annex the two provinces on the understanding that Austria would co-operate with Russia in a Balkan settlement and avoid " everything which might engender friction or mistrust." The Sandjak business was regarded by Russia as a violation of the spirit of this Treaty, and the 1908 negotiations were in theory opened for the purpose of adjusting the 1897 Treaty to the new situation thus created. The closure of the Straits to ships of war was governed by Article LXIII of the Treaty of Berlin which reaffirmed the provisions of the Treaty of Paris of 1856, and the Treaty of London of 1871.

annex Bosnia and Herzegovina, then Russia would adopt a " favourable and friendly attitude." In return for this Austria would evacuate the Sandjak, and agree to a " confidential and friendly exchange of views " in regard to the Straits.[1]

Between the dates of these two memoranda, that is between June 19 and August 27, an event of great importance occurred. In July of 1908 the Young Turks overthrew the system of Abdul Hamid and announced that the new Turkey would give equal rights to all her subject nationalities.[2] For the moment it appeared as if the Balkan question had solved itself, and the Concert of Europe desisted with a sigh of relief from any further effort to introduce Macedonian reforms. Baron von Aehrenthal and Prince Ferdinand of Bulgaria interpreted the Young Turk Revolution in a less acquiescent manner. They considered that the suspension of the Concert of Europe, the inexperience of the new men at Constantinople, and the temporary weakening in Turko-German relations caused by the discomfiture and practical disappearance of Abdul Hamid, had presented them with an ideal opportunity for realising their desires. By the end of July Baron von Aehrenthal had prepared

[1] The Text of these Agreements is given in *G.P.*, xxvi A, pp. 190 ff.

[2] The following are the main dates in the Young Turk revolution. On July 22, 1908, Niazi Bey raised the standard of revolt at Resna. On July 23 the Committee of Union and Progress proclaimed the Constitution at Salonika and threatened to march on the capital. On July 24 Abdul Hamid capitulated and restored the Constitution of 1876. On April 5, 1909, a counter revolution broke out in Constantinople, on April 25 the Committee troops under Mahmoud Shevket entered the capital, and on April 27 Abdul Hamid was deposed in favour of his brother. He was interned at Salonika, but when the Greeks were approaching that city in 1912 he was hurriedly removed in the German Embassy yacht and imprisoned in the Palace of Beylerbey on the Bosphorus. In 1915 during the Dardanelles campaign, he was shifted to Magnesia, where he died on February 10, 1918.

for his impending gesture.[1]   Prince Ferdinand came
to Ischl on August 5. There can be little doubt that
everything was in readiness as early as August 10.

On August 19 M. Iswolsky left St. Petersburg upon
his ill-starred journey.   His idea was to proceed to
Carlsbad and thereafter to visit Italy, Paris, London
and Berlin. He had no desire to meet Baron von
Aehrenthal until he had first obtained from the other
Powers their consent to the opening of the Straits.
Unfortunately, however, Count Berchtold, Austrian
Ambassador in St. Petersburg, was also taking the cure
at Carlsbad. He persuaded M. Iswolsky to visit him
at his castle of Buchlau in Moravia, where Baron von
Aehrenthal was also expected. The meeting took
place on September 15 and 16.

It is beyond the scope of this biography to enter into
the controversy which thereafter raged as to what
actually happened at Buchlau. It may be assumed that
Iswolsky gave an unconditional assent to the annexation of Bosnia and Herzegovina, whereas Baron von
Aehrenthal's agreement to the opening of the Straits
was conditional upon the concurrence of the other
signatory Powers. Two things alone are certain.
Firstly, that M. Iswolsky committed himself to Baron
von Aehrenthal to an extent which he never dared to
disclose either to his own people or to the Governments of France and England. Secondly, that Baron
von Aehrenthal, realising that M. Iswolsky's lips were
sealed, proceeded to what can only be described as
blackmail. The result in any case was most unfortunate. From that moment M. Iswolsky became
obsessed with a burning desire for revenge against the

[1] Musulin, *Das Haus am Ballplatz*, pp. 164 ff.

man who had duped him. From that moment he flung himself heart and soul against the Central Powers.[1]

On October 5 Prince Ferdinand declared the independence of Bulgaria and proclaimed himself King. On the following day Baron von Aehrenthal announced the annexation of Bosnia and Herzegovina. He denied warmly that there was any connection between the two events.[2] His action created a storm of indignation throughout Europe. The unfortunate Count Mensdorff was sent up to Balmoral to break the news to King Edward. He met with a cold reception. " Mensdorff," so wrote Hardinge to Arthur Nicolson, " is not fully representative of a policy of duplicity such as Aehrenthal's." [3] Our Ambassador at Vienna was instructed to protest. Baron von Aehrenthal expressed " his extreme astonishment and regret " that His Majesty's Government should regard his action as

[1] The Buchlau problem can be warmly recommended to students of diplomatic mysteries. The accepted explanation is that Aehrenthal tricked Iswolsky by annexing the Provinces before the other Powers had been approached regarding the Straits. This explanation is contradicted by the facts. (a) On September 23 Iswolsky wrote to Aehrenthal telling him that he had drafted a reply to the Austrian memorandum of August 27 and sent it to the Tsar for approval. (b) Two days later he told von Schoen at Berchtesgaden that he *expected* the annexation to be declared on October 8. (c) He received the first news of the annexation while in Paris and took it quite calmly. It was only later when he got to London that he exploded.

It is impossible not to feel that what really happened was that it was not till he got to London that Iswolsky realised that what we and he meant by the " opening of the Straits " were two entirely different things. He dared not confess to the Tsar that he had failed to foresee this vital divergence in interpretation. He thus seized on Aehrenthal's alleged " duplicity " as an excuse. We shall find him seeking a similar red herring in the matter of the German " ultimatum " of March 22.

[2] Unfortunately Count Rudolph Khevenhüller, Austrian Ambassador in Paris, informed the French Government that Bulgaria would " precede Austria by one day." On hearing this afterwards the Emperor William minuted " Der Rudi hat was schönes angerichtet "—" Rudi has let them down proper " (*G.P.*, xxvi., 8987).

[3] Sir Charles Hardinge to A. N., Private, October 13.

a violation of the Treaty of Berlin. It was, he said, " with painful surprise " that he had received a protest from England.[1] Signor Tittoni, the Italian Foreign Minister, was equally indignant. He denied that Baron von Aehrenthal had on the occasion of their Salzburg meeting given him any serious warning of his intentions. In Russia, as was to be expected, the blast of indignation turned against Iswolsky. Not only had the man been duped at Buchlau, but he had completely misunderstood the nature of Russian feeling on the subject. He had sold the Serbs for the freedom of the Straits. And of what possible advantage to Russia, with her weak naval forces, was the freedom of the Straits ? It only meant that foreign fleets could pass the Dardanelles and Bosphorus and bombard Odessa. The Emperor of Russia took a more personal view. In speaking to Nicolson he described Baron von Aehrenthal's conduct as " positively ignominious." [2] The Serbians, who were still smarting from the " pig-war " of 1905, and against whose kinsmen this blow had been aimed, immediately placed large orders with Creusot. Their Foreign Minister, M. Milovanovich, proceeded on a tour of the foreign capitals stating that Serbia would perish sooner than suffer this infamy, demanding autonomy for the two provinces, and compensation for Serbia in the shape of a port on the Adriatic.

The reaction in Germany was of even greater interest. Baron von Aehrenthal had, it is true, given his German allies some vague warning of his intentions : these warnings had, however, been conveyed in a jocular and hypothetical form and had not been

---

[1] B.D., vol. v., No. 318.　　　　[2] B.D., vol. v., No. 425.

taken seriously : the more specific announcement of
the impending annexation had been conveyed only
three days before the event and at a moment when the
Emperor was at Rominten, the Chancellor at Nordeney
and the Foreign Secretary at Berchtesgaden. The
Emperor William was furious, and Baron Marschall
from Constantinople added fuel to the flames. It was
evident that Austria's action in annexing two provinces
nominally under Turkish suzerainty would bitterly
offend the Porte. " And so," the Emperor wrote,
" my Turkish policy, built up laboriously for twenty
years, goes smash ! A great score over us for Edward
VII ! " [1] " Er hat uns," he wrote again, " unerhört
düpiert "—" he has tricked us disgracefully." The
Emperor was all for dissociating Germany from
Austria's action. The German Foreign Office, for the
first few hours, were also in favour of such repudiation.
They informed the British Ambassador that " Austria's
action had placed Germany in a position of great
embarrassment, as she was forced to choose between
her ally Austria and her friends the Turks." [2] Prince
Bülow, that disastrous man, telegraphed wildly from
Nordeney. Whatever happened, he said, Germany
must support Austria or what remained of the Triple
Alliance would be dislocated. The slogan must be
" la loyauté sans phrases." [3] Austria must be given a
blank cheque and to the Turks they must explain that
Germany knew nothing about it. The Turks, for
their part, declared a boycott of all Austrian goods.

In his diary for October 12 Nicolson made the following entry : " Attacks on Iswolsky very bitter.

[1] *G.P.*, vol. xxvi., No. 8992.   [2] *B.D.*, vol. v., No. 316.
[3] *G.P.*, vol. xxvi., No. 8937.

Feeling against Austria terribly strong. Don't like the aspect of affairs."

The problem, meanwhile, was what could be done to rescue M. Iswolsky. He had arrived in London on October 9 wearing a somewhat guilty look. Sir Edward Grey described his appearance in a vivid passage : " Directly I began to speak to him his eyes became very dull and defensive." [1] The Russian Foreign Minister at once raised the question of the Straits. He stated that he must return with something to show to Russian public opinion or else he would have to resign and his place would be taken by some reactionary. " It is evident," Sir Charles Hardinge wrote to Nicolson, " that we must do our best to support him, such as he is." M. Iswolsky asked for the right of egress from the Black Sea for Russian ships but without the right of ingress for foreign vessels. He was told that in view of the situation in Turkey the moment seemed hardly opportune for such a proposal. He was bitterly disappointed. He again talked of resignation. Nicolson, when consulted, was not wholly sympathetic. He wrote :

" I think that Iswolsky exaggerated in intimating that a refusal on our part to entertain his wishes as to the Dardanelles might lead to his downfall and to that of Stolypin, to a return of the reactionaries and other disastrous consequences. In the first place, the Dardanelles is not regarded here as a question of vast importance. And secondly, if Iswolsky were to lose his portfolio it by no means follows that Stolypin would also resign. The two are not inseparable, though they may have many views in common." [2]

[1] Sir E. Grey to A. N., Private, October 26.
[2] A. N. to Sir Charles Hardinge, October 26.

At the same time Nicolson was anxious to defend Iswolsky against any imputations against his personal honour. On October 8 he had written privately to Sir Edward Grey as follows :

> " I know Iswolsky very well, and I do not think that he gave his ' concurrence ' to the Austrian project ; but I think it is quite possible that he went a little further than was prudent, and did not show that decided opposition which the circumstances demanded. He is often not firm in personal conversation,—and is unwilling to say anything which might appear to be displeasing to his interlocutors, especially when he is their guest—this is a weak trait in his character. He loves academical discussions in which he can review the world from China to Peru, but he does not like the hard give-and-take of an argumentative conversation. My own opinion is that he was a little yielding in his opposition and a little too discursive in examining possible compensations."

It was decided, therefore, that King Edward should write to the Emperor Nicolas recommending Iswolsky to his mercy. And that His Majesty's Government should meanwhile give support to the Russian proposals for an international Conference which should regulate the situation and save the face of M. Iswolsky.

Encouraged by this support, M. Iswolsky proceeded to draft a programme for the Conference, which he divided under nine headings. The British Government accepted M. Iswolsky's nine points with some minor modifications. The Russian Foreign Minister then travelled to Berlin. He met with a cold reception. He asked the German Government to press the Austrian Government to agree to the proposed Conference. They refused to do anything of the sort.[1]

[1] G.P., vol. xxvi., No. 9064.

The situation which then ensued is best described in terms of a private letter which Sir Edward Grey addressed to Nicolson on November 10 :

LONDON, *November* 10, 1908.

" MY DEAR NICOLSON,

"In the course of general conversation to-day Benckendorff told me he had received a private letter from Iswolsky who was evidently in low spirits about his reception in Berlin.

"The Germans had been very stiff : they had told Iswolsky practically nothing except that they were going to support Austria ; and, generally, he had received the impression that the Germans were in distinctly ill-humour with regard to Russia and very much changed in their feeling towards her. He found that the Reval visit still rankled.

"I told Benckendorff that this talk in Germany about being ' ringed-in ' was nonsense. Germany had two allies in Europe. France and Russia had one each : namely each other. We had our agreements with France and Russia, which were public to the whole world. Germany stood in the middle of Europe, with two allies and the strongest Army in the world, and no one dreamt of attacking her. We were the only Power against whom Germany could invent even a fiction about attack without being completely ridiculous, and of course we had not the least intention of attacking her. She could invent such a fiction about us only because we were the one Power that was out of her reach.

" Benckendorff went on to say that he had an impression that, in some way or other, Germany's alliance with Austria had been extended, and was now construed to cover the Balkans in a way which it had not done before.

" Then Benckendorff told me that he was going to be very indiscreet, and asked me what England would do supposing a crisis arose in the Balkans and Germany took the part of Austria as her ally.

" I said it was no good for me to say anything on such a matter unless I was authorised by the Cabinet to do so, and it was impossible for me to ask the Cabinet to consider such a contingency or to come to a decision with regard to it.   For the last week, I had been considering another contingency : what should we do if Germany attacked France in connection with the Casablanca incident.   The French had not, I thought, been seriously alarmed about this ; they had not asked us any questions ; and the incident was now settled.   He would have seen how strong the feeling of the English Press had been against any aggression upon France.   I had always felt that if Germany fastened war upon France in connection with Morocco, the world would say that France was being attacked because she had made friends with us, and for us to fold our hands and look on would not be a very respectable part.

" But in all these questions it was impossible to come to a decision beforehand : so much depended upon how the quarrel came, and who was the aggressor.   British sympathy would naturally be against the aggressor in any war.

" I asked Benckendorff what Russia would have done if there had been war between France and Germany about Morocco.

" He replied that he had not read the terms of the alliance with France, but he knew that they were wide.

" I then asked him what the action of France would be if Austria and Russia came to blows about the Balkans, and Germany supported Austria.

" In such an event, he said, of course France would be brought in, and all four Powers would be involved.   But, should such a crisis arise, he was optimistic enough to think that sharp, decisive action on our part would keep the peace.   If the British Government were at once to ask for a vote of credit from the House of Commons : he thought that would make the whole difference between peace and war.

" I concluded, as I had begun, by saying that it was not to be expected that a Cabinet would come to a decision on a question of this kind except under the pressure of a crisis. I could not submit such a question to my colleagues unless it became urgent : and it was no good for me to say anything unless I was authorised to do so by them.

" Benckendorff ended by asking me not to forget what he had told me about the unfavourable impression made upon Iswolsky by his visit to Berlin.

" Yours sincerely,

E. GREY."

One cannot but feel sympathy for M. Iswolsky at this juncture. His English friends, as was abundantly evident, would refuse to commit themselves in advance. His French ally was at the moment engaged in an acute and alarming controversy with Germany over the ill-treatment of certain German Consular officials at Casablanca. Russia was isolated and unprepared. It would perhaps have been wiser if M. Iswolsky had at once capitulated to the necessities of the situation. He endeavoured, however, to save his face. He endeavoured to conciliate Russian opinion by showing every sympathy for the Serbs. Nicolson feared that he had gone too far :

" I do not think," he wrote, " it very wise on the part of Russia to have gone so far in the way of assurances to Serbia. The Serbian Minister here has been told that Russia will do all that is possible to help her, and that Russia preserves her entire liberty of action, whatever arrangements may be made between Austria and Turkey. The meaning of these assurances will doubtless be amplified at Belgrade and may give rise to hopes which it will be difficult to realise." [1]

[1] A. N. to Sir E. Grey, Private, January 21, 1909.

Difficulties and embarrassments crowded upon the Russian Foreign Minister. The German Ambassador, to whom he appealed in his desperation, was not encouraging. He spoke of Reval : he stated that as M. Iswolsky had chosen to side with the Western Powers, Germany must deduce the consequences from the situation thus created : that " she must hesitate to afford to Russia that assistance which, had the grouping of Powers been different, she might have been willing to offer." [1] Baron von Aehrenthal was not proving himself in the least accommodating regarding a Conference. He had no objection to a Conference so long as it was clearly understood that the Powers would merely ratify the annexation and not discuss it. There could be no question, moreover, of any territorial compensation to Serbia or Montenegro. " If Russia," he said, " wants war, she shall have it." [2] It was known that General Conrad von Hoetzendorff, Chief of the Austrian Staff, was pressing for a " preventative " war against Serbia. It was known also that opinion in Russia did not desire a war in the very least :

> " I firmly believe," Nicolson wrote on November 18, 1908, " that in official and responsible military circles there is no desire for war : on the contrary there is a strong desire that war should be averted : but if Austria and Serbia were to come to blows it would be most difficult to restrain a popular outburst which might carry with it the Government and the more sober-thinking people."

On November 4, 1908, Nicolson was received by the Emperor in private audience at Peterhof. He found His Majesty pacing up and down the room

---

[1] *G.P.*, vol. xxvi., No. 9085.   [2] *B.D.*, vol. v., No. 430.

dressed in a peasant's blouse of red silk. The Emperor spoke with embittered venom against Baron von Aehrenthal. He then launched out into a diatribe against William II. Upon the writing table in the bow window lay a copy of the *Daily Telegraph* of October 28, heavily scored with a blue pencil. It contained an interview [1] accorded by the Emperor William to an English friend, in which credit was claimed for having resisted a Russian scheme for intervention during the Boer War. The Tsar was enraged by this breach of faith. He informed Nicolson that it was the Emperor William who had desired intervention and that all that Russia had proposed was the most friendly form of mediation. He walked to his writing table and searched among his papers, while Nicolson gazed out into the mists of the Gulf of Finland. The Tsar returned with a document which he explained was a private communication which he had received from the Emperor William " during the worst days of the war." Nicolson, who could not see the date of the document which the Tsar held in his hand, imagined not unnaturally that His Majesty was referring to the Boer War. In this he was wrong. The passage which the Emperor then proceeded to read spoke of English Jingoes and English impertinence, and urged that Russia should make some attack upon the frontier of India. We are now in the position to identify this document. It was a personal communication from the Emperor William to the Tsar dated

[1] This unfortunate though well-intentioned interview was the work of Colonel Stuart Wortley, whose house the Emperor had rented for the summer. The interview was repudiated by Prince Bülow in the Reichstag on November 10 in terms which led the Emperor to claim that he had been betrayed. The incident was the main cause of Prince Bülow's dismissal in July of 1909 and the appointment of Herr von Bethmann Hollweg.

November 17, 1904,[1] and therefore written during the campaign in Manchuria and not during the Boer War. The passage which the Tsar read to Nicolson runs as follows : [2]

"An excellent expedient for cooling British insolence would be to make some military demonstration on the Perso-Afghan frontier, where they think you powerless to appear with your troops during the war. Even should your forces not suffice for a real attack on India, they would do for Persia which has no army; and pressure on the Indian frontier from Persia will have a remarkably cooling effect upon the hot-headed Jingoes in London."

This disclosure produced on Nicolson a deep and durable impression. Hitherto, except at rare moments of irritation, he had been able to regard the clumsiness of German diplomacy with amused and, as it were, benevolent detachment. From this moment, however, his judgment was coloured by the conviction that Germany cherished tortuous and malignant designs against the British Empire. He had already seen how, in the first Morocco crisis, Germany had trampled on the dignity of France in order to show her that neither the Alliance with Russia nor the Entente with England could be of any avail. He feared that the German Government would now initiate a similar policy of intimidation at St. Petersburg. He knew that Russia was too weak to stand alone, and he was obsessed by the nightmare lest Germany, allied with Russia, Austria

[1] Briefe und Telegramme, Wilhelm II an Nicolas II. Von Gerlach, Vienna, 1920.

[2] This famous incitement was drafted not by the Emperor but by Prince Bülow, who sent it to his Sovereign in a letter of November 4, 1904, with a request that the latter should translate it into " good English " and send it to the Tsar as his own. The original German text is even more violent than the Emperor William's translation.

and Turkey, and thus possessed of every geographical and strategical advantage, should frighten France into neutrality and face England with an overwhelming menace on the Indian and Egyptian borders. Prince Bülow, at one of those rare moments when he ceased to be clever and became intelligent, remarked that the tension between Germany and England was due " to some vast misunderstanding." One is tempted to attribute this misunderstanding to the fact that neither country realised that the other was also terribly, and unnecessarily, afraid.

In the autumn of 1908 Sir Frank Lascelles retired from the post of British Ambassador in Berlin, and the German Emperor let it be known in London that Nicolson would be welcome as his successor. According to Count Metternich this bold but admirable suggestion was made " on the principle that poachers make the best game-keepers." The British Government did not respond to the idea, which was perhaps unfortunate. Had Nicolson gone to Berlin in 1908 he would have acquired a deeper and clearer understanding of German policy. So intelligent and fair-minded a man would have seen at once that under all the vaunting, violence and vanity of the German Emperor and Empire there existed a deep layer of pacificism and good sense. He would have realised that their restlessness was largely due to thwarted energy ; their boasting to lack of self-confidence ; and their untruthfulness to the circumstance that, as with so many musical people, they possessed fancy but no constructive imagination. It is doubtful whether he would have been any more successful than were Sir Edward Goschen or Lord Haldane in securing the limitation of naval armaments or preventing thereby the war of 1914. But at least, during the vital years that followed, he would have concentrated the splendid energies of his mind and character upon a problem more central than that of the maintenance of the Anglo-Russian Entente.

XI

THE HUMILIATION OF RUSSIA

[1909-1910]

Situation at the end of 1908—German attitude—The Conference proposal
—Iswolsky attempts to win over Bulgaria—King Ferdinand in St. Peters-
burg—King Edward's visit to Berlin—M. Iswolsky's alarm—Anglo-
Austrian negotiations—German decision to intervene—Austria tries to
blackmail Iswolsky—The German ultimatum of March 22—Nicolson's
regret and indignation—He urges an Anglo-Russian Alliance—He warns
Grey of danger of German predominance—His fears of the future—
Russian indignation against Germany—German complaints of Nicolson
—Effect of Bosnian Crisis—Russian internal situation—The Cowes visit
—Death of King Edward—Nicolson asked to become Under Secretary
at the Foreign Office—His hesitation to accept the appointment—His
farewell audience with the Emperor Nicolas—He leaves Russia.

(1)

THE situation, as it stood in the late autumn of 1908,
was as follows. M. Iswolsky, while realising that
Russia could not count on England or France and was
too weak to fight alone, hoped none the less that by
adopting a firm attitude he could drag Austria before
the tribunal of a European Conference and even obtain
some compensation for Serbia and Bulgaria. Baron
von Aehrenthal was not in the least impressed by M.
Iswolsky's menaces : he informed the British Ambassador that " he knew Russia like his pocket and felt
sure that she was not in a position to go to war." [1]
He denied, moreover, that Russia had any right to
assume a protectorate, " une papauté ethnologique,"
over the Slavs, and contended that the issue was merely

[1] B.D., vol. v., Nos. 483 and 490.

one between Austria and Turkey—the Power suzerain over Bosnia and Herzegovina. Germany was, on second thoughts, not at all displeased that circumstances should thus work to her advantage. The crisis would make it clear to the Austrians that Germany was their only friend. Moreover, if Germany remained benevolently aloof, it was possible that France in her anxiety would urge counsels of moderation upon Russia. " If," so wrote Prince Bülow to his Imperial master, " we have the sense to keep quiet, then France must take action on her own, and then the encircling ring around us (' der Einkreisungsring '), which is already showing cracks, will be permanently snapped. . . . All we need is to adopt the rôle of benevolent observers, while concealing within ourselves the secret pleasure that we feel." [1]

It was not, however, in the nature of German diplomacy to remain an observer, benevolent or otherwise, for long. An attempt to sow elaborate distrust between the Powers of the Triple Entente was in December engineered by Captain von Hintze, the Emperor William's " Military Plenipotentiary " and personal representative attached to the Imperial Russian Court. This ingenious naval officer informed the Tsar that Germany was prepared to offer Russia the freedom of the Straits but that the difficulty was to overcome British reluctance. He suggested, therefore, that the Russian Government should ask the French Government to exert pressure in London. He hoped in this way to cause trouble and misunderstandings between the three capitals. The Tsar replied, however, that the moment was not propitious for raising

[1] G.P., vol. xxvi., No. 9197.

the Straits question in any form, and Captain von Hintze's manœuvre was thus without result.[1]

On December 23 Baron von Aehrenthal, who was becoming impatient at M. Iswolsky's insistence upon a Conference, decided to apply a little gentle pressure. In a circular which he on that date addressed to the Powers he made a passing reference to the secret agreements between Austria and Russia. M. Iswolsky became alarmed lest further revelations might lead to the publication of his own unfortunate letters. He went so far as to beg the German Government privately to restrain Baron von Aehrenthal from any further disclosures,[2] and he informed the Austrian Embassy in Petrograd that in view of this further breach of good faith he would be unable to conduct with Austria any further confidential negotiations. Nicolson was amused by this incident. He wrote to Sir Charles Hardinge as follows :

" Iswolsky is more embittered than ever against d'Aehrenthal as he considers the publication of the Austrian Aide Mémoire and of the correspondence, without previous reference here, as a most irregular and incorrect proceeding. He is especially annoyed with the reference to certain previous arrangements with Russia which he says can only refer to the secret agreements of 1897. There must be a considerable literature of an interesting character in the private archives of Vienna and St. Petersburg ; and it must be a bore when one conspirator gives away his accomplice." [3]

By the end of 1908 it was clear that the Conference

[1] G.P., vol. xxvi., chap. 199, especially No. 9185.
[2] G.P., vol. xxvi., No. 9172.
[3] Letter of December 30, 1908.

scheme was receding further and further into the background. Austria was on the verge of coming to a direct agreement with Turkey on the basis of a monetary payment and the renunciation of the Sandjak. It was obvious that Baron von Aehrenthal would, once this agreement had been concluded, merely ask the Powers to ratify it without further comment. M. Iswolsky thereupon decided to win Bulgaria to the Russian side. An agreement was made whereby Turkey agreed to Bulgarian independence in return for a large sum of money which Russia provided for Bulgaria by renouncing a corresponding amount in the Turkish indemnity for the War of 1878. M. Iswolsky went even farther. The death of the Grand Duke Vladimir provided an excellent excuse for an accidental visit to St. Petersburg of Prince Ferdinand. He was received, on February 1, 1909, with Royal honours. He stood by the grave of his relative throwing little pink rose buds upon the coffin. He had changed considerably since that afternoon twelve years ago when he had cut Nicolson upon the lawn of Buckingham Palace. He no longer bore any resemblance to a fox, his hair and beard having changed to a wolf-like grey, his figure having swelled to regal proportions. He was extremely affable to Arthur Nicolson. The latter profited by the occasion to beg of him in all earnestness to use his influence for the maintenance of peace in the Balkans. The King of Bulgaria placed one finger beside his enormous Coburg nose. " Je serai doux," he said, " comme un petit petit agneau."

Baron von Aehrenthal was indignant at M. Iswolsky's intrigues with Bulgaria. He proceeded again to talk of war, and Conrad von Hoetzendorff was allowed to mobilize a few further divisions against Serbia. Meanwhile, however, a temporary improvement was introduced by the visit of King Edward to Berlin on February 8. " I found," Sir Charles Hardinge wrote to Nicolson, " a community of interest with Germany in her desire for the preservation of peace in the Balkans, and the maintenance of the *status quo*. Bülow's disapproval of Aehrenthal's procedure was most marked, and I left with the impression that Bülow would, in certain circumstances, act with France and ourselves in the Near East and proceed in conformity with Anglo-French and Russian views." [1] A communiqué was issued at Berlin to the effect that the conversations which had taken place on the occasion of the Royal visit had " disclosed a complete understanding between Germany and Great Britain in regard to affairs in the Balkans." This communiqué threw M. Iswolsky into a panic. He sent for Nicolson, who found him in a condition bordering on hysteria. The following passage occurs in Nicolson's diary for February 13, 1909 :

> " Iswolsky is, or pretends to be, convinced that we have settled with Germany on Balkan questions, and that means with Austria also, as the two go hand in hand : France has settled Morocco with Germany : Russia is thus isolated. Evident that Austria intends to have a military execution in Serbia, as the result of her feeling safe that France and England will not budge. I tried to convince him that there was no question of our deserting Russia. He would not have this : he repeated that Pourtalès was always rubbing in to him that Germany would march with Austria : he would have it that we had thrown over Russia and that France had done likewise. This meant complete

[1] *See also* G.P., vol. xxvi., No. 9930.

collapse of his policy : he would have to admit that he had
steered the wrong course, to abandon alliance and entente,
to take another line. Berlin had always told him he was
on the wrong tack and making combinations which at the
critical moment would prove of no value. He doubted
whether Germany would preach peace and moderation at
Vienna, as both Germany and Austria thought Russia
would do nothing and could be ignored. Serbia was
perfectly quiet : it was a wanton act which Austria was
preparing to commit. Russian opinion would be incensed
and a general conflagration might follow."

Nicolson was not unduly perturbed by this outburst.
" When all is said and done," he wrote, " we come
back to the question on which so much hangs—will
Russia actively intervene in a conflict of Austria with
Serbia and Montenegro ? " [1] For a moment he feared
an explosion of Slav opinion, but he subsequently
modified this opinion. The German Ambassador, for
his part, was seriously uneasy : his warnings were not
listened to in Berlin : " Nicolson Iswolsky Co. Ltd.
are carrying on a policy of Bluff "—it was with these
words that the Emperor William minuted the warnings
of Count Pourtalès.[2] Sir Edward Grey was anxious
and uncertain. Both England and Germany desired a
peaceful issue to the dispute, and yet neither of them
dared to speak with any firmness either at St. Petersburg
or at Vienna. On February 19 Sir Edward Grey suggested that Italy, France and Germany should make
joint representations at Vienna to the effect that an
attack on Serbia might lead to a European war. Baron
von Aehrenthal was to be asked what exactly were his
grievances against Serbia and the Powers would then

[1] A. N. to Sir Edward Grey, Private, February 24, 1909.
[2] G.P., vol. xxvi., No. 9400.

use their best efforts at Belgrade to remove the causes of complaint.[1] On hearing of these proposals Baron von Aehrenthal informed Prince Bülow that Austria preferred to deal with the matter by herself, even if this entailed a risk of war.[2] The German Government thereupon informed Sir Edward Grey that it was at Belgrade and not at Vienna that the Concert of Europe should intervene, that the Serbian Government should at once disband her forces, renounce all claim for territorial compensation, and place herself in the hands of the Great Powers. M. Iswolsky, on learning, to his dismay, that the French Government were inclined to support the German proposal—(an inclination which he characterised as a " denunciation of the Alliance " [3])—determined to forestall it by direct action. He made immediate and independent representations at Belgrade urging the Serbian Government to adopt a " pacific attitude " and to claim no territorial compensation. Sir Edward Grey at the same time opened direct negotiations with Baron von Aehrenthal in the hope of finding a formula which both Vienna and Belgrade could accept. It appeared probable that the crisis would be settled by Anglo-Russian intervention at Belgrade and Vienna. This prospect was unwelcome to the German Foreign Office. They were not at all inclined to allow Sir E. Grey and M. Iswolsky to score a diplomatic success. Nor did they wish Baron von Aehrenthal to attain his objective independently of German assistance. They decided therefore upon immediate action.

---

[1] B.D., vol. v., No. 585, and G.P., vol. xxvi., No. 9377 ff.

[2] G.P., vol. xxvi., No. 9386.   [3] B.D., vol. v., No. 614.

(2)

On February 26 Turkey formally recognised the
Austrian annexation of Bosnia and Herzegovina.
Baron von Aehrenthal now contended that as the
Power most interested had signified her assent it would
be wilful provocation on the part of Serbia or any
other country to raise further difficulties. M. Iswolsky, learning that the Austrian Government were about
to order a general mobilisation, and anticipating that
they were determined to force Serbia into war, again
urged the latter to place herself in the hands of the
Powers. On March 10 the Serbian Government gave
an absolute assurance of their pacific intentions and
signified that it was for the other powers to see that
justice was done. On the following day the Austrian
Government stated that Serbia's submission must be
unconditional and refused to recognise her right of
invoking the good offices of the other Powers. On
March 12 Count Berchtold, Austrian Ambassador in St.
Petersburg, informed the Russian Press that owing to
the unsatisfactory nature of the Serbian assurances it
" would be necessary to send her an ultimatum." On
the same day he visited the unfortunate M. Iswolsky
and informed him that unless he advised Serbia to
surrender, Baron von Aehrenthal would be obliged
" to communicate to London, Paris and Belgrade
certain secret letters written to him by M. Iswolsky
in the previous summer." [1] The Russian Foreign
Minister once again was seized with panic. He appealed to Berlin, beseeching them to restrain Baron
von Aehrenthal : he stated that he was ready to revive

[1] G.P., vol. xxvi., No. 9436.

the League of the Three Emperors ; he threatened if
Aehrenthal published his letters to disclose other
documents which would demonstrate the disloyalty of
Austria and Germany to their Italian partner in the
Triple Alliance. At the same time he telegraphed to
Belgrade advising them to come to direct terms with
Austria.[1]

The German Foreign Office (or more precisely the
Acting Under Secretary, Herr von Kiderlen Waechter)
acted quickly. Kiderlen was anxious to avoid war,
partly because the Emperor feared a revolution in
Russia, but " especially " (so he informed the French
Ambassador) " as we are not as yet ready for one ourselves." [2] But he was not willing that the crisis should
be settled independently of Germany. On March 17
he received information that at a Crown Council
held at Tsarskoe Russia had definitely decided that she
could in no circumstances go to war. " There ! "
wrote the Emperor William on learning this, " something definite at last ! Now we can go ahead." [3] On
March 17, therefore, the German Ambassador at St.
Petersburg proposed to M. Iswolsky that all idea of a
Conference should now be dropped, and that the
Powers should merely recognise the annexation by an
exchange of Notes. M. Iswolsky temporised. He
answered vaguely and he consulted Paris and London.
He informed Nicolson that his reply to the German
proposal had been " purposely obscure " since he did
not wish to " lay all his cards upon the table." This
discretion on the part of the Russian Foreign Minister
proved, however, of no avail.

[1] B.D., vol. v., No. 669.   [2] B.D., vol. v., No. 680.
[3] G.P., vol. xxvi., No. 9451.

On March 21, 1909, Herr von Kiderlen instructed Count Pourtalès to obtain from M. Iswolsky an unconditional acceptance of the German proposal. Russia was to consent immediately and without ambiguity to the abrogation of Article XXV. of the Treaty of Berlin, and thereby to recognise the annexation of the two provinces. " You should," so runs this famous telegram, " at the same time make it quite clear to M. Iswolsky that we expect a precise answer—Yes or No. Any evasive, complicated or ambiguous reply will be regarded as a refusal. In such an event we should withdraw and allow matters to take their course. The responsibility for all that follows will rest exclusively on M. Iswolsky." [1]

The incident is recorded in Nicolson's diary for March 23, 1909 :

" Found Iswolsky in great alarm. He told me that Pourtalès had yesterday presented him with a ' peremptory summons ' that Russia should declare without ambiguity that if Austria asked the Powers to acknowledge the abrogation of Article 25, Russia would accept it. If a refusal, or an evasive reply, were given, then Germany would ' lâcher l'Autriche sur la Serbie.' It was not, he said, an ultimatum since it did not actually threaten war ; but it was a ' diplomatic ultimatum ' of the most violent character. A Cabinet Council had been called together and they had decided to accept the German demand so as to avoid a war. Iswolsky acknowledged that this was a humiliation for Russia, but as the latter was isolated and as France could not be depended upon there was nothing to do but to accept. The Central Powers combination was too powerful for Russia to resist alone. A complete submission. I tried to induce him to delay an answer until France and England had been consulted or until the

---

[1] G.P., vol. xxvi., No. 9460, p. 694.

Vienna discussions were concluded, but he said he must send in his reply that evening. Which he did to Pourtalès at 9.30 p.m. A sad ending. He told Touchard that his political career was finished. This is too pessimistic. We must see what the papers say. But if they could find a successor he would doubtless be dismissed."

Later, March 31.

" As to the general situation he was gloomy, and foretold that this Austro-German hegemony would be the source of much future trouble. I advocated the consolidation of the Alliance and the Entente. With this he agreed. He talked of resigning, as he could not bear these unjust attacks. I advised him to buck up and not to give in. He was in a poor condition, and trying to wriggle out of the bog into which he has fallen. I dined with the Berchtolds. Music afterwards. Thaws during the night."

Nicolson, as a matter of fact, was somewhat relieved that M. Iswolsky had not thought fit to consult England and France before deciding upon the acceptance of the German ultimatum. A request for advice would have been difficult to evade. Even as it was, he found himself in an embarrassing position. M. Iswolsky, on the afternoon of March 23, read to him the terms of Russia's capitulation. Nicolson reported the interview in a long despatch to the Foreign Office : " I was, I confess, puzzled as to what to say. I should, I admit, have liked to have said a good deal on what seemed to me a surrender on the part of Russia." [1] As it was, Nicolson was able to indulge in vague expressions of regret.

It was in this way that the Bosnian crisis was settled. Serbia, after some slight wriggling, capitulated completely. The other Powers grudgingly gave their

[1] *B.D.*, vol. v., No. 753.

assent. The Central Powers had scored a diplomatic victory more disastrous to themselves than any possible defeat.

(3)

Nicolson's first impression was that the ultimatum of Germany had attained its object, and that unless the Triple Entente could be cemented into an Alliance the balance of power was doomed. He expressed his views frankly in a despatch and in a private letter to Sir Edward Grey, both of March 24. In the first he recorded in greater detail the substance of his conversation with M. Iswolsky :

" Russia," M. Iswolsky stated, " did not want a war. She was just beginning to bring order into her finances, was reorganising her army, and internal unrest was quieting down.   A war would throw back all the progress effected, and would probably revive all the troubles from which Russia was just emerging.   The whole matter was thoroughly threshed out during the Cabinet Meeting, which lasted three hours ;   and the decision was arrived at to accept the German proposal.   It was a hard pill to swallow, having to submit to what was practically an ultimatum.   The whole Austro-German plan had been skilfully conceived, and the right moment chosen.[1]   Three or four years hence Russia would have so far recovered herself as to be able to speak in a different tone.   This the two Central Powers knew well, and they did not intend to let the moment pass by.   I asked in that case whether he was quite sure that further demands would not be formulated.

[1] That there was a certain amount of premeditation and collusion between Germany and Austria is shown by Aehrenthal's letter to Bülow of February 20, 1909, in which he " opened his political heart " to his German ally (G.P., xxvi., No. 9386).   It is evident also, as explicitly stated by the Emperor in a minute of February 25 (G.P., xxvi., No. 9389 and notes), that German policy was based on the assumption that France and England would not stand by Russia.

His Excellency said that very possibly they would be, but he could only wait till they arrived. In short, he added, the Austro-German combination was stronger than the Triple Entente. I said that I totally disagreed with him. Great Britain, France and Russia were more than equal to any combination. His Excellency said that this might be so in a sense : but there was no alliance binding the three Powers together, and there was not that firmness and cohesion as existed between Austria and Germany. . . .

" I repeated to M. Iswolsky my regret that he had not, before replying to Count Pourtalès, consulted with His Majesty's Government and the French Government. He said that he had not had time. I must observe in connection with this point that M. Iswolsky had received the German communication on Monday afternoon at 4.30. He saw the French Ambassador immediately afterwards, but did not mention the matter : and it was only on the following afternoon that he made Admiral Touchard and myself acquainted with what had passed, and after the decision of the Cabinet Council. He communicated his reply to Count Pourtalès in the night after his return from taking the orders of the Emperor." [1]

In a private letter written on the same day, but a few hours later, Nicolson indulged in pessimistic forecasts :

" After this easy victory, I should not be surprised if greater demands were made of Russia, and if she, like Servia, were asked to change her course of policy. If this were to come about a wide field would be opened out. My firm opinion is that both Germany and Austria are carrying out a line of policy and action carefully prepared and thought out. Algeciras had to be revenged : the ' ring ' carefully broken through : and the Triple Entente dissipated. The Franco-German agreement was the first step ; and France is a quarter of a way towards a fuller

[1] B.D., vol. v., No. 761.

understanding with Germany.[1]   Russia is temporarily
weak, with a timorous Foreign Minister.   She had to be
frightened out of the Entente, and the first step towards
this had been eminently successful.   The Franco-Russian
alliance has not borne the test : and the Anglo-Russian
entente is not sufficiently strong or sufficiently deep-rooted
to have any appreciable influence.   The hegemony of the
Central Powers will be established in Europe, and England
will be isolated.   The activity in building up the German
navy is significant : [2] and the sudden entry of Germany on
the scene here is also significant.   When we have passed
through the present ' Sturm und Drang ' period, I should
not be surprised if we were to find both France and Russia
gravitating rapidly towards the Central Powers, as neither
of the former, distrustful of each other, feels that she can
stand alone against the power of the central combination.

" Our Entente, I much fear, will languish and possibly
die.   If it were possible to extend and strengthen it by
bringing it nearer to the nature of an alliance, it would then
be possible to deter Russia from moving towards Berlin.
The bulk of intelligent opinion is at present in favour of
working with us, and is hostile to Austria and Germany ;
but if it be found that the Entente cannot save them from
humiliating concessions, public feeling would, perhaps
reluctantly, recognise that terms had better be made with

[1] The French Government, after the settlement of the Casablanca incident,
had negotiated a pact with Germany whereby the latter recognised French
political interests in Morocco in return for what amounted to a partition of
all economic concessions between France and Germany.   This pact, which
was signed on February 8, 1909, was regarded by England and America as
violating the principle of the open door.   It did not outlast the Morocco
crisis of 1911-1912.

[2] The German Navy Law of 1908 had reduced the life of capital ships from
25 to 20 years.   In the autumn of that year the British Admiralty learnt that
the German 1908-1909 naval programme was being anticipated.   In January,
1909, Sir Edward Grey warned the German Government that British naval
estimates would have to be increased.   On March 16 Mr. McKenna disclosed
to the House of Commons that Germany would possess by April, 1912, a
minimum of 13 and a maximum of 17 Dreadnoughts.   This inaccurate
forecast caused great alarm in England.

the other parties. The ultimate aims of Germany surely are, without doubt, to obtain the preponderance on the continent of Europe, and when she is strong enough, and apparently she is making very strenuous efforts to become so, then she will enter on a contest with us for maritime supremacy. In past times we have had to fight Holland, Spain and France for this supremacy, and personally I am convinced that, sooner or later, we shall have to repeat the same struggle with Germany.

"If we could keep France and Russia on our side it would be well ; and if we could contract some kind of alliance with Russia, we should probably also steady France and prevent her from deserting to the Central Powers.

"You will, I daresay, consider that I am pursuing nightmares, but I will run this risk and lay my opinion before you. It seems to me that we are approaching a critical period when a regrouping will take place in Europe and hostile and indignant as is public opinion at present in Russia against Germany and Austria, this is no reason for concluding that it will be a permanent sentiment. We were not beloved a short time ago. We should not forget that in a very few years Russia will have regained her strength, and will again be a most important factor.

"I wish that Iswolsky and his colleagues had stiffened their backs. Stolypin unluckily has gone to recuperate in the Caucasus. I think that they magnified the danger, as, even admitting that Russia is for the moment weak and that her western provinces might be overrun, a greater man than exists at the present day found himself baffled and unable to subdue this country. Besides, a great nation should not tamely accept a peremptory summons."

Sir Edward Grey was alarmed by the suggestion that the Triple Entente should be brought squarely into the open. On April 2 he replied as follows :

"I am not surprised at your reflections in your letter to me. I do not think that it is practicable to change our agreements into alliances ; the feeling here about definite commitments to a continental war on unforeseeable conditions would be too dubious to permit us to make an alliance. Russia too must make her internal Government less reactionary—till she does, liberal sentiment here will remain very cool, and even those who are not sentimental will not believe that Russia can purge her administration sufficiently to become a strong and reliable Power."

Nicolson was much disappointed by the above letter. His long experience of European politics had convinced him that we were approaching a period which boded life or death to England. He feared that British high-mindedness, optimism and good-humour would not in themselves suffice to avert the impending disaster. He felt that Germany, with her deplorable lack of political imagination, was impressed only by concrete facts : that so long as our relations with France and Russia were not openly and accurately defined, Germany would still cherish hopes of dislocating the Entente by force. He had thus urged the Government to take the only step which, in his judgment, could avert catastrophe ; and he was answered in terms of " liberal sentiment."

His depression during these months is reflected in his private letters to his wife. " It is difficult," he writes, " to wake up the British public as to what is ahead of them. We slumber on and think we shall muddle through everything somehow. Occasionally I feel quite despondent." " We are," he writes again, " an illogical and inconsequent people—shortsighted and insularly arrogant." " I shall be glad," he writes on May 3, 1909, " of a change of Government. I am afraid we are not likely with the present people to have

a well defined firm foreign policy. We shall drift on
amiably from day to day. I shall not continue to
plead for an alliance with Russia, as it is clearly useless
to do so." The uselessness of any such proceeding
was brought home to him a few days later. A
despatch from the Foreign Office received on May 6
conveyed to him the following intimation :

"The attention of the Secretary of State has been drawn
to the use in official telegrams and despatches of the
expression 'triple entente' when referring to the joint
action of England, France and Russia. The expression is
one which is no doubt convenient, but if it appeared in a
Parliamentary Bluebook it would be assumed to have some
special official meaning and might provoke inconvenient
comment or inquiry.

"I am requested by Sir E. Grey to ask you to avoid
using it in future in your official telegrams and despatches."

This intimation was significant of the state of feeling
not only in the House of Commons, but in the Cabinet.
Nicolson received private information to the effect that
a group of Ministers, headed by Lord Harcourt, were
at this date anxious to allow the understanding with
Russia to die a natural death. Sir Charles Hardinge
was at one with Nicolson in regretting and in opposing
this tendency. They both realised that Russia was too
weak to stand alone, and that if she were abandoned
by England she would cleave to Germany. They had
little doubt that Germany would endeavour to force
both France and Russia into a declaration of neutrality
in the event of war with England.[1] This prospect

[1] See Sir Charles Hardinge's admirably moderate memorandum of May,
1909. That their apprehensions were not imaginary is indicated by the
Emperor William's Minute of February, 1909, to the effect that France should
be obliged by force to repudiate the Franco-Russian alliance in the event of Germany joining Austria in war against Russia (G.P., vol. xxvi., No. 9391 note).

filled them with despair. They could not but recognise that British public opinion was not ripe for an
alliance, but they regretted that the Cabinet should lull
themselves into a false sensation of security and should
hide from the House of Commons the dangers which
to the expert eye were only too apparent.

For the moment, however, the indignation aroused
in Russia by Germany's action was too intense to permit
of any further capitulation to Berlin. " I have been
assured," Nicolson wrote to Grey on March 29, " that
there has never previously been a moment when
Russia has undergone such humiliation. Though
Russia has had her troubles both internal and external
and has suffered defeats in the field, she has never had,
for apparently no valid cause, to submit to the dictation of a foreign Power." The German Government
were surprised and pained by the resentment which
their action had aroused. At first they had been
triumphant. " For the first time," writes Prince
Bülow, " the Austro-German Alliance proved its
strength in a grievous conflict. The group of Powers
whose influence had been so much over-estimated at
Algeciras fell to pieces when faced with the tough
problems of continental policy." [1] This self-satisfac-
tion was not of long duration. " I do not think,"
Count Pourtalès wrote on May 6, " that I exaggerate

---

[1] Prince Bülow persisted in this opinion. After his retirement he wrote as
follows : " The sword of Germany has been flung into the scales, directly on
behalf of our Austrian Ally, indirectly for the preservation of European peace,
and above all and before all on behalf of German prestige and her position
in the world. . . . The result of the Bosnian crisis was in fact the end of
Edward VII's policy of encirclement. . . . The artificial encirclement and
isolation of Germany (which for a time had been the bogey of a few timid
souls) was shown up as a *diplomatic* illusion, and one that lacked the pre-
conditions of any practical policy " (Furst Bülow, *Deutsche politik, Volksausgabe*,
pp. 51, 52).

when I say that at present the feeling against Germany is even more bitter than that against Austria." [1] Prince Bülow felt constrained to warn the Emperor, who was to meet the Tsar in Finnish waters, " not to say much about the events of the last few weeks." The Emperor William was distressed. " I very naturally expected," he wrote to the Tsar, " that you and I would win universal applause. But to my regret and astonishment I observed that a great many people blame us both instead." [2] It was decided, therefore, to make it clear that the ultimatum of March 22 had not been an ultimatum at all, still less a " peremptory summons," but merely an amicable attempt to extricate Russia from a difficult position.[3] It was decided also that Nicolson should be selected as a scape-goat.

Already in the early days of March the German Ambassador in London had complained officially that Nicolson " who held M. Iswolsky in the hollow of his hand," had been encouraging the Russian Government to resistance.

" This," Nicolson answered, " is absolutely untrue. I have spoken freely to Iswolsky as to the difficulties which Aehrenthal has created, but I have never gone further than

[1] G.P., vol. xxvi., No. 9532.   [2] G.P., vol. xxvi., No. 9533.

[3] It is difficult to see how German historians can seriously contend that the German communication of March 22 was not of a minatory character. It is possible that M. Iswolsky, in order to conceal the fact that he was concurrently being blackmailed by Count Berchtold, threw the maximum emphasis upon the communication of Count Pourtalès. But the actual text of Herr von Kiderlen Waechter's instruction is before us. It describes itself as a " last attempt " to secure a solution, and it asks for a definite answer, " Yes or No." Moreover, Kiderlen himself boasted afterwards of having humiliated Iswolsky (see E. Jackh, Kiderlen Waechter, ii. pp. 26 ff.), and in a subsequent conversation with Také Jonesco he referred to it as follows : " I knew that the Russians were not ready for war, that in no case would they make war, and I wished to draw profit from this knowledge. . . . Never would Schoen and Co. have dared to do what I did on my own responsibility " (Také Jonescu, Souvenirs, p. 49).

was justifiable or indeed than what has been said in London to Mensdorff and Metternich. I have never urged him to adopt a line which might widen the breach between him and Vienna. As to my ' running him '—the idea is ridiculous. We know each other very intimately, and I may say without vanity that he has confidence in me, and likes to talk matters over with me. I am pleased that he should do so, and I think that it is of advantage. But he forms his own judgments and takes his own decisions. . . . The charges brought by Prince Bülow are rather serious, and though I have no wish to magnify them, I hope that he will be induced to give further information."

This request for further information put a stop to the complaints, but the attacks continued underground. In March Nicolson received the following letter from his friend, Sir Donald Mackenzie Wallace :

" Perhaps you do not know that you are regarded in the German camp as the prime mover in all the diabolical intrigues for weakening German influence in Petersburg, and that you are described by very competent authorities as a double-dyed Machiavelli ! ! ! I daresay you never saw that life-like portrait of yourself before ! Grey was greatly amused at my account of your unenviable diplomatic reputation. ' These foreigners,' he remarked, ' must be terrible intriguers themselves to suspect us as they do. I suppose they spend a great deal of money on their secret service, whilst I spend nothing.' . . . With the first part of the remark I quite agreed, but on the last part I must have looked a little incredulous, for he hastened to add, ' Well, *if* we spend anything, it must be very trifling, because it never comes to my knowledge.' As a remedy for foreign intrigues he suggested that foreign statesmen ought to receive their education at an English public school."

The opinion that Nicolson was in fact at the bottom of Iswolsky's resistance was sincerely held by perfectly

honourable German officials.[1] Count Pourtalès, for
instance, to whom Nicolson had made some biting
remarks about the effects of German bullying, imagined
quite sincerely that if the British Ambassador could
say such things to his face he must say far worse things
behind his back.[2] He even complained to M. Sazonow
who had then been appointed Under Secretary of
Foreign Affairs at the Pevtchesky Most. " This statement," the latter recorded, " calls for no comment, but
it is all the more characteristic since it emanated from
the least chauvinistic of German diplomatists." [3] The
assertion is repeated even by the admirable Erich
Brandenburg,[4] who writes : " The British Ambassador
Nicolson, who had already proved himself an enemy
of Germany at Algeciras, did his best to embitter the
resentment of the Russians." [5]

[1] These views have been reflected by Professor Sidney Fay in his admirably
objective book *The Origins of the World War* (vol. i. p. 391). It is possible that
Iswolsky exaggerated the German action in order to distract attention from
his own secret commitments to Austria. Nicolson was not at the time aware
of the blackmail being applied by Berchtold, and quite sincerely believed that
Russia was being faced by an ultimatum. Professor Fay, at this single point,
appears to lose his unfailing sense of fairness.

[2] *G.P.*, vol. xxvi., Nos. 9498 and 9503.

[3] Sazonow, *Fateful Years*, English edition, p. 19.

[4] Erich Brandenburg, *Von Bismarck zum Weltkriege*, p. 293.

[5] Less reputable were the attacks made upon Nicolson by Captain von
Hintze, subsequently German Minister for Foreign Affairs, but at that date
the Emperor William's personal representative at the Court of the Tsar.
" Sir Arthur Nicolson," he wrote, " is an active and unscrupulous opponent.
If you have any material against him it should without hesitation be turned
to account, particularly as he himself knows no scruple." Herr von Hintze's
proposals were not approved by his Government. Herr von Schoen wrote
as follows to Count Pourtalès : " Von Hintze writes of the warnings that he
has given to his friends in the entourage of the Tsar against Sir A. Nicolson,
and hints that he wishes to be even more active in this direction. Such
gambits sometimes give one a momentary advantage, but the directive lines
in the relations of foreign Powers are governed by other factors." Captain
von Hintze shortly afterwards " lost the confidence of the Tsar," and had to
be recalled (*see G.P.*, vol. xxvi., No. 9573 and note).

These manœuvres were of little effect. The German Embassy continued to be cut by Petersburg society, and Nicolson continued to enjoy unmeasured popularity. The attitude of the Tsar was particularly encouraging. At an audience of April 14 he assured Nicolson that the only result of the crisis had been to strengthen the Entente. His Majesty clasped his hands together, interlocking the fingers with significant emphasis : " We must," he said, " keep closer and closer together."

The effect of the Bosnian crisis was not, therefore, either what Prince Bülow had hoped or what Nicolson had feared. The Central Powers had scored a resounding diplomatic victory, but, as is the nature of diplomatic victories, it was of the Pyrrhic variety. They had succeeded in humiliating Russia, Serbia, France and England. But what had they gained ? Austria had secured the *de jure* occupation of two provinces which she possessed already. On the other hand she had created a Balkan block under Russian auspices. Germany, with her Nibelungen fidelity to the Austrian Alliance, had led the dual Monarchy to regard themselves as indispensable, and to expect further favours to come, and further blank cheques. Italy, the third partner in the Triple Alliance, was indignant at having been ignored. And Russia found herself irrevocably committed to France and England.

" The importance," writes Erich Brandenburg,[1] " of these events was very great. The preponderance of the German-Austrian block in continental questions had been clearly manifested. Russia saw herself driven more than ever to lean on the Western Powers and

[1] Erich Brandenburg, *Von Bismarck zum Weltkriege*, p. 294.

from that moment she regarded the consolidation of the Entente as a matter of life and death. Iswolsky, who till then may have hesitated whether an understanding with the Central Powers might not better suit his book . . . was from now on in his heart of hearts completely committed to the Entente."

(4)

The protracted calm that followed upon the tempest of the Near Eastern crisis was employed by Nicolson in resuming his study of the Russian internal situation. Things were undoubtedly improving : the activities of terrorist and agrarian agitators had been checked : the Duma, although a packed body, was gradually acquiring a little prestige : Stolypin was slowly but surely elaborating his scheme for the creation of a stable class of peasant proprietors : the finances were recovering under the able direction of M. Kokovtsoff : and the Emperor appeared to have acquiesced in a programme of evolution by which his country would be transformed into an organic community under a paternal Government and based upon millions of peasant families each owning a few *desiatines* of soil. Such shafts of watery sunlight as pierced from time to time the dark pall that hangs for ever over Russia were quickly shrouded by delation, persecution, uncertainty and fear. People disappeared mysteriously, never to return. The old network of spies and *agents provocateurs* still spread throughout the country twisting the minds of men into diseased and crooked shapes.

A healthy prejudice against Russia, and the Russian Entente, still filled the minds of English Liberals. Uneasy mutterings were heard when it became known

that the Tsar intended to return the Reval visit. Mr.
Asquith, who was aware that even in his own Cabinet
there were those who disapproved of the Entente,
suggested that it might be well if M. Stolypin and M.
Iswolsky were to proceed no further than Cherbourg.
The Imperial Russian visit could then be represented
as a purely family affair. Sir Edward Grey and Sir
Charles Hardinge over-ruled this proposal, which
would have caused offence and encouraged the reactionary elements in St. Petersburg. It was thus in
the full panoply of an official visit that the Emperor
and Empress proceeded from France to England.
Nicolson, who had joined the Royal yacht at Cowes,
recorded his impressions in daily letters to his wife :

> H.M. YACHT *Victoria and Albert*,
> *August* 2, 1909.
> " DARLING LITTLE WIFE,—I wonder if you received the
> letter I wrote early this morning—just a line. This I am
> writing just before dinner and we have had rather a long
> day. Before 11 we had to get into full rig, then steamed to
> Spithead and awaited the Emperor, who came up punc-
> tually at 12. The King and Royalties went off to the
> *Standart* while we waited on board here,—and then we had
> luncheon, a lengthy business. About 3 we weighed
> anchor and went down the lines of the Fleet. It was
> blowing a little but was clear and the sight was magnificent.
> We came to our berth about 4.30. I have now got out of
> my full rig into which I shall have to re-enter at 8. It
> was cold owing to the north breeze. I must say these
> functions bore me, as the novelty has worn off."

> *August* 3.
> " A big banquet last night. You will have read the
> speeches. I sat between Grey and Seymour and so was
> very happy. The illumination of the Fleet was magnificent

and impressed the Russians. All was over at 11 p.m. and I was rejoicing at an early bed when the King sent for me and kept me and Jacky Fisher talking till 12 with the Prince of Wales."

August 4.

" Still lovely weather. I pottered about the yacht in the morning and lunched with Grey, Asquith and Iswolsky in the *Enchantress*. We had a long business talk from 2.30 till 5. Very satisfactory. Then I went off to the *Thistle* and tea with the Empress Eugenie. She was looking very well. We had a big banquet on the *Standart* not very well done. We came back at 11.30. I was just going to bed when the King sent for me and I had to sit with him till 12-15—rather tiring. The Emperor is in great force and even the Empress has livened up. I shall be glad when I am quiet again as I hate these functions."

August 5.

" I get off this afternoon. Last night an informal dinner on the *Standart*. Very pleasant. I sat between the Empress and the Princess of Wales. They were both most amiable. The guitar band of the ship played and sang after dinner and as it was a lovely night it was all most agreeable."

The conversation which took place in the *Enchantress* between the British and Russian Ministers was not of great importance. M. Iswolsky, after his invariable exordium of abuse of Aehrenthal, expressed the fear that now that Austria had imposed her will on Serbia she might wish to draw Bulgaria also within her orbit. He urged that the Western Powers should do all within their power to support the Young Turks and to prevent the impending dissolution of Turkey in Europe. He spoke also of Persia, where the British and Russian Legations were again at loggerheads. He expressed a desire " for a frank and full interchange of views between the two Governments in all questions." Mr. Asquith mumbled his assent. Nicolson recorded the conversation afterwards in a memorandum which he sent to the Foreign Office.[1]

In the autumn of 1909 Nicolson returned to St. Petersburg. Iswolsky, when passing through Berlin, had visited the new Chancellor, Herr von Bethmann Hollweg. He assured this great European (one of the few completely unassailable figures in pre-war diplomacy) that there was nothing in the Anglo-Russian Entente which was aimed at Germany, that no agreement had been concluded at Reval, " not one single comma," of which Germany had not been informed. He expressed the fear that Austrian ambitions in the Balkans might one day lead to a European war, a catastrophe which Russia, at any cost, desired to avoid. Herr von Bethmann Hollweg recorded this conversation in a memorandum to the Emperor William. The latter minuted each separate assurance of M. Iswolsky with the one word : " Lüge " or " Lie." The passage in which M. Iswolsky gave the most specific assurance that no secret agreements had been concluded at Reval was minuted similarly : " Lie No. 6." And yet in this the Russian Foreign Minister had spoken nothing but the truth.[2]

(5)

Nicolson had now been nearly four years in Russia and was supremely contented with his lot. He loved the Russians and their fickle ways : he loved the great

---

[1] A. N. to F.O., August 3, F.O. Archives, Russia, 29989/09.
[2] G.P., vol. xxvi., No. 9568.

red palace in which he lived, the ease, the precision and
indeed the luxury of his daily life. He would rise
early and walk with his wife—an unfailing companion
—along the boarded alleys of the Summer Garden.
Four times would they complete the circuit of that
dismal rectangle, and then there would be work till
luncheon, and a sleigh-drive behind swift black horses
to the Islands, and then work again, and in the evening
some dinner or reception. The crowd parted as he
entered those stifling drawing-rooms—a bent and smiling figure leaning on an ebony stick. They regarded
him as a personage of extreme importance, the friend
of King Edward and of their own Emperor, the
confidant and supporter of Stolypin and Iswolsky, the
man who had made the Anglo-Russian Entente. This
atmosphere of general awe and liking enabled Nicolson
to forget his fundamental shyness and there was then no
cloud in those alert blue eyes, no hesitation in the gaiety
of his smile. His domestic circumstances, in that year
1910, were also satisfactory. The old financial troubles were now things of the past. His eldest and his
favourite son, Frederick, was with his regiment, the
15th Hussars, in India : his second son, Erskine, was
Flag-Lieutenant at Malta : his third son had a few
months before entered the Foreign Office : his little
daughter Gwendolen was the sunshine of his days.
Within the Embassy itself all was concord. Never, he
felt, had any Ambassador been blest with so delightful
or so efficient a staff. There was the Counsellor, Mr.
Hugh O'Beirne, the most brilliant of companions, the
most loyal and intelligent of assistants.[1] There was

---

[1] Mr. O'Beirne was drowned in the *Hampshire* when accompanying Lord
Kitchener to Russia.

the Naval Attaché, Captain Victor Stanley, with his
friendly and delightful wife. There were Ernest
Scott, George Kidston, Gerald Wellesley, and Tom
Spring Rice. There can be no question but that these
last years in Russia were the happiest in his life.

On April 7 Nicolson heard from Sir Frederick
Ponsonby at Biarritz that they were anxious regarding
the King's health. A month later, King Edward was
dead—it was the end of an epoch, and for Nicolson
also it was a cloud across the evening sky. He returned to England in June, and he there learnt that
Sir Charles Hardinge was likely to succeed Lord Minto
as Viceroy. Sir Edward Grey urged Nicolson to
accept the post of Permanent Under Secretary at the
Foreign Office. Nicolson had no desire whatever to
accept this appointment. On June 8 he wrote to his
wife :

"I sat between Charlie Beresford and Bigge.[1] The
latter told me that Hardinge was certain to have India.
He said that everyone hoped I should accept the F.O.—
that I was the only man to fill it now—that he knew that
it was a great sacrifice both of salary and position to ask of
me, but that the public service required it. I told him that
I was of two minds. I was a poor man and the financial
sacrifice was serious. Bigge said he realised all I should
be giving up but he expatiated on the King requiring
someone well up in foreign affairs to whom to refer, etc.,
etc. Now honestly speaking I should *much* prefer if I were
not placed in the position of having to decide. I would
far rather stay at St. Petersburg for many reasons. But if
it is put to me that the public service requires my coming
here I could not refuse. I doubt whether I ought to do so,
as public duty comes first of all. I earnestly trust, how-

[1] Lord Stamfordham.

ever, that some other arrangement may be made and that I shall not be asked to go to the F.O."

On June 11 a formal offer was made and accepted. Next day he wrote again to his wife :

" I did hesitate much, and even now I am not enthusiastic. It is a great change coming somewhat late in life. I suppose it is a compliment but I am too old to feel flattered. Bigge said something about taking it for two or three years and then going to Paris. I am not bothered about the money side, but I do deeply regret giving up diplomatic life. I really loved it. I do not disguise from myself that I am undertaking very hard and responsible work of a character very different from that to which during the last 35 years I have been habituated. I told Grey that the only grudge I ever had against Hardinge was that he made it so exceedingly difficult to succeed him adequately. Haldane, with whom I lunched, was very insistent. He said that the Head of the F.O. was one of the most important posts in the Government and that it was essential not to have there a civil servant but a ' diplomatist statesman.' More in that vein. All very well, but my heart is really sore at the prospect of leaving diplomacy and Russia. We were both so happy. May we be equally so in our new life."

Nicolson returned alone to St. Petersburg to take leave of the Emperor. A State luncheon was given in his honour at Tsarskoe. Two days before, Nicolson —who when his wife was absent was liable to take liberties with his health—had eaten some caviare which, as cholera was still raging, was strictly forbidden. He was violently ill. The doctor informed him that he could not possibly go down to Tsarskoe. He insisted on not breaking so formal an engagement, and he forced the doctor—a weak and foolish man—to give him some potent drug which would tide him over the few hours of the ceremony. The doctor prepared two pills. The Ambassador might take one before starting, but he was on no account to take the second unless absolutely obliged. Nicolson swallowed both pills and journeyed in agony to Tsarskoe. He managed to survive the luncheon without fainting. He said farewell to the Emperor and Empress. Ten days later he was well enough to travel home to England. But for three years afterwards he was obliged to follow a careful diet and was subject to frequent recurrences of his attack.

He gloomily rejoined the Foreign Office, after an absence of thirty-five years, on October 1, 1910.

BOOK IV

THE ANGLO-GERMAN ENTENTE

XII

THE AGADIR CRISIS

[1910-1911]

Lord Hardinge's reforms in the Foreign Office—Nicolson does not extend
them to the Diplomatic or Consular Services—Sir Eyre Crowe—Sir
William Tyrrell—The two schools of thought in the Foreign Office—
Nicolson's belief in the German menace—His desire to render the
Entente stronger and more avowed—Sir Edward Grey's difficulties—
Examination of the German menace—Sir Edward Grey's justification—
Nicolson's dislike of Foreign Office work—His failings and value as
Permanent Under-Secretary—The Potsdam visit—Effect in France—
Anglo-German negotiations—Nicolson's distrust of these—The Agadir
incident, July, 1911—Franco-German negotiations—Mr. Lloyd George's
speech—War Preparedness in England—Collapse of the crisis—The
Caillaux disclosures—Result of Agadir crisis—Strained relations with
Russia over Persia—The Shuster incident.

(1)

THE Foreign Office, in the interval, had changed
considerably. The revolution introduced by Lord
Hardinge, on Sir Eyre Crowe's suggestion and initiative,
had transformed what had been a stuffy family business
into an efficient Department of State, second only to
the Treasury. In the old days people folded papers
four times across, leaving but exiguous rectangles for
comments or suggested action. These rectangles were
reserved for the great. Lord Hardinge, a progressive
and ruthless administrator, had altered all that. He
had forced the Department to adopt a different method
of presenting and preserving their papers. He had
introduced " jackets." The vital importance of this
reform may escape the attention of the uninitiated.
In its essence it secured that a sheet of foolscap, instead

of being folded four times, and thus diminished, was not folded at all. It was placed in a cover, the wide and cleanly space of which allowed full scope for minutes. In the old days there had been room only for the cramped and congested minutes of Lord Sanderson. Lord Hardinge, by his reforms, allowed all sorts of young men to write what they pleased. His was indeed a democratic innovation. The juniors in the Department were from that moment enabled to make suggestions. From that moment the Foreign Office had become an institution to which it was well worth the while of an industrious, intelligent and ambitious young man to belong. Unfortunately, Hardinge left the Foreign Office before he was able to extend to the Diplomatic Service a similar inducement to the gifted junior. Nicolson was too diffident in administrative matters to carry his predecessor's reforms to their logical conclusion. The result is that whereas the Foreign Office is to-day run on the system of 1930, the Diplomatic Service is still to a large extent conducted on the system of 1842. And the energetic Civil Servant, when relegated to Diplomacy, is thus apt to resign.

Nicolson, on entering the Foreign Office as a super-imposed outsider, was full of admiration for the machinery which Lord Hardinge had created. He liked the new archivists, docketers, typists, printers, stenographers, binders, and second division clerks. He accepted the system as he found it. He was too busy to consider the possibility of advancing these reforms a stage further. It had all been very different in the time of Lord Granville. But Lord Granville was dead. Nicolson admitted that Charlie Hardinge, for whom he had an affectionate and deeply loyal admiration, had done wonders. But he felt that the moment had come when wonders should cease. It never occurred to him that the Diplomatic and Consular Services were also in crying need of reform. When it was suggested that a scheme should be prepared for the fusion of the two—a scheme by which the Diplomatic Service could get rid of its countless incompetents and the Consular Service could reward its numerous competents—he took refuge behind the Treasury. There were problems of increment and pensions. The Public Accounts Committee was a body behind which it was very easy to take refuge.

Meanwhile the Foreign Office, as he found it in that autumn of 1910, was dominated by two outstanding personalities. These were Sir Eyre Crowe and Sir William Tyrrell. The former was head of the Western Department and subsequently, in January of 1912, Assistant Under Secretary of State. Sir William Tyrrell was Private Secretary to Sir Edward Grey. It is difficult to conceive of two men more diverse from each other in temperament and attainments.

Sir William Tyrrell was intuitive, conciliatory, elastic, and possessed a remarkable instinct for avoiding diplomatic difficulties. Sir Eyre Crowe was the perfect type of British Civil Servant—industrious, loyal, expert, accurate, beloved, obedient, and courageous. Sir William Tyrrell, who was inspired by a deep personal devotion to Sir Edward Grey, concentrated his efforts on sparing his chief all unnecessary complications or worries. Sir Eyre Crowe, on the other hand, had an unfortunate habit of indicating to the Foreign Secretary, and his colleagues in the Cabinet, that they

were not only ill-informed but also weak and silly.
Sir William Tyrrell did more than any man to increase
the prestige of the Foreign Office in circles which had
hitherto regarded British diplomacy as mysterious and
aloof : he was on excellent terms with journalists and
Members of Parliament. Sir Eyre Crowe had an abid-
ing horror of all amateur diplomatists, whom he would
characterise as " meddlesome busybodies ": it was
only within the Foreign Office that the nobility of Sir
Eyre Crowe's nature was fully realised. Sir Eyre
Crowe believed that in the conduct of public affairs it
was essential that everything of importance should be
recorded in writing and without ambiguity. Sir
William Tyrrell relied upon the spoken, rather than
upon the written, word. Sir Eyre Crowe felt that it
was consonant with the mission of England to resist
the powerful and to support the weak. Sir William
Tyrrell, while kindly towards the smaller brethren,
treated the strong brother with cautious solicitude.
Sir Eyre Crowe believed in facts ; Sir William Tyrrell
believed in personal relations : the former relied upon
lucidity ; the latter upon atmosphere ; the minutes
of Sir Eyre Crowe were precise and forcible ; the conversations of Sir William Tyrrell were intangible but
suggestive ; the former concentrated his energies upon
penetrating the matter in hand without regard to col-
lateral contingencies ; the latter, who kept aloof from
the machinery of office life, excelled in examining the
outer radius of international problems. They were
both imbued with the highest sense of public duty, but
whereas Sir Eyre interpreted that duty as a faithful
observance of the Civil Service creed, Sir William
approached it in terms of personal loyalty to Sir

Edward Grey. Sir Eyre Crowe's magnificent qualities
of brain and soul were sometimes marred by an excess
of rigidity : it was by pliant and adaptable gaiety that
Sir William Tyrrell conquered so many hearts.

(2)

At the outset Nicolson was on terms of equal confidence with both his associates. As the years passed,
however, he tended to rely to a greater extent upon
Sir Eyre Crowe, to whom both politically and tem-
peramentally he was more akin. There thus arose in
the Foreign Office (and almost imperceptibly) two
schools of thought ; the one represented by Sir Edward
Grey and Sir William Tyrrell ; the other by Nicolson
and Crowe. The latter school wished to define the
situation : the former school desired to remain elusive
and non-committal. It would be an exaggeration to
represent these two schools as conflicting or even
competitive. Loyalty, confidence, collaboration were,
as between Grey, Crowe and Nicolson, continuously
maintained : there was nothing in their divergence of
opinion which detracted from their respective liking
and esteem. The divergence did, however, exist ; and
as a result Sir Edward Grey tended to be guided by
those who sympathised with his Parliamentary difficulties, rather than by those who insisted on his
responsibility to Europe. It is necessary at this stage
to define these two conflicting tendencies, since it is
only in the light of his latent disagreement with Sir
Edward Grey—a disagreement which was continually
a subject of amicable and even humorous discussion
between them, but which for obvious reasons was
never stated on paper—that Nicolson's letters and

minutes of the pre-war period can properly be
understood.

Nicolson believed profoundly in " The German
Menace." He believed, that is, that the German army,
and above all the German navy, were larger and more
fully equipped than was necessary for purposes of mere
defence. He believed that there existed a compact
minority in Germany (powerful enough to force the
hands of the civilians) who desired to use these two
mighty engines of war in order to impose the will of
Germany upon other nations. And he felt that, since
these people believed in force, it was by force alone
that they could be restrained.

For this purpose the Triple Entente was not, in his
judgment, strong enough. He considered Russia a
factor of vital importance and great uncertainty. If
Russia deserted to Germany, not only would France be
paralysed and our naval position in the Mediterranean
correspondingly weakened, but England would also
be immeasurably hampered by the Russian menace in
Central Asia. It was for this reason that he pressed
continuously for the strengthening of the fragile bond
that united us with Russia. He desired, above all, that
the solidarity of the Triple Entente should be patent
and proclaimed. He regarded the existing arrangements with France and Russia as possessing all the
disadvantages, and none of the benefits, of an alliance.
He feared that the Ententes were sufficiently binding
to encourage people in St. Petersburg and Paris,
but not sufficiently binding to discourage people in
Berlin. He considered that in this vital matter the
indolent British indulgence in half-measures was not
only dangerous but unfair. Unfair to Germany :

unfair to France and Russia : unfair, above all, to
British public opinion.   He urged Sir Edward Grey,
in season and out of season, to make it clear to the
world exactly where we stood.

The Secretary of State, somewhat naturally, was
annoyed by this persistence. It is always irritating for
a gentleman in a false position to be assured by other
gentlemen that his position is false. And from 1906
onwards Sir Edward Grey's position had been very
illogical indeed. His ignorance of Continental psychology had tempted him in the early days of his office
to under-estimate the importance which would be
attached abroad to " conversations " between the
General Staffs. His expert knowledge of Ministerial
and Parliamentary psychology convinced him, on the
other hand, that, once these conversations had been
taken seriously by the foreigners, the Cabinet would
be extremely annoyed at not having been informed at
the time. Sir Edward Grey endeavoured therefore to
reconcile the hopes that he had, largely on his own
responsibility, aroused in France, with the doubts
which he had aroused in the enlightened, but somewhat envious, hearts of his colleagues. He embarked
on a shilly-shally business of trying simultaneously to
alleviate the anxieties of M. Cambon and those of Mr.
Lulu Harcourt. In this he failed.

Never has any man been faced with so appalling a
dilemma. Obviously the easiest course would have
been to deny the existence of any German menace, and
thereafter to allow the French and Russian Ententes to
die a natural death. No Foreign Secretary could possibly take such a risk or expose his country to the
danger of isolation in face of a dictatorial militarism.

He was bound to take the German menace as an axiom. Two alternatives were then open to him. He could have tried to purchase German disarmament by vast colonial concessions. This policy (and it offered every prospect of success) would not at the time have been approved by Parliament; it would have been interpreted as a breach of faith by France and Russia; and would in any case have left Germany still dominant upon the Continent. The second alternative was to define the Ententes in terms which left no doubt that France and Russia and England would co-operate in resisting all aggression; and then to come to an understanding with Germany for the removal of all future causes of friction. It was all very well for Nicolson and Crowe to urge this latter policy upon their chief: it was obvious that he could only impose such Continental commitments upon a Cabinet and Parliament frightened by the bogey of an Anglo-German war. How could he possibly exhibit such a bogey? The Cabinet itself was split into two parties. Grey's essential difficulty was that whereas the rulers of Germany could commit their country in secret, he himself could only definitely, or rather constructively, commit his country with Parliamentary sanction. It was thus inevitable that he should fall back on half-promises and day-to-day expedients. The issue in fact was one between oligarchic and democratic methods. And when it comes to secrecy it is the former which possesses the advantage.

We are able to-day to be wise after the event. We can argue, if we like, that the whole theory of " The German Menace " was a subjective fallacy. We can contend that anything was better than the discredit of co-operation with a country such as Russia. We can insist, with better justification, that even if the dominant party in Germany did desire to impose its will upon the British Empire, it would have been better if the British Government had submitted to such crass dictation rather than risk the death or mutilation of ten million young men. But these, at the time, were not the points at issue. The essential controversy, given the psychology at that date inevitably prevailing, centred around the problem whether it was more conducive to peace to menace Germany or to conciliate her. This riddle, and it is vital, cannot be answered by our present shell-shocked generation. For the moment it is necessary only to affirm that in wishing to come into the open, to show the solidarity and reliability of the Ententes, Nicolson desired solely to avert a European war. Whereas Grey's apprehensions were disturbed by his simultaneous desire to avert a Parliamentary crisis.

These criticisms of Sir Edward Grey must be qualified by one vital reservation which renders them nugatory. Nicolson and Crowe both felt that a military victory in the last resort was preferable to a national humiliation. Grey considered that war was justified only by the fight for life and death. Had he belonged to a later generation he would have felt (as some of us now begin to feel) that war is justified by no possible or conceivable provocation. His feet were tangled by the briars of pre-war conceptions : he stumbled and fumbled at places where Nicolson and Crowe saw clearly and incisively : their aim was to clear a way through the immediate thicket : his aim was to reach something wider. But if he stumbled, it was because his eyes—those sad eagle eyes—were fixed upon an ultimate and distant ideal. And it is for this reason that Sir Edward Grey shares with Bethmann Hollweg the honour of being, alone of pre-war statesmen, morally unassailable.

(3)

On becoming Head of the Foreign Office, Nicolson found himself concerned, not only with the administration of the Department and the attendant Diplomatic and Consular Services, but with the task of advising Sir Edward Grey upon all important matters of foreign policy. Hitherto he had specialised upon certain angles, upon Morocco or Russia, and had enjoyed composing those admirable despatches which even to-day impress one with their lucidity and judgment. He was now overwhelmed with a mass of subsidiary questions—some of them trivial, all of them exacting, and for most of which he had but little aptitude or interest. He would labour onwards unceasingly, cursing the fate which had condemned him to so cruel a penitentiary. He was by then sixty-one years of age, and in constant pain from rheumatism and arthritis. The first batch of Foreign Office telegrams would be brought to him at nine in the morning and the last batch at ten at night. Hours of his day were occupied in interviewing Foreign Ambassadors. Meanwhile the red despatch boxes—ten, twelve, fourteen, sixteen of them—would accumulate upon the table beside him. They filled him with nausea and despair. Never has any man so cordially disliked being Permanent Under Secretary of State.

To the sheer irksomeness of his daily functions was

added the unhappiness of feeling that he was scarcely suited to his task. He would remark sadly that he had been a good General in the Field, but that as Chief of the Staff he was a failure. He wrote to his youngest son as follows :

> " I am afraid that I am not a good head of an office. I am too easy-going in a way, and I always trust to men all cordially joining in keeping the machine going—but I hope that I never shirk myself. I do so hate rows."

It seems indeed that his resentment of the harassed and harried routine imposed upon him—the actual effect of this constant overwork upon his health—induced a mood of pessimism and self-dispraise which were not wholly justified by the facts. His wide knowledge and experience of all the essential problems, the confidence with which he was regarded by the French and Russian Governments, the complete intimacy of relations existing between him and the foreign Ambassadors, the actual authority of his prestige, were all assets of great value. His presence at the Foreign Office was a guarantee of the preservation of the Ententes. Moreover, he conducted with our representatives abroad an unceasing flow of private correspondence in which he kept them regularly informed of the atmosphere at home, and through which they also were able to provide him with information not suitable for inclusion in an official despatch. These letters were circulated only to Sir Edward Grey and the Cabinet, and did not pass through the Department. It is from this important correspondence that material for the following chapters has been derived.

Within a few weeks of his arrival at the Foreign

Office, Nicolson's knowledge of Russian conditions
and personalities was of advantage in removing a
misunderstanding which arose in connection with the
Tsar's visit to Potsdam on November 4, 1910. Iswolsky by then had appointed himself Ambassador at Paris,
from which vantage ground he proceeded to indulge in
a whole network of revengeful intrigues. His Under
Secretary, M. Sazonow, a fox-faced man, was appointed
Acting Minister for Foreign Affairs, an appointment
which was confirmed a few weeks later. M. Sazonow
accompanied his Sovereign to Potsdam and had several
long interviews with the Chancellor and Herr von
Kiderlen Waechter, who had by then been appointed
Foreign Secretary. Bethmann Hollweg assured M.
Sazonow that Germany would not encourage any
Austrian adventures in the Balkans, while Sazonow
assured Bethmann Hollweg that Russia would never
allow the Anglo-Russian Entente to assume an anti-
German complexion. " I do not think," Nicolson
wrote to Hardinge, who had already arrived in India,
" that anything occurred at Potsdam which need give
cause to the slightest uneasiness." [1] It subsequently
transpired, however, that Sazonow had promised
Germany a free hand, so far as Russia was concerned,
in the completion of the Baghdad Railway. It was
felt in Paris and London that the Russian Foreign
Minister should not have committed himself to a
scheme in regard to which he knew that his partners
in the Triple Entente desired to formulate certain
reservations. " Ce Monsieur," M. Pichon remarked
to Sir F. Bertie, " est insupportable." [2]   M. Jules

[1] A. N. to Lord Hardinge, November 30, 1910.
[2] Sir F. Bertie to A. N., February 8, 1911.

Cambon, at Berlin, was even more indignant. Sir
E. Goschen, on January 7, 1911, wrote to Nicolson
as follows :

" Cambon is furious with the whole thing. He told me
yesterday that officially he took the line that nothing that
had occurred at Potsdam, or afterwards, could disturb the
relations between France and Russia ; but he added
' Voulez-vous que je vous dise mon opinion ? Eh bien,
c'est que l'alliance Franco-Russe est f——.' I think that
we may take it for granted that Kiderlen's policy is to detach Russia from France and us, and that he has already
gone some way towards its realisation. He has evidently
been too much for Sazonoff, and I think that the latter is
much mistaken if he thinks that he can wriggle out of what
he has been brought to say and write."

M. Sazonow endeavoured to reassure his partners
by stating that by the expression " Baghdad Railway "
he had meant only " the railway as far as Baghdad."
Nicolson, for his part, took the whole incident calmly.
He did not wish to discourage M. Sazonow from
coming to an agreement with Germany :

" I am always afraid," he wrote, " that if Berlin considers
Russia is hesitating unduly she may herself break off all
further negotiations. This would be most deplorable, as
it would render the relations between Russia and Germany
worse than they were before and would also undoubtedly
give occasion for a furious campaign in the German press
against ourselves." [1] To Sir George Buchanan, who had
succeeded him as Ambassador in St. Petersburg, he expressed the same opinion : " It would be a misfortune
were these negotiations to have no result as, if they were
absolutely to fall through, relations between Germany and
Russia would be considerably impeded, and this is the last

---

[1] A. N. to Sir George Barclay, February 15, 1911.

thing which either we, or, I presume, Sazonow, would desire." [1]

These are the opinions of one whom Germans insist upon regarding as the main artificer of the policy of encirclement. No such policy existed.

(4)

Although Nicolson was thus anxious, within reason, to facilitate good relations between Germany and Russia, he viewed with some apprehension the course of the discussions which were then proceeding between Germany and England.[2] He knew that Herr von Bethmann Hollweg could only induce Admiral Tirpitz to consent to a substantial reduction in German naval construction if England offered in return, not only to make important colonial concessions, but also implicitly to abandon her Ententes with France and Russia. In other words, Germany would only pledge herself to recognise our permanent superiority at sea if we pledged ourselves to recognise Germany's permanent

---

[1] A. N. to Sir George Buchanan, January 17, 1911.

[2] The previous history of these negotiations is as follows : On July 14, 1909, Bethmann Hollweg succeeded Bülow as Chancellor. On August 21, 1909, he suggested to Goschen a naval arrangement between the two countries " as part of a general understanding." On September 1, 1909, we replied, cordially welcoming these overtures. On October 15, 1909, a preliminary discussion took place between Goschen and Bethmann Hollweg, from which it appeared that in return for a political agreement Germany would retard, but not reduce, her naval construction. On November 4, 1909, Bethmann Hollweg disclosed that by " political agreement " he meant some formula binding Great Britain to neutrality in the event of an attack by a third party on Germany, plus concessions in the colonies and regarding the Baghdad Railway. In view of the constitutional and parliamentary crisis in England we then suspended the negotiations. They were resumed in July of 1910, and on August 11, 1910, we offered to give assurances that we had no hostile intention against Germany, to discuss other matters, and to agree to temporary retardation of naval construction. It is at this point that the main narrative begins.

superiority on the Continent. This latter admission
constituted, in Nicolson's judgment, too great a risk.
What he feared was that the Cabinet, in their ignorance
of the ultimate authority exercised by Tirpitz and the
pan-Germans, would be inveigled into some arrangement which, while not safeguarding our naval security,
would weaken the security we derived from our understanding with Germany's neighbours. His attitude is
well illustrated in the following letters. On February 6,
1911, he wrote to Sir E. Goschen :

> " The utmost, so far as I can gather, that we have
> obtained from Germany in respect to a naval programme
> is that the Germans may possibly retard the dates of con-
> struction under their present naval law and that, if we
> do not desire to see an extension of that law, or rather if
> we wish to obtain from them a promise that that law will
> not be extended, we must arrive at a political agreement
> with them. Now retardation of the dates of construction
> may in practice be of great advantage rather than of
> disadvantage to the Germans. It would enable them to
> profit by experience of the present types of Dreadnoughts,
> and to introduce the improvements or developments
> which practice may have shown to be necessary. The
> final output in 1917 would remain precisely at the figure at
> present fixed, and so, by promising a retardation, they by
> no means afford us guarantees of such a nature as would
> permit us to diminish our own shipbuilding programme.
> Therefore anything which we can obtain from Germany
> in respect to naval construction can only come into effect
> six years hence, and in the meantime they wish us to tie
> our hands by some political agreement. This is far too
> one-sided an arrangement to please me, and, to tell you the
> truth, I do not see any way of arriving at a solution of the
> question between ourselves and Germany which would be
> satisfactory to both parties."

To Lord Hardinge he was even more explicit : [1]

"I hope that our Government now fully realise that the aim of Germany in these negotiations is to smash up, as far as she is able to do, the Triple Entente and that her chief object is to isolate France as much as possible. I am not completely at ease in my own mind that she may not succeed in this respect to a limited extent as it is known that at the present moment there is a wave in many circles here towards a friendly understanding with Germany. It is impossible to convince the adherents to this policy that Germany does not admit a friendship on equal terms and that we should find ourselves before long compelled to act in accordance with German wishes in every question which might arise. On the other hand it is, of course, impossible for us to take up an attitude adverse to the friendly understanding as we should be immediately accused of placing obstacles in the way of what these good people consider to be one of the strongest guarantees for peace. I look forward to a troublesome time during the next few months, but so far as my voice is heard it will always be in favour of a firm maintenance of our under-standing with France and Russia."

His doubts were confirmed by a letter which he received from Sir Cecil Spring Rice, at that time Minister in Stockholm : [2]

"The Swedish Foreign Minister told me that the German Chancellor had told him that negotiations were going on between him and Goschen about limitation of armaments but that there was not likely to be a practical conclusion arrived at ; because England could not accept any other condition except one giving her command of her own seas, in order to secure the safety of her supplies,

[1] To Lord Hardinge, April 19, 1911.
[2] From Sir C. Spring Rice, May 23, 1911.

and her own freedom from invasion—while no German Government could defend before the German public a convention which acknowledged for all time the German naval inferiority as part of the law of Europe."

The negotiations, meanwhile, dragged on in an inconclusive manner. " It looks to me," Nicolson wrote, " as if we were walking round each other, hesitating to come to close quarters ; and I am not sure that our Admiralty have any clear idea as to what proposals they could put down on paper." In May of 1911 the German Emperor paid a visit to London for the unveiling of the Victoria Memorial. He was, as always, received with friendly admiration. The anti-Russian party in the Cabinet and Parliament were much encouraged. The prospects for direct agreement with Germany appeared brighter than ever. It was this very moment that was selected by Herr von Kiderlen Waechter to make a gesture which brought England and Germany to the verge of war.

(5)

On the afternoon of July 1, 1911, Count Metternich, the German Ambassador, entered Nicolson's room at the Foreign Office and informed him that he had an important message to deliver. His manner " was extremely nervous and constrained." The Ambassador stated that owing to the disturbed condition of affairs in Morocco, and in response to the appeals which they had received " from certain German merchants," the German Government had decided to send a warship, the *Panther*, to Agadir. Nicolson expressed some surprise at this announcement and observed that Agadir was not one of the Moorish ports which were open to trade, and that he was unaware that there were any German residents or merchants in the vicinity. Count Metternich replied, with obvious embarrassment, that his instructions were simply to announce the fact and not to enter into any discussion on the subject. Nicolson suggested that the despatch of a warship to a Moorish port was a violation of the Act of Algeciras. " That," answered Count Metternich, " has already lost its validity." The Under Secretary of State confined himself to stating that he would transmit the message to Sir Edward Grey, who was returning the next day from his holiday, and that the latter would consult the Cabinet. Count Metternich then withdrew. On the same day, July 1, 1911, the *Panther* appeared in front of Agadir.

The Agadir incident provides an admirable illustration of the ineptitude of German diplomatic methods. On paper, the German Government possessed an excellent case. It was perfectly true that the Act of Algeciras had to all intents and purposes become a dead letter. The French had gradually extended their influence by methods not contemplated by that instrument,[1] and in April, 1911, M. Cruppi had announced the impending despatch of a French column to Fez. The German Government had at once intimated to Paris that such action would be considered an infringement of the Act of Algeciras and would entitle them to resume their liberty of action. They could thus

[1] The following are the stages by which the Act of Algeciras was violated. In 1907 General Lyautey occupied Oujda. In July of that year the French, owing to the murder of some French workmen, bombarded Casablanca. In 1908 Abdul Aziz was turned out by his brother Muley Hafid, who was considered to be in German pay. In 1910 a rising broke out in Fez and the French officials and colony appealed for protection. A column was despatched which entered the capital on May 21, 1911.

argue, with perfect justification, that they were fully entitled to send a warship to Agadir.

Such arguments, however, failed to carry conviction. In the first place, by the Franco-German Convention of February 9, 1909, Germany had already agreed to " disinterest herself politically " in Morocco in return for economic concessions. The details of these concessions had led to protracted negotiations between M. Jules Cambon, French Ambassador in Berlin, and Herr von Kiderlen Waechter. Only a week before despatching the *Panther* to Morocco, the German Foreign Minister had been engaged at Kissingen in a very friendly negotiation with M. Cambon. It is not surprising, therefore, that no well-informed person either in Paris or London believed for one moment in the explanations and assurances of the German Government. Nor did Herr von Kiderlen Waechter expect his statements to be taken at their face value. He at once informed M. Cambon that he would withdraw the *Panther* and give France a free hand in Morocco in return for substantial compensations elsewhere. When asked to disclose the nature of these compensations he indicated that what Germany wanted was practically the whole of the French Congo.

Foreign opinion was therefore correct in assuming from the outset that the " *Panther's* spring " was in no way connected with German rights or interests in Morocco but represented a desire on the part of the German Government to obtain something in hand for the purpose of future bargaining. Herr von Kiderlen's action was, in fact, a reversal to the old " Geiseltheorie " of Holstein—the theory that it is a clever diplomatic move to seize some pledge or

" Faustpfand " and to refuse to surrender it except in return for payment. Such a manœuvre is seldom successful. In the first place it is not often remunerative to ask for one thing when you want another. And in the second place this duplication of intention is apt to arouse distrust and opposition. Within a few weeks of Herr von Kiderlen's gesture it was admitted, even in Berlin, that he had committed a blunder. " German public opinion," wrote Goschen, " is beginning to realise that Agadir was a mistake and that it has put the Morocco question on a sabre-rattling footing from which it is difficult to retreat and dangerous to advance." [1]

It is questionable whether Herr von Kiderlen would have placed his country in so false a position had he not counted on the isolation of France. He did not believe that Russia would support her ally in a Moroccan question, and he was quite certain, such was the benignity being shown in London, that English public opinion would not be aroused. " It is curious," Nicolson wrote to Sir Fairfax Cartwright, " but I believe that this is the third occasion after an Imperial visit to London that something disagreeable has arisen. I imagine that the warmth of the reception which is always undoubtedly accorded to the Emperor in England completely misleads him as to its real purport and meaning, and he goes away with the firm conviction that he has got us comfortably in his pocket." [2]

Such illusions were quickly dispersed. On July 4 Sir Edward Grey told Count Metternich that our attitude could not be one of disinterestedness, and that

---

[1] Sir Edward Goschen to A. N., August 26, 1911.
[2] A. N. to Sir Fairfax Cartwright, July 24, 1911.

" we could not recognise any new agreements which might be come to without us." The German Government ignored this hint, and for twenty days they maintained an obstinate silence. On July 15 they opened direct negotiations with France. On July 21 Mr. Lloyd George, at a Mansion House luncheon to the City Bankers, made a statement on behalf of the Government. " If," he said, " a situation were to be forced upon us in which peace could only be preserved by the surrender of the great and beneficent position Britain has won by centuries of heroism and achievements ; by allowing Britain to be treated, where her interests were vitally affected, as if she were of no account in the Cabinet of Nations : then I say emphatically that peace at that price would be intolerable for a Great Country like ours to endure."

This statement, coming from such a source and at such a moment, burst like a bomb-shell upon Europe. It was only then that Herr von Kiderlen realised that it was a mistake to have chosen as his terrain a region of the world where Great Britain was bound by Treaty to give diplomatic support to France. " I have every belief," Nicolson wrote, " that the maintenance by us of our present attitude—and I am quite convinced that there will be no flinching on our side—may eventually render Germany more compliant and reasonable. She will see that the Triple Entente is not so weak a combination as she apparently imagined. She has in fact committed a great blunder. I think she will have great difficulty in extricating herself from it without losing considerable prestige." [1]

Meanwhile the negotiations between Herr von

[1] To Sir G. Buchanan, August 1, 1911.

Kiderlen and M. Jules Cambon were progressing. On July 19 the former had warned the French Ambassador that Germany, if she did not obtain what she desired in the Congo, would go " to the bitter end." On July 25 Count Metternich made to Sir Edward Grey a communication of so minatory a character that the latter felt obliged to warn the Admiralty that " the fleet might be attacked at any moment." [1] By August M. Jules Cambon was constrained to report to his Government that " it would be mere levity not to foresee a conflict," and von Kiderlen at the same date was proclaiming that " the attitude of France made war almost inevitable." The crisis reached its height in the middle of September. On September 17 Sir Edward Grey, who was at Fallodon, wrote as follows to Nicolson :

" The negotiations with Germany may at any moment take an unfavourable turn, and, if they do so, the Germans may act very quickly, even suddenly. The Admiralty should remain prepared for this. It is what I have always said to McKenna. Our fleets should, therefore, always be in such a condition and position that they would welcome a German attack, if the Germans should decide on that suddenly. We should, of course, give the Admiralty news immediately of any unfavourable turn in the Franco-German negotiations, but German action might follow so soon after this, that there would not be time to get our ships together if they were not in positions whence this could be done quickly. I should like to be sure that the Admiralty are keeping this in mind. I am puzzled by the German optimistic reports of the prospect of the Franco-German negotiations. They may be, and probably are, intended to prepare the way for a climb down : but they

---

[1] Winston Churchill, *The World Crisis*, vol. i., p. 48.

may be intended to mislead and lull suspicions before a rapid coup."

Our preparations were in fact far more advanced than was realised by British public opinion. It was not known, for instance, that from September 8 to September 22 of 1911 we were in constant expectation of hostilities, and that the tunnels and bridges on the South Eastern Railway were being patrolled day and night. It was not till the morning of September 22, on the receipt of news from Berlin that Herr von Kiderlen was weakening, that Nicolson was able to give the word that a state of " war preparedness " might be relaxed. The extent of this preparedness can be gauged by the letter which he wrote to Lord Hardinge on September 14 :

" I spent a week at Balmoral last week, but nothing very important occurred during my visit. I was glad to find that the King is perfectly sound as regards foreign affairs. I have had some talks since my return with Haldane, Lloyd George, and Winston Churchill ; I am glad to find that all three are perfectly ready—I might almost say eager —to face all possible eventualities, and most careful preparations have been made to meet any contingencies that may arise. These three have thoroughly grasped the point that it is not merely Morocco which is at stake. It really amounts to a question as to whether we ought to submit to any dictation by Germany, whenever she considers it necessary to raise her voice. I may tell you in confidence that preparations for landing four or six divisions on the Continent have been worked out to the minutest detail. On the other hand reports which we have received from our various military informants all point to the fact that the French army has never been in a better state of equipment, organisation and armament, or been inspired by so strong a feeling of perfect confidence and unity, and in short they would enter into a campaign feeling that they were able to meet their adversary on very nearly equal terms, and that the issue will not necessarily be, as I believe many people in Germany consider, unfavourable to the French arms. At the same time I cannot conceive that Germany would desire to push matters to an extremity, unless they are deluded by the overweening confidence which the German Emperor has more than once expressed to several people with whom he has had conversations lately. If one can attach credence to what he says, he is firmly convinced that Germany would have a military promenade through France ; that Russia would be slowly lumbering up on its eastern frontier, and would arrive far too late to throw any serious weight into the scale before the French had been thoroughly defeated and humiliated ; and as regards ourselves he believes that we could take no active part. If such be his real opinion he might possibly be attempting a venture at hostilities ; but I think he would find himself most gravely deceived in his forecast."

The attitude adopted by the English Cabinet produced a panic upon the Berlin Stock Exchange, and von Kiderlen immediately abated his demands. He no longer asked for practically the whole of the French Congo. He asked only for such concessions as France would readily be able to afford. On October 11 he agreed to recognise France's position in Morocco ; on November 3 a Convention was signed by which France ceded certain Congo territory to Germany. The crisis was over.

It cannot be denied, however, that what Grey described as " this fit of political alcoholism " left Europe with an aching head. German public opinion vented upon Great Britain their fury at having been exposed to a diplomatic defeat : they contended that, but for

Mr. Lloyd George, they could easily have come to an amicable arrangement with the French Government. It subsequently transpired that they were correct in this assertion. Unknown to us, as also to the French Foreign Office, M. Caillaux, then President of the French Council of Ministers, had all the time been conducting subterranean negotiations of a most capitulatory character through the medium of international finance. It was not till the end of the year that these negotiations were disclosed. On January 15, 1912, Nicolson wrote to Sir Edward Goschen as follows :

"I should very much like to hear what view Jules Cambon takes of the revelations which have recently occurred in France in respect to the extraordinary line followed by the former President of the Council. I must say that the disclosures which have been made explain to a certain extent the irritation which arose in Germany in regard to our attitude and the charges which they brought against us of having impeded a satisfactory settlement with France. We were, of course, entirely ignorant of the secret negotiations which Caillaux was carrying on through financiers and other channels. No doubt the German Government considered that they would be able to come to terms with him of a far more satisfactory kind than was eventually the case. Our action naturally ran across these underhand negotiations, though, as far as we are concerned, we acted in perfect innocence of what was proceeding. I think it is a very good sign that the French nation has declined to be a party to such proceedings and have demanded that their diplomacy should be open and above board and conducted by those who are responsible for it. Caillaux seems to have kept the President of the Republic, as well as his colleagues, completely in the dark, and I think that it is a matter of satisfaction that he has been definitely removed from office."

The issue, however, had been far wider and deeper than a mere controversy as to whether France should obtain Morocco or Germany the Congo, or whether Joseph Caillaux was, or was not, a crook. From the outset Nicolson had realised that here again arose the problem of whether or no Germany was to dominate the Continent. On July 24, 1911, he had written as follows to Sir Edward Goschen :

"There is no use in disguising the fact that the situation is a serious and delicate one, and it is not simply a question as to whether the French will give such and such concessions to Germany or whether the establishment of Germany in such and such ports in Morocco is or is not a vital question for us. The whole question is whether we intend to maintain the Triple Entente, and I think that it is upon this broad ground that the situation should be viewed. If the French really saw any weakening on our part in that respect, they would, in all probability, make terms with Germany, quite irrespective of us, and they would never forgive us for having failed them at a critical moment. The result would be that we should then have a triumphant Germany and an unfriendly France and Russia and our policy since 1904 of maintaining the equilibrium, and consequently the peace, of Europe would be completely wrecked. Moreover, the change in our relations both with France and Russia would materially alter our naval situation in the Mediterranean and elsewhere, and would eventually entail increased naval estimates, and would also render our position in Central Asia both unstable and insecure. I think that our Government fully realise this, so that I am not uneasy that such a catastrophe will occur. At the same time we are face to face with a very grave problem which will require very careful and cautious handling."

Nicolson kept on reverting to the necessity of

rendering the Ententes more dependable and more open. Even before the Agadir crisis, in a letter of May 17, 1911, he had expressed his views to Sir F. Bertie :

" You can quite understand that there is considerable hesitation here to binding ourselves to any definite course of action in view of possible eventualities. Personally I should wish that some arrangement in the nature which you indicate could be made. I gather that there has been a certain amount of desultory talk between our military authorities and the French military authorities but nothing definite seems to have been laid down. To my mind this is unfortunate, and I quite agree with you that if a crisis does arise it will be sudden and probably unexpected."

The results of the Agadir panic induced no relaxation of the prevailing tension. In France it led, in January, 1912, to the removal of M. Caillaux and the emergence of M. Poincaré and the policy of revenge. In Germany it produced a feeling of humiliation. In England it evoked increased uneasiness. " That Germany," Nicolson wrote, " will seize the first opportunity for recovering her position I have very little doubt. We are evidently entering into a period in which we shall be obliged still further to increase our naval estimates in order to be ready to meet all possible contingencies. Paul Cambon considers that even if negotiations succeed a conflict will by no means be improbable within the next two or three years. The bitter feeling against us will necessitate our being constantly on the watch. The future, therefore, is not very bright." [1]

---

[1] A. N. to Sir Fairfax Cartwright, September 18, 1911, and to Sir E. Goschen of the same date.

(6)

Nicolson's anxieties during the Agadir crisis had been increased by acute apprehension regarding our relations with Russia. The Russian Government (as might perhaps have been foreseen) did not share our desire to render Persia a prosperous buffer State immune to external interference. They laid marked stress upon those clauses of the Anglo-Russian Convention which bound England not to oppose Russian penetration in northern Persia ; and they ignored the clauses of the same Convention which pledged Russia to respect Persian integrity and independence.[1]   In June of 1908 M. Hartwig, their Minister in Tehran, instructed Colonel Liakhoff of the Cossack Brigade to bombard the Persian Parliament and to assist Mohammed Ali Shah to re-establish an autocracy. This action aroused much criticism in England, and Sir Edward Grey was hard put to it to answer Parliamentary questions in such a manner as not to give offence. Mohammed Ali Shah, for his part, was too unscrupulous even for the gentle fatalism of his subjects. This monarch has been described as " the most perverted, cowardly, and vice-sodden monster that has disgraced the throne of Persia in many generations." [2]   In April

[1] The following events had occurred in Persia since Nicolson's departure in 1887. On May 1, 1896, Nasr-ed-Din Shah had been assassinated, and had been succeeded by Mazaffer-ed-Din, a very foolish old potentate. In 1906 an agitation took place against him, the populace demanded a Constitution, 16,000 people took refuge in the British Legation, and the Shah promised a Constitution and the election of a Parliament or Majlis. Muzaffer-ed-Din died on January 4, 1907, and was succeeded by Mohammed Ali. The latter was completely in Russian pay, and his subservience to M. Hartwig led to increasing friction between the Court and the Majlis. It was to suppress this opposition that Colonel Liakhoff made the coup d'état of June 23, 1908.

[2] Morgan Shuster, *The Strangling of Persia*, pa. xxi.

of 1909 his country rose against him : the Persian nationalists flew to arms in the northern provinces : the Bakhtiari Khans advanced on the capital from the south : the Russians, for their part, shipped two regiments from Baku which, on July 11, 1909, occupied Kasvin, a shambling city about ninety miles from Tehran. The Nationalist and Bakhtiari troops were able, however, to dodge round the Russian forces ; to enter the capital unopposed ; and to proclaim the deposition of Mohammed Ali Shah in favour of his infant son Sultan Ahmed. Mohammed Ali, clasping the great diamond, the Darya-i-Nur, in his podgy hand, bolted into the Russian Legation. After protracted negotiations he was allowed to proceed to Odessa where the Russian Government undertook to keep him under supervision. The Constitution was re-enacted ; and on November 15, 1909, the Majlis was again opened amid scenes of great public enthusiasm.

These events led to a certain divergence of attitude between the Russian and the British Legations. The latter sympathised with the constitutional movement ; the former sympathised only with Mohammed Ali. As a result of repeated representations addressed by Sir G. Buchanan to the Russian Government, M. Hartwig was transferred to Belgrade, where his abundant energy was devoted to encouraging Serbia to intrigue against Austria-Hungary. He was succeeded by M. Poklewsky Koziell, a gentleman who had enjoyed great popularity in London society by being continuously willing to play bridge as a partner of King Edward. The arrival of M. Poklewsky, who was quite incapable of controlling his subordinates (or indeed anything else), did not lead to more scrupulous

z

observance on the part of Russian agents of the Anglo-Russian Convention. " The English," M. Sazonow wrote to M. Poklewsky on October 8, 1910, " pursuing as they do vital aims in Europe will, if necessary, sacrifice certain interests in Asia in order to maintain the Convention with us. These circumstances we can naturally turn to our advantage." This meant that M. Poklewsky was expected to treat Northern Persia, and the Persian Government, as the vassals of St. Petersburg. He completely fulfilled these expectations. Complaint after complaint poured in upon Downing Street. Nicolson was at pains to defend Russian misdeeds. It is still recounted in the Foreign Office that he minuted a bulky memorandum on Russian violations of the Convention with the words : " I have not read this document. But if, as I assume, it contains criticisms of Russian procedure in Persia, it is largely based on prejudice and false assumptions."

In the summer of 1911 events occurred which even so convinced a Russophil as Nicolson found it difficult to defend. In May of that year Mr. Morgan Shuster, a young, optimistic and convivial American, arrived in Tehran for the purpose of acting as Financial Adviser to the Persian Government. He at once let it be known that he for his part was not prepared to recognise the Anglo-Russian Convention. He was warmly supported by the Nationalist deputies in the Majlis, who invested him with almost dictatorial powers. He proceeded to execute these powers with great energy, promptitude and indiscretion. In July of 1911 Mohammed Ali, the ex-Shah, escaped from Russian detention at Odessa and landed in Persia. Mr. Shuster organised a force for his capture and offered the command of this force to Major Stokes, an energetic officer who had at the moment completed his term of service as Military Attaché to the British Legation. The Russian Government stated that if Major Stokes were in any capacity employed in Northern Persia they would regard such employment as a violation of the Anglo-Russian Convention. Their representations were inevitably supported by the British Legation, but neither Mr. Shuster nor Major Stokes could be induced to surrender. The dispute raged throughout the summer ; and meanwhile Mohammed Ali's forces were defeated and the ex-Shah was himself obliged again to bolt. MM. Poklewsky and Sazonow felt that the failure of the ex-Shah, and the arrogance displayed towards them by Mr. Shuster, had damaged their prestige.

Nicolson found it necessary to warn our Minister in Tehran, who was finding it increasingly difficult to conceal his warm sympathy for Mr. Shuster. " It would be disastrous," Nicolson wrote, " were the understandings between Russia and ourselves to be weakened in any way whatever." [1] To Lord Stamfordham Nicolson admitted " that it will be difficult for us to defend Russian action in Parliament as the Russians on this occasion have not got a strong case." [2] He at the same time wrote to Mr. O'Beirne at St. Petersburg begging him to restrain M. Sazonow's ardour. These representations were of no avail. On November 29, 1911, the Russian Legation, profiting by a dispute between some Treasury gendarmes and the Russian Cossacks, addressed an ultimatum to the Persian Government in

---

[1] To Sir G. Barclay, October 24, 1911.
[2] To Lord Stamfordham, November 13, 1911.

which they demanded the dismissal of Mr. Shuster within forty-eight hours. On December 1 this ultimatum was rejected by the Persian Government acting under pressure from the Majlis. On December 2 Sir Edward Grey summoned Count Benckendorff and informed him that he himself would be unable to retain the post of British Foreign Secretary if Russia were to occupy and administer Northern Persia in violation of the Convention. The Russians in their reply were profuse in assurances that their action was merely temporary. On December 14 Major Stokes left Persia for England. On January 11, 1912, Mr. Shuster left Persia for the United States. " It is enough," so wrote our Minister at Tehran, " to make the angels weep to see all Shuster's machinery fall into incapable hands. Even if we were able to get the Persians to appoint Mornard in his place the latter is nothing but a pigmy compared to Shuster. I *really* liked that man."

The crisis, for the moment, had passed. The Russians remained in occupation of certain towns in Persia, but they did not proceed to any regular occupation of the country.[1] The whole incident, however, left an unfortunate impression. Mr. Shuster was banqueted by the Liberals on his way through London, and M. Sazonow was outraged by this demonstration. Nicolson, for his part, was ordered by his doctor to take a complete rest for several weeks.

---

[1] The Russian troops, however, remained in occupation of several Persian towns. In March of 1912, they proceeded, without provocation, to bombard the town of Meshed, and damaged the sacred Mosque of the Imam Reza. Shia opinion was outraged by this gratuitous iniquity. By then, however, British opinion, and therefore the House of Commons, were more interested in the loss of the *Titanic*.

XIII

THE BALKAN WARS

[1912-1913]

The Italian seizure of Tripoli—Its effects in Europe—Split between the civilians and military in Vienna—M. Tcharykoff's scheme—Strained relations between Berlin and Vienna—Death of Aehrenthal and appointment of Berchtold—Nicolson attempts in vain to leave the Foreign Office—Cassel and Ballin—The Haldane Mission—The subsequent negotiations for a neutrality formula—Failure of the negotiations— Anxiety in Paris—The Naval Agreement with France—Colonial negotiations with Germany—Russian intrigues in the Balkans—The Balkan League—Outbreak of the First Balkan War—Germany restrains Austria—The Grey-Cambon letters—The Tyrrell-Kühlmann conversations—Improvement in Anglo-German relations—The Ambassadors' Conference—The Peace negotiations between the Balkans and Turkey— The Second Balkan War—The Treaty of Bucharest—Resultant situation —Sir F. Cartwright's warning.

(1)

For the sake of our Entente with France we had been brought, during the Agadir crisis, to the very edge of War. For the sake of our Entente with Russia we had become accessories to the strangling of Persia. In the autumn of 1911 a further incident occurred in which our freedom of moral and political action was hampered by our subservience to Russian ambitions and prejudices.

On September 27, 1911, Marchese Imperiali, the Italian Ambassador in London, called upon Nicolson and announced that Italy had decided to occupy the Turkish provinces of Tripoli and Cyrenaica. Nicolson suggested that this was an act of war, if not of spoliation. Marchese Imperiali admitted that a state of war might result between Turkey and Italy, but he asked for the " moral support " of the British Government. Nicolson replied that the attitude of England towards Italy's action was not one which could be lightly decided, and that Sir Edward Grey would desire to consult the Cabinet. In reporting this conversation to the Secretary of State Nicolson suggested that, while we had no desire to alienate the sympathies of Italy, yet it would be difficult for us to approve of Italian action. " I should be inclined," he wrote, " to avoid the expression ' moral support.' " Sir Edward Grey replied from Fallodon : " I rather think my absence at this moment, though undesigned, is not undiplomatic."

On September 28, 1911, Italy declared war on Turkey. On October 5 she landed troops at Tripoli and Benghazi. In November she proclaimed the annexation of the two provinces and proceeded to occupy the Islands of the Dodecanese. The Powers, for their part, were anxious to mediate, foreseeing that if the war were protracted there was a danger that the Balkan States might take advantage of Turkey's difficulties. Neither Turkey nor Italy were, however, particularly anxious for mediation. They did not seriously desire to make peace since they were not seriously engaged in waging war. The importance of the Tripoli incident is to be sought rather in its effect upon the grouping of the several Powers.

Both France and Russia were bound by secret Treaty to raise no objection to Italy's spoliation of Turkey. England desired to remain neutral and aloof, and a similar attitude was imposed on Germany, who felt herself unable to intervene in a war declared by an ally on a friend. The attitude of Austria, however, was peculiar and interesting.

Baron von Aehrenthal had never forgiven Germany for taking to herself the whole credit for the solution of the Bosnian crisis. From 1909 onwards Vienna had tended to become more and more independent of Berlin. The military party, headed by the Archduke Franz Ferdinand and General Conrad von Hoetzen-dorff, had for long been urging that Italy would be far less dangerous as an enemy than as an ally. They desired to take advantage of the Tripoli expedition to fall upon Italy from behind. They desired, by means of what they called a " preventative war," to secure that in the impending struggle with Russia their southern ally should not stab them in the back. Baron von Aehrenthal, although he had no illusions as to the military or moral value of Italy, felt that politically she was a useful member of the Triple Alliance. Without her, Vienna would have to face Berlin alone. He therefore opposed the Archduke and Conrad von Hoetzendorff, and when they endeavoured to force his hand he extracted from the old Emperor an order dis-missing General Conrad from his post. By this action he created an undying feud between the Ballplatz and the General Staff, a feud which was to have disastrous consequences in July of 1914.

A second subsidiary development of the Tripoli war should also be noted. On October 23, 1911, the Russian Ambassador at Constantinople, M. Tcharykoff (a man whom Nicolson described as a " vain and ambitious busybody "), offered the Turkish Govern-ment a Russian guarantee of Constantinople and ad-joining territory in return for the freedom of the

Straits. The Turks were much alarmed by this offer, and on October 31 they approached London with a proposal for an Anglo-Turkish Alliance. The British Government, owing to their desire not to offend Russia, were obliged to return a most evasive reply to these overtures. The Turks then turned to Marschall von Bieberstein. From that moment the bond between Germany and Turkey became indissoluble.

The relations between Berlin and Vienna were, on the other hand, increasingly strained. The German General Staff were alarmed and angered by Baron von Aehrenthal's summary removal of Conrad von Hoetzendorff. In November it became known that the Austrian Foreign Minister intended to float an enormous loan upon the Paris Bourse. The French Government, it was felt, would not permit the quotation of such a loan unless they had received positive assurances of Austrian neutrality in the case of war. The German Government were thus delighted when they learnt in December of 1911 that Baron von Aehrenthal was suffering from leucocythaemia. He died on February 17, 1912. He was succeeded by Count Berchtold, Austrian Ambassador in St. Petersburg and a former colleague of Arthur Nicolson's. Count Berchtold was a man of excellent intentions and engaging manners : Nicolson doubted, however, whether he would have sufficient strength or capacity to resist the Archduke and Conrad von Hoetzendorff. He expressed his apprehensions to the Ambassador in Vienna. " I have the greatest doubts," he wrote, " whether Berchtold will be able to take an independent line of his own in any matters of foreign policy. I do not think, however, that he will try to establish more intimate relations with St. Petersburg : it is of essential importance that Russia and Austria should come to an agreement in regard to the affairs of South Eastern Europe." [1] Writing to Lord Hardinge he was even less optimistic :

> "I am afraid that with the death of Aehrenthal the Archduke may have a far more open field before him. The old Emperor, of course, is opposed to this policy, but he dreads, I am told, having scenes with his Heir-apparent, and the latter does not scruple to put the strongest pressure upon his uncle. I think you know Berchtold very well and I am sure that you will agree with me that, however charming and amiable may be his qualities, he is scarcely of sufficient calibre or strength of will adequately to fill the place of Aehrenthal." [2]

Intimate relations between Berlin and Vienna were, in fact, soon established, and the slight disturbance caused by the Tripoli war was soon forgotten. The Triple Alliance was renewed in December of 1912 for a period of fourteen years.

Nicolson, under the strain of office work and arthritis, had aged considerably in the eighteen months he had been at the Foreign Office. He longed to escape again into diplomacy. He suggested to Sir Edward Grey that he might be allowed, on the retirement of Sir Fairfax Cartwright, to obtain the Embassy at Vienna, where his intimacy with Count Berchtold might prove of some value. Sir Edward Grey at first saw no objection to this proposal. It was represented to him, however, by those who did not wish the post of Permanent Under-Secretary to fall into the hands of a

---

[1] A. N. to Sir Fairfax Cartwright, February 19, 1912.
[2] A. N. to Lord Hardinge, February 22, 1912.

younger man, that the appointment of Nicolson as Ambassador in Vienna would arouse the suspicions of the German Government. Sir Edward Grey informed Nicolson that he was indispensable in Downing Street.

(2)

In the late winter of 1911 Sir Ernest Cassel had a bright idea. He felt that the increasing rivalry between his home-land and his father-land was leading both countries to the verge of disaster. He placed himself in communication with his friend, Albert Ballin of the Hamburg-Amerika Line. Cassel was to tell the British Government that the Emperor had expressed a wish to receive a Cabinet Minister in Berlin. Albert Ballin was to tell the Emperor that the British Government desired to send a special representative to Germany to discuss an accommodation. The arrangement worked admirably. The Emperor signified his willingness to receive such an emissary : the British Cabinet were delighted to accept such an invitation. They selected Mr. Haldane as their representative. He arrived in Berlin on February 8, 1912.

" Sir Arthur Nicolson," writes M. Poincaré, " augurait mal de cette tentative et avait essayé de l'empêcher." [1] This statement is only partially correct. Nicolson knew that whatever he might say would make no impression on the Cabinet, nor did he attempt to raise objection to Mr. Haldane's mission. On the other hand he regarded that mission with anxiety and dismay. He foresaw that in the last resort Herr von Bethmann Hollweg would not be strong

---

[1] Raymond Poincaré, *Au service de la France*, vol. i., p. 165.

enough to impose upon Admiral von Tirpitz any substantial reduction of the naval programme. He feared,
on the other hand, that Mr. Haldane might be inveigled
into making political concessions in return for some
flimsy assurance of naval retardation. His apprehensions were largely confirmed by the event.

On learning of the Franco-German agreement regarding Morocco,[1] Admiral von Tirpitz at once took
the train to Berlin. " I went," he records in his
memoirs, " to Berlin in the autumn and represented to
the Chancellor that we had suffered a diplomatic check
and must meet it by a supplementary Naval Bill." The
details of this supplementary estimate, or " Novelle,"
were not known to Mr. Haldane when he arrived in
Germany. He was given a copy of it by the Emperor,
which he put in his pocket for examination on his
return. It provided for the creation of a reserve
squadron, and thus secured that four-fifths of the
German navy would continuously be upon a war
footing : it provided also for a substantial increase of
personnel, and the extra construction of three battleships and two armoured cruisers. Mr. Haldane, however, did not glance at this formidable document until
his return to London. During his two days' visit to
Berlin he confined himself to crooning over past misunderstandings, to offering Germany such things as
Zanzibar, Pemba and other colonial compensations,
and to discussing a formula for British neutrality in the
event of war. He returned on February 10 bringing
with him no definite assurances upon the naval question, but a German formula of neutrality which, if
agreed to, would have effectually prevented us from

[1] *See* p. 348.

supporting France or Russia in the event of Germany becoming " entangled in war " with either of these two countries.[1] The only concession which Germany offered in return for our abandonment of the Ententes was to " slow down " the rate of construction, not of the existing naval programme, but of the additions thereto proposed in the Draft Novelle of 1913. It seems incredible that the German Government, realising as they did that the Haldane mission was an absolutely serious gesture, should have responded to it in so negative a manner. Of all problems of German pre-war diplomacy this is the one which it is most difficult to understand or to explain.

The resultant situation was well summarised in a letter which Sir Edward Goschen addressed to Nicolson on February 10, 1912 :

" What does it amount to ? That, if what has been suggested is carried out, the Germans get what, under Grey's instructions, I have been opposing for two years, namely, a political understanding without a naval agreement. For I cannot regard a relaxation in the ' tempo ' of a brand new and additional naval programme as a naval arrangement. We more or less rejected a relaxation of the ' tempo ' of the original Naval Law as a rather worthless concession, and now it is proposed that we should accept a relaxation of a new Law which will add a number of ships to the German Navy and bring its personnel up to about 80,000 men as a *quid pro quo* for the realisation of Germany's dearest wish, namely, a political understanding —an agreement, which, however carefully drawn up as regards the ' aggressive ' point, is only too likely to hamper us in the future. I pointed out most of this to Haldane, and to tell you the truth he is rather depressed at

[1] The text of this amazing document can be found in Mr. Haldane's admirable book, *Before the War*, p. 64.

not getting more—but he said that after all a political
understanding was the main thing—so said the Emperor,
and so said the Chancellor, and so they have said for two
years. That it was possible for Haldane to get more, I do
not believe, but I am not surprised that both the Emperor
and the Chancellor were ' in a good mood.' Besides the
understanding, we appear to be willing to give them
Zanzibar, and facilitate at a given moment their acquisition
of certain Portuguese possessions, besides a share in our
concessions in South Persia. On the other hand, what do
we get ? No naval arrangement such as might relieve our
taxpayers, only a relaxation in the ' tempo ' of construction
outside the old Naval Law, and fair promises about Timor
and the Baghdad Railway. I told Haldane that I thought
they were getting, more or less, their heart's desire at a
cheaper price than we had fixed before : and I think this is
a pity, as recent events have shown that our position,
unhampered by a political understanding, is a strong one,
and our price should therefore have been raised, not
lowered. Thank goodness, Haldane has been firm enough
on the two keels to one question. That is a practical
argument which may yet have some influence on their
construction programme. Tirpitz is evidently much
exercised by Haldane's assurance that the two keels to one
are inevitable. Cambon is pale but calm : but whatever
he says I can see that he is not comfortable : and I hear
that the Russian Embassy is rather in dismay : but then
they do not in the least know what Haldane has been
doing."

The negotiations initiated by Mr. Haldane did not
cease on the latter's return to London. He impressed
upon his colleagues in the Cabinet that it was impossible to hope for any naval offer from Germany unless
we could first provide Herr von Bethmann Hollweg
with such political concessions as would enable him to
convince the pan-Germans. Discussions continued,

therefore, upon the question of the "neutrality formula." On March 12 Count Metternich indicated to Mr. Haldane that the German Government might not merely suspend, but even modify, the draft Novelle, in return for a "suitable political formula." He was told that no formula would be acceptable which committed us to unconditional neutrality in the event of Germany becoming "entangled" in war. The Ambassador stated that his Government did not insist upon the word "entangled" and would accept the phrase "if war is forced upon Germany." We for our part offered to undertake "neither to make nor join in any unprovoked attack upon Germany." This phrase, in its turn, did not meet with the approval of the German Government. Sir Edward Grey during these discussions was fully occupied by the coal strike, and the onus of the negotiations fell upon Nicolson, who remained in close contact with Mr. Haldane. It became increasingly clear that the discussion of neutrality formulas was not likely to lead to any result. Nicolson wrote to Grey on April 4, 1912, as follows :

"Let us definitely abandon formulas, which are at the best dangerous and embarrassing documents, and the signature of which would, in present circumstances, apparently affect our relations with France. Were we to continue to endeavour to find words which would satisfy Germany, we should gradually be led into signing a document restrictive of our liberty of action, and which would, thereby, remove, to my mind, one of the best guarantees of peace. So long as Germany cannot rely on our abstention or neutrality, so long will she not be disposed to disturb the peace."

The final decision, however, came from the side of

Germany. Bethmann Hollweg stated that as we considered the German neutrality formula went too far,
and as they did not consider that our formula went far
enough, it would be better to abandon all further discussion of the matter. He therefore proposed to lay
before the Reichstag the proposed Novelle which he
had offered to suspend or even to modify. He was
at the same time quite ready to discuss in an amicable
spirit the question of territorial exchanges in Africa.
The Novelle finally became law on June 14, 1912.

(3)

Mr. Haldane's visit to Berlin and the subsequent
discussions of a neutrality formula aroused the greatest
anxiety in Paris. The French Government considered
it necessary to review their whole international position
and they summoned M. Paul Cambon to their deliberations. M. Cambon returned to London on April 14,
1912, and on the following day he visited Nicolson at
the Foreign Office. Nicolson recorded their conversation in a minute to Sir Edward Grey. This minute
throws so important a light on the past, present and
future relations between the French and British
Governments that it is permissible to reproduce it
textually and at length :

> " M. Cambon spoke to me to-day in regard to our
> relations with France. He said that in 1905, when
> Germany was pressing France hard, Lord Lansdowne had
> mentioned to him that H.M. Government would be
> disposed to strengthen and extend the understanding with
> France, and would be ready to discuss the matter. M.
> Cambon had conveyed this proposal to M. Delcassé, then
> Foreign Minister, who had replied by telegraph authorizing

M. Cambon to enter upon discussions. M. Cambon did not act upon those instructions ; and wrote to M. Delcassé explaining that he would prefer, before entering upon discussions with Lord Lansdowne, to be assured that M. Rouvier, then President of the Council, agreed with M. Delcassé and desired to strengthen and extend the understanding. M. Delcassé, therefore, brought the question before the French Cabinet, and M. Rouvier declared that he was opposed to any extension of the understanding. M. Delcassé, therefore, tendered his resignation. M. Rouvier at that time was initiating his negotiations with Germany in regard to Morocco, and was unwilling to take any steps which might hamper these negotiations. Later M. Rouvier discovered that he had made a blunder, and that Germany was leading him into a position which would be detrimental to French interests, and was, indeed, manœuvring him into a situation which was humiliating and irksome, and from which France would have difficulty in extricating herself. He, therefore, changed his attitude, and expressed his willingness to enter into discussions with H.M. Government with a view of securing to France the assistance of Great Britain in the event of France being forced into hostilities with Germany. In the meantime the Conservative Government had resigned office, and on M. Cambon approaching Sir E. Grey with the object of opening discussions on the lines indicated by Lord Lansdowne, he ascertained that the new British Government were unwilling to go as far as M. Rouvier desired, and the matter was dropped. Now M. Poincaré was frequently being asked by men of standing and influence in France as to how far France could count upon British support in the event of any difficulties with Germany. Public opinion, M. Cambon continued, had been much aroused in France over the Agadir incident and subsequent developments, and there was a universal feeling in France, of a strength and extent which was surprising, that should Germany endeavour to place on

France any affront the country must resent and repel it. In Germany too there was a strong chauvinistic feeling prevailing, of which the large increases in the German army and the active military preparations were symptomatic. The French Government were convinced that an opportunity would be seized, perhaps not this year, but possibly the next year or the year after, by Germany to create some incident which would arouse public feeling on both sides of the frontier, and which would, viewing the temper in both countries, very probably lead to war. The German Emperor and the German Chancellor were, doubtless, pacifically inclined, but they were not, in reality, the influential and deciding factors. The Pan-Germans, the Navy League, and other chauvinistic elements, the military, etc., were the factors which had the greatest weight and influence. In these circumstances, M. Poincaré considered that it was necessary to take stock of the position of France, and to see on what outside assistance she could rely when the moment arrived. It was evident that the attitude of England was a very important factor, and the recent endeavours of Germany to neutralise her clearly indicated that England was regarded as the Power which held largely the balance for or against peace. Were Germany assured that England would remain neutral, her hands would be free for dealing with France. Were she in doubt, she would hesitate. But it was of great importance to France also to be assured what would be the attitude of England, and if she could count upon her. M. Poincaré was anxious to be clear in his mind on that point, and the very recent assurances and communications which he had received from H.M. Government had not been sufficiently clear and precise thoroughly to satisfy and enlighten him.

"I told M. Cambon that, in a question of such importance, I naturally could only give him my personal opinion. I would tell him frankly that personally I was, as he knew, a warm adherent of the understanding with

France, and no one would be better pleased than myself if
it were strengthened. But there were certain facts which
should be borne in mind. In the first place I doubted
extremely if H.M. Government would be at all disposed
to tie their hands in any way as to any line of action which
they would adopt in any possible contingencies. They
would, I felt sure, desire to preserve complete liberty of
action. Moreover, among large sections of the community
of late there was a strong feeling, which was shared
possibly by some members of the Government, that some
' understanding ' should be arrived at with Germany ;
there was no very clear conception as to what was meant
by an understanding, but it was felt that perhaps we had
been a little obstructive towards Germany, limiting her
expansion and keeping her out of her place ' in the sun.'
Personally I considered that these misgivings and self-
reproaches had no basis in fact ; but they existed. Those
who were well acquainted with recent history would
hardly regard Germany as an injured innocent, but there
were many here who did : and of late there had been a
very active propaganda by financiers, pacifists, faddists
and others in favour of close relations with Germany, and
this propaganda had made considerable headway. No one
would wish not to retain friendly relations with Germany,
so long as they could be secured with due regard to
British interests. If, at this moment, France were to come
forward with proposals so to reshape our understanding
as to give it more or less the character of an alliance, I felt
pretty sure that neither the Government as a whole nor
large sections of British public opinion would be disposed
to welcome such proposals, which would be regarded by
many as offering umbrage and a challenge to Germany.
It would be far wiser to leave matters as they were ; and
not to strain an understanding which was at present
generally popular, and did not by itself afford the
slightest reason to any other country to resent or to
demur to it."

This important minute was sent to Sir E. Grey and the Prime Minister. The former wrote : " You could have taken no other line with Cambon than you did take. I shall have to say the same. I shall, however, impress upon him that though we cannot bind ourselves, under all circumstances, to go to war with France against Germany, we shall also certainly not bind ourselves to Germany not to assist France." Mr. Asquith was less explicit. " I entirely approve," he wrote, " the language used by Sir A. Nicolson."

The endeavour of the French Government to ascertain how far they could rely on British assistance in the event of war was thus again checked by the refusal of the British Government to commit themselves in advance to any binding undertakings. Within a few weeks, however, of their rejection of M. Cambon's overtures circumstances caused the Cabinet to make certain dispositions and arrangements which, in effect, committed the British Empire to intervention in any war between France and Germany.

The Admiralty experts, on examining the draft Novelle which Mr. Haldane had brought back from his visit, discovered that von Tirpitz's scheme was far more menacing than had at first been supposed. The Government became seriously alarmed, and the question was examined whether it would not be necessary to withdraw ships from the Mediterranean and concentrate them in home waters. Nicolson was asked to give his opinion upon the political aspects of such a reversal in naval policy. On May 6, 1912, he recorded his views in a minute to Sir Edward Grey :

" If the Admiralty consider that it is essential to concentrate all their naval forces in the Channel and the North

Sea, and that, therefore, the naval forces in the Mediterranean must be very materially reduced, I can conceive only three alternative courses open to us :

A. To increase the Naval Budget so as to enable an additional squadron to be created for permanent service in the Mediterranean. This solution would presumably be ruled out as imposing too heavy a charge on the estimates.

B. To come to an Alliance with Germany so as to free a large portion of the fleets at present locked up in home waters for the purpose of watching Germany. Such a measure would

   (i) place us in an inferior position to Germany, who would then be very much the predominant partner, and able to put unendurable pressure upon us whenever she thought it necessary to do so. Moreover the safety of our vital parts would be left dependent on the goodwill of Germany.

   (ii) It would throw the three Scandinavian States, Belgium, Holland into the arms of Germany, who would in general estimation be the dominating power.

   (iii) It would cause France and Russia to be at least cold and unfriendly ; and our position throughout the mid East and on the Indian frontier and elsewhere would be seriously shaken and imperilled. These are three indisputable facts. I do not allude to the probabilities of German pressure on France, and the risk of a European war, the loss of our prestige throughout the world which would regard us as having been compelled to make terms with Germany, and to become practically dependent on her. I would, therefore, rule out this solution.

C. An undertaking with France, whereby she would
undertake in the early part of a war, and until we
could detach vessels from home waters, to safeguard
our interests in the Mediterranean. She would,
naturally, ask for some reciprocal engagements
from us which it would be well worth our while to
give. This to my mind offers the cheapest, simplest,
and safest solution."

The solution which Nicolson recommended to the
Cabinet was indeed the only solution available. Discussions in this sense were opened with the French
Government and eventually led to an agreement by
which we undertook to safeguard the security of the
northern coasts of France, whereas the latter, in conjunction with such naval forces as we could maintain
in the Mediterranean, would safeguard our interests
and communications in those waters.

The vital importance of this arrangement was not
recognised by the Cabinet at the time. " The significance," Nicolson notes in his Narrative, " of the
undertaking which we then gave came out clearly in
the days immediately preceding the outbreak of war
in 1914." In 1912, however, few members of the
Government seem to have realised that these naval
dispositions committed us far more inextricably than
we had ever been committed before. It was not till
the early days of October, 1912, that the Cabinet as a
whole discovered that military conversations had also
been proceeding with France and Belgium for the last
five years. They insisted that the situation should be
defined. The French Government asked for nothing
better. On October 22, 1912, an exchange of Notes
took place between Sir Edward Grey and M. Cambon

in which, to the relief of the British Cabinet, it was formally laid down that these discussions between military and naval experts did not constitute " an engagement that commits either Government to action in a contingency that has not yet arisen and may never arise." But in the same exchange of Notes it was also laid down that " if either Government had grave reason to expect an unprovoked attack by a third Power . . . it should immediately discuss with the other whether both Governments should act together to prevent aggression and to preserve peace and, if so, what measures they would be prepared to take in common."

In eliciting this document from the Cabinet M. Cambon had obtained something beyond his most optimistic expectations. It seems almost incredible that the British Government did not realise how far they were pledged. They had in fact committed themselves to a guarantee which would involve England either in a breach of faith or a war with Germany. And it was the Novelle of Admiral von Tirpitz which produced this curious result.

(4)

In order to complete the full story of the Anglo-French Naval Agreement, and therefore to include the Grey-Cambon letters of October 22, 1912, it has been necessary to anticipate the main thread of the narrative. We must now return to February, 1912, and to the ensuing developments in Anglo-German relations.

The failure of the Haldane mission, the endeavours of the German Government to commit Great Britain

to unconditional neutrality, had suggested even to the
most optimistic politician that the experts might after
all be right when they contended that Germany could
only consent to recognise our naval domination if we
recognised her own domination upon the Continent.
The Haldane negotiations had at least served the purpose of elucidating the real points at issue. Mr.
Asquith's Cabinet were not, however, able to take a
decided line. Public opinion would not allow them
either to conclude a definite alliance with France and
Russia, or to withdraw definitely from the Ententes
and thus to leave to Germany, in return for substantial
naval concessions, the complete mastery over Europe.
The Cabinet endeavoured, as was natural, to make the
best of both worlds. They continued, via Mr. Harcourt and Herr von Kühlmann, to negotiate an agreement with Germany regarding our own and other
peoples' colonies, as well as a settlement of the Baghdad
Railway. From time to time Mr. Winston Churchill
threw out hints that we were still prepared to discuss
a naval accommodation. In his Glasgow speech he
irritated the pan-Germans by informing them that their
navy was merely a luxury. On March 18 he offered
an automatic limitation of armaments. " If Germany,"
he said, " will build no ships in any single year, we
shall follow their example." These hints provoked
no response from Berlin. Relations, however, continued to improve. Count Metternich, the German
Ambassador in London, was recalled in May. Nicolson much regretted the removal of this wise and
comprehending diplomatist. " The departure of
Count Metternich," he recorded in his Narrative, " was
regrettable, as he thoroughly understood this country,

and was anxious to maintain the friendliest relations.
I have reason to believe that he did not approve of all
the acts of his Government, and was conscious that
their methods were not always prudent and not always
far-sighted. I remember that on saying good-bye to
me he expressed the wish that we should meet again
when we were both out of office and free to talk frankly
as ' we might have some interesting things to tell each
other ! ' " Count Metternich was succeeded by Baron
Marschall von Bieberstein who had for years, assisted
by Mr. Paul Weitz, been the elephantine voice of
Germany in the East. Baron Marschall died but a few
weeks after his arrival. For two months the German
Embassy was in charge of Herr von Kühlmann—a
diplomatist of great intelligence and one who was
inspired by sincerely pacific intentions. Prince Lichnowsky was appointed Ambassador on October 13,
1912. He was a personal enemy of Herr von Kiderlen
and carried no weight whatever with the German
Foreign Office. It is difficult to understand why, at
so important a juncture, the German Government
should have selected as their representative a man who
had for thirteen years been buried in his castle at Grätz,
and whose opinion they regarded as of no value. Mr.
Asquith has expressed the view that Baron Marschall,
had he lived, could have prevented the European War.[1]
It should be added in fairness to Prince Lichnowsky,
who was not only a great gentleman but also a great
European, that had the Wilhelmstrasse listened to his
opinion and judgment the war might also have been
prevented. But to Prince Lichnowsky no patriotic
German lent an ear.

[1] Asquith's *The Genesis of the War*, p. 104.

The British Government, while flirting with the German Embassy in London, did not abate their desire to re-insure themselves with France and Russia.

> "I am much afraid," Nicolson wrote to Hardinge, "that the tendency of the present day is to avoid taking any responsibility whatever, or indeed of adopting (*sic*) any policy which has an element of vigour or foresighted-ness. This I see evidenced throughout the world. I suppose it is a malady which attacks every Government." [1]

This lack of any firm directive was all the more to be regretted since it was by then clear that serious trouble was brewing in South Eastern Europe. On January 18, 1912, Sir Henry Bax Ironside, our able Minister at Sofia, warned Nicolson privately that an alliance was secretly being negotiated between Bulgaria and Serbia under Russian auspices. Nicolson regarded this policy on the part of M. Sazonow and M. Hartwig as highly dangerous. His apprehensions were recorded in a letter written, after the event, to Lord Hardinge:

> "To my mind the primary cause of all that has happened is the secret alliance which Russia encouraged the four States to conclude. I imagine that Sazonoff had in his mind in the first instance merely to gain a diplomatic success over Austria and to re-establish Russian prestige in the Balkan peninsula. He should, however, have foreseen that by encouraging and promoting the close understanding between the four Balkan powers he was practically raising hopes and aspirations which they had some grounds for thinking Russia would enable them to realise. Moreover, unless our information is quite erroneous, Bulgaria and Servia even went so far as to peg out between themselves districts in Macedonia which

[1] To Lord Hardinge, July, 1912.

would fall to each other when the Turkish Empire broke up." [1]

For the moment, Nicolson concentrated all his efforts on furthering a situation in which Austria and Russia could act jointly in the Balkans as the mandatories of the Concert of Europe. In February, 1912, M. Poincaré suggested that the three Entente Powers should take joint action at Constantinople and Sofia to prevent a revival of Macedonian trouble. Nicolson was strongly opposed to any isolated action. On February 5, 1912, he wrote to Sir Fairfax Cartwright, our Ambassador at Vienna, as follows :

> " We have told Cambon that we are disinclined to take
> any active part in any discussions which would be limited
> to ourselves, France and Russia. We consider that it
> would be of far more advantage that the two Powers most
> interested in Balkan matters, *i.e.* Austria and Russia,
> should come to an agreement between themselves as to
> what steps, if any, are necessary. We are also strongly of
> opinion that if any steps are taken either at Sofia or at
> Constantinople, they should be undertaken by all five
> Powers and not by any special group. It is clear that it
> would be extremely undesirable that we and France and
> Russia should undertake the duty of taking steps at Sofia
> and Constantinople in which Austria and Germany are
> not participators, and we are most averse from any action
> in these questions which would lead to any separate, and
> possibly antagonistic, groupings of powers."

Neither M. Sazonow nor Count Berchtold were, however, in the least desirous of co-operating with each other. The former had never forgiven Austria for her Bosnian bullying ; the latter was angry with Sazonow for his endeavours to found a Balkan block

[1] To Lord Hardinge, October 9, 1912.

under Russian auspices, and for his manifest attempts
to secure the co-operation of Italy. " I must say,"
Nicolson wrote, " that it is regrettable that there is not
a real statesman at Vienna who would do his utmost
to smooth relations with Russia. Much as I like
Berchtold personally, I do not think that he has a very
wide outlook." [1]

The Serbo-Bulgarian Treaty was signed on March
13, 1912. The Treaty between Bulgaria and Greece
was signed on May 29, 1912. Both these Treaties were
supplemented by military conventions aimed at Turkey.
M. Poincaré, on learning of the conclusion of these
agreements, was alarmed. He suggested to London
and St. Petersburg that the three Entente Powers
should sign a " pacte de désintéressement " in the
Balkans. The effect of this proposal in Russia is well
described in a private letter addressed to Nicolson by
Hugh O'Beirne, Chargé d'Affaires in St. Petersburg :

" Sazonow has been greatly put out during the last few
days by Poincaré's proposal for a declaration of principle
by the three Powers regarding mediation, and by the suspicion of Russia which dictated those proposals, and in
his irritation he had spoken to me with great openness
about Russia's policy. His main objection to Poincaré's
suggested declaration of disinterestedness was, of course,
with reference to the impression which it would produce
on the Balkan Slavs. He told me, what I had naturally
surmised, that the Bulgarian and Serbian delegations
which had just visited Russia, ostensibly on the occasion
of the Moscow celebrations, had in reality come in connection with the Serbo-Bulgarian secret Treaty. He explained that the delegations had come to ' present ' the
signed Treaty to the Emperor. Russia thus appears as a

[1] To Sir F. Cartwright, July 8, 1912.

kind of high protecting Power in the alliance concluded between the two Slav kingdoms, and the Emperor gives his formal sanction to the secret arrangement which contemplates, in certain eventualities, the partition of Macedonia. That Sazonow attaches real importance to this arrangement, and that in fact he means business by it, is shown by the way in which he took the proposal to sign a ' pacte de désintéressement.' He said that, coming immediately after the arrival of the Slav delegations, it would be regarded as a renunciation by Russia of her historic rôle in the Balkans, that it would have a disastrous effect, and that it would undo at a stroke the work accomplished by Russian policy during the last two years. He regarded the suggestion as positively dangerous, and described it as playing with fire, by which I take him to mean that it is a dangerous thing to force Russia to show her hand about the Balkans, because she might have to make a declaration which would have far-reaching consequences."

From that point onwards events in the Balkans proceeded according to plan. In September M. Sazonow paid a visit to England, and on his return from Balmoral Nicolson met him at Crewe Hall. It was there, on September 29, 1912, that they both received the news that Bulgaria had mobilised. They hurried back to London. The Concert of Europe was immediately, if somewhat belatedly, cemented.

The wires buzzed with conflicting formulas suggesting intervention, and non-intervention, and the preservation of the *status quo*. " To my mind," Nicolson wrote to Grey, " all these declarations in the present welter are mere verbiage and will produce no impression anywhere. I do not think that the intention to maintain the *status quo* will be taken very seriously." [1]

---

[1] Nicolson to Grey, October 3, 1912.

A formula was agreed upon by October 7 whereby the united Powers notified the Balkan States that if war broke out no territorial changes would be permitted. On the next day, the King of Montenegro—who was having a flutter on the Vienna Bourse—anticipated the date agreed on with his allies and declared war on Turkey. Serbia, Bulgaria and Greece, within a few hours, followed his example. The Balkans were ablaze.

" This is not," so Nicolson wrote to Hardinge, " a chapter in European diplomacy which will be very satisfactory to look back upon." [1]

(5)

Europe now found herself faced with the very crisis which she had for years been dreading. It seemed inevitable that the hour had struck when Russia and Austria would decide between them their age-long conflict for supremacy in South Eastern Europe. Two factors, however, combined to postpone this catastrophe until August, 1914.

In the first place the Balkan States showed an unexpected initiative. The rapidity and completeness of their success took both Austria and Russia by surprise. On October 22 the Bulgarians routed the Turkish eastern army at Kirk Kilissé. On October 26 the Serbians routed the Turkish western army at Koumanovo. On November 8 the Greeks entered Salonika. A week later the windows of Constantinople rattled to the distant bruising of the Bulgarian guns. Within a month of the outbreak of hostilities Turkey had lost

[1] To Lord Hardinge, October 9, 1912.

all her possessions in Europe outside the rampart of Tchataldja—that is twelve miles from Constantinople itself. It was no longer open, either for Austria to oppose or for Russia to assist, the cause of the Balkans for the Balkan peoples. That problem had settled itself.

It has since transpired that, in spite of this fortunate " fait accompli," Austria had, in November, 1912, determined on war. The Serbians, in their victorious advance, had joined hands with Montenegro across the Sandjak. The Austrian Government decided to turn them out. The reserves were mobilised, the Austrian representatives abroad were furnished with instructions to prepare for war, and Conrad von Hoetzendorff was re-appointed Chief of the General Staff.[1] Herr von Kiderlen Waechter became alarmed. He despatched the Chancellor on a visit to Berchtold and asked him to make it perfectly clear that the Austrian Government " must keep us informed of their intentions *in advance* and not, as has so often happened, face us with a *fait accompli*. We will not become the satellites of Austria in the Near East." [2] The Emperor William was equally perturbed. " This," he wrote, " may mean a European war and ultimately a life and death struggle for us against three Great Powers." [3] He therefore arranged a meeting with the Archduke Franz Ferdinand and warned him that Germany would not support Austria in a war to turn Serbia out of the Sandjak or to prevent her from reaching the Adriatic. " I think," he said, " that you are rattling my sabre a little too

[1] *See* an interesting article published in *Der Krieg*, No. 22, October 1929, p. 148.

[2] *G.P.*, vol. xxxiii., No. 12135.   [3] *G.P.*, vol. xxxiii., No. 12404.

loudly." It is unfortunate that similar advice was not given in July of 1914.[1]

Sir Edward Grey, no less than the Emperor William, regarded the situation with anxiety. He explained to the Cabinet that the crisis was such that it might well lead to a European war. He indicated to them also that, in such an event, circumstances might arise which would entail British intervention. They asked him to define exactly the nature of our commitments to France and Russia. He replied that the Cabinet, as a Cabinet, were not committed in the least. All that had happened was that the soldiers and sailors had " conducted conversations." They asked him to explain the scope of these conversations. He replied (as was indeed true) that he had no conception of what had passed. They asked him whether M. Poincaré and M. Sazonow were equally certain that the British Empire retained an absolutely free hand in the event of European complications. Sir Edward Grey expressed the sincere and heartfelt hope that the French and Russian Governments were equally vague on the subject as he was himself.

The precisionists in the Cabinet were not contented with this assurance. They insisted that the freedom of our hand should be stated and recorded on paper. Sir Edward Grey thereupon drafted the famous Note to M. Cambon.[2] He imagined that by these instruments England had secured her complete liberty to act as she chose. M. Poincaré, on the other hand, was

---

[1] The problem why Germany restrained Austria in 1912 but did not restrain her in 1914 is one that can be warmly recommended to the student. It is not convincing to attribute this difference of attitude and action to such subsidiary causes as the improvement of relations between Germany and England, the horror evoked by the assassination of Franz Ferdinand, or the death of Kiderlen Waechter.

[2] See pp. 373, 374.

convinced that Sir Edward Grey's letter committed England beyond the possibility of recall. This misunderstanding persisted until August 3, 1914.

In the interval Sir Edward Grey attempted to re-insure himself with Germany. It must be admitted that some uncertainty still exists as to how far he was himself responsible for what followed.[1] The incident has been disclosed only through the publication by the German Government of Herr von Kühlmann's telegrams. On October 14, 1912, Sir William Tyrrell, Private Secretary to Sir Edward Grey, dined with the German Chargé d'Affaires in the latter's private house. He informed Herr von Kühlmann that he had been charged by Sir Edward Grey to make " a serious and decisive proposal," and one which he hoped, he sincerely hoped, would be so regarded in Berlin. He was authorised to offer Germany and Herr von Kühlmann " heartfelt and durable conciliation." He wished to stretch out to Herr von Kühlmann and, through him, to Germany, " the olive-branch of peace." Not only did he desire, not only did the British Government desire, to join with Germany in localising the existing Balkan crisis, but they also wished to co-operate for all time with Germany in China, Persia, Turkey and Africa. Germany and England, from that moment, would walk " hand in hand." [2]

Herr von Kühlmann—a sincere and constant believer in Anglo-German co-operation—telegraphed ecstatically to Berlin. " This," he remarked delightedly, " marks the beginning of the end of the

---

[1] The record of what follows is derived from German sources. No mention of this incident is found in the British archives.

[2] G.P., vol. xxxiii., No. 12284.

Ententes." The next morning Sir William Tyrrell warned Herr von Kühlmann that he must exercise particular discretion regarding their after-dinner conversation : he had been expressing merely Sir Edward Grey's personal opinions : the conversation must be regarded as absolutely confidential; even Sir Arthur Nicolson had not been informed.[1]

Herr von Kiderlen, on receiving this information, displayed some doubts. He replied to Herr von Kühlmann that it seemed very odd that Sir Edward Grey should have enshrined so " serious and decisive " a message in an after-dinner conversation of Sir William Tyrrell. (" Eine Tischunterhaltung zwischen Ihnen und Herrn Tyrrell.") It was also strange that Sir Edward Grey should have gone out of his way to warn the German Embassy that this conversation had been concealed from the Permanent Under Secretary. He begged Herr von Kühlmann not to be carried away by any undue optimism. The German Government were all for localising the Balkan conflict and were prepared to co-operate towards that end with Sir Edward Grey. As regards the " hand in hand " business, Herr von Kiderlen required something more definite. He would require :

(A) An undertaking that all negotiations should be kept absolutely secret, but that the ensuing agreement should be published to the world, and

(B) That during the progress of these secret negotiations the British Government should promise not to support the interests of " third parties " in any matter " where she herself has no vital interest." As Erich Brandenburg remarks, this reply meant that

[1] G.P., vol. xxxiii., No. 12285.

Kiderlen was prepared to offer German co-operation only at the price of our abandoning the interests of France and Russia.[1]

There exists no written record, either in the German or British archives, of the ultimate result of Sir William Tyrrell's conversation.

The fact remains, however, that Germany did support the efforts of England to localise the Balkan conflict. On December 3, 1912, the Turks asked for an armistice. On December 16 Turkish and Balkan delegates met at St. James's Palace to discuss terms of peace. On December 17 a Conference of Ambassadors was instituted in London, under Sir E. Grey's chairmanship, to preserve the peace of Europe.

(6)

It would be beyond the scope of this biography to recount in any detail the amicable but protracted proceedings of the Ambassadors' Conference. " The details," writes Sir Edward Grey, " with which we dealt were insignificant—in themselves mere sparks. But we were sitting on a powder magazine." [2] The object of Austria was to prevent Serbia and Montenegro obtaining a larger increase of territory than was inevitable ; and above all to bar their access to the Adriatic. For this purpose a State of Albania was created, and the efforts of the Austrian and German Ambassadors were directed towards incorporating within Albania as much as was possible of the territory claimed by Serbia and Montenegro. A rupture almost arose over the village of Djakova, and a serious crisis

[1] Erich Brandenburg, *Vom Bismarck zum Weltkriege*, p. 389.
[2] Grey, *Twenty-Five Years*, vol. i., p. 265.

threatened when Montenegro, against the orders of the Ambassadors' Conference, occupied the Albanian town of Scutari. Both these difficulties were surmounted by the conciliatory spirit manifested by the five Ambassadors and by Sir Edward Grey's authoritative handling of his colleagues. The main lines of the Albanian frontier were agreed to by mutual concession, and a mixed commission was sent to the spot to delimit the border. This commission had not completed its labours by August of 1914. Once the main crisis was over the deliberations of the Ambassadors became less and less frequent, and even in 1914 there were certain points, such as the attribution of the islands at the entrance to the Dardanelles, which had not been decided.

In spite of this, the Ambassadors' deliberations of 1912-1913 furnish an example of the old diplomacy at its best, and it is regrettable that Sir Edward Grey failed in his endeavour to revive this excellent conclave in July of 1914.

The concurrent conference of the Balkan belligerents was marked by less moderation. After protracted wrangles the Turks at last agreed, at the end of December, 1912, to sign a preliminary Treaty, by which they surrendered to the Balkan Allies all territory north of the Enos-Midia line including the town of Adrianople. The news of this cession led to a military revolution at Constantinople. Enver Bey burst into the room in which the Cabinet were sitting, murdered the Minister of War with a revolver, and denounced the armistice. This action did not, however, alter the military situation; a further armistice had to be concluded on April 16, 1913, and the peace delegates again resumed their seats in St. James's Palace. The Turks refused, at this second Conference, to accept the Enos-Midia line, and grave differences of opinion were also disclosed between the Balkan allies themselves. Sir Edward Grey became impatient. On May 25 he summoned the delegates to his room at the Foreign Office and asked Nicolson to assist him in explaining to them the urgent necessity of signing peace. The delegates of Serbia, Bulgaria, Greece, Montenegro and Turkey, somewhat sheepish in their frock-coats, were ranged one by one upon the carpet. Sir Edward Grey advanced towards them and fixed them with his eagle eye : he pointed towards them with an outstretched and imperative finger : he summoned to his assistance the total resources of his Wykhamist French. " Ou signer," he shouted at them, " ou partir ! "

The Treaty of London was signed between Turkey and the Balkan States on May 30, 1913.

Bulgaria, Greece and Serbia at once proceeded to quarrel over the spoils. On June 29 King Ferdinand ordered his troops treacherously to attack Serbia. The remaining allies, including Rumania, turned upon Bulgaria and within a few weeks forced her to capitulate. A final Treaty was signed at Bucharest on August 10, 1913, by which Serbia and Greece gained further territory, whereas Bulgaria was despoiled of most of what she had won from Turkey. The latter, for her part, recovered Adrianople. That was the conclusion of the first and second Balkan wars.

Nicolson himself had little direct share in the labours of the Ambassadors' Conference, and strove rather to lighten the burden upon Grey's shoulders by taking

on himself the current work of the Department. From
time to time, however, Grey would disappear to his
cottage in Hampshire and Nicolson would take his
place at the Conference. The records of proceedings
were sent down to Grey in the country and he would
return them with pencilled comments. These comments were often interspersed with more human passages. There is, for instance, a note from Rosehall
P.O. in Scotland, dated April 19, 1913 :

> " There is some prospect of rain and if so the sport will
> be very good. It seems almost too much to expect that
> everything including both Balkan crises and salmon
> should go well simultaneously, but things seem to prosper
> so well in my absence that it would not be in the public
> interest for me to curtail it. I am in rude health with an
> appetite for everything except office work." There is
> another such comment of May 4. " It was difficult at my
> cottage to-day to believe that war in so beautiful a world
> had ever occurred or was even possible."

The Balkan Wars of 1912-1913 had, however, prepared the way for a catastrophe more terrible than the
world had ever contemplated. Not only were Bulgaria and Turkey decided on revenge, but Austria and
Russia were determined that they would not a third
time mobilise in vain. The former emerged from the
crisis to find Serbia increased in arrogance, territory
and aspirations. The latter had been obliged to surrender to the Triple Alliance in such matters as Albania,
Scutari and the Serbian access to the Adriatic. On this
occasion each of the disturbers of the peace felt that
she had suffered a defeat.

Austria, for her part, had some justification for
her apprehensions. Sir Fairfax Cartwright, an acute

observer, sounded a note of prophetic warning. He wrote to Nicolson privately as follows :

" As soon as peace is restored in the Balkans, the Austrian authorities anticipate that Serbia will begin a far-reaching agitation in the Serb-inhabited districts of the Dual Monarchy, and as this country cannot allow any dismemberment of her provinces without incurring the danger of the whole edifice crumbling down, we have all the elements in the near future of another violent crisis in this part of the world, which may not unlikely end in the final annexation of Serbia by the Dual Monarchy. That, however, will lead to a war with Russia, and possibly to a general conflict in Europe." [1]

In another letter he went even further :

" Serbia will some day set Europe by the ears, and bring about a universal war on the Continent. I cannot tell you how exasperated people are getting here at the continual worry which that little country causes to Austria under encouragement from Russia. It will be lucky if Europe succeeds in avoiding war as a result of the present crisis. The next time a Serbian crisis arises I feel sure that Austria-Hungary will refuse to admit of any Russian interference in the dispute and that she will proceed to settle her difference with her little neighbour coûte que coûte." [2]

[1] Sir F. Cartwright to A. N., May 23, 1913.
[2] Sir F. Cartwright to A. N., January 31, 1913.

XIV

THE OUTBREAK OF WAR
[June-August 1914]

(1)

PRINCE LICHNOWSKY arrived in London in November, 1912. Never has any foreign Ambassador achieved such rapid or such resounding popularity. In the first place there existed a very anxious desire to improve relations with our Teutonic kinsmen. In the second place the personality of Prince Lichnowsky was admirably attuned to the transitional mood in which English public life was then indulging. The rulers of England, at that time, had lost none of their reverence for the territorial aristocracy, but they liked their patricians to be decorative without becoming patronising. The Lichnowskys completely fulfilled these requirements. They gave most sumptuous and regal entertainments at which the footmen were arrayed in

liveries dating from the time of John Sobiesky. And
next morning Princess Lichnowsky, laughing and hat-
less, could be seen running races with her dogs and
children in the park. English people like that sort of
thing. They liked the Ambassador's youthful and
interested manner ; his intellectual, though slightly
querulous voice ; the obvious fact that he also was a
dilettante and an amateur. The Lichnowskys were
welcomed with open arms, not only by London society
but also in political, academic and commercial circles.
It was only in Berlin that the German Ambassador was
not believed.

Prince Lichnowsky, from the moment of his arrival,
flung himself heart and soul into his task of reaching
some agreement with the British Government. In this
he was loyally assisted by the Counsellor of Embassy,
Herr von Kühlmann. Other members of his staff were
not so loyal, and wrote privately to Berlin warning
them that Prince Lichnowsky had gone completely over
to the English and was sadly gulled by Grey. The
Ambassador, at the outset, concentrated upon obtaining some agreement regarding the Baghdad Railway,
as also a revision of the 1898 Convention regarding
the Portuguese Colonies.[1] Both these negotiations
were in the end successful. A Convention regarding
the Baghdad Railway was initialled on June 15, 1914.
That regarding the Portuguese Colonies, although concluded as early as August of 1913, did not enter into
operation owing to the unwillingness of the German
Government to allow the whole arrangement to be
published. Both instruments, however, were ready
for completion by July of 1914.

[1] *See* above, p. 127.

Nicolson himself took little part in these negotiations. He was no expert on the Baghdad Railway,
and he heartily disliked the Convention regarding the
Portuguese Colonies. He described it as " the most
cynical business that I have come across in my whole
experience of diplomacy." His feelings on the subject
were recorded in a letter to Lord Hardinge :

> " The new German Ambassador has arrived and seems
> to be a pleasant but not a very conspicuously intelligent
> man. He has lost no time in re-opening discussions as to
> the Portuguese colonies and although he only presented
> his letters three days ago he has contrived to induce Grey
> and Harcourt to draw up a draft project dividing the
> spoils between us. I consider the whole transaction to be
> most discreditable and I desire to have as little to do with
> it as possible. Of course, the defence of the Government
> is that they are merely revising an arrangement which was
> made by their predecessors. This may be so but if you
> revise and confirm an arrangement, it practically means
> that you thoroughly approve of it and, bad as the adminis-
> tration of Portugal and her possessions may be, I do not see
> how, on grounds of political honesty and equity, you can
> partition with another Power these possessions which you
> have yourself engaged to defend and to maintain intact." [1]

Prince Lichnowsky, in his Memoirs, has given a
perfectly fair and accurate picture of his relations with
Arthur Nicolson : [2]

> " Sir A. Nicolson and Sir William Tyrrell were, after
> the Minister, the two most influential men at the Foreign
> Office. The former was no friend of Germany's, but
> his attitude towards me was scrupulously correct and
> courteous. Our personal relations were excellent. He,

[1] To Lord Hardinge, November 21, 1912.
[2] Prince Lichnowsky, *Heading for the Abyss*, pp. 69-70.

too, did not want war ; but as soon as we advanced against France, he no doubt worked in the direction of an immediate intervention. . . .

" Sir William Tyrrell, Sir Edward's private secretary, possessed far greater influence than the Permanent Under-Secretary. This highly intelligent official had been at school in Germany . . . and became a convinced advocate of an understanding. He influenced Sir Edward Grey, with whom he was very intimate, in this direction."

During the Balkan Conference in London Prince Lichnowsky, although somewhat hampered by his in-structions to afford unstinted support to his Austrian colleague, had shown himself conciliatory and well-in-tentioned. " An exceedingly amiable man," so Nicol-son wrote to Goschen on March 5, 1913, " but he does not strike any of us as having a very clear business head, and I doubt if he reports very accurately to his Government." This latter judgment was not justified : Prince Lichnowsky's reports are now available and are very accurate indeed : the only fault about them is that they were not credited by those to whom they were addressed. The fact remains, however, that Prince Lichnowsky was able during the first few months of his mission to introduce a marked improvement in Anglo-German relations. This improvement was manifested to the world by the success of King George's visit to Berlin in May of 1913.

Anglo-German friendship remained, however, largely superficial. Beneath the sugar-coating of these amenities the old fear and rivalry had lost nothing of its bitterness. Mr. Winston Churchill, on March 26, 1913, offered Germany " a naval holiday," but his proposals were refused on the ground that a suspension

of naval construction would cause unemployment in
the German yards. It was not only at sea that Germany was increasing her war preparedness. In 1913
a new law was passed adding to the size of the German
army, and a levy on capital was enforced for the purpose of strengthening the frontier fortresses and aug-
menting the war-chest at Spandau. Other countries
then took similar precautions. In France the three
years' period of military service was re-enacted.
Russia, Austria, Belgium and Italy made feverish
efforts to improve the efficiency of their fighting forces.
It has been estimated that in the year 1913 the military
expenditure of the Continental Powers was increased
by £50,000,000.

Other considerations, of a more personal nature,
tended to enhance the anxiety and vigilance of the
British Government and their advisers. Herr von
Kiderlen Waechter, German Foreign Secretary, died
suddenly on December 30, 1912. He was succeeded
by Herr von Jagow, Ambassador at Rome, who was
the very soul of gentleness. Kiderlen, it is true, would
bang his beer mug upon the table, and shout and
glower at Ambassadors as if they were poachers and he
(as he indeed appeared) a gamekeeper. But Kiderlen
had one great advantage. He disliked war in general
and Admiral von Tirpitz in particular. He considered
that no man's feelings were worth the price of one of
his own Hamburg cigars. But he had a predilection,
in spite of his virility, for the humane ; and in him
Herr von Bethmann Hollweg found a powerful but-
tress and support. In January of 1913 Goschen
warned Nicolson that Jagow for his part was not made
of reinforced concrete : he feared that, should a sudden

crisis occur, both Bethmann Hollweg and Jagow would be swept away. He urged the Government " not to slacken their efforts to place the country in a secure and unassailable position." [1]

(2)

Sir Edward Goschen had no need to apprehend a slackening of our effort. The question of British military and naval preparedness was the concern, not so much of the Cabinet as of the Committee of Imperial Defence. The latter body, as was inevitable, was largely guided by the Admiralty and the War Office. The Cabinet, feeling secure in their belief that the ultimate decision would always rest with them, allowed a certain latitude of preparation to the service departments. It was more convenient for them not to permit their right hand to know what their left was doing. Their left hand, however, was exceedingly active : its most efficient finger was General Sir Henry Wilson, Director of Military Operations.

This ambitious soldier had been appointed to the War Office in August, 1910. He was distinguished, as his biographer remarks, by a " bland ingenuousness of manner which he had cultivated successfully." It is an endearing quality of the British race that they are suspicious of nothing except intelligence. Sir Henry Wilson, being aware of this, was careful to conceal his intelligence under a cloud of facetiousness. By this means he was able, without arousing uneasiness in the Cabinet, to maintain with the French General Staff relations of the closest intimacy. He was in constant communication with General Foch. He induced the

[1] Sir Edward Goschen to A. N., Private, January 24, 1913.

latter to come to London and showed him everything.
He brought him to see Nicolson at the Foreign Office.
Nicolson considered Foch to be " a sensible and
charming little man." This was so long ago as
November, 1910. Since then Sir Henry Wilson had
elaborated an admirable scheme for the eventual despatch to France of a British Expeditionary Force.
Year by year he would proceed to Paris and perfect
these arrangements. That, after all, was his job ; nor
can he be blamed for his acute efficiency. There were
moments, however, when Sir Henry Wilson appears
to have gone further than is recommendable in a purely
executive officer. The following minute is among
Nicolson's private papers of this period :

"SIR EDWARD GREY.

" I met General Wilson last night, who has just come
back from Switzerland and on his way through Paris[1] saw
some of the leading military men. He tells me that the
soldiers are of the opinion that it would be far better for
France if a conflict were not too long postponed. Their
reasons are that if it would come now it would be in
consequence of the Balkan difficulties, and therefore they
would be able to secure the whole-hearted support of
Russia. Were a conflict to be postponed and eventually
to arise over some difficulty between Germany and France
alone, they had some doubts, treaty notwithstanding,
whether Russia would go whole-heartedly on their side.
They impressed upon Wilson that Russia was now
exceedingly strong, both in her military organisation and
also in her financial condition, and was therefore far less
dependent on French support, either in a military or a
financial sense. In short, that Russia was now well able
to look after herself, and might be inclined to take a line

[1] General Wilson had not been to Paris. He had been to visit General
Foch at Bourges.

of her own. (This I gather is not quite the view of the French Government, who are nervous lest they should be dragged into a war over Balkan affairs in which the French public have no great interest.) He further said that he found some doubts in the minds of the military men as to what would be our attitude—whether we should really in the case of a conflict give them any material assistance on land, and whether, indeed, such assistance would be efficient and above all timely.

(Sgd.) A. N.   February 24, 1913.

(*Minute by Sir Edward Grey* :) The French Government clearly do not want to be dragged into war over the Balkans and are working to prevent Russia precipitating a conflict over that. We on our side can be no party to France precipitating a conflict for the revanche.

E. G."

The efficient watchfulness of the Committee of Imperial Defence extended even to combinations outside the mere question of Anglo-French co-operation. Nicolson was asked by the Committee to ascertain the probable attitude of Belgium in the event of French or British forces being obliged to defend Belgian neutrality. He put the question privately to Sir Francis Villiers, our Minister in Brussels. The correspondence is here reproduced, not because it led to any definite arrangement, but since it shows that the Committee of Imperial Defence were, by the beginning of 1913, aware that the Germans would advance through Belgium, but unaware what attitude the Belgian Government would adopt. The letters are as follows :

" There is one point on which I have been for some time past anxious to write to you, but which pressure of business has continually prevented me from doing. I should much like to have your opinion as to whether, in

the event of a European war, Belgium would be likely to
be on our side or against us ? What I mean is that should
we and France, for instance, be compelled to advance
through Belgium for the purpose of repelling a German
aggression in those quarters, whether we could count on
Belgium receiving us as friends or enemies ? It is a matter
of some importance, though I quite understand that it will
be difficult to give any decided answer to it. I was asked
the question by our military people, and I said that I
thought that, if anything, the balance inclined to Belgium
regarding us as most unwelcome visitors, and that she
would be more likely to incline to Germany. You see
that the point is that we and France might have to move
troops across the Belgian frontier in order to meet the
approach of German troops on the other side, and
naturally it would be a matter of great importance to the
military commanders if they felt that on their left flank
they had friends and not dubious enemies. Of course in
the case of hostilities really breaking out, so many considerations which it is at present impossible to foresee
might have to be taken into account, and, therefore, it is
exceedingly difficult, if not impossible, to count with
certainty on what attitude Belgium might be disposed to
adopt. I thought that I would put the case before you and
I shall quite understand if you are unable to express a
positive opinion one way or the other." [1]

On January 11, 1913, Sir Francis Villiers replied as
follows :

" The view held, or at any rate expressed by the Government here is that so far as the guarantee of Belgian
neutrality is concerned, the position has materially
changed since the establishment of our Entente with the
French. In the event of a European conflict England
would be involved, Belgium would be included within
the theatre of war, the neutrality of the country would not

[1] A. N. to Sir Francis Villiers, Private, December 30, 1912.

necessarily be taken into account, and might be violated by British forces as well as by those of the other belligerents. Belgium can, therefore, no longer depend upon the guarantee, but must provide for her own defence against three possible enemies instead of against two as before—that is to say against England as well as against France and Germany. This question has been dealt with in some of my recent despatches, and in reports by Bridges (the Military Attaché) which I have forwarded. How far these feelings are really entertained it is difficult to judge. Their actual expression only began just at the time when the Belgian Government had made up their minds to propose a large increase of the army. So to some extent allowance must be made for the desire to frighten those who are opposed to military reorganisation. On the other hand, there is some distrust of us, due to the impatience, rapidly growing, at our delay in recognising the annexation of the Congo. There is also on the part of the Government a leaning towards Germany. Our reception as friends or enemies should we advance troops into Belgium to repel a German aggression would depend upon circumstances. From my own observations and from conversations with Bridges I am of opinion that if we were to take action before the Germans actually entered Belgium, or in any case without agreement with the Belgian Government, or without an invitation from them, we should be considered to have violated the neutrality of the country and thus to be enemies. This would not be the feeling, I believe, among the people or in the army, but the Government would treat our troops as hostile, not probably to the extent of actively opposing us, but they would not afford any assistance or in any way facilitate our operations."

In the final event the action of Germany relieved us from all doubt as to the correct procedure in this matter of Belgian neutrality.

ARTHUR NICOLSON AT THE DATE OF HIS
RETIREMENT FROM THE FOREIGN OFFICE

Photo by Russell.

(3)

In February of 1913 Nicolson had once again begged Grey to release him from the shackles of the Foreign Office and to permit him to return to diplomacy. Sir Edward suggested that if he would stay on till August, 1914, he might then succeed Sir F. Bertie in Paris. Nicolson pointed out that shortly after that date Lord Hardinge would be due to return from India and would hope to obtain Paris for himself ; Grey overcame these scruples.

"I have," Nicolson wrote to his youngest son on February 27, 1913, "accepted Grey's proposal to stay on here till Paris is vacant and have written to Charlie Hardinge. I do hope the latter will not think that I am not playing straight with him, but I really did plead his cause with Grey." Hardinge replied from India that in his opinion Nicolson had a prior claim on Paris, and there was no question of either of them standing in each other's way. The matter was thus amicably settled, as between life-long friends.

Nicolson looked forward with eagerness to this impending though still distant release. His distaste for his functions at the Foreign Office was augmented, towards the end of 1913, by his inability to share Sir Edward Grey's doctrines on internal as well as on external politics. The Irish controversy was by then cleaving English opinion into two hostile camps, and, as was inevitable, Nicolson took the side of his Ulster relations. He wrote to his friend, Hugh O'Beirne, on October 7 :

"I have not the slightest idea what are the intentions of the Government in regard to Ulster, as I carefully refrain

2 C

from ever discussing home politics with any friends of mine in the Cabinet." "We are quite dominated," he wrote to Goschen a few days later, "by the Ulster question."

Whatever restraint Nicolson might impose upon himself in this burning and embittered problem, Sir Edward Grey was well aware that their opinions were diametrically opposed. A certain personal constraint thus stole as a veil between them. Their mutual respect remained untarnished : their mutual loyalty was as firm as ever : but the old frankness and un-reserve was gone.

This almost imperceptible estrangement was not diminished by Nicolson's persistence in contending that the test of Germany's desire for good relations was not the Portuguese Colonies but the Novelle of Admiral von Tirpitz. Grey was irritated at having so unpleasant a fact brought home to him. Nicolson was in despair at his inability to induce people to take any definite line :

"I am convinced," he wrote, "that if the Triple Entente could be converted into another Triple Alliance, the peace of Europe could be assured for a generation or two. Ententes are all very well for a certain time, but they are most unsatisfactory transactions as they have none of the benefit of an alliance, and are always liable to break down when there is the slightest friction or difference of opinion." [1] "I am afraid," he wrote again, "supposing a collision did occur between France and Germany, that we should waver as to what course we should pursue until it was too late. It is unfortunate that the Govern-ment will not lay the state of the case frankly and openly before the country, and endeavour to stimulate the public

[1] A. N. to Sir Louis Mallet, March 21, 1914.

to follow the example of every country in Europe, and be ready to make certain sacrifices for their own defence." [1]

It is not surprising that Grey should have been irritated by these exhortations to " lay the case frankly and openly before the country." He knew all too well that the Cabinet would never listen to any nonsense like that.

In November, 1913, the Archduke Franz Ferdinand paid a private visit to England. Nicolson hoped that the occasion might be taken to urge upon him the necessity of closer relations between Austria and Russia. The Archduke, however—a large man with an ungainly mind—was not responsive to such overtures. Nicolson was disappointed. He wrote to Goschen :

> " I was down at Windsor for two days where I made the acquaintance of the Archduke. He was all smiles and amiability and was on his best possible behaviour. Practically no politics were talked, except the usual very unilluminating kind. When I mentioned that Aehrenthal had been my colleague at St. Petersburg, he gave a sniff, and said that he had been little acquainted with that gentleman. He praised up Berchtold very highly—but that was to be expected."

Writing to his youngest son, Nicolson was less discreet : " I met the Austrian Heir Apparent at Windsor. A sly and stupid man. I tried to draw him but without success."

(4)

Russia, meanwhile, was causing anxiety. Disquieting information reached the Foreign Office of Russian

[1] A. N. to Lord Hardinge, October 29, 1913.

encroachments in Mongolia, Kashgar, and Chinese
Turkestan. Northern Persia was being treated as a
Russian province. The protests of our Legation at
Tehran became increasingly urgent and embarrassing.
And in November of 1913 an incident occurred which
threatened once again to put the Anglo-Russian
Entente to the test.

The Turkish Government, after their collapse in the
Balkan Wars, asked the German Government for the
loan of a German military mission for the purpose of
improving the defences of Constantinople. It was
felt in Berlin, and quite rightly, that it was useless to
undertake so invidious a task unless the mission were
accorded wide executive powers. General Liman von
Sanders was selected for the appointment, and was
charged with the command of the Turkish forces at
Constantinople. On hearing of this, M. Sazonow
completely lost his head. He contended that the
executive command entrusted to Liman von Sanders
would place the Ambassadors at Constantinople at the
mercy of a few German officers. The German Government replied, with unanswerable logic, that von
Sanders' position was in no sense more dominant or
authoritative than that enjoyed by Admiral Limpus,
the English instructor to the Turkish navy. The
British Government were disconcerted by the importance attached by M. Sazonow and by M. Delcassé (at
that time serving as French Ambassador at St. Petersburg) to an incident which they felt was not intended
to be provocative. M. Sazonow, however, insisted
that " this question must be the test of the value of the
Triple Entente." Nicolson, for once, was not inclined
to adopt the Russian point of view :

" The difficulty," he wrote to Mr. O'Beirne, then Chargé d'Affaires at St. Petersburg, " in dealing with Sazonow is that one never knows precisely how far he is prepared to go. Though we may be quite ready to admit that the appointment, if it be really of the character which we are given to believe, is of a very serious nature, still we should look very foolish if we took the question up warmly and then found that Sazonow more or less deserted us. In fact there is a certain disinclination on our part to pull the chestnuts out of the fire for Russia." [1]

This incident was eventually settled by a compromise, but the impression remained with M. Sazonow that we had let him down. He spoke seriously on the subject to Sir G. Buchanan on the latter's return. He complained that England " would never allow the Triple Entente to take any action in which the Triple Alliance would not join, for fear of causing a division among the Powers." [2] These apprehensions were evidently shared in higher quarters. M. Kokovtsoff, who had succeeded M. Stolypin as President of the Council, was dismissed, and the post was given to old M. Gorémykin—who was well known for his reactionary and anti-British feelings. Nicolson, who had reason to dread M. Gorémykin, was perturbed by these changes. It was rumoured even that M. Sazonow was to be replaced by M. Hartwig—a singularly dangerous man. At the same moment, moreover, the Government of India had entered into an agreement with China which would entail the revision of that section of the Anglo-Russian Convention which dealt with Thibet. The Russians were complaining of our opposition to the Trans-Persian Railway and of our grasping

[1] A. N. to Mr. O'Beirne, December 2, 1913.
[2] Sir G. Buchanan to A. N., February 5, 1914.

attitude in the matter of the Kerman Mining Concession. They refused to consider a revision of the Thibetan Convention unless we agreed to give them " more elbow room " in Persia. They threw out hints that what they really wanted was some form of triple agreement, between us, Russia and Japan, guaranteeing the *status quo* in the Far East. It looked as if the whole Anglo-Russian Convention was about to totter in fragments to the ground.

M. Poincaré was filled with acute anxiety at these developments. He was alarmed also at the evident improvement of the relations between London and Berlin. He therefore took advantage of King George's visit to Paris in April, 1914, to suggest to Sir Edward Grey, who accompanied his Sovereign, that something should be done to re-affirm the Anglo-Russian Entente. Sir Edward Grey suggested an exchange of Notes similar to those which, in October of 1912, had passed between himself and M. Paul Cambon. M. Poincaré urged that something more explicit was required. Sir Edward suggested " naval conversations." M. Poincaré warmly welcomed this proposal.

Nicolson, as was to be expected, was in favour of such a step. " I do not know," he had written to Sir G. Buchanan on first hearing of the proposal, " how much longer we shall be able to follow our present policy of dancing on a tight rope, and not be compelled to take up some definite line or other. I am also haunted by the same fear as you—lest Russia should become tired of us and strike a bargain with Germany." [1]

The naval conversations with Russia were opened in May of 1914. They were devoid either of importance

[1] A. N. to Sir G. Buchanan, April 21, 1914.

or result, but unfortunately the fact that they were proceeding was communicated to the German Government by their pet spy in the Russian Embassy. The German Government jumped to the conclusion that England and Russia were about to concert plans for a landing in Pomerania. They caused the *Berliner Tageblatt* to publish a sensational version of this conspiracy. This, in its turn, led to a Parliamentary question, which Sir Edward Grey, on June 11, 1914, endeavoured to counter by a reply which was, to say the least, evasive. Prince Lichnowsky was then instructed to demand further explanations. Grey assured him that he, for his part, would never allow the Entente between England and Russia to assume an anti-German direction. Lichnowsky was for the moment satisfied with this answer and proceeded on leave of absence to Germany. On July 6 he returned and intimated to Sir Edward Grey that if naval conversations with Russia were really taking place " it would foster the desire felt in Germany for increased armaments and would make it more difficult for the German Government to keep within the limits fixed by law for naval and military expenditure." This, in its essence, amounted to a threat. The following minutes passed on the subject between Nicolson and Grey :

F.O.

" SIR E. GREY.

" I hope that you will allow me to make an observation to you in regard to that portion of the conversation which Prince Lichnowsky had with you yesterday relating to a naval understanding with Russia. He practically warned us that if we were to enter into any kind of naval arrangement with Russia certain unpleasant consequences would

ensue and we may, therefore, infer that if we wish to avoid
consequences we must abandon any naval conversations
with Russia. In short we are to abstain from taking the
most elementary precautions and from discussing any
arrangements which might be necessary to our defence in
certain contingencies. This request or suggestion is a
pretty strong one for one Power to make to another and
it comes oddly from a Power who quite rightly makes
secret arrangements with her allies—arrangements which
for aught we know may comprise certain measures
against us in possible eventualities. We must not forget
that only a year or two ago Germany pressed Russia to
engage to remain neutral in the event of hostilities
between Germany and England—as she also strove to
secure our neutrality in case of a Franco-German conflict.
She, therefore, very rightly looks ahead, and seeks to
avert any possible danger or combination against herself,
whether near or remote. This liberty apparently she
wishes to deny to us. I sincerely trust we shall not walk
into this trap but keep our hands perfectly free and our
friendships unimpaired.

A. N.   *July* 7, 1914.

Minute by Sir E. Grey : Certainly what Lichnowsky has
said is not going to alter our conversations with Russia
or France or our relations to them. The difficult question
is whether I should say nothing to Lichnowsky or whether
I should admit that we have had and may continue to have
such conversations both with France and Russia. I will
talk this over with you.

E. G."

On July 9, therefore, Sir Edward Grey informed
Prince Lichnowsky that " as he had no wish to mislead
him " he was unable to deny that " conversations had
taken place between the naval and military authorities
on the two sides." [1]

[1] Lichnowsky, *Towards the Abyss*, p. 372.

By that time, however, the crisis was already hurrying to its solution.

(5)

At 4 p.m. on Sunday, June 28, 1914, the following telegram reached the Foreign Office from Mr. Jones, Vice-Consul at Sarajevo :

> " According to news received here Heir Apparent and consort assassinated this morning by means of an explosive nature."

Mr. Jones had been careful not to overstep the bounds of accuracy : the first weapon, a bomb, had missed its objective : it was with his revolver that Gabriel Princip actually committed the murder.

A court of enquiry was immediately opened in the Bosnian capital. It was established that although the perpetrator of the outrage was a Bosnian student, the bomb and revolver had been supplied from Belgrade. It was not, at the time, clearly proved that the Serbian General Staff or the Serbian Government had been accessories before the fact. The Austrian authorities none the less decided, and with every justification, to inflict punishment upon Serbia. On July 2 they intimated to Berlin the nature, although not the exact nature, of their intentions : Berlin (imprudently perhaps) replied that Vienna could, in any circumstances, rely on German support. On July 7 the Crown Council of Austria-Hungary, encouraged by this assurance, decided upon extreme action. They omitted, however, fully to warn their German ally. The Emperor William departed upon his annual cruise in Norwegian waters, while the British Government embarked upon a conference on the affairs of Ireland. " The tragedy," wrote Nicolson, " which has recently occurred at Sarajevo will, I hope, not lead to any further complications." [1]   In this he was mistaken.

It was realised, of course, both in Berlin and London, that the Austrian Government would be obliged to make some demonstration such as would convince their own Jugo-Slavs that there could be no further tolerance of Serbian propaganda.   It was thought, however, that Vienna would act with such rapidity and decision that Belgrade would be occupied before Slav opinion in Russia had recovered from the shock of the assassination.   The Austrian Government, most un-fortunately, delayed taking action for sixteen days, and even after they had committed themselves to a punitive expedition against Serbia they were unable to move their forces for a further three weeks.   It was this unexpected delay that upset the optimistic calculations of Downing Street and the Wilhelmstrasse.   In neither place did there exist the slightest sympathy for Serbia. They were both anxious to see that country brought to book.   The delay of Conrad von Hoetzendorff, which was due to sheer muddle-headedness, gave time for what was merely a frontier question between Austria and Serbia to develop into a conflict between Slav and Teuton, and thus between the Triple Alliance and the Triple Entente.

On July 6 Prince Lichnowsky, who had just returned from Berlin, warned Sir Edward Grey " privately but very seriously " that the intentions of Austria were somewhat excessive.   He begged him to preach mod-eration at St. Petersburg.   Sir Edward sent for the

---

[1] A. N. to Sir George Buchanan, June 30, 1914.

Russian Ambassador and urged him to request his Government to do nothing which might cause umbrage to the Triple Alliance. The Austrian Foreign Minister, for his part, kept on assuring the Ambassadors at Vienna that the situation was not one of any gravity.[1]

On July 23 the Austro-Hungarian Government addressed to Serbia an ultimatum such as no independent Power could accept. On July 25 the Serbian reply was received at the Ballplatz. It was of a contrite and conciliatory nature. It was immediately rejected by the Austrian Government, who instructed their representative to leave Belgrade and at the same time mobilised against Serbia. The excessive terms of the Austrian ultimatum ; their summary rejection of the Serbian reply ; made it clear that the Austro-Hungarian Government would rest content with no ordinary reparation but were determined, at any cost, to extirpate the Serbian danger root and branch. By the morning of Sunday, July 26, there could be no possible doubt that Europe was on the verge of war.

The history of the ensuing twelve days has led to much controversy and much research. Each Power manœuvred for position and many historians have been tempted to treat these manœuvres as of serious importance. It may be questioned, however, whether

---

[1] Professor Fay in his second volume draws attention to the warning given to Sir M. de Bunsen by Count Lützow, on July 12 (see B.D., xi. 55 and 56), and blames Grey for not acting upon this warning. This is a slight misunderstanding of the atmosphere and expectations then prevailing in London. Everybody expected Austria to take strong action, and Count Lützow's warning was taken for granted. It must be remembered that he was at the time a private individual and that his pessimism was not confirmed by Berchtold.

the events which happened between that Sunday, July 26, and that Tuesday, August 4, possess any but a dramatic interest. The war was caused by an unhealthy state of mind in Europe : that state of mind had been created by the amassed unintelligence of international thought from 1878 onwards : it displays a false sense of historical values to lay disproportionate stress upon the intricate diplomatic evolutions which took place during the last twelve days.

Nor is the issue, even historically, so very confused. The main facts are sufficiently clear, in spite of the clouds of mud stirred up by the several propagandists. The main onus of responsibility falls upon Serbia, Russia and Austria. England and Germany were also deficient in foresight and decision. France, during those twelve days, was scarcely to blame at all. Serbia was to blame for having deliberately encouraged conditions which rendered Austrian intervention, as they well knew, inevitable. Austria was to blame for her lack of moderation and frankness in preparing her punishment of Serbia. Russia was to blame for taking advantage of a local incident to further her pan-Slav ambitions. England was to blame for hesitating to declare her attitude, or her disapproval of Russian methods, while there still was time. Germany was to blame (and we may doubt whether it is more than a tactical reproach) for having without due consideration promised Austria her unconditional support. Europe was to blame for having twisted herself into competing alliances.

The whole proportions of the problem are vitiated by dwelling unduly upon the rights and wrongs of those twelve indecisive but decisive days. In the present narrative care will be taken to tell the story in terms only of Nicolson's personal experience.

(6)

The whole story, from his point of view, falls into three distinct phases. During the first phase, from June 28 to July 23, he regarded the crisis as one between Austria and Serbia and hoped that it would be confined within the limits of a diplomatic incident. During the second phase, from July 24 to July 30, the crisis widened into one between Austria and Russia, and Nicolson's efforts were concentrated upon doing nothing which might be interpreted at St. Petersburg as disloyalty to the Entente. During the last phase, from July 31 to August 4, he was obsessed by the nightmare lest England might hesitate to honour her moral engagements, and lest her inevitable intervention might be postponed until Paris had fallen and France had been crushed.

The text of the Austrian ultimatum was received at the Foreign Office on Friday, July 24. On Saturday, July 25, Sir Edward Grey went away for the week-end to Itchen Abbas and Nicolson was left in charge of the Foreign Office. On the morning of Sunday, July 26, a telegram was received from Sir G. Buchanan from which it appeared that Russia would be prepared to see the crisis " placed on an international footing." Nicolson at once proposed that a Conference of the disinterested Powers, that is Germany, France and England, should be summoned in London and that meanwhile Russia, Austria and Serbia should be asked to suspend " all active military *operations*." " It seems to me," he wrote to Grey, " the only chance

of avoiding a conflict—it is I admit a very poor
chance—but in any case we shall have done our
utmost." [1]   The German Government, while not re-
jecting the British proposal outright, gave to the
Austrian Government " the most convincing assurances " that they in no way identified themselves with
any such suggestion.[2]

Meanwhile M. Sazonow from St. Petersburg was
releasing a whole covey of suggestions.   The German
Government, for their part, made the sensible suggestion that all ideas of European mediation should be
dropped and that Austria and Russia should be encouraged to negotiate direct.   " I should like,"
Nicolson wrote, " to see some practical action.   If
direct conversations are to take place between Vienna
and St. Petersburg we had better not confuse the
matter by making any fresh proposal." [3]

On Tuesday, July 28, Austria declared war on
Serbia.   The situation as it then stood is summarised
in a private letter of that date from Nicolson to Sir
George Buchanan :

> " I can quite understand Russia not being able to
> permit Austria to crush Servia.   I think the talk about
> localising the war merely means that all the Powers are to
> hold the ring while Austria quietly strangles Servia.   This
> to my mind is quite preposterous, not to say iniquitous.
> I do not understand after the very satisfactory way in
> which Servia has met the Austrian requests how Austria
> can with any justification proceed to hostile measures
> against her.   If she deliberately provokes war with Servia
> with the intention of giving her what she calls a lesson,

[1] B.D., vol. xi., No. 144.
[2] Austro-Hungarian Documents, vol. ii., No. 68.
[3] B.D., vol. xi., No. 215.

she is, I think, acting most wrongly, for she must know very well that such an action on her part would in all probability lead to a general European conflagration, with all its untold disastrous consequences. Germany has not played a very straight game—at least so far as we are concerned—in all this business. On two occasions we asked her to use moderating language at Vienna and we promised to support her if she did so. She contented herself with simply passing on our proposal as our proposal, which of course was not what we desired or requested, and again she brushed on one side the idea of a small conference here as being an impractical suggestion. Then Lichnowsky says that he is so pleased that Anglo-German co-operation seems likely to be successful. His interpretation of the word ' co-operation ' must be totally different from that which is usually accepted.

" What has preoccupied, and I confess has troubled, me very much, is satisfying Russia's very natural request as to what we should do in certain eventualities. I foresaw as well as you did that this crisis might be taken by Russia as a test of our friendship, and that were we to disappoint her all hope of a friendly and permanent understanding with her would disappear. We, of course, living under such conditions as we do here, when no Government practically can take any decided line without feeling that public opinion amply supports them, are unable to give any decided engagements as to what we should or should not do in any future emergencies ; but I think we have made it perfectly clear that in any case neither Germany nor Austria could possibly rely with any certainty upon our remaining neutral, and I think this fact has been much impressed upon them by one or two incidents which have occurred within the last two or three days. The decision to keep our battle fleet together instead of allowing it to disperse in order to give leave to its crews was officially notified and given prominence in the papers, and has been immediately taken as a sign by Germany and others that

we are prepared to take our share in hostilities if circumstances arose to make it necessary for us to do so.   Moreover, you will see that the tone of our press after the first
shock which was occasioned by the Austrian ultimatum,
has come round to the fact that it would be difficult, if not
impossible, for us to stand outside a general European
conflagration.   There is no doubt whatsoever that were
we drawn into this conflagration we should be on the side
of our friends.   Although therefore we were unable to
give Sazonof a definite undertaking as to what our attitude
would be, I think you will see that there is very little
doubt, supposing we were called upon to take a share, that
we should not hesitate to do our duty."

Wednesday, July 29, was a crucial day.   Sir Edward
Grey, in making an urgent appeal to Lichnowsky for
Anglo-German co-operation to prevent a general con-
flagration, warned him that if France were attacked
England could not for long stand aside.   The receipt
of this much belated warning produced a panic in
Berlin.   An urgent and violent telegram was sent to
Vienna stating that the German Government " must
immediately and emphatically recommend " the acceptance of outside mediation, and that Germany " must
decline to be irresponsibly dragged into a world war."
It is possible that Herr von Tschirschky, German
Ambassador at Vienna, delivered this message in a
modulated form.   It was in any case too late.   Russia
began to mobilise on July 29, and general mobilisation
was decreed in St. Petersburg at 6 p.m. on Thursday,
July 30.   A state of " immediate danger of war " was
proclaimed in Germany ; even in England a " precautionary period " was announced.   It became evident
that France might now at any moment be attacked.

(7)

Nicolson had been on intimate terms with M. Paul Cambon for upwards of thirty years. This intimacy had been increased by four years of close co-operation in London, and by their common experiences during the Agadir crisis and the protracted crisis of the Balkan wars. Almost daily, during those four years, the French Ambassador had visited Nicolson at the Foreign Office. A small but distinguished figure, with startlingly white hair and beard, with prominent glaucous eyes, he would enter the room slowly, place his grey top hat upon its accustomed table, sink into his accustomed leather chair, and exclaim, as he drew off first one kid glove and then the other, " Eh bien, mon cher, voici encore votre pain quotidien ! " During those five dark days from July 30 to August 3 Paul Cambon did not for one instant lose his imperturbability, his dignified precision, or his outward calm. Nicolson felt ashamed, however, to meet the anguish in Paul Cambon's eyes.

On July 25 M. Cambon was summoned urgently to Paris. He returned on July 28. On Thursday, July 30, he visited Sir Edward Grey and reminded him with exquisite courtesy of the letters which they had exchanged on October 22 of 1912. It had been agreed in that correspondence that if the peace of Europe were seriously threatened the two Governments would consult together as to what action should be taken. The Secretary of State replied that the Cabinet was to meet next morning and that he would see the Ambassador again that afternoon. On Friday, July 31, Sir Edward Grey informed M. Cambon that the Cabinet were

2 D

unable to give any pledge at the present juncture. He added that he was addressing an official enquiry to Berlin and Paris asking whether the two Governments would undertake not to violate the neutrality of Belgium. M. Cambon was well content with this assurance : he had reason to know that the German reply would not be satisfactory. Nicolson on the same day addressed the following minute to the Secretary of State :

July 31, 1914.

SIR EDWARD GREY.

" It seems to me most essential, whatever our future course may be in regard to intervention, that we should at once give orders for mobilisation of the army. It is useless to shut our eyes to the fact that possibly within the next 24 hours Germany will be moving across the French frontier—and if public opinion, at present so bewildered and partially informed, is ready in event of German invasion of France to stand by the latter, if we are not mobilised our aid would be too late. Mobilisation is a precautionary and not a provocative measure—and to my mind is essential."

A. N.

(*Minute by Sir Edward Grey*) :

" There is much force in this. We ought to prepare and I think it should be considered early to-morrow."

E. G. *July* 31, 1914.

Shortly before midnight on that Friday, July 31, Nicolson was awakened at his private house in Cadogan Gardens by an urgent message from the French Embassy. It enclosed a telegram reporting (wholly incorrectly) that the French frontier had been violated. At 7 a.m. the next morning, Saturday, August 1, he sent across to Sir Henry Wilson in Draycott Place.

They went together to Lord Haldane's house in Queen
Anne's Gate where Sir Edward Grey was staying. The
Secretary of State was still in bed. Nicolson, who was
unwilling to disturb his chief, returned to breakfast at
Cadogan Gardens. Sir Henry Wilson, for his part,
dashed off on an excited errand to mobilise the leaders
of the Unionist opposition. Nicolson refused to be a
party to this cabal. He walked, as usual, to the
Foreign Office. He was met by the news that Germany had declared war on Russia and that France was
mobilising. The Cabinet met again to consider their
position and at the conclusion of the meeting Sir
Edward Grey again sent for M. Cambon. He informed him that " France must take her own decision
at this moment without reckoning on an assistance
which we are not now in a position to promise."
M. Cambon stated that he must refuse to transmit such
an answer to his Government. A few minutes later,
white and speechless, he staggered into Nicolson's
room. Nicolson went towards him and took his
hands to guide him to a chair. " Ils vont nous lâcher,
ils vont nous lâcher," was all that the Ambassador
could say. Nicolson went upstairs to interview Sir
Edward Grey. He found him pacing his room, biting
at his lower lip. Nicolson asked whether it was indeed
true that we had refused to support France at the
moment of her greatest danger. Grey made no answer
beyond a gesture of despair. " You will render us,"
Nicolson said angrily, " a by-word among nations."
He then returned to M. Cambon. The Ambassador
had by then recovered. He suggested that the moment had arrived to produce " mon petit papier."
This document referred to the 1912 arrangement and

made it clear that France, relying on our word, had
deprived her northern coasts of all means of defence.
Nicolson advised him not to send in an official Note
to this effect in view of the high tension then prevailing.
He promised, however, to convey the reminder to Sir
Edward. An hour later he sent the following minute
to the Secretary of State :

53 CADOGAN GARDENS,
August 1, 1914.

SIR EDWARD GREY.

" M. Cambon pointed out to me this afternoon that it
was at our request that France had moved her fleets to the
Mediterranean, on the understanding that we undertook
the protection of her Northern and Western coasts. As I
understand you told him that you would submit to the
Cabinet the question of a possible German naval attack on
French Northern and Western Ports it would be well to
remind the Cabinet of the above fact."

(*Minute by Sir Edward Grey*) :

" I have spoken to the P.M. and attach great importance
to the point being settled to-morrow."

E. G.   1.8.14.

M. Cambon, meanwhile, had returned to the French
Embassy. He was there visited by Mr. Wickham
Steed, Foreign Editor of *The Times*. The latter asked
him : " Que faites-vous, M. Cambon ? " " J'attends
de savoir," he answered, " si le mot honneur doit être
rayé du vocabulaire anglais." [1] This is the sole recorded instance of an impassioned remark on the part
of M. Cambon.

On the morning of Sunday, August 2, a telegram
was received to the effect that French territory had been

[1] Charles Roux, " Veillée d'Armes à Londres," *Revue des Deux Mondes*,
August 15, 1926, p. 739.

violated in the region of Longwy. Nicolson sent the telegram on to Sir Edward Grey with the annexed minute :

> " I presume you have received the enclosed telegram. The action of Germany clearly constitutes her the aggressor, and in these circumstances there should be no hesitation as to our attitude. I am sure that the country would fully endorse when the facts are stated our coming to the aid of our friends. I have also little doubt that the opposition leaders in this case would, if consulted, be of the same mind.
>
> " We should mobilise to-day so that our expeditionary force may be on its way during next week. Should we waver now we shall rue the day later."

On the same day Grey gave Cambon a written assurance that we should protect the French coast in the event of a naval attack : he added verbally that he could give no promise of any further assistance. On that Sunday, August 2, the German Government addressed to Belgium an ultimatum demanding free passage. This ultimatum was refused. On Monday, August 3, Germany declared war on France. At 4 p.m. on that afternoon Sir Edward Grey at last informed the House of Commons and the country of the real nature of the crisis. Nicolson, in an agony of suspense, waited in his room at the Foreign Office. The scene has been well recorded by Mr. Wickham Steed :

> " At that hour I called on Sir Arthur Nicolson. He asked me how I thought ' it would go.'
> " ' If you mean Grey's speech,' I answered, ' it will go excellently. He has only to tell the truth and he will have the House and the Country with him.'

" ' I wish I felt as sure as you,' Sir Arthur replied, ' there is a good deal of active opposition and the crisis has come so rapidly that the country does not know what it is all about.'

" We discussed the situation until a secretary came into the room with a slip of paper from the tape machine :

" ' They have cheered him, Sir,' he said.

" ' Thank goodness ! ' ejaculated Sir Arthur in a tone of relief.

" Soon after 5 o'clock Lord Onslow, Sir Arthur Nicolson's private secretary, burst into the room. He had come straight from the House of Commons.

" ' He has had a tremendous reception, Sir,' he said, ' the whole House was with him.'

" Sir Arthur Nicolson sank back in his chair, in the attitude of a man from whose shoulders a crushing burden of anxiety had been lifted.

" ' Thank God ! ' he said fervently, ' now the course is clear, but it will be a terrible business.'

" Such was the ' bellicose ' spirit in the Foreign Office on the eve of the war. If Sir Edward Grey or the Government made mistakes, they were certainly not the mistakes of men who looked upon the prospect of war otherwise than with horror." [1]

An hour later Sir Edward Grey returned to the Foreign Office. Nicolson went upstairs to see him. The Secretary of State was leaning gloomily by the window. Nicolson congratulated him on the success of his speech. Sir Edward did not answer. He moved into the centre of the room and raised his hands with clenched fists above his head. He brought his fists with a crash upon the table. " I hate war," he groaned, " I hate war."

---

[1] Wickham Steed, *Through Thirty Years*, vol. ii. pp., 26-27.

(8)

At 2 p.m. on Tuesday, August 4, Sir Edward Grey telegraphed his ultimatum to Berlin. The German Government were asked to furnish assurances that they would respect the neutrality of Belgium. A reply was requested by midnight, German time, that is by 11 p.m. in London. If no satisfactory reply were forthcoming Sir Edward Goschen was to ask for his passports and to say that the British Government would feel bound to " take all steps in their power to uphold the neutrality of Belgium and the observance of a Treaty to which Germany is as much a party as ourselves."

It was expected that the German Government would return no reply to this ultimatum and that a state of war would arise at 11 p.m. A communication was thus prepared for delivery to Prince Lichnowsky when the ultimatum expired. The text of this communication was as follows :

FOREIGN OFFICE, *August* 4, 1914.

YOUR EXCELLENCY,

" The result of the communication made at Berlin having been that His Majesty's Ambassador has had to ask for his passports, I have the honour to inform Your Excellency that in accordance with the terms of the notification made to the German Government to-day His Majesty's Government consider that a state of war exists between the two countries as from to-day 11 o'clock p.m.

" I have the honour to enclose passports for Your Excellency, your Excellency's family and staff."

I have, etc.,

E. GREY.

The staff of the Foreign Office were working at full pressure under the blaze of countless electric lights.

The mobilisation scheme prepared in 1910 by the Committee of Imperial Defence had worked from the first moment of the " precautionary period," without a hitch. All that remained, by 9 p.m. on August 4, was to despatch the warning telegrams to every British Consul on the face of the globe. These telegrams had already been printed in advance and had reposed for years in what was known as the " war-press " in the Western Department. All that was required was to affix with the rubber stamp provided, the one word " Germany " in the blank space left between the word " War " and the ensuing phrase " Act upon instructions." To relieve the tension of their nerves the senior members of the Foreign Office participated in this pastime. While they were so engaged, one of the private secretaries dashed in to say that Germany had declared war on England. It was then 9.40 p.m. and the Note prepared for Prince Lichnowsky was hurriedly re-drafted and typed. The amended version began with the words : " The German Empire having declared war upon Great Britain, I have the honour, etc." The passports were enclosed in this amended letter and Mr. Lancelot Oliphant, at that time assistant in the Eastern Department, was despatched to Prince Lichnowsky. He returned at 10.15. A few minutes later an urgent telegram arrived *en clair* from Sir Edward Goschen at Berlin. It reported that the Chancellor had informed him by telephone that Germany would not reply to the ultimatum, and that therefore, to his infinite regret, a state of war would arise by midnight.

The Foreign Office were appalled by this intimation. Immediate enquiries were made as to how the previous information had been received to the effect that

Germany had taken the initiative in declaring war. It was ascertained that this information was based on an intercepted wireless message by which German shipping were warned that war with England was imminent. It was the Admiralty who had made the mistake. The Foreign Office then realised with acute horror that they had handed to Prince Lichnowsky an incorrect declaration of war. It was decided that at any cost this document must be retrieved and the right one substituted. It was decided also that the youngest member of the staff should be selected for this invidious mission, and the choice therefore fell upon Nicolson's youngest son.

Grasping the correct declaration in a nervous hand, he walked across the Horse Guards Parade and rang the bell at the side-door of the Embassy which gives on the Duke of York's steps. It was by then some five minutes after eleven. After much ringing a footman appeared. He stated that Prince Lichnowsky had gone to bed. The bearer of the missive insisted on seeing His Excellency and advised the footman to summon the butler. The latter appeared and stated that His Highness had given instructions that he was in no circumstances to be disturbed. The Foreign Office clerk stated that he was the bearer of a communication of the utmost importance from Sir Edward Grey. The butler, at that, opened the door and left young Nicolson in the basement. He was absent for five minutes. On his return he asked Sir Edward Grey's emissary to follow him and walked majestically toward the lift. They rose silently together to the third floor and then proceeded along a pile-carpeted passage. The butler knocked at a door. There was a screen behind the door and behind the screen a brass bedstead on which the Ambassador was reclining in pyjamas. The Foreign Office clerk stated that there had been a slight error in the document previously delivered and that he had come to substitute for it another, and more correct, version. Prince Lichnowsky indicated the writing table in the window. "You will find it there," he said. The envelope had been but half-opened, and the passports protruded. It did not appear that the Ambassador had read the communication or opened the letter in which the passports had been enclosed. He must have guessed its significance from the feel of the passports and have cast it on his table in despair. A receipt had to be demanded and signed. The blotting pad was brought across to the bed, and the pen dipped in the ink. While the Ambassador was signing, the sound of shouting came up from the Mall below, and the strains of the Marseillaise. The crowds were streaming back from Buckingham Palace. Prince Lichnowsky turned out the pink lamp beside his bed, and then feeling he had perhaps been uncivil, he again lighted it. " Give my best regards," he said, " to your father. I shall not in all probability see him before my departure."

Thirteen years later this same Foreign Office clerk visited Prince Lichnowsky at his shooting box in Silesia. For two hours they walked together in the snow-clad woods. The Englishman burned to ask a question which had been troubling him for all those years. " Did you ever know," he longed to ask, " that we gave you, that night in London, the wrong declaration of war ? "

He did not ask this question.

XV

EPILOGUE

[1914-1928]

(1)

WITH the outbreak of war British foreign policy ceased to have any separate identity : it was pooled in the general policy of the Allies. Nicolson remained on for another two years as head of the Foreign Office, but he confined himself to relieving Sir Edward Grey of the routine work of the Department and neither attempted nor desired to take a leading part in the conduct of war-time diplomacy. He was able, it is true, to draft the " Pact of London " by which a be-lated alliance was concluded with France and Russia. For the rest, however, he felt himself out of harmony with the crudities of war-time politics as well as with the hysteria of belligerent patriotism. He thus aban-doned to other hands the negotiations which culmi-nated in Italy's desertion of the Triple Alliance. He much disliked the suffering caused to civilians by a policy of ruthless internment and by the sequestration of enemy property. His whole attitude towards the war was, indeed, old-fashionable. He objected to the blockade : he hated the secret service work and the spy-fever which it produced : he was particularly dis-tressed by the excesses of war-time propaganda. His simplicity in this respect was at moments almost

427

startling. He would state quite openly that he was certain that the stories of German atrocities in Belgium were grossly exaggerated. He was pained and surprised on receiving from Spring Rice at Washington a copy of some German propaganda attack upon himself. " Why," he wrote to Grey, " should I be brought in ? " " You do not seem to know," Grey answered, " that in Germany I am said to be stupid and a mere tool of that arch-devil Nicolson. And the German who said this had been in England and had met me, which makes it all the more striking ! "

Nicolson's sense of chivalry was also wounded by the cruel attacks made in the Press upon such public servants as Prince Louis of Battenberg and Sir Eyre Crowe. He was distressed also at the unfair and ignorant criticism directed against Sir Louis Mallet, our Ambassador at Constantinople. He had watched with admiration the skill with which Sir Louis had deferred the inevitable adhesion of Turkey to the Central Powers, and he thought that the Ambassador's reputation should have been defended at the time with greater vigour.[1] He was saddened by what he felt to be a deterioration in that sense of fairness which he knew to be his country's most important asset.

He thus, through those sad months of 1914 and 1915, ploughed on at his desk, taking upon himself a mass of merely routine labour, leaving to others the execution of those war-necessities for which he knew himself to be without aptitude or inclination.

He had no illusions as to the duration of the war. He wrote to Lord Hardinge in March, 1915 :

[1] A generous tribute to Sir Louis Mallet is made by Lord Grey in his *Twenty-Five Years.*

" When you have a great nation like Germany, with its wonderful organisation and patriotism, engaged in a struggle for what is practically her existence as a great nation, one cannot expect that she will surrender until she has been brought down to the very last of her resources. People here talk gaily of the war being over in June, and I do not know on what data so cheerful an expectation is founded. Myself I have little doubt that if Germany were left fighting entirely alone she would put her back to the wall and fight to the bitter end."

" One cannot," he wrote to the same a few months later (July 21, 1915)—" disguise the fact that it is a most marvellous performance that after nearly a whole year of war against three such powerful nations as the Allies, Germany should still be in possession of Belgium, several Departments of France and a considerable portion of Russian territory, while not a single foreign soldier is on her own soil except as a prisoner of war."

In particular he was alarmed lest the propaganda directed against Germany in England should lead public opinion to forget the moderation which at that date was with us traditional, and to insist upon humiliating conditions of peace. " I look forward," he wrote to Sir G. Buchanan on May 3, 1915 :

" I look forward with some trepidation to the time when peace terms have to be discussed. I am always in favour of Bismarck's policy not to exact conditions which will compel your former adversary to await his time for revenge. At the same time we must no doubt secure to ourselves some guarantee of a fairly durable peace. We should all be liberated from this overburdening competition in armaments."

His health meanwhile was not adequate for the strain of conducting a great Department of State during the feverish pressure of the war. It had been decided in August, 1914, to extend Lord Bertie's tenure of the Paris Embassy, and Nicolson now thought only of retirement into private life. Lord Grey begged him to remain at the Foreign Office, since there was no one at the moment to take his place. In the spring of 1916, however, he saw an opportunity for release. On April, 1916, he wrote to Grey as follows :

" Hardinge should be home in about a fortnight. He wants to have about a month's holiday and is then anxious to find employment in connection with the Foreign Office. I should like to tell you that, if you agreed, I should be perfectly ready to cede my post to him. I consider that, in these times, it is most essential that you should have at your disposal the best available knowledge. I think that it would not be fair to you, nor in the public interest, were I to continue to fill the post if there is a younger, more active, and better equipped man than I am to take my place. I have not written a word to Hardinge on this proposal."

Grey and Hardinge both agreed to this suggestion. On June 20, 1916, Nicolson retired from the public service. On the day before he left the Foreign Office Sir Edward Grey addressed the following minute to the Department :

" To-morrow Sir Arthur Nicolson retires, and I cannot let to-day pass without putting on record my sense of the great service he has rendered by staying at his post during the war and my personal gratitude to him for the help and support he has given me. In 1914 Sir Arthur Nicolson had asked to be relieved of the work of Under Secretary and had indeed been advised in the interests of his health to give it up. On the outbreak of war he threw aside this consideration and for nearly two additional years has with great public spirit borne the strain and shared the unusual burden that has fallen upon all of us. When the War comes to a successful end, the part that he has taken in holding his post through the worst and most anxious months will be remembered to his credit and honour."

(2)

Nicolson, after nearly half a century of close connection with public affairs, found himself a little lost on retiring into private life. This severance from official employment was particularly irksome at a moment when the fate of his country hung in the balance and when an outsider would find it almost impossible to obtain reliable information. He was saved from this painful deprivation by the thoughtfulness of his Sovereign. King George represented to him that Lord Stamfordham was terribly overworked, and that it would be of great assistance if on leaving the Foreign Office Nicolson would come to Buckingham Palace and act as an additional private secretary. This was merely an excuse dictated by His Majesty's tact. All that happened was that for several months Nicolson would drive down to the Palace in the morning and would be shown by the King the official reports received from the several theatres of war. To the hour of his death Nicolson would speak with grateful emotion of the delicacy which inspired this action. In 1917 he was offered, and accepted, a post on the Board of the London City and Midland Bank. This entailed his abandoning his so-called employment at the Palace. He enjoyed his attendance at the Bank, and he much appreciated the welcome extended to him by his fellow directors.

Gradually, as the years passed, the arthritis which had tortured him between his fiftieth and sixtieth years became completely rigid and less painful. He was bowed almost double, but his sufferings and consequent sleeplessness were less intense. For a year or so he continued to enjoy such limited social intercourse as he allowed himself. For the summer months he would go to Bath, Harrogate or Buxton, and in August he would pay a round of country visits. He would stay with the Novars at Raith, and then on to Balmoral. His annual visits to Balmoral were a great pleasure to him : he would go to picnics with Queen Mary and the children, talking to her about books and politics. " I love this place," he wrote to his youngest son, " I really think it is the pleasantest house of all to stay in. People are so simple here and happy."

After 1917, however, he no longer embarked upon these expeditions. His increasing frailties made him self-conscious. He retired into what had always been the centre of his life, the devotion of his wife and family. His interest in foreign affairs remained as acute as ever. He was not a believer in " la victoire intégrale." He approved warmly of Lord Lansdowne's peace efforts and wrote to tell him so. The latter replied from Bowood on December 2, 1917 : " I attach a special degree of importance to your opinion on such a question—and I am glad to find that it is widely shared by men whose judgment cannot be challenged." He was incensed by the theory, which was even then being propagated, that Germany had provoked the war. He set himself to write an article which he sent to one of the leading quarterlies, in which he tried to put the German case more fairly.

He concluded this article with a note of warning, " All," he wrote, " are anxious for a durable peace, but there will be little hope of durability if it were thought to impose on great communities terms which would be regarded as intolerable or humiliating, and which would sow the seeds of revengeful animosity. A peace to be durable—though nothing in this world is durable or permanent—should, so far as human foresight can provide, be moderate and just." The Editor sent him back his manuscript. " What you say," he wrote, " about the two views of the origin of the war being equally intelligible is no doubt true, but I should hardly like to publish it without adding a caveat. Can you really maintain that the German fear of the Einkreisungspolitik was ' genuine ' ? Again you say that Germany devoted much attention to gaining the goodwill of Great Britain. Ostensibly perhaps, but was it genuine ? You say also ' That no great Power desired war.' Was this true of Germany ? " Nicolson was discouraged by these queries : the article was never published.

He followed the peace negotiations with interest and apprehension. He was appalled by the Treaty of Versailles. Particularly did he resent the paragraph which obliged Germany by force to admit that she was solely responsible for the war. He considered that paragraph both undignified and meaningless. " I cannot understand it," he would say, " you cannot impose a moral judgment on a whole people. I feel sure that we old diplomatists would not have done such a thing. I think some people *were* more responsible than others, such as Aehrenthal, but not a whole nation."

(3)

He thus withdrew further and further into the shell of his own domestic happiness. His sons, his son-in-law Francis St. Aubyn, for whom he had a great affection, survived the war. His later years were gladdened by the voices of his grandchildren.[1] He would sit there quietly, watching the years slip by. " He had the gift," writes his daughter, " of making big events seem natural through his quiet simplicity. He had no knowledge of modern life but somehow a clear understanding of its difficulties. He never gossiped : he never, in a way, lived in this world : politics and his family were for him the only reality : for the rest, his reserve kept secret what he felt."

The following portrait of him in his last years has been furnished by his daughter-in-law :

" It was impossible to come into his presence without immediately becoming aware of his physical personality. A little figure huddled in an armchair, the hands resting on an ebony stick—that was the first impression : and then would come the sudden flash of the blue eyes, and the charming smile of welcome, and the instinctive effort to get up. 'Don't move,' one would hastily say ; and one would hastily sit down oneself, and begin to tell him something that might amuse him. He was easily amused. Although he could scarcely turn his head, he would watch his visitor with alert attention, and his laugh came readily

[1] His second son, Erskine, married in October, 1919, Katherine, daughter of Sir Henry and Lady Albertha Lopes, and had two sons, David and Peter, and one daughter, Naomi. His third son married in October, 1913, Victoria Sackville-West and had two sons, Benedict and Nigel. His daughter married in October, 1916, Francis St.Aubyn, and had three sons, John, Piers and Giles, and two daughters, Jessica and Philippa. His eldest son remained unmarried.

LORD AND LADY CARNOCK WITH SOME OF THEIR GRANDCHILDREN, 1927

over any trivial anecdote, or he would give the little nervous exclamation so characteristic of him, like a sharp in-taking of the breath : ' Ha ! ' he would say, and one would wonder if it were not half an exclamation of pain. For all the time one was acutely conscious of his physical frailty. His extreme smallness, his difficult and crippled movements, his bowed shoulders, all combined to make the fine head and intellectual forehead appear almost too heavy for that tiny body to support. I remember that once, and once only, he tried to describe the exact sensation of ankylosis. ' It's as though,' he said with a smile, ' you had a stiff neck all over all the time.'

" Nevertheless, although physically so small and fragile, his manner was conceived upon a scale of ample but authoritative courtesy. He was impressive, not insignificant. With all his gentleness, all his simplicity, he contrived to impose his personality so that in a company of several people it was of *his* presence that one remained aware, and to *him* that one naturally deferred. He might sit silent in his armchair, watching, trying to hear—for he was growing deaf—but one could never forget that he was there. This quality must be due, one inevitably thought, to something essential in the man himself : what, I used to wonder, is at the root of one's deference, respect, and affection ? for, in spite of his irreproachable manners and his charm, he is aloof, slightly unreal, removed from life by reason of his age, his disabilities, and the absent-mindedness which comes over him as he grows tired. But the answer was not hard to find. It is not often that one meets a man whose absolute goodness and integrity proclaim themselves in the first glance of his eyes as one first shakes hands, not often that one feels compelled to acknowledge the moral attributes as the basis of a personal impression. Thus, however, it was with him. One's perception of him was most curiously and vividly compounded of physical compassion and spiritual homage."

In the spring of 1924 he developed a weakness of the heart which would have proved fatal but for the skill of his doctors and the force of his own vitality. For five further years he remained an invalid, avoiding all but the most essential exertions. His mind was vigorous and unclouded to the end. He died, without fear and without regret, on the 5th of November, 1928, in his eightieth year.

APPENDICES

APPENDICES

APPENDIX I

(SUMMARY OF INSTRUMENTS EMBODYING CAMBON-LANSDOWNE AGREEMENTS OF APRIL 8, 1904.)

A. *Convention respecting Newfoundland and West and Central Africa.*

ARTICLES I-IV. Regulate Newfoundland Fisheries.

ARTICLE V. Small concession made to France on frontier between Gambia and Senegambia.

ARTICLE VI. Great Britain cedes to France Iles de Los.

ARTICLE VII. Regulations regarding nationality of persons in territory thus ceded.

ARTICLE VIII. Frontier rectifications on Niger and Lake Chad.

ARTICLE IX. Convention to be ratified.

B. *Declaration regarding Egypt and Morocco.*

ARTICLE I. H.M.G. declare that they have no intention of altering the political status of Egypt. French Government declare " that they will not obstruct the action of Great Britain in that country by asking that a limit of time be fixed for the British occupation or in any other manner." French Government will also assent to a Khedivial decree containing amended guarantees necessary for the protection of the Egyptian bondholders. This decree not to be modified without the consent of the Powers signatory of

439

the London Convention of 1885. Director General of Antiquities shall continue
to be a French citizen. French schools
in Egypt to continue to enjoy same
liberty as in the past.

ARTICLE II. French Government declare that they
have no intention of altering the political status of Morocco. H.M.G. recognise that it appertains to France, more
particularly as a Power whose dominions
are conterminous for a great distance
with those of Morocco, to preserve
order in that country and to provide
assistance for the purpose of all administrative, economic, financial and military
reforms, which it may require. They
declare that they will not obstruct the
action taken by France for this purpose,
provided that such action shall leave
intact the rights which Great Britain in
virtue of Treaties, Conventions, and
usage, enjoys in Morocco, including the
right of coasting trade between the ports
of Morocco enjoyed by British vessels
since 1901.

ARTICLE III. H.M.G. will respect French rights in
Egypt in respect of coasting trade.

ARTICLE IV. " The two Governments being equally
attached to the principle of commercial
liberty both in Egypt and Morocco,
declare that they will not, in those
countries, countenance any inequality
either in the imposition of customs
duties or other taxes or of railway trans-
port charges." Trade of both nations in
Morocco and Egypt shall enjoy same
treatment in transit through the French

and British possessions in Africa. This engagement to be binding for thirty years. Two Governments at same time reserve to themselves in Morocco and Egypt right to see that railway, port and road concessions, etc., " are only granted in such conditions as will maintain intact the authority of the State over these great undertakings of public interest."

ARTICLE V. H.M.G. will use their influence to safeguard position of French officials in Egypt. French will do same for Britain's officials in Morocco.

ARTICLE VI. H.M.G. guarantee free passage of Suez Canal in accordance with stipulations of Treaty of October 29, 1883. On the other hand execution of para. 1 and 2 of Art. 8 of that Treaty will " remain in abeyance."

ARTICLE VII. No fortification to be erected on Moorish coast of Straits of Gibraltar.

ARTICLE VIII. French Government to come to an understanding with Spain regarding Spanish interests in Morocco.

ARTICLE IX. The two Governments to " afford to one another their diplomatic support in order to obtain the execution of the clauses of the present Declaration."

C. *Secret Articles.*

ARTICLE I. " In the event of either Government finding themselves constrained by the force of circumstances to modify their policy in respect to Egypt and Morocco," the engagements under Articles IV, VI, and VII of the Declaration to remain intact.

ARTICLE II. H.M.G. have no present intention to abolish the Capitulations in Egypt, but should they wish to reform present judicial system the French Government "will not refuse to entertain any such proposals." We give similar assurance regarding Morocco.

ARTICLE III. Spain to have coast from Melilla to River Sebou, subject to her agreeing to Articles IV and VII of the Declaration, and undertaking not to alienate the territory thus acquired.

ARTICLE IV. If Spain refuses, then Declaration holds good between H.M.G. and France.

ARTICLE V. Should other Powers refuse to accept Khedivial Decree French Government will not object to repayment at par of the Guaranteed Privileged and Unified Egyptian Debts after July 15, 1910.

D. *Declaration concerning Siam, Madagascar and New Hebrides.*

I. *Siam.* Country west of Menam basin to be in British sphere of influence, that to the east of that basin in the French sphere. Neither party to annex Siamese territory.

II. *Madagascar.* H.M.G. withdraw their protest against French customs tariff.

III. *New Hebrides.* Two Governments agree to draw up an Arrangement which shall put an end to difficulties arising from absence of jurisdiction over natives of the New Hebrides. Commission to be appointed to settle disputes between French and British nationals regarding landed property.

APPENDIX II

(SUMMARY OF FINAL ACT OF ALGECIRAS APRIL 7, 1906.)

CHAPTER I. *Police.*

1. Conference declare that following measures should be taken :
2. Police to be under authority of Sultan, recruited from native population, and stationed in the eight trade ports.
3. In order to assist Sultan in the organisation of this force French and Spanish officers and non-commissioned officers will be engaged.
4. Their employment to be for five years. The detailed arrangements to be drawn up by senior French and Spanish officers in consultation with Moorish authorities and Inspector General. They will be submitted to diplomatic body at Tangier for approval.
5. Number of police not to be more than 5,000 or less than 2,000. French and Spanish officers to be sixteen to twenty in number, non-commissioned officers to number of thirty or forty.
6. Necessary funds to be supplied by State Bank.
7. Inspector General to be a Swiss citizen.
8. Copies of his reports to be furnished to diplomatic body at Tangier.
9. Latter can in case of need call on Inspector General for a report.
10. Salary of Inspector General.
11. His contract to be communicated to Diplomatic Body.

12. Instructors to be Spanish at Tetuan, mixed at Tangier, Spanish at Laraiche, French at Rabat, mixed at Casablanca, and French at three remaining ports.

CHAPTER II. *Arms traffic.*

13-29. Detailed regulations affecting import of arms, etc., into Morocco.

30. France to apply these regulations on Algerian frontier and Spaniards in Spanish zone.

CHAPTER III. *State Bank.*

31. Bank to be called " State Bank of Morocco."

32. And have sole right of issuing paper money.

33. Will act as Treasury of Morocco.

34. Will have exclusive right of short-term loans and priority right for public issues.

35. May on conditions make advances to Moorish Government.

36. Will keep separate account for special tax of $2\frac{1}{2}\%$ *ad valorem* on foreign imports.

37. Will assume functions of Royal Mint.

38-41. Regulations concerning Bank buildings and establishments.

42. Moorish Government may appoint High Commissioner to represent them on the Board, but without right of interference in management of Bank.

43. Subsequent agreement to determine exact relations between Bank and Moorish Government.

44. Bank to be under French law.

45. Actions against the Bank will be heard by Special Tribunal composed of three consular magistrates and two assessors. Cases will be heard under French commercial law. Right of Appeal to Federal Court at Lausanne.

46. Latter will also act as Court of Arbitration in disputes regarding Bank concession.
47. Statutes of Bank to be drawn up by Special Committee provided for in Art. 57 below, and on following principles.
48. Board of Bank to be at Tangier.
49. And to be constituted by representatives of all States participating in the Capital.
50. Directors to be proposed to General Meeting of Shareholders by groups subscribing to capital of Bank.
51. Censors to be nominated by Deutsche Bank, Bank of England, Bank of Spain and Banque de France.
52. Censors will see that concession and statutes of Bank are observed. They will have no right to interfere in actual management of Bank. They will meet at least once in every two years and will draw up an annual report.
53. Salary and travelling expenses of Censors.
54. Commission of Tangier notables to advise Board on question of discount and credit.
55. Capital to be not less than fifteen and not more than twenty million francs.
56. Capital to be equally divided among Powers represented at Conference who wish to subscribe. In any case two shares equal to those reserved for the participating groups shall be given to French consortium in compensation for their abandoning rights obtained under contract of June 12, 1904.
57. Special committee of subscribing banks to meet to draw up Statutes of the Bank.
58. Modifications to be voted by three thirds majority of shareholders on proposal of Directors approved by the Censors.

CHAPTER IV. *Revenue and Taxation.*

59. Foreign nationals to pay *tertib.*
60. And may purchase land and erect buildings.
61. Moorish Government can raise a tax on urban property. Proportion of these receipts to be devoted to town improvement and hygiene.
62-65. Minor fiscal proposals.
66. Moorish Government can temporarily impose $2\frac{1}{2}\%$ *ad valorem* duty on foreign imports. Revenue thus derived to be devoted to public works designed to improve trade and commerce. Public works contracts to be under supervision of diplomatic body.
67. Reduction of export duties on peas, mais, etc.
68. Increase in cattle export quota.
69-76. Minor disposition—coasting, trade, warfare, opium, tobacco monopoly.

CHAPTER V. *Customs.*

77-96. Regulations to improve customs administration and diminish smuggling.
97. Customs to be under permanent Commission constituted by one representative of Moorish Government, one representative of Diplomatic Body, and one representative of State Bank.
98-102. Penalties and safeguards.
103. Application of customs regulations to be entrusted to France and Spain on the frontiers of their possessions.
104. Customs regulations can be revised bv Diplomatic Body deciding by unanimity.

CHAPTER VI. *Public works and services.*

105. No public services can be alienated to private interests.

106. Signatory Powers reserve to themselves the right to see that any concessions granted to foreign capital are not of a nature to weaken control of Moorish Government over important public services.
107. Public tender for all concessions without distinction of nationality.
108. Moorish Government to submit all contracts to diplomatic body.
109. Tenders to contain no conditions inimical to free competition.
110-119. Dispositions giving Diplomatic Body rights of supervision over concessions for mines, quarries, forests, and all matters of expropriation.

CHAPTER VII. *General Dispositions*
    regarding ratification, etc.

APPENDIX III

(SUMMARY OF ANGLO-RUSSIAN CONVENTION OF AUGUST 31, 1907.)

Convention regarding Persia.

PREAMBLE. The two Governments " having mutually agreed to respect the integrity and independence of Persia and sincerely desiring the preservation of order throughout that country and its pacific development as well as the permanent establishment of equal opportunities for the commerce and industry of all other nations " : and in view of the special interests which each possesses in the country owing to their geographical and commercial situation, have agreed as follows :

ART. I.   Great Britain undertakes not to seek for herself or to support in favour of British subjects or of nationals of third Powers any commercial or political concessions north of a line from Kasr-i-Shirin to the point of intersection on the Perso-Afghan frontier, and not to oppose either directly or indirectly any Russian demand for such concessions within that area.

ART. II.   A similar renunciation on the part of Russia for the territory south of a line from Bunder-Abbas to the Afghan frontier.

ART. III. Neither party to oppose the grant of concessions to the other within the neutral zone between these two lines. All existing concessions to remain valid.

ART. IV.   Customs revenues pledged to the service of British or Russian loans in either zone not to be affected by the provisions of Articles I and II.

ART. V.   In the event of default on these loans the two Governments will consult each other.

Persian Gulf Declaration. (Sir E. Grey to Sir A. Nicolson, No. 325, August 29, 1907.) H.M.G. have taken note of Russian Government's statement that they do not deny special interests of Great Britain in the Persian Gulf. H.M.G. will continue " to direct all their efforts to the preservation of the *status quo* in the Gulf and the maintenance of British trade ; in doing so they have no desire to exclude the legitimate trade of any other Power."

Convention regarding Afghanistan.

PREAMBLE. The two Governments " in order to assure perfect security on the respective frontiers of

Central Asia and the maintenance in those regions of permanent peace " are agreed as follows :

ART. I.   Great Britain declares that she has no intention of altering the political status of Afghanistan, or encouraging that country to adopt measures which might threaten Russia. Russia recognises that Afghanistan is outside the Russian sphere of influence and agrees only to enter into political relations with that country through the intermediary of H.M.G. Russia will also agree not to send any agents into Afghanistan.

ART. II.   Great Britain agrees not to interfere with the internal administration of Afghanistan or to annex or occupy Afghan territory provided that the Amir fulfills his treaty obligations.

ART. III. Specially designated Russian and Afghan officials can settle directly matters of non-political import affecting the frontier or the frontier provinces.

ART. IV.   All advantages hitherto accorded to Anglo-Indian trade will also be accorded to Russian trade. If Russia wishes to send commercial agents into the country she shall do so only after agreement with H.M.G.

ART. V.   Convention only to enter into force when consent of Amir obtained. (*N.B.*—The Amir never consented. The Russian Government, however, loyally agreed to the Convention being regarded as in force even without that assent.)

Convention regarding Thibet.

PREAMBLE. Two Powers recognise suzerain rights of China over Thibet. Russia admits that Great Britain, owing to her geographical position

" has a special interest in seeing that the existing system regulating the external affairs of Thibet is maintained in its integrity."

ART. I.   Both Powers recognise territorial integrity of Thibet and agree not to interfere in its internal administration.

ART. II.   Both Powers undertake not to treat with Thibet except through the intermediary of the Chinese Government. This does not affect direct commercial negotiations between British commercial agents and Thibetan authorities as provided in Younghusband Convention. British and Russian Buddhists may enter into religious relations of a strictly non-political nature with Dalai Lama.

ART. III. Neither Government to send representatives to Lhassa.

ART. IV.   Neither party to obtain concessions.

ART. V.   No Thibetan revenues to be pledged to either party.

Annex regarding Chumbi Valley.

Great Britain confirms assurances made by Viceroy to effect that British troops will be withdrawn after payment of three annuities of the indemnity. Should the occupation be for any reason prolonged, a friendly exchange of views will take place between the two Governments.

Exchange of Notes regarding Scientific Missions.

Neither Government to send any mission for three years. At the expiration of that period the two Governments to discuss what further measures should be taken.

INDEX

Caillaux, M. Joseph, 349, 350, 351.
Calpouzos, Sergeant, 55-58.
Cambon, M. Jules, French Ambassador at Madrid, and subsequently in Berlin, ix, 163, 187, 337, 343, 346, 349, 365.
Cambon, M. Paul, French Ambassador at Constantinople, and subsequently in London, ix, 90, 91, 100, 132, 138, 142, 147, 149, 174, 177, 331, 351, 367, 368, 369, 371, 373, 374, 378, 383, 406, 417-421.
Caprivi, Count, 87.
Cartwright, Sir Fairfax, British Ambassador in Vienna, 344, 361, 378, 389, 390.
Cassel, Sir Ernest, 361.
Cassini, Count, 173, 190.
Castletown, Lord, 144.
Chamberlain, Mr. Joseph, 127, 128, 131, 132 and note, 137.
Chesney, Sir Francis, 92.
Churchill, Mr. Winston, xv, 347, 375, 394.
Clemenceau, M. Georges, 35, 193, 194.
Constantine, Grand Duke, 246.
Cromer, Earl of, 35, 47, 96.
Crowe, Sir Eyre, 325, 327-329, 332, 333, 428.
Cruppi, M., 342.
Currie, Sir Philip, (Lord Currie), 11, 67, 82, 100.
Curzon of Kedleston, Marquess of, 240, 241, 256-257.

D

D'Abernon, Lord (Sir Edgar Vincent), 91, 95.
Delcassé, M., xv, 127, 130, 131, 142, 148, 149, 150, 151, 157, 159, 163, 164, 253, 367, 368, 404.
Derby, Earl of, 13.
Dolgorouki, Prince, 67, 68, 245.
Dournovo, M., 210.
Dufferin and Ava, Marquess of, 26, 28, 31, 32, 36-49, 62, 65, 75, 76, 94, 108, 126, 129.
Dufferin and Ava, Marchioness of, 28, 29, 45, 48.

E

Eckardstein, Baron, 132, 141-142.
Edward VII., King, 58, 125, 140, 147, 148, 154, 174, 196, 206, 255, 269-274, 279, 283, 296, 315, 316, 318, 319.
Egerton, Sir Edwin, 54.
Enver Bey, 387.
Errington, Viscount, 204.
Eugénie, Empress, 316.

F

Fay, Professor Sidney, 312 note, 411 note.
Ferdinand, Prince of Bulgaria, 103, 104, 105, 106, 107, 277, 278, 279, 295, 388.
Fisher, Sir John (Lord Fisher), 209, 274, 315.
Foch, Marshal, 396, 397.
Ford, Sir Clare, British Ambassador at Constantinople, 54, 81-83, 89, 92, 94, 95, 96, 97, 98.
Franz Ferdinand, Archduke, 359, 382, 383 note, 403, 409.
Franz Josef, Emperor of Austria, 359, 361.
French, Sir John (Lord French of Ypres), 269, 274.
Freycinet, M. de, 35, 36, 37, 38.
Freytag, Gustav, 14.
Friedrickz, Baron, 214, 271.

G

Galtier, M., 173
Gambetta, M., 34, 35, 37.
Gapon, Father, 209.
Gaselee, Mr. Stephen, i.
George, Mr. Lloyd, 345, 347, 349.
George V., King, 347, 406, 431.
Giers, M. de, 103.
Gladstone, Mr., 26, 27.
Gooch, Dr., i.
Gorémykin, M., 210, 211, 220, 224, 405.
Goschen, Sir Edward, British Ambassador in Vienna, and subsequently in Berlin, 29, 233, 290, 337, 338 note, 339, 340, 344, 349, 350, 364, 394, 395, 396, 402, 413, 423, 424.